THE
FENIAN
RISING

T0386227

THE
FENIAN
RISING

JAMES STEPHENS
AND THE
IRISH REPUBLICAN
BROTHERHOOD,
1858-1867

MICHAEL T. FOY

The
History
Press

First published 2023

The History Press
97 St George's Place, Cheltenham,
Gloucestershire, GL50 3QB
www.thehistorypress.co.uk

© Michael T. Foy, 2023

The right of Michael T. Foy to be identified as the Author
of this work has been asserted in accordance with the
Copyright, Designs and Patents Act 1988.

All rights reserved. No part of this book may be reprinted
or reproduced or utilised in any form or by any electronic,
mechanical or other means, now known or hereafter invented,
including photocopying and recording, or in any information
storage or retrieval system, without the permission in writing
from the Publishers.

British Library Cataloguing in Publication Data.
A catalogue record for this book is available from the British Library.

ISBN 978 1 80399 262 4

Typesetting and origination by The History Press
Printed and bound in Great Britain by TJ Books Limited, Padstow, Cornwall.

Trees for LYfe

Contents

Dedication

This book is dedicated to Walter Grey and Tricia Ramsay.
These two wonderful friends died before the book was completed.

Acknowledgements

I owe a great debt to Dr Michelle Brown who meticulously read and corrected every chapter and made valuable suggestions for improvement. I also appreciate the help I received from Stewart Roulston, Dr Timothy Bowman, Nick Dexter, Len O'Driscoll. Anne O'Mahony and Mary Horgan. Finally I want to thank Nicola Guy who commissioned the book, editor Dan Coxon and project editor Ele Craker.

Michael T. Foy

1

The Birth of Fenianism

Fenianism has been called the political force that sporadically dominated Irish politics from the 1850s until recent times.[1] First manifesting itself in America as the Fenian Brotherhood under John O'Mahony, and in Ireland as the Irish Republican Brotherhood under James Stephens, its role has been described as that of a watchdog acting on behalf of an Irish separatist tradition that was committed to winning Irish freedom through physical force.[2] Defeated often, Fenianism's tremendous resilience meant it rose time and again, phoenix-like from the ashes, to eventually inspire the 1916 Easter Rising and finally an Anglo–Irish war that established an independent Irish state.

The origins of Fenianism lay in five decades of Irish history that culminated in the tumultuous 1840s, when Ireland simultaneously experienced momentous political, social, economic and demographic upheavals. Ever since the Act of Union in 1800 had abolished the Irish parliament and made Westminster supreme, the country constantly seethed with discontent, political, religious and agrarian. Within three years, Robert Emmet led a brief unsuccessful rebellion, after which he and the other leading conspirators were executed. Subsequently, Ireland often seemed more like an occupied country in which the Irish government maintained control through a large military garrison, a paramilitary police force and a panoply of repressive legislation. In the 1820s, the nationalist politician Daniel O'Connell mobilised popular disaffection into a movement that in 1829 secured Catholic Emancipation, a triumph that saw him be acclaimed as 'The Liberator' and 'The Great Dan'. For the next decade, O'Connell concentrated on influencing successive Whig governments to enact legislation benefitting Ireland but his supremacy remained undimmed. A prominent supporter declared that 'it seemed Celtic Ireland had lodged its proxy in his hands alone, to be used at his unquestioned discretion'.[3]

In 1840, O'Connell resumed mass campaigning through a Repeal Association that demanded the restoration of an Irish parliament. Although O'Connell was now 65 years old, his new organisation attracted a younger generation enthusiastic for political change that included John Blake Dillon, Thomas Davis, Charles Gavan Duffy and William Smith O'Brien. Dillon and Davis had become friends at Trinity College, Dublin, and in 1842 they founded *The Nation* newspaper, which successfully propagated a generous nationalism inclusive of all classes and creeds. Soon, Dillon and Davis (who died prematurely in 1845) were joined by Duffy, a Northern Catholic experienced in the newspaper industry, and O'Brien, a Protestant landowner from Co. Clare.

Inside the Repeal Association, the quartet's followers became known as Young Ireland, and unlike most members they did not uncritically idolise O'Connell, resenting as they did his dictatorial methods, his susceptibility to flattery from an inner circle of sycophants, and the way O'Connell increasingly identified nationalism with Roman Catholicism. They respected him even less in 1843, when O'Connell cancelled a major meeting at Clontarf after the prime minister Sir Robert Peel banned it. Although the British government did not destroy O'Connell, the climb-down had damaged his authority, seriously eroded confidence in the idea of peaceful political change, and emboldened Young Irelanders to challenge the direction in which O'Connell was leading them. By now Young Ireland had concluded that, if necessary, revolution could be justified to achieve its goals. The dispute came to a head in July 1846 when the Repeal Association endorsed O'Connell's resolution rejecting physical force except in self-defence. Young Irelanders immediately seceded and established their own organisation, The Irish Confederation, which operated through a network of Confederation Clubs.

By now, a devastating potato famine had gripped Ireland in the nineteenth century's greatest natural catastrophe. Over the next four years a million people died and another million fled the country as unforgettable scenes of horror became seared into the memories of traumatised survivors. At Bantry in west Cork, many inhabitants awakened to find, leaning against their front doors, the emaciated corpses of victims who had taken shelter on their porches overnight. Daily, two drivers on a horse and cart collected the bodies. A lady whose companions rowed her out to an island was puzzled by the death-like silence and an absence of life when the dogs were fat and healthy. But her friends shied away from revealing the terrible truth. On countless roadsides lay corpses that were partly green from eating nettles and partly blue from cholera and dysentery. Lacking the money, strength or material to make coffins or dig graves, people often tied bodies to a plank of wood and sank them in bogs. Communal wailing at funerals in overflowing graveyards was everywhere. Evictions, a mass exodus of people, families and even entire communities ripped apart and a government and landlords almost universally perceived as callous had profound consequences. With considerable understatement, a Fenian, John O'Leary, declared that the Famine inflamed the minds of men both then and after against England.[4] In fact, it dug a bottomless well of hatred and fury that for many decades thereafter poisoned Anglo–Irish relations and strengthened the claim of radicals that the only language the British government understood came from the barrel of a gun. Revolutionaries also argued that famine made an insurrection necessary as delay meant that there might soon be nobody left to rebel.

After O'Connell died in 1847, the Repeal Association went into steep decline and Young Ireland gained the political ascendancy. But an influx of new members contained ultra-radicals like John Mitchel, who in *The Nation* advocated a social revolution and the destruction of landlordism. Alarmed, the Home Secretary, Sir George Grey, described Mitchel's violent rhetoric as the ravings of a disordered imagination. Mitchel's incitement had now trapped O'Brien, Duffy and Dillon in the same predicament into which they had previously put O'Connell. In early 1848, political tensions rose steeply when Mitchel demanded an immediate rising. After the Young Ireland leadership rejected his aggressive policy, Mitchel seceded and established his own newspaper, the *United Irishman*. Unsurprisingly, the British government arrested Mitchel and sentenced him to fourteen years' transportation in Van Diemen's Land.

Mitchel's conviction inflamed Confederation clubs, which were already arming and drilling. Accusing the British government of repression and provocation, they began preparing for rebellion, but the leadership's plans were half-hearted, ill thought-out and over-optimistic. The intention was to rise in September after harvest time, but Dublin Castle had already devised detailed countermeasures and planted spies inside Young Ireland. Then, in mid-July 1848, the government struck pre-emptively by proclaiming Dublin, Cork, Drogheda and Waterford and suspending Habeas Corpus. O'Brien, Dillon and Thomas Meagher responded by travelling through Kilkenny and Tipperary, attempting with minimal success to rouse a demoralised peasantry into rebellion. Finally, they reached the village of Ballingarry, where fifty policemen barricaded themselves inside a large two-storey house owned by a Mrs Margaret McCormack. After a tense stand-off, the police opened fire and began a desultory exchange that lasted until police reinforcements appeared. Despite being fired on, they kept coming until the rebels, low on ammunition, faded away. Effectively the rising was over. The Ballingarry shootout became known derisively as the Battle of Widow McCormack's Cabbage Patch: Duffy called it an ignominious failure.

At Special Commission trials in September and October, prominent Young Irelanders like William Smith O'Brien, Terence Bellew McManus and Thomas Meagher were condemned to be hanged, drawn and quartered, though their sentences were commuted to life imprisonment. Arrested before the rising, Charles Gavan Duffy was eventually acquitted of all charges. Many nationalists succumbed to despair. O'Connell's constitutional politics was seemingly discredited and revolutionary violence had ended in fiasco. There appeared no way out. But not everyone gave up hope, especially those Young Ireland leaders who had sought refuge in America. In fact, prominent Fenians agreed that their movement was born from the wreckage of 1848. John Devoy described it as the child and successor of the Young Ireland uprising, while John O'Leary claimed Fenianism was the direct and inevitable outcome of '48.

The failure of the rising had scattered Young Ireland leaders across the globe.[5] Some were transported to Van Diemen's Land and others wandered far away, including Darcy McGee, who sojourned for a while in Constantinople. A number were smuggled out of Ireland by sympathetic local populations: disguised as priests, Michael Doheny and Richard O'Gorman escaped separately to America, where they joined John Blake Dillon. John O'Mahony and James Stephens stayed for some years in Paris. But everyone except for O'Brien, Martin and Stephens eventually ended up in America. O'Mahony and McGee arrived in New York, while Mitchel, McManus and Meagher would escape captivity and sail to freedom in the United States.

In America, not everyone kept the faith. John Blake Dillon had always opposed even the idea of insurrection and only turned out at Ballingarry as a gesture of solidarity with his leader William Smith O'Brien. In New York, he concentrated on his successful legal practice until 1855, when he returned home after an amnesty and permanently abandoned revolutionary politics. William Smith O'Brien and John Martin also availed themselves of amnesty to return home, where they also embraced entirely constitutional methods. Richard O'Gorman became a partner in Dillon's law firm and like him renounced revolutionary violence, before fading into harmless obscurity. Even more strikingly, Darcy M'Gee effectively went over to the enemy. After moving to Canada, he entered politics and played a leading role in establishing the Federation of Canada in 1867. McGee also became bitterly hostile to American and Canadian Fenians, who retaliated by assassinating him in April 1868 on his way home from parliament in Ottawa.

But from their analysis of the 1848 rising, Doheny and other exiles had concluded that it had been doomed from the start because leaders like William Smith O'Brien, John Blake Dillon and John Martin were never serious revolutionaries. Socially and intellectually refined, disconnected from militant followers and frequently Protestants of the Ascendancy landowning class, these hesitant theoretical revolutionaries had thought insurrection should only be undertaken reluctantly as a last resort if the British government left them no alternative or even provoked them into rebellion. Many performed half-heartedly during the rising and appeared almost relieved when it rapidly collapsed with little physical and material damage. But to their more radical supporters, revolution was an all-consuming passion for which they were prepared to sacrifice everything. For them, constitutional nationalism, repeal, devolution and federalism were all chimeras best left to political daydreamers, and there was no alternative to violently toppling British rule in Ireland. Accordingly, if a new resistance movement emerged, its leaders had to be hard-headed and dedicated revolutionaries, completely focussed on the single goal of an independent Irish Republic. And this could only be achieved by mobilising every resource in Ireland and America in order to forcefully sever the connection with England.

In the United States, these irreconcilables had considerable potential support among a growing Irish-American population.[6] Transatlantic migration had existed from colonial times and continued during the country's early decades, when newcomers settled in northern cities, the south and emergent western states. They expressed their Irish-American identity through cultural societies and nationalist organisations but many remained passionately interested in Irish politics. Overwhelmingly supportive of Daniel O'Connell's constitutional nationalism, few envisaged violently separating Ireland from England, but the huge influx of Famine refugees radicalised Irish-American attitudes, regarding themselves as they did innocent victims of an almost biblical tragedy, deliberately made strangers in a foreign land by a heartless British government. And their bitterness intensified when English newspapers like *The Times* rejoiced that: 'in a few years more, a Celtic Irishman will be as rare in Connemara as the Red Indian on the shores of Manhattan'. Unsurprisingly, Irish-America became a factory of grievances, its anti-English hostility constantly fanned by political demagogues, incendiary pamphlets and ballads demanding vengeance. An Irish journalist declared that the Famine sowed 'dragon's teeth from the Hudson to the Mississippi. The maddened fugitives of the dreadful Famine and eviction times hated the English power with quenchless hate.'[7]

Dublin Castle's expectation that transportation or banishment thousands of miles away from Ireland would eliminate Young Ireland refugees as a threat proved erroneous. After voyaging far beyond the British government's reach, Doheny, Mitchel, O'Mahony and others were free to dream of an independent Ireland and strive to realise it. A journalist drily observed that the Queen's writ did not run in Manhattan.[8] These irreconcilables formed a nucleus from which a new revolutionary organisation might emerge to renew the war against England, and New York was a haven from which they could strike at the enemy. Over time in America, many Irish migrants gravitated towards the exiled rebel leaders, in part because America was not after all a Promised Land. Starting at the bottom, they often remained trapped there. The exiled leaders offered them the hope of climbing out of poverty and some migrants even envisaged a great return to Ireland, like the Jews out of Egypt and Babylon. Consequently, a significant minority of Irish-Americans shifted from constitutional nationalism to revolutionary separatism, extolling exiled Young Ireland leaders as heroic martyrs and in the process endowing them with great moral authority. Potentially, they had a large base of support, because between 1848 and 1851, 848,000 Irish migrants entered America, in particular massively swelling New York's small Irish community.[9] By 1859, 134,000 Irish-born residents comprised 26 per cent of the city's population. New York's Irish newspapers, bars, clubs and societies, churches and St Patrick's Day parades dominated Irish-America's political, cultural and social life. Furthermore, despite living in the city's poorest areas, Irish-Americans accumulated political power through a legendarily corrupt Democratic party machine, and gradually New York became the beating heart of Irish-American separatism. Uniquely among immigrant communities, the Irish remained deeply involved in the affairs of their homeland and new migrants kept their grievances alive. Over half a century earlier, Lord Cornwallis had speculated that Irish-Americans might one day become very dangerous. 'They will embark with a spade and return with a musket.'[10]

Some exiled Irish leaders hoped to quickly resume the armed struggle against England. In 1851, Doheny dispatched Michael Phelan, a famous billiards champion, to Ireland, ostensibly for an exhibition tour but secretly on a reconnaissance mission to communicate with those '48 men who had remained at home. However, Phelan soon concluded that revolutionary conditions did not exist in a country whose exhausted population had mostly abandoned politics altogether.[11] A contemporary observer had discovered 'districts where the land being exceptionally good, the tenantry were still able to live, but when they met at market time or church, there were such gaps visible in the familiar muster that even in these districts the population looked like the remnant from a shipwreck'.[12] Moreover, despite a declining death rate, human misery was unabated. Smallholders who accepted poor relief had legally forfeited ownership to landlords known chillingly as 'Exterminators', whose pitiless clearances meant that 'a traveller in any southern or western county saw the ruins of human habitation from morning till night'.[13] With hundreds of thousands of tenants evicted, more surviving on relief and poorhouses overflowing, Phelan's bleak report disappointed Doheny but he grudgingly accepted that a long haul was inevitable – especially as no single powerful separatist organisation existed in both America and Ireland.

However, it was difficult uniting Irish-American organisations that constantly squabbled, and only a charismatic leader could fuse the warring parties into a single separatist movement with a clear sense of purpose. Irish-American morale was still at a low ebb in 1853 when John Mitchel escaped from captivity and reached New York on 29 November 1853.[14] Even Young Irelanders, who distrusted Mitchel's judgement, acknowledged his brilliance as a polemicist, someone whom Charles Gavan Duffy called a constant trumpet of resistance to England[15] and who to many nationalists seemed the embodiment of the revolution.[16] Mitchel's strong personality, the fear he inspired in enemies, and his formidable intelligence and journalistic talent quickly established him as America's foremost Irish émigré. But unifying the warring Irish-American factions required a conciliator, a skilled politician adept at compromise and who could understand other people's opinions. As someone who alienated legions of people, Mitchel was the last person in the world fit for that role. Divisive and vituperative, he regarded politics as war and believed that even fellow nationalists who differed from him should be crushed.

Almost immediately, Mitchel founded the *Citizen* newspaper, which fuelled an atavistic hatred of England by preaching that the Famine was a British government conspiracy to annihilate an entire nation and completely anglicise Ireland. When the Crimean War began in March 1854, Mitchel created the Irishmen's Civil and Military Republican Union, New York's first pre-Fenian society, to recruit volunteers and raise funds for arms and ammunition. Optimistically, Mitchel promised that if the war lasted another year, an Irish-American naval invasion would land in Ireland. Next, he asked Russia's minister in Washington to provide ships for the expedition, offering in return an insurrection in Ireland that would weaken England militarily. However, the Russians were indifferent and negotiations petered out, causing the Union to collapse. Then Mitchel's brief political career in New York imploded spectacularly when he publicly feuded with John Hughes, the city's Roman Catholic Archbishop and himself an Irish immigrant. After Mitchel defended the right of Papal States inhabitants to overthrow their ruler the Pope, Hughes denounced him. As a titan of New York public life who had built churches, schools, hospitals and orphanages for Irish-Americans, the Archbishop was well-connected to politicians, businessmen and the city's social elite, and accustomed to obedience and respect. But Mitchel had never bowed the knee to any establishment figure, political. social or clerical, and as a Presbyterian Ulsterman least of all to a Roman Catholic archbishop. Instinctively, he retaliated by accusing Hughes, the Roman Catholic hierarchy and priesthood of 'having twice in '98 and '48 delivered over the Catholic people of Ireland. Therefore, no terms are to be kept with such inveterate and treacherous enemies.' Nicknamed 'Dagger John', Hughes hit back, calling Mitchel a 'vitriol flinger'. After years of firing literary bullets, Mitchel had finally shot himself in the foot.

Battling the archbishop alone was political insanity, but incredibly, Mitchel doubled down and recklessly antagonised New York's powerful abolitionists. He not only defended Southern slavery but endorsed a resumption of the transatlantic slave trade so that poor whites could also become slave-owners. Long a white supremacist – and anti-Semite – Mitchel regarded Northern industrial capitalism as a threat to the Southern way of life. These two different cultures, he contended, meant that Southern states had gradually evolved into a separate nation. In March 1854, Mitchel provocatively declared that, 'We deny that it is a crime, or a wrong, or even a peccadillo, to hold slaves, to buy slaves, to keep slaves to their work by flogging: we, for our part, wish we had a good plantation, well-stocked with healthy negroes in Alabama.' Outraged, abolitionists demanded Mitchel's political scalp.

Warring simultaneously with two powerful New York institutions was political suicide, one that shredded Mitchel's base, decimated the *Citizen*'s circulation, and in December 1854 forced his resignation as editor. Tin-eared and ham-fisted, Mitchel had embarrassed followers who realised – if he did not – the fatal contradiction between demanding Irish freedom and simultaneously championing human bondage in America. At the end of December, public outrage at Mitchel's moral blindness effectively ran him out of town. Just like his political career, he went south to Tennessee, a slave state where Mitchel farmed land outside the city of Knoxville. Behind, he left an Irish-American community in turmoil.

Responsibility for filling a leadership vacuum now fell to 50-year-old Michael Doheny,[17] originally a Tipperary lawyer who during the 1848 Rising had begun a life-long friendship with John O'Mahony. After settling in New York, Doheny was admitted to the bar, founded a legal practice, and also became a well-known speaker on the political lecture circuit. In November 1853, Doheny and 40-year-old O'Mahony resumed their partnership when the latter moved from Paris to New York. Steeped in Irish culture, Celtic folklore and ancient manuscripts, O'Mahony had studied classical texts at Trinity College, Dublin, but he left university prematurely when his father died in November 1835 and returned home to manage the family's farm holdings in Cork and Tipperary.[18] At 6ft 2in tall, immensely strong and charismatic, O'Mahony became a commanding local leader but shied away from politics until he joined the 1848 rising. Afterwards, O'Mahony led a prolonged guerrilla campaign along the Suir valley from

22 August to late September. Attacking police and army posts, O'Mahony proved himself a talented military commander, but as British forces closed in he fled to France. As a penniless and jobless political exile, O'Mahony survived in Paris teaching Gaelic at the Irish College until Napoleon III overthrew the Second Republic, after which he left for America.

As Mitchel's successors, Doheny and O'Mahony worked well together, but the former was senior partner, a well-known attorney prominent in Irish-American politics and the stronger personality, a brawler who frequently gatecrashed opponents' meetings. By contrast, the relatively unknown and impoverished O'Mahony relied heavily on Doheny as he adjusted to his new American life.[19] Moreover, O'Mahony was temperamentally a dreamer, often impractical and at times emotionally fragile. Soon after arriving in America, he briefly abandoned Catholicism, founded a spiritualist circle, and became a medium before suffering a mental breakdown. 'I really was delirious – insane if you will – for several days in consequence of long mental and physical suffering and extreme nervous excitement.'[20] This manifested itself as religious euphoria during which O'Mahony's great physical strength became almost preternatural. Once he hurled two policemen down steps and another half-dozen officers were needed to subdue him. O'Mahony attributed his recovery to the Virgin Mary's divine intervention. Even so, Doheny made O'Mahony the public face of Irish-American separatism, preferring to exercise power from behind the scenes. Doheny's aggressive and rather uncouth behaviour had alienated important Irish-Americans like Archbishop Hughes, whereas O'Mahony's dignified bearing made him widely acceptable, an emollient figure bent on restoring harmony in the separatist movement.

Doheny and O'Mahony began reviving separatism by replacing the defunct Irishmen's Civil and Republican Union with an Emmet Monument Association.[21] This was a shrewdly chosen title as Robert Emmet's life and death exercised a tremendous hold over the imagination of Irish-Americans. By November 1855, the Association had over 3,000 members pledged to embark for Ireland when a rising began. As the Crimean War was still raging, Doheny and O'Mahony again tried to enlist Russian aid, by asking the New York consul to provide ships to transport 2,000 Irish-American volunteers to Ireland and weapons for 50,000 rebels. The Russian diplomat took them seriously and reported their proposal sympathetically to St Petersburg.

Doheny and O'Mahony also hoped that revolutionary prospects had improved in Ireland since Phelan's mission in 1851, as an attempt by prominent Young Irelander Charles Gavan Duffy to effect peaceful change had recently collapsed.[22] Sensationally acquitted in April 1849, Duffy was the only Young Ireland leader left free in Ireland. After resurrecting *The Nation* newspaper, he had toured Ireland and witnessed immense poverty and starvation. In Kilkenny an Exterminator landlord had evicted hundreds of people, and local priests responded by establishing a Tenant Protection Society. Soon, similar organisations proliferated across Ireland, and in August 1850 they united to form a Tenant League that demanded fixity of tenure and lower rents. Having rejected the idea of another rebellion, Duffy believed that fusing land reform and parliamentary representation could produce radical change, especially if a strong nationalist group of MPs held the balance of power at Westminster. Packed Tenant League meetings showed considerable support for Duffy's programme and revived nationalist hopes. The first step was contesting a general election and removing ineffective Irish MPs, whom Duffy scathingly denounced as 'never more discredited and distrusted than at this time. The few honest men among them were too feeble to count for much; the majority were habitual jobbers and some were accused of selling for hard cash the petty local patronage placed at their disposal by the Treasury.'[23] More pithily, a journalist derided them as a miserable parody of reality.[24]

In the general election of July 1852, the Tenant League endorsed candidates who supported an independent parliamentary opposition that would extract concessions from the British government. But many candidates had simply jumped on the populist bandwagon and were no better than the incumbent MPs. Duffy recalled 'wealthy nincompoops who had joined the League in the vague hope of getting into parliament'.[25] Despite triumphing with fifty-eight MPs, Duffy was saddled with deadwood like Daniel O'Connell's eldest son, Maurice, who had achieved nothing during twenty years in parliament. Duffy branded him 'a moral wreck' whose life of dissipation and philandering scandalised Dublin society; he was probably relieved when Maurice died from a brain haemorrhage in June 1853. Even so, Tenant League MPs now held the balance of power at Westminster, and in December 1852 they helped topple Lord Derby's minority Tory government. Duffy believed that to avoid the same fate, Lord Aberdeen's new coalition Cabinet of Whigs and Peelites would concede reforms in Ireland, but instead, Aberdeen bought off some of Duffy's MPs. William Keogh, the ambitious member for Athlone, performed a spectacular political somersault, reneged on his pledge of independent opposition, and accepted office as Solicitor-General for Ireland. Having long paraded himself as a nationalist champion, Keogh's unscrupulous behaviour astounded even the most cynical politicians and – against stiff competition – made him the most hated man in Ireland. John Sadleir, a Carlow MP, also defected and became a Treasury Lord, taking with him a brother and three cousins, all of them MPs. Edmund O'Flaherty, MP, a wheeler-dealer, was appointed a Commissioner of Income Tax. Outraged, Duffy claimed that until the last moment they had emphatically promised him not to take office.[26] However, some Tenant League MPs hoped the defectors could actually influence government policy, while others quietly gravitated to the government side. By-election losses also steadily eroded the League's parliamentary strength, while Duffy lacked the steely resolve to impose iron discipline on his MPs. Furthermore, Aberdeen's government adamantly resisted land reform in Ireland and after March 1854 it focused entirely on the war in Crimea.

By 1855, Duffy led only twenty-two MPs in parliament, where his speeches made little impact. From America, John Mitchel relentlessly caricatured him as 'Mr Give-Away-Duffy', always kow-towing to the British government. Absurdly, Duffy also continued to edit and write lengthy parliamentary reports for *The Nation*, whose treasurer absconded with its funds. Depressed and haunted by a sense of failure, Duffy decided to quit his 'blind and bitter land' for a new life in Australia, where he hoped to recover his health and become a successful lawyer. Duffy's gloomy valedictory address in *The Nation* on 4 August 1855 announced his retirement as MP; unless conditions changed dramatically, there was no more hope for Ireland than for a corpse on the dissecting table.[27] On 6 November, the virtually penniless Duffy and his family left Ireland, a departure that for many people seemed proof that constitutional politics had ended in miserable failure.

Duffy could hardly imagine matters getting worse, but they did because of John Sadleir.[28] Sadleir's almost rags-to-riches story had begun in Tipperary, where he bought up estates from ruined landlords and also established the Tipperary Joint-Stock, a bank whose branches throughout Ireland attracted large deposits. After moving to the City of London, Sadleir became chairman of the London and County Bank, speculated in Italian, American and Spanish railways, invested in iron mines and reputedly owned every cargo of sugar from the West Indies. By 1852, 36-year-old Sadleir's supposed Midas touch had elevated him to the status of financial wizard, a millionaire surrounded by the trappings of luxury whose Hyde Park mansion hosted grand receptions for the capital's social elite. His election to parliament made Sadleir valuable political connections; a peerage seemed only a matter of time.

However, the law then required that MPs accepting government posts underwent re-election and Sadleir was humiliatingly defeated in Carlow. Despite finding another seat in Sligo, his political career stalled when a Mr Dowling sued him, claiming that during the Carlow by-election, Sadleir had him kidnapped to prevent Dowling voting for Sadleir's opponent. In court Sadleir perjured himself blind, but in January 1854 the jury found for Dowling, effectively calling Sadleir a liar and forcing his resignation from the government. Two months later, after exploiting his official position to steal £15,000, Edmund O'Flaherty absconded just ahead of pursuing Scotland Yard detectives. In America, Edmund O'Flaherty MP resurfaced as William Stuart, a successful theatrical impresario and respectable businessman who was feted in high social circles. O'Flaherty's vanishing act strengthened a growing suspicion in Ireland that MPs were less politicians and more a criminal conspiracy of charlatans, sanctimonious guardians of public morality who enriched themselves at taxpayers' expense. Moreover, unlike men he had prosecuted for tax evasion, O'Flaherty eluded justice and never spent a day in jail.

But O'Flaherty's offences were petty compared to Sadleir's criminality. Despite dismissing his resignation from government as a minor bump in the road, Sadleir's fortunes went relentlessly downhill. During 1854 and 1855, a series of high-risk investments flopped spectacularly, losses that he covered by recruiting more investors in a giant Ponzi scheme. But still Sadleir's debts mounted inexorably. Trapped, he forged deeds and share certificates and treated the Tipperary Joint-Stock as his private piggy bank, all the while maintaining a façade of glittering success. Despite the enormous strain of his double life, Sadleir continued circulating parliament, glad-handing politicians and gloating over Charles Gavan Duffy's troubles. But behind the mask, Duffy saw a desperate man: 'His face was appalling. He had always been a dark, mysterious person but now he looked wild; haggard and repulsive. It seemed that thwarted ambition had turned his blood to liquid mud.'[29]

On Saturday, 16 February 1856, the Tipperary Bank ran out of cash and Sadleir's complex web of fraud finally unravelled. After his brother James requested £30,000 to keep the bank afloat, Sadleir spent the day frantically trying to raise funds but he was repeatedly turned down. And when one investor, whose deeds had been forged, began investigating, Sadleir realised that his rickety financial empire was about to collapse. However, unlike O'Flaherty, he saw no way out. Facing financial ruin, social disgrace and lengthy imprisonment, Sadleir committed suicide. On 17 February, pedestrians on Hampstead Heath found his body lying beside a silver tankard smelling of prussic acid and a note in which Sadleir admitted sole responsibility for his crimes. Others suffered not at all. William Keogh rose ever higher, first becoming Attorney-General for Ireland and then a senior judge.

When news of Sadleir's death reached Ireland, panic erupted among thousands of investors facing financial ruin. Technically this did not trigger a bank run; there was no money in the bank. A prominent journalist, A.M. Sullivan, recalled that:

> The Tipperary Bank closed its doors; country people flocked into the towns. They surrounded and attacked the branches; the poor victims imagined their money must be within and they got crowbars, picks and spades to force the walls and 'dig it out.' Old men went about like maniacs, confused and hysterical; widows knelt in the street and, aloud, asked God was it true they were beggared for ever. Even the poor-law unions, which had kept their accounts in the bank, lost all and had not a shilling to buy the paupers' dinner.[30]

By April 1856, the colossal scale of malfeasance became known: £1,250,000 and counting. John Sadleir was exposed as nineteenth-century Ireland's most prolific white-collar criminal.

Coming soon after the Tenant League's demise, the financial crash of February 1856 unleashed popular revulsion against a system that had apparently debauched public life, ruining the innocent while powerful guilty men evaded justice. And Sadleir perfectly epitomised a culture of greed and corruption rampant in 'respectable' society. A.M. Sullivan claimed that:

> not even in the darkest days of the eighteenth century a lower level of public spirit, a lower tone of political morality, prevailed in Ireland

than at this time. Public life was almost wholly abandoned to the self-seeking and adventurous. Good faith, honesty, consistency, sincerity in public affairs were cynically scoffed at and derided. The political arena was regarded simply as a mart in which everything went to the highest bidder; and the speculator who netted the most gains was the man most applauded.[31]

Nationwide disgust fuelled a widespread conviction that an entire rotten system should be swept away. However, though many Irishmen believed the 1850s were Ireland's locust years, Sullivan asserted that others found stagnation and apathy strangely comforting, and that:

If the absence of political life and action could be called tranquillity, or torpor be deemed repose, Ireland from 1852 to 1858 enjoyed that peaceful rest, that cessation from agitation which so many authorities declared to be the one thing wanting for her prosperity and happiness. To the eye of superficial observers, Ireland was in 1856 more really and completely pacified than at any time since the time of Strongbow. The people no longer interested themselves in politics. Who went into or who went out of parliament concerned them not. The agitator's voice was heard no more. All was silence. Rest and peace some called it.[32]

It was the quiet and peace of a political graveyard. Like a river when dammed, Irish nationalism always sought another outlet. Over previous decades, revolution, mass agitation and parliamentary politics had all been tried unsuccessfully, but defeat never ended the story; instead, it was merely a prelude to another chapter. The Tenant League's disintegration and Duffy's departure from Ireland simply meant that many nationalists would henceforth travel a different political path.

Capitalising on constitutional nationalism's disarray, Doheny and O'Mahony dispatched an emissary to Ireland, Joseph Denieffe, a 22-year-old tailor and EMA member.[33] However, proof of their scarce resources was that the EMA had well under fifty members, and they chose Denieffe as a cheap option because he was travelling to say farewell to his dying father in Kilkenny. Moreover, Denieffe was astonished when Doheny and O'Mahony ordered him to establish a revolutionary organisation in Ireland as the EMA had no important contacts there. Even more surprisingly,

Doheny told Denieffe that in September 1855 a naval expedition of 30,000 Irish-American volunteers would descend on Ireland, a promise that only made sense if Doheny had secured Russian assistance. Naively reassured, Denieffe left for Ireland. Upon finding his father completely recovered, he began his political mission. First, Denieffe enlisted John Haltigan, a *Kilkenny Journal* foreman, and together they recruited EMA members in neighbouring towns and villages, helped by an economic depression that had paralysed business and swamped the poorhouses. Denieffe recalled that although it was merely the nucleus of an organisation, the prospects seemed good.[34]

Haltigan next advised Denieffe to visit Dublin and meet Peter Langan, the owner of a Lombard Street timber yard at which radicals discussed revolutionary prospects. The group included John Hickey, a foreman builder from Kingstown with three militant brothers well-connected to the building trade: Garrett O'Shaughnessy, a metal worker; Philip Gray, a bookkeeper; and Thomas Clarke Luby, a Protestant journalist. Luby had never heard of the EMA, was sceptical about Denieffe, and completely dismissed the idea of an American naval invasion in September without extensive preparations having been made in Ireland. Unlike Langan, Gray and O'Shaughnessy, Luby refused to join the EMA and he was apparently vindicated when the promised fleet never materialised. As his savings diminished, Denieffe was about to return home when a Dublin friend gave him a job in Carrickmore, Co. Monaghan.

September passed uneventfully because Russia hesitated to risk an American naval expedition that the Royal Navy would probably have annihilated. Nevertheless, Doheny and O'Mahony continued negotiating with the Russians until the Crimean War ended in March 1856 and the Emmet Monument Association disbanded – though a committee was left in place to revive it if circumstances changed. However, by autumn, Irish-American politics had descended into renewed bickering. Sickened, O'Mahony contemplated founding an Irish colony in the west, but after a year spent translating a seventeenth-century Gaelic history of Ireland, he returned to politics in late 1857 as hopes of an Irish rebellion revived.[35] Deteriorating Anglo–French relations threatened a major European war and the Indian Mutiny had diverted British military resources from Ireland to the sub-continent. The EMA was swiftly reconstituted, though for another eighteen months it remained nameless, until in 1859 it would finally re-emerge as the Fenian Brotherhood.

Meanwhile, an almost penniless Denieffe had heard nothing from Doheny and O'Mahony, and he was about to leave for America when a letter from Haltigan announced that a former political exile, James Stephens, wanted to meet him. Denieffe's decision to delay his departure transformed everything. Born in Kilkenny, 32-year-old Stephens had worked in Dublin during the 1840s as a civil engineer, while gravitating politically to Young Ireland. At Ballingarry on 29 July 1848, Stephens led rebels in a skirmish with police and was shot in a hip and thigh. After he fled to the Tipperary/ Kilkenny border, an angry mob mistook Stephens for a British spy and almost lynched him. 'The moments I passed in the midst of this infuriated and exasperated multitude were the most terrible moments of my life.'[36] Just in time, a visitor from Kilkenny recognised Stephens and saved him.

Stephens and Michael Doheny then went on the run together, hounded for weeks by police as they trekked from town to town, physically and emotionally exhausted. The flight established Stephens's reputation for daring, courage and resourcefulness, and he greatly impressed Doheny. 'During the whole time which we spent, as it were, in the shadow of the gibbet, his courage never faltered and his temper never once ruffled.'[37] Stephens's family and friends helped out by placing in the *Kilkenny Moderator* a report of his death from serious injuries. Stephens's father then arranged a mock funeral in which a stone-filled coffin was buried at the city's ancient cathedral.

After he and Doheny parted, Stephens sailed for England, caught a ferry to France, and on 16 September reached Paris, where he recuperated from his wounds in a run-down hotel. Unemployed for over a year, Stephens survived on loans, handouts and teaching English. Paris broadened him culturally, especially after he lodged in the Latin Quarter while studying logic, ethics and philosophy at the Sorbonne. From August 1849, Stephens shared accommodation with John O'Mahony, who was 'dearer to me than any man I ever knew. O'Mahony and I then were almost inseparable.'[38] Once O'Mahony threw over a banister a Polish Jew who demanded Stephens repay a loan. Afraid the debt-collector was dead, they collapsed in laughter when he scampered away.

Both men followed political events in Ireland closely while associating with the secret revolutionary societies that abounded in Paris. Gradually, Stephens became less political refugee and more a professional revolutionary, inspired by European conspiracies like the Italian Carbonari. Pondering Ireland's political future, he eventually concluded that Irish nationalism had three possible courses of action.[39] Firstly, it could again resort to the constitutional agitation for legislative independence that O'Connell had organised. But the British government had rebuffed even the Liberator. Where O'Connell had failed no one else could succeed. Secondly, Ireland could lash out 'wildly and insanely' at England, a strategy that had led straight to the ill-fated Cappoquin Rising in 1849. This was the 'politics of Bedlam' whose advocates were 'criminals or lunatics'. Scorning both constitutional agitation and spontaneous violence, Stephens declared that armed revolt was the only possible course but only after a secret oath-bond society had spread all over Ireland, armed its members with rifles like soldiers, and disciplined them like an army. Stephen later claimed that after Ireland was liberated, he would gladly leave public life a happy man. Often depicted as a blinkered fanatic, he outlined a generous vision of independence, draining the poison from Anglo–Irish relations and inaugurating an Entente Cordiale between Ireland and England. 'Nothing would please me better than to see England and Ireland forget mutual pains, wrongs and frettings and insure their common future by an alliance, offensive and defensive.'[40]

At the end of 1855, Stephens returned to Ireland, probably because he felt isolated after O'Mahony left for America two years earlier, and also alienated from Napoleon III's authoritarian monarchical regime. Moreover, after the Tenant League's collapse, the Irish political situation seemed more favourable to revolutionaries. Stephens also longed for a sense of purpose in his life. 'I hated the sedentary life of the litterateur, and my desk appeared to be an instrument of torture. I passionately longed for work – to do something.'[41] By early January 1856, Stephens was back in Dublin, penniless and literally on his uppers. After former comrades from 1848 told him that Ireland was in a hopeless state, he left Dublin in the bleak mid-winter, walking towards his family home in Kilkenny city. Sometimes trudging through the night, Stephens's continental clothes and long flowing beard had him often mistaken for an Oriental and sometimes as part of a travelling circus. After losing contact with his family, he discovered, at journey's end, that his two brothers had vanished and their father was dead. 'My only sister (Anna) had followed him to the grave in the prime of girlhood and thus was a household ruined and broken up.'[42] Virtually alone in the world, an exhausted Stephens was nursed back to health by an uncle and three aunts.

In Kilkenny, Stephens found political opinion 'at a very low ebb, cold, dead and passionless, as if Young Ireland had never existed'.[43] An exodus of people, especially natural leaders, had completely demoralised even his 1848 comrades. 'All my enthusiasm was frozen for the moment. I looked like one who had come on a wild goose chase after all and whose mission had been prematurely ended.'[44] But Stephens soldiered on and decided to undertake a walking tour of Ireland, funded by occasional French tutoring and dependent for bed and board on friends and the kindness of strangers:

> I was anxious to see the people for myself, to walk through as much of the island as possible, to go to the city and speak to the toiling artisan, to walk into the rural districts and chat with the farmer or the labourer, to make scrutinising tours through the minor towns and villages, seeking to find out, wherever I went, the sentiments real of the masses.[45]

In a sense this was an anatomy study to test Duffy's contention that Ireland resembled a corpse on the dissecting table, an analogy that had gripped popular imagination. Like a doctor, Stephens planned to discover whether the body politic was indeed dead, slowly expiring, or capable of a full recovery: 'In fact, I wanted to feel Ireland's pulse.' If the situation was indeed hopeless, Stephens intended resuming his exile and living permanently in Paris. 'With this fixed and firmly-rooted idea I took up my pilgrim's staff and commenced my walk of three thousand miles through the country.'[46]

Travelling as 'an seabhac', 'the wandering hawk' (after his hawk-like eyes) Stephens calculated that between spring and autumn 1856 he actually covered about 3,500 miles, a testing distance for someone prone to hypochondria and who claimed to have suffered from fading memory, famine fever, rheumatism, depression and a fear of blindness. All the while he battled aristocratic hostility, farmers' apathy and what he considered bourgeois pig-headedness. But labourers, tradesmen and peasants' sons listened sympathetically, a reception that left Stephens well satisfied at journey's end: 'My three-thousand miles walk through Ireland had convinced me of one thing - the possibility of organising a proper movement for the independence of my native land.'[47] However, after consulting with Dublin republicans, Stephens decided against establishing a revolutionary movement immediately – though the time would come. 'From what I had seen I could say that the cause was not at all dead, but sleeping. The corpse on the dissecting table was a myth. Ireland lived and glowed but lived and glowed

– in a trance.'[48] Stephens believed decisive action was vital in the near future because Ireland was in a race against time for survival. Otherwise, a much-diminished population would continue an irreversible decline ending in a complete extinction of the Irish race:

> I was as sure as of my own existence that if another decade passed without an endeavour of some kind or another to shake off an unjust yoke the Irish people would sink into a lethargy from which it would be impossible for any patriot however Titanic in genius or for anybody of patriots however sincere and zealous to arouse them into anything like a healthy existence. To save my race from this dream, to revive old hopes and aspirations. Such was my aim, such my ambitions.[49]

In late 1856, Stephens caught a lucky break when a bookseller friend informed O'Mahony that he was back in Ireland. O'Mahony immediately re-established contact with Stephens, though initially he had no political role for him in mind. Indeed, having withdrawn from Irish-American affairs, O'Mahony was himself actually drafting a farewell speech. Even so, he and Doheny realised Stephens's return was significant and that he was a far more important person than Denieffe for their project of an Irish revolutionary movement. In letters, Stephens criticised O'Mahony's enemies and urged him to stay in politics; when O'Mahony eventually returned to the EMA, Stephens took the credit for changing his mind.

Although determined to avoid the 'drudgery' of full-time teaching, Stephens survived by tutoring in French the children of three suburban families and two sons of John Blake Dillon, the former Young Ireland leader. He also invited Dillon to join his conspiracy but was rebuffed; Dillon now wanted nothing to do with revolution. Stephens also unsuccessfully approached John O'Leary, a 26-year-old medical student from Tipperary whom he had known for a decade. O'Leary had no principled objections to rebellion but argued that the time was not yet right for an insurrectionary movement.

In 1857, Stephens learned from John Haltigan about Denieffe's Irish mission. When they met, Stephens urged Denieffe to remain in Ireland and together they would establish a secret revolutionary organisation. Dazzled by Stephens, Denieffe cancelled his journey home and returned to his job. Over the following months Stephens consolidated his relationship with Doheny and O'Mahony, who were making the still unnamed Fenian Brotherhood supreme in Irish-America and were confident now that Stephens could build a viable counterpart in Ireland. Two days before Christmas 1857, an American emissary, Owen Considine, delivered to Stephens a letter from a committee whose chairman, Michael Doheny, wanted to know whether Ireland was ripe for rebellion and, if so, would Stephens establish a revolutionary organisation. Significantly, though, Considine also handed over a private message from O'Mahony cautioning Stephens about the American side's meagre resources, a proviso that Stephens ignored.[50]

Reading aloud his reply to Denieffe, Stephens declared that Ireland was ripe for insurrection and that he would lead it. Provided Irish-America sent £80–100 for three months, Stephens promised to organise 10,000 men, 1,500 of them armed with rifles. But, 'the Centre of this or any similar organisation should be perfectly unshackled; in other words, a provisional dictator. On this point I can conscientiously concede nothing.'[51] Irish-American leaders did not realise that this was an ultimatum. Some wanted to control a transatlantic relationship and others envisaged an equal partnership but everyone had misjudged Stephens, whom most knew little and understood less. Even Doheny's and O'Mahony's passing friendship with Stephens was in bygone times when neither had fathomed his lust for absolute power, his inability ever to work harmoniously with anyone on an equal basis. Nor was Stephens's demand for total control confined to Ireland; his ambition encompassed the entire revolutionary movement on both sides of the Atlantic. This misunderstanding right from the start as to where authority ultimately resided would bedevil transatlantic relations and help bring about defeat in 1867.

Denieffe brought Stephens's reply to New York, encountering Doheny outside the New York City Halls of Justice in Manhattan and handing him the letter. 'He tore it open and read a few lines; the tears came to his eyes; he folded the letter and we hastened on to his office.'[52] Assembling his inner circle, Doheny organised a whip round, but although everyone chipped in their last cent and later collected more money from friends, only £80 was raised over the next two months. Finally, Denieffe left for Ireland and reached Dublin on 17 March 1858, bringing a letter from 'the Irish revolutionary committee' that appointed Stephens 'chief executive of the Irish revolutionary movement' with 'supreme control and absolute authority over the movement in Ireland'.

Despite a shortfall in cash, Stephens seized the historically symbolic Day of Saint Patrick. At his lodgings in McGuinness Place near Lombard Street, he, Luby, Langan, O'Shaughnessy, Denieffe and Considine launched a new revolutionary organisation. None could have imagined that their creation, after struggling for existence, would eventually succeed beyond their wildest expectations and become what one historian has called the most enduring and successful revolutionary secret society in Europe.[53] Under Stephens's guidance, Luby devised an oath that pledged members' loyalty to an Irish Republic and obedience to their superior officers. Initially, the organisation lacked even a name and members referred to Our Body, Our Movement, The Society, The Organisation and The Brotherhood. Luby referred to the Irish Revolutionary Brotherhood, while Stephens sometimes mentioned the Irish Republican Brotherhood. Only after mass arrests in September 1865 would the last name become popular, starting among Irish fugitives in America and eventually finding favour in Ireland. However, for convenience, historians habitually speak of the Irish Republican Brotherhood (IRB) from 1858 onwards.

In late spring 1859, the EMA holding committee would remodel its organisation and elect O'Mahony as president. Influenced by his Gaelic studies and the imaginary world of ancient Ireland that he often mentally inhabited, O'Mahony then persuaded the EMA to rename itself as the Fenian Brotherhood.[54] Almost 2,000 years earlier the Irish national militia was the '*Fiana Erion*' or Fenians, a name derived from its famous commander, variously known as Fenius, Fin and Fion. O'Mahony's choice was inspired. Short, strong and Irish, it denoted modern Fenians as warriors in an army of liberation. Moreover, by harking back many generations, O'Mahony had located Fenianism in a long line of resistance that would only end with final victory over England. By giving his Irish-American organisation a unique name, O'Mahony was asserting the existence of two separate but equal wings of the same movement, united in a common purpose but each contributing in different ways. Yet, ironically, many IRB members in Ireland found O'Mahony's choice of title appealing and began calling themselves Fenians as well. Regardless of names, the Fenian Brotherhood and IRB shared the same raison d'etre, which one historian has identified as the 'violent struggle against British rule; parliamentary and other constitutional action were anathematised'.[55]

Stephens structured the IRB as an army, emphasising hierarchy, discipline and secrecy. As Central Organiser of the Irish Republic ('C.O.I.R') he was effectively commander-in-chief, exercising total authority over the entire movement. Many members were uncomfortable with this untrammelled power, but John O'Leary believed that the leader of a conspiracy was much more like the chief of an army than the chief of a state: 'His power must be theoretically absolute. All unlimited power, as all restraints upon liberty, are in themselves evils. A conspiracy is in itself an evil, but is sometimes necessary to oppose a greater.'[56] Recruits were enrolled in circles, analogous to an army regiment, with every circle presided over by a centre or A, equivalent to a colonel. Centres chose nine Bs or captains, who in turn selected nine Cs or sergeants. Finally, Cs chose nine Ds who comprised the rank and file. Every IRB member was to unquestioningly obey his superior officers. In order to shield the IRB from British espionage, Stephens tried to hermetically seal the organisation by insisting on each rank knowing only the identity of his immediate superior, though in practice this rule was often violated. From the start, then, Stephens was a provisional dictator, universally acknowledged as The Boss, The Captain. Yet he hardly looked an imposing leader – unlike O'Mahony, who stood over 6ft tall, and whom John O'Leary considered perhaps the manliest and handsomest man he had ever seen.[57] By contrast, at 5ft 7in, Stephens was stout with fair hair balding around the top of his head and a long flowing sandy beard, tinged with grey. While Stephens had a massive forehead, his hands and feet were remarkably small, and he had a disconcerting habit of closing his left eye when speaking.

However, Stephens exuded an absolute conviction that the revolution would ultimately triumph and that only he could lead it to final victory, a spellbinding certainty that banished all doubt. His followers' blind faith and adulation resembled a semi-religious devotion which, one prominent Fenian claimed, made Stephens 'an object of wonder, almost worship'.[58] Denieffe regarded him with boundless admiration:

I would undertake anything for him. He seemed to have me under a spell. There was an earnestness in his every move. He was abstemious, frugal – in fact, in adversity his greatest qualities were shown to perfection. He was all that could be desired as a leader. Strict attention to duty, perseverance, privation, toil – no rest until the object was reached and victory achieved. We were willing to bear all and follow him to the end.[59]

Even A.M. Sullivan described Stephens as 'a man of marvellous subtlety and wondrous plausibility; crafty, cunning, and quite unscrupulous as to the employment of means to an end'.[60] He believed that Stephens's great manipulative ability and strength of will made him a born conspirator; in fact, 'one of the ablest, most skilful and most dangerous revolutionists of our time'.[61]

By portraying himself as a man of action bent on a rising at the earliest opportunity, Stephens sowed the seeds of transatlantic discord. Cautious and methodical, O'Mahony came to regard Stephens as an irresponsible firebrand who would probably destroy Fenianism. He believed that an open Fenian Brotherhood should be independent from but closely allied to a secret IRB organised on military lines, and furthermore, unlike Stephens, O'Mahony doggedly adhered to a gradualist policy about starting the rising. Only when the Fenian Brotherhood and IRB had achieved sufficient discipline and resources should they should launch a combined onslaught against England. Until then, both organisations should be kept in a state of constant, watchful preparedness, biding their time and waiting for an opportunity to strike, especially when England became embroiled in a foreign war.

As the IRB's provisional dictator from the start, Stephens had avoided the long climb to supreme power that most politicians must endure and, in the process, also superseded another potential leader, Thomas Clarke Luby. The son of an Anglican clergyman from Dublin and a Roman Catholic mother, 33-year-old Luby was a law graduate of Trinity College, Dublin. After abandoning his family tradition before joining O'Connell's Repeal Association, he wrote for *The Nation* newspaper, before defecting to Young Ireland. During the 1848 rising, Luby commanded rebels on the borders of Dublin and Meath and audaciously planned for 200 Dublin volunteers to seize Blanchardstown police station, but fewer than twenty men mustered at Blanchardstown. Luby then went south, intent on joining the Young Ireland leaders, only for the rising to suddenly collapse in fiasco at Ballingarry. A year later, Luby helped lead the so-called Cappoquin rising, along with fellow radicals Fintan Lalor, John O'Leary and Joseph Brennan, who planned to simultaneously attack police stations in Waterford, Kilkenny,

Clare and Limerick on 16 September 1849. But turnout was poor and the only fighting occurred at Cappoquin in Co. Waterford, where Brennan unsuccessfully attacked a police barracks.

After a brief imprisonment, Luby left for Paris in 1851 to join the Foreign Legion and gain military experience. Since recruiting for the Legion had been temporarily suspended, he spent a year in Australia before returning to Ireland in 1853, his revolutionary ardour undiminished. Teaming up with comrades from 1849, Luby edited *The Tribune*, a newspaper whose belligerent rhetoric echoed that of Mitchel. However, after two unsuccessful risings, even Luby reacted cautiously when Denieffe turned up in Dublin, but when Stephens appeared his impeccable revolutionary credentials won Luby over.

Although both Stephens and Luby essentially created the IRB, Stephens was always its single unchallenged leader, despite Luby's stronger claim through his social rank, university education, literary ability, conspiratorial history and greater standing among Dublin revolutionaries. But whereas Stephens craved primacy and power, Luby lacked personal ambition: even his best friend, John O'Leary, acknowledged Luby's 'weakness of will' and that he was 'too ready to be swayed by inferior, though in a sense, stronger men'.[62] Luby considered Stephens 'an able organiser' and was content to remain his loyal but never utterly subservient second-in-command. Sometimes, he deflated Stephens's inflated ego as well as his literary, artistic and philosophical pretensions, even openly teasing Stephens about his talking 'hocus pocus trash. I used in our jollier moods to make him laugh by calling him to his face "the great Sir Hocus Pocus".'[63]

As IRB leader, Stephens began creating a mass movement. He had already absorbed Langan's Dublin friends, while the Hickey brothers recruited in Kingstown and among the capital's building trade. However, two years later the Dublin IRB would still have only about fifty members. On 19 February 1858, Stephens and Luby started a southern recruiting tour and assumed control of a secret network that O'Mahony had established in Cork, Waterford, Limerick and Tipperary before the 1848 rising, and left in place when he fled Ireland. O'Mahony later claimed that from France and then America he maintained contact with these rebel artisans and labourers, 'some thousands of stalwart fighting men. This I considered a good basis to build an organisation on. And I have not been disappointed in my expectations.'[64] Stephens and Luby also integrated Denieffe's Kilkenny network into the IRB and urged Haltigan to continue recruiting. Denieffe recalled that:

The object of Stephen's tour was to secretly visit and personally interview the most influential Nationalists in each town, explaining to them as far as was permissible at that time the plan and scope of the organisation in America and Ireland and what it hoped to accomplish. He invariably succeeded in getting them interested to the extent of their becoming active local organisers and always, before leaving, instructed them regarding the expected growth and future government of the society in that section. The meetings were carried on with great secrecy behind closed doors and, in each place, Stephens was given the name of reliable men in the next town, men whose patriotism he could rely on to the death; these in turn referred him to others further along and in that way the entire South was organised. Later on, other men were sent North and West, men widely acquainted in those sections repeated the good work performed by Stephens, Luby and others in the South and Southeast.[65]

In Cork, Stephens and Luby absorbed the Phoenix Society, a revolutionary but not oath-bound organisation that repudiated British rule in Ireland. Founded in 1856 in famine-devastated Skibbereen, it flourished throughout an Irish-speaking area of west Cork with a long revolutionary tradition. When Stephens visited the town in May 1858, he claimed Irish-Americans had promised him men, money, weapons and drill instructors. Jeremiah O'Donovan Rossa, owner of a hardware shop, immediately joined the IRB and quickly became the town's centre. Within weeks, 90 of 100 Phoenix men in Skibbereen had enrolled in the IRB, and in October 1858 an American army officer came from Dublin to train them. Rossa boasted that 'Before the autumn months had passed away, we had the district in a blaze.'[66] As the IRB expanded across Co. Cork, recruitment soared, secret drilling in woods and on hillsides was widespread, and the county's political mood changed. But at Skibbereen, Stephens's and Luby's momentum stopped abruptly after they ran out of money and returned to Dublin.

Denieffe recalled this period as:

a most gloomy one. Everything was not only at a standstill, but the outlook for the future was dark indeed. There had been no news from America since my return and it looked as if our friends there had given up all thought of us. This state of inertia was demoralising. Each day came and passed into yesterday but still no tidings.[67]

Exasperated, Stephens sent Denieffe back to America to discover why transatlantic communications had apparently broken down and funds dried up. But IRB finances could not even cover Denieffe's boat fare and only a member's gift of £8 saved the day. In New York, Denieffe learned that $100 had been sent, totally cleaning out the Fenian treasury. After scraping together another $200, Denieffe returned to Ireland a month later and warned Stephens about the bleak situation in New York. Far from the Fenian Brotherhood being a large and well-funded organisation, it probably consisted of O'Mahony, Doheny and the sixteen co-signatories of their December 1857 letter to Stephens. Moreover, further funding for the IRB was unlikely as Irish-Americans were now sceptical that a credible revolutionary society could ever be established in Ireland.

But Stephens still needed money, and lots of it, for his and Luby's organising tours, IRB couriers who travelled to Britain and America and also to purchase weapons and ammunition. However, Denieffe's two money-raising trips to New York had raised only £140 – barely covering his travel expenses. Suspecting that Irish-American leaders had lied about their financial strength, Stephens decided to investigate the American situation for himself, and establish a financial pipeline along which cash would flow into IRB coffers. In his quest for money, Stephens also needed prominent Irish-Americans to endorse him, because since 1848 there had existed in New York a large fund controlled by an Irish Directory consisting of Young Ireland exiles like Meagher and O'Gorman. Established to help Irish revolutionaries, the fund had grown rapidly to £10,000, which financed the escapes of Mitchel, McManus and Meagher. By 1858, well over £5,000 remained and Stephens wanted it. On 13 October, Stephens arrived in New York.

From the moment he landed, Stephens's arrogance and ingratitude were on full display. Utterly self-centred, he complained about his treatment, despite himself being virtually penniless and dependent on others to cover his hotel and travel expenses. Disappointed at the Fenian Brotherhood's stagnation, he lambasted everyone except O'Mahony. Even Doheny, his former comrade-in-arms, was 'pitiful and wretched. Also, he is jealous, envious and false.'[68] Doheny and O'Mahony immediately advised Stephens that to secure the Directory's assets he must win over Meagher and Mitchel, who although not a director, remained hugely influential in Irish-America. After escaping from Van Diemen's Land and reaching New York in May 1852, a destitute Meagher had prospered by marrying Libby Townshend, an heiress whose wealthy family gave them a mansion on Fifth Avenue. Meagher also owned a weekly newspaper, the *Irish News*.

On 14 October 1858, Stephens and O'Mahony visited Meagher, whose patronising manner instantly alienated Stephens, as did Meagher's vast bulk – living testimony to hopeless gluttony. But Stephens was a talented storyteller and his glowing tales of the IRB's growth led Meagher to hail him as the Wolfe Tone of his generation. Meagher promised to help Stephens get money from the Directory, provided he secured Mitchel's endorsement. Accordingly, Stephens travelled to Knoxville, Tennessee, on a railway ticket that Doheny bought for him. Having business in the capital, Meagher accompanied Stephens as far as Washington; but on the train, he disgusted Stephens by downing a bottle of brandy and gorging himself from a food-laden table. On 21 October, an exhausted Stephens reached Knoxville, Tennessee, where Mitchel had built a large house and established a newspaper that stridently advocated slavery. In vile weather and soaking wet, Stephens arrived at Mitchel's residence. The two men had never met, though Mitchel knew something about Stephens's organising ability and his presence at Ballingarry in 1848. For his part, the abolitionist Stephens carefully avoided mentioning slavery but there was no personal chemistry between him and Mitchel. Both men radiated immense self-esteem and looked down on almost everyone else. Furthermore, Mitchel thought Stephens was grasping and possibly a fantasist: 'For two days he remained with us, telling me romantic tales of his armed, sworn and organised forces. All he wanted was that I should publicly call on my fellow countrymen in America for money, and no end of money, to be remitted to him for revolutionary purposes.'[69] Yet Mitchel received few visitors and Stephens had travelled far to win his approval. Consequently, Mitchel gambled a $50 cheque – for him a substantial sum – on Stephens's prophecy that the IRB would soon overthrow British rule in Ireland. Furthermore, despite rejecting Stephens's plea for a public endorsement, Mitchel wrote a supportive letter to the Irish Directory.

For a while after returning to New York, Stephens revelled in success. On 9 December the still unnamed Fenian Brotherhood appointed him Chief Executive of the Irish revolutionary movement, with supreme authority in Ireland and America. Unsurprisingly, henceforth Stephens assumed the Fenian Brotherhood was subordinate to him, and in January 1859 he appointed O'Mahony as his supreme organiser in the United States and Director of the Revolutionary Brotherhood in America. Then things fell apart. Dizzy with success, Stephens behaved arrogantly towards men who were once his superiors. At a meeting in Washington, Stephens told Mitchel and Meagher that he now wanted their total commitment and obedience. Mitchel recalled that Stephens 'demanded of us in a somewhat high tone, that we should enter his conspiracy, and should use all the credit and influence that he supposed us to possess among the Irish citizens, in order to procure money for the purpose of the conspiracy. It was a startling proposal'.[70] Thereafter Mitchel's and Meagher's confidence in Stephens ebbed away.

On Wednesday, 26 January 1859, Stephens encountered Meagher at the *Irish News* office in New York and immediately sensed his discomfort. After a brief conversation, Meagher handed over a letter declaring that he could not endorse a revolutionary movement seemingly doomed to failure. This change of mind has never been satisfactorily explained. Perhaps Meagher knew about Mitchel's own doubts; possibly he was reluctant to jeopardise his new-found place in New York's high society. Stephens himself blamed Young Ireland leaders and accused his old mentor John Blake Dillon of poisoning Mitchel against him. When the Directory refused to hand over any funds, Stephens realised that months of exertion had all been for nothing. Enraged, he accused Mitchel and Meagher of deception. 'Not that I had a high opinion of – or even believed – in their patriotism. But I believed they would not dare hold out because by doing so it would be evident to all that they were shams, had been shams probably at all times and had abandoned their country.'[71] Stephens denounced Mitchel as a 'disgruntled egoist'; Mitchel scorned Stephens as a humbug and a lying rogue.

Spurned, Stephens denounced Young Ireland leaders as an obsolete political elite of middle-class professionals whose social and intellectual snobbery had warped their judgement. For his part, Stephens despised them as ghosts who had failed utterly in 1848 but remained imbued with a sense of entitlement, invincibly certain they remained the natural leaders of Irish nationalism. The Young Ireland exile, Richard O'Gorman, epitomised this delusion: only good now for ceremonial roles at St Patrick's Day parades, he clung to his seat on the Directory. For Stephens this was a parting of the ways with this old guard. John O'Leary claimed that henceforth Stephens 'had not a good word to say of the Young Ireland party; and he infused his own feelings largely into the mass of his followers'.[72] Stephens would not have long to wait for his revenge.

Stephens's relations with American Fenian leaders also deteriorated after he realised they had achieved little and vastly inflated their resources – just as he had grossly exaggerated the IRB's strength. To help, Stephens took it upon himself to establish Fenian branches outside New York in cities like Boston, Chicago and Philadelphia. Although prone to self-pity and hypo-chondria, Stephens's travels were exhausting and doing the work of others only increased his antipathy to Fenian Brotherhood leaders. Even O'Mahony did not escape his wrath; the first seeds of doubt about 'Big John' had been planted. 'He lacked so to speak complete mastery over his intellectual tools and materials. Indeed, hundreds of men with not a tithe of O'Mahony's intel-lect have cut far more brilliant and showy figures on the stage of history.'[73]

Transatlantic relations cooled further, soon after Stephens departed America. Despite Stephens's belief that he had achieved supremacy over the American leadership, the reconstituted EMA finally went public as the Fenian Brotherhood not the Irish Revolutionary Brotherhood. Furthermore, O'Mahony had exchanged his Stephens-designated title of Chief Executive for that of President. And, while retaining the IRB's organisational structure and goals, the Fenian Brotherhood's ethos reflected O'Mahony's open and consensual nature, being neither illegal, conspirato-rial, oath-bound nor authoritarian. By rejecting Stephens's blueprint, he was clearly asserting American independence and henceforth a genuine transatlantic partnership depended on Stephens's willingness to compro-mise – a quality alien to his nature.

Stephens had intended sailing home on 5 February 1859, but delayed his departure after Dublin Castle suppressed the Phoenix Society. Spooked, Stephens suspected it knew about the American trip, was tracking his movements and would arrest him when his ship reached an English port. Deciding against returning on a British liner, he waited a month for a vessel travelling directly to France, where he intended to stay indefinitely. Using the extra time profitably, Stephens toured New Orleans and other major cities raising funds for the IRB. More money flowed in after January 1859, when American Fenians established an Irish Patriotic Defence Fund, whose ambiguous title implied it was financing the legal defence of Phoenix

Society members recently arrested in Ireland. In fact, contributions were secretly channelled to Stephens and the IRB. To what extent – if at all – Stephens was implicated in the deception remains unclear, but incontrovertibly he took funds from a money-laundering scam. However, until the Fund's cover was blown in July 1859, donations for Irish revolutionaries rolled in, and Stephens finally left New York on 1 March 1859 flush with cash – £600–700 in gold.

During Stephens's absence in America, the Irish Constabulary had warned Dublin Castle about Phoenix Society subversion in Cork, Kerry, Tipperary and Limerick. Chief Secretary Lord Naas sent troops to Bandon, Bantry and Clonakilty, stationed a gunboat in Bantry Bay, and dispatched a hard-line Resident Magistrate, George Fitzmaurice, to Skibbereen. Suspecting America might become a hostile Irish base, Naas also located an Irish Constabulary Sub-Inspector, Thomas Doyle, in New York to investigate Irish-American politicians, societies and newspapers. Doyle reported that the Fenian Brotherhood existed and claimed it was encouraging the Phoenix movement in Ireland.

In October 1858, anxiety in Ireland about the Phoenix Society went public after A.M. Sullivan had William Smith O'Brien pen a letter for *The Nation* newspaper criticising the organisation, while in a strong editorial, Sullivan claimed conspirators in Skibbereen were drilling and procuring arms.[74] His intervention brought down on Sullivan a torrent of abuse. From America, Stephens branded him a 'felon-setter'; a government agent. Even so, Sullivan was satisfied that his actions had done the trick. But the Irish government wanted to eradicate the Phoenix menace once and for all, especially as priests, magistrates and loyalists still feared an imminent rebellion. On 6 December, police simultaneously raided Skibbereen, Bantry, Kenmare and Killarney, rounding up Rossa and other suspects. These arrests and the deplorable conditions in which prisoners were kept generated considerable public sympathy for young men widely regarded as naive dupes. Even Sullivan raised money for their legal defence. But Naas wanted draconian punishment and appointed a special commission to conduct trials in Cork and Kerry. Attorney-General Whiteside led the prosecution, and the presiding judge was none other than the now Justice William Keogh. When the Kerry trials began in Tralee, in March 1859, it required two trials and an all-Protestant jury to convict the first defendant, Daniel O'Sullivan, who was sentenced to ten years' penal servitude. Hanging over the proceedings had been the mastermind who supposedly lured the defendants into treason. Attorney-General Whiteside told the jury that this person, who had unfortunately escaped arrest, had first appeared a year earlier in County Cork under the nom-de-plume of Hawk – 'But his real name was Stephens. He proceeded through the county enrolling persons in an illegal secret society by promises that the Americans and French were about to invade Ireland.' Dublin Castle was on to the IRB leader.

Before the Cork trials began on St Patrick's Day, 17 March 1859, the state decided to cut its losses and offered a deal whereby the accused would plead guilty and be released without punishment. But Rossa and the others were unwilling to abandon Daniel O'Sullivan. On St Patrick's Day the defence was ready, but after Keogh consulted the Crown, he suddenly postponed proceedings until the next assizes. Rossa and his co-defendants remained in prison until July 1859, when the deal offer was renewed. Although Rossa was prepared to fight to the end, he claimed:

> the Cork City men who were in communication with us gave us to understand that James Stephens had left Ireland after our arrest, that he was in France, that no word was received from him, that the work seemed dead and that we may as well accept the terms of release offered to us.[75]

Provided Daniel O'Sullivan was also freed, Rossa and the others complied and were released on 27 July 1859.

Once again, A.M. Sullivan believed the Phoenix danger was over. But arrest, detention and trial had not chastened the defendants, only strengthening their commitment to revolution. Rossa emerged from prison a bitter, angry young man. 'My business in Skibbereen was ruined, the creditors came down on the house after my arrest'; the ownership of the house got into law; my wife with four children had to move into another house.'[76] O'Leary saw in Rossa a much-changed man, 'soured in temper,' 'a terribly uncompromising person'.[77] Unsurprisingly, Phoenix members craved vengeance against informers. After identifying one, Denieffe recalled that he needed Luby's authorisation for an assassination. 'I shall never forget the effect that the proposition had on him. Pacing up and down, he said "By God, it cannot be permitted. I will not take the responsibility of such a course upon myself." The matter was reluctantly given up.'[78]

Having arranged to meet Luby and O'Leary at Boulogne, Stephens arrived in late March 1859. Confident about the IRB's future and in good humour, he awakened Luby at the Hotel de Folkstone, banging loudly on his bedroom door and in a booming voice ordering him in French to open in the name of the Emperor.[79] But instead of a posse of gendarmes, Luby saw a grinning Stephens. Next day the trio left for Paris, where Stephens rented lodgings near the Champs-Elysees. He intended remaining in France indefinitely and making its capital a European New York, a more convenient base from which his couriers would communicate with the IRB in Ireland and the Fenian Brotherhood in America. In July, Luby left for Ireland, instructed by Stephens to expand an IRB that had made little progress during the leader's absence.[80] On Luby's return, the Dublin IRB still consisted mainly of Peter Langan's circle and the Hickey brothers' followers in Kingstown, only about fifty members in all. But Luby was an excellent organiser and he was helped by Con O'Mahony, a young schoolmaster from Skibbereen based at the teacher training school in Marlborough Street. O'Mahony also brought in James O'Callaghan, a Cork friend working at Cannock and Whites, a well-known drapery emporium in Mary Street. Luby claimed that in an almost incredibly short time they created a virtually new and formidable Dublin IRB. Through O'Callaghan the IRB infiltrated drapery businesses, recruiting their smartest commercial assistants and numerous intelligent tradesmen. Many newcomers were former members of the so-called Pope's Irish Brigade, who had returned from Italy, while others were soldiers discharged from the East India Company's Artillery. Prominent new recruits included Nicholas Walsh, Edward Ryan, Andrew Nolan, Maurice O'Donoghue and Edward Duffy. Luby's regular letters to Stephens boasted that his 'New Organisation' had transformed Dublin into possibly the IRB's capital, though cautiously he only promoted new recruits at most to Bs or captains, leaving it to Stephens on his return to make them As – centres or colonels.

O'Leary recalled Stephens being 'semi-slumberous' in Paris, summoning prominent Fenians to the French capital for extended periods and regaling them with his ambitious plans for the IRB.[81] These included bringing centres from Ireland for military courses and establishing a training school for leadership cadres. Neither scheme ever materialised. Moreover, Stephens and O'Mahony had agreed that Irish-Americans should be sent to Ireland as drill masters and organisers, but they often found no IRB circles in their districts and dwindling funds forced many to return home. Instead of giving his Irish coterie in Paris creative work, Stephens acted more like a tour guide as he escorted Dan McCartie, Denis Mulcahy, Joseph Denieffe and others to landmarks like Versailles and the Arc de Triomphe. Despite his enriching them culturally, these excursions left them none the wiser about the IRB's future. By early summer 1859, as funds ran low and bills and rents went unpaid, a disenchanted Denieffe got permission to return to Dublin. The more Stephens burned through money, the less John O'Leary respected him. 'There was a certain flabbiness of moral fibre about him. As Stephens's indebtedness proportionately increased, and his temper naturally did not improve, his general way of regarding men and things, which at the best was the reverse of charitable, took an extra tinge of pessimism.'[82] By late 1860, Stephens probably felt a jaded sense of déjà vu, experiencing the same personal and financial desperation that had blighted his first Parisian exile.

His fraught relations with the Fenian Brotherhood also troubled Stephens, angry as he was at O'Mahony's repeated failure to send funds. For his part, O'Mahony resented Stephens's incessant demands for money when a financial crash in 1857 had decimated the savings of Irish-Americans. And since Stephens never allowed proper accounting of his spending, O'Mahony found himself in effect signing blank cheques. Gradually O'Mahony's doubts broadened into misgivings about Stephens's entire leadership of the IRB and whether his boasts tallied with reality. Accordingly, O'Mahony began dispatching envoys to investigate the IRB, the first being Edmund Boyle in 1860, an elderly Fenian from St Louis. James Cantwell from Philadelphia followed but he stayed on to marry a widowed ex-girlfriend who owned an hotel in D'Olier Street. O'Leary regarded these envoys as harmless irritants, especially as Luby controlled their itineraries and ensured that they endorsed Stephens's glowing assessments. But their very presence incensed Stephens, whom O'Leary recalled fulminating at 'a certain inquisitorial tendency on the part of O'Mahony who kept forever sending men over to Ireland'.[83] Yet far from backing down, O'Mahony's suspicions that Stephens had manipulated his envoys only mounted until finally, in November 1860, he decided to discover for himself the true state of affairs.[84]

Stopping off first in Paris, O'Mahony listened as Stephens waxed lyrical about an IRB expanding on all fronts. Upon reaching Dublin just before Christmas, O'Mahony then lodged at Cantwell's Star and Garter Hotel, where an ultra-loyal Peter Langan validated Stephens's appraisal: everything was going superbly. Indeed, after meeting IRB centres and new recruits, O'Mahony congratulated Luby on the organisation's progress. He then embarked on a triumphal tour, proof that even after his decade-long exile, O'Mahony remained a legendary hero in Cork, Tipperary, Waterford and Limerick. But by staying on in Ireland much longer than intended, O'Mahony provided a lightning rod for IRB discontent with Stephens's leadership. In Clonmel, O'Mahony met Denis Mulcahy, who had returned from Paris utterly disheartened, telling everyone that Stephens would have done better to bring the Louvre back to Ireland with him. Dan McCartie also returned with similarly unflattering stories about Stephens.

Having borne the brunt of government repression, the Phoenix men resented an IRB leader who, from the safety of Paris, had not helped them during their lengthy detention. By contrast, O'Mahony was in Ireland, while still officially a wanted man. When Luby and O'Mahony reunited in Dublin, Luby realised immediately that O'Mahony's attitude to Stephens had significantly cooled. O'Mahony now complained about Stephens's inertia and joked that he had spent two years in Paris 'doing nothing, with his head wrapped up in a blanket'.[85] O'Mahony also wanted the IRB to establish a council that would act as Stephens's Cabinet and run the organisation in his absence. When Luby resisted unilaterally reducing Stephens's power, O'Mahony demanded that Luby contact him. Luby's letter urged Stephens to return immediately if he wanted to save the IRB. Stephens was shaken and suspected O'Mahony of organising a coup against him. Abruptly ending his Parisian sojourn, Stephens immediately left for Dublin.

At Peter Langan's timber yard, Stephens ambushed O'Mahony, relentlessly accusing him of breaking promises and starving the IRB of funds. Spellbound, Denieffe watched as:

Stephens reproached him in words of the most cutting sarcasm, telling him of his shortcomings, feebleness and insincerity and wound up reminding him how he, Stephens, had dragged him out of obscurity and put him in a position he never dreamed of. O'Mahony did not answer this terrible arraignment and remained sitting while Stephens paced, restlessly up and down the floor.[86]

Luby vividly described Stephens lounging on a settee and twirling an open penknife as he berated O'Mahony like an insubordinate underling.

O'Mahony responded by 'hurrying up and down the room like a caged animal and beating his forehead nervously with his fingers'.[87]

Luby recalled that when Stephens had softened O'Mahony up, he suddenly dangled before him an apparently honourable compromise. The IRB would establish regional councils responsible for purely local affairs – a proposal Stephens never intended keeping but which satisfied O'Mahony. Next day, they formalised an agreement. But despite a superficial harmony the wounds never fully healed, and their relationship would never be the same again. Luby admitted that, 'From this day onwards feelings of jealousy between him (O'Mahony) and Stephens grew daily more intense and bitter.'[88] O'Mahony's last official act in Ireland was meeting Dublin's IRB centres in March 1861. He learned then for the first time what American aid the IRB needed for a rising: 5,000 disciplined men armed with rifles or muskets, competent officers and abundant munitions, a target O'Mahony promised to work towards and hoped to achieve. Two months later he sailed to Liverpool – but just before leaving for New York, O'Mahony learned that the American Civil War had begun.

2

Fenianism in the Doldrums

Soon after O'Mahony left Ireland in May 1861, Stephens and Luby spent several weeks traversing Cork, Kerry and Clare on their most successful tour yet, meeting IRB centres, establishing new circles and recruiting members. Simultaneously, IRB organisers founded circles in England, Scotland and Wales. Stephens also mended relations with the Phoenix defendants, whom he took on a yacht cruise across Bantry Bay. Relaxed and smoking his pipe, Stephens predicted that Queen Victoria would be the last English monarch of Ireland, impressing O'Donovan Rossa with 'the strong faith he had in the success of his own movement. The way he always spoke to his men seemed to give them confidence. That was one of his strong points as an organiser.'[1] For his part, Stephens recognised that Rossa was bold, courageous and imbued with an unbreakable will; finally, he realised that even a provisional dictator needed a talented inner circle – men like Rossa, Edward Duffy, Charles Kickham and John Devoy.

Twenty-one-year-old Duffy hailed from Co. Mayo. After his father died, Duffy left school prematurely and worked as an apprentice at a dry goods business in Castlebar before moving to Dublin, where he joined the IRB. Dynamic and gregarious, Duffy swiftly became known as the Fenian Emmet, though even his great friend John O'Leary regarded this praise as excessive.[2]

Thirty-three-year-old Kickham was from Tipperary, the son of a drapery shop owner.[3] Aged 13 he had suffered catastrophic injuries after a gunpowder flask accidentally exploded, leaving him almost blind and deaf as well as facially disfigured. Unable to work, Charles overcame his visual impairment to read the classics and publish poetry, while he also gravitated politically to militant nationalism. Kickham impressed Stephens, who tried recruiting him for the IRB, but he preferred open defiance of British rule to a conspiracy. Three years later, Charles changed his mind after meeting O'Mahony during the latter's Irish mission. Converted to Fenianism, he joined the IRB in March 1861.

Nineteen-year-old John Devoy came from a small townland in Co. Kildare, where his father William farmed a tiny patch of land.[4] In 1849 the family relocated to Dublin, where William eventually became managing clerk at Watkin's Brewery. At school, John's rebelliousness landed him in perpetual trouble. He refused to sing 'God Save the Queen', kicked a teacher who tried to cane him, and punched another sadistic teacher who wrung his ears. Upon leaving school, Devoy attended night classes in Irish that covertly propagated militant nationalism, and in early 1861 he joined the IRB. Totally inexperienced in warfare, Devoy decided to join the French army, and he even rebuffed Stephens's advice to fight instead in an imminent American Civil War. Stephens remarked: 'That young man is very stubborn.' But in Paris, a virtually penniless Devoy discovered that foreign citizens could not join the French Army, and enlisted in the Foreign Legion instead. Devoy served briefly in Algeria before returning to the family home in Dublin. Stephens realised he had matured and appointed him IRB organiser at Naas in Kildare.

By now, Stephens and the IRB were suffering from a lack of money, especially Irish-American funding. Between April 1861 and April 1862, the Fenian Brotherhood sent Stephens just £113, a sum that he told O'Mahony was pitiable. Stephens also claimed falsely that he was actually raising more in Ireland, when in fact the IRB was almost completely dependent on America. By mid-1862, Stephens himself would be almost penniless, forced to borrow 10s for food from Luby – who himself was loaned the money.[5] But, as always, Stephens saw everything through the prism of his own needs, even when civil war in America threatened the Fenian Brotherhood's very existence. Whole circles vanished, the majority that survived were skeletons, and the most active members had left to fight. Between 150,000 and 170,000 men of Irish descent joined the Union Army, and 40,000 fought for the Confederacy, six of whom became Southern generals. Philip Sheridan, the son of Irish migrants from Cavan, established an Irish Brigade and became a Union major general. Another Union major general, Michael

Corcoran, just managed to dissuade O'Mahony from enlisting by insisting this would leave the Fenian Brotherhood rudderless.

Despite his strong support for the Union cause, the war's seemingly endless slaughter depressed O'Mahony, who declared that the sheer scale of Irish-American casualties had left thousands 'whitening Virginia with their bones. This is a real blood-market.'[6] Perhaps 35,000 died between 1861 and 1865. The Battle of Antietam in September 1862 decimated the Irish Brigade, which suffered 600 fatalities. Three months later, when General Robert E. Lee crushed the Union Army at Fredericksburg in the war's most one-sided battle, the Brigade lost another 545 soldiers. This carnage reached its apogee in July 1863 at the three-day Battle of Gettysburg, a bloodbath that virtually wiped out what remained of the Brigade, which lost 320 out of its remaining 530 men. Civil war shredded the Fenian Brotherhood. Fifty branches folded as O'Mahony struggled virtually single-handedly to keep the movement alive. This disarray caused a scarcity of money for the IRB, but more importantly as long as civil war lasted, it made an Irish rising impossible because an American naval expedition to Ireland was out of the question.

As American funding dwindled to a trickle, IRB expansion in Ireland stalled, leaving it just one – and not the most important – political organisation vying for the leadership of nationalist Ireland. Most prominent were Young Irelanders like William Smith O'Brien, John Blake Dillon and John Martin, who had returned from exile in the mid-1850s and reconciled themselves to constitutionalism. However, although widely respected, these three grandees had retired from direct political involvement and exercised influence through public pronouncements and private advice. Instead, after 1855, George Henry Moore, MP for Co. Mayo, commanded the Tenant League's shattered ranks, assisted by A.M. Sullivan, proprietor of Ireland's biggest-selling daily newspaper, *The Nation*. But, after the general election, Moore was expelled from parliament for electoral intimidation. His successor, the Tipperary M.P. Daniel O'Donoghue, known universally as The O'Donoghue, was a superb orator and widely regarded as the most popular man in Ireland.

By 1860–61, popular interest in Irish politics was reviving. Frustrated at his stalled career, George Moore resurfaced and proposed an Irish Volunteer force that would compel the British government to concede legislative independence. However, Dillon told Moore that without an Anglo–French war he should either accept British rule and assimilate, or migrate to a more hospitable country. Crushed, Moore abandoned his project. Instead, on 5 May 1861, A.M. Sullivan launched a national petition for an Irish plebiscite on legislative independence. Despite knowing that the British government would not grant an Irish parliament, he hoped that huge support for his campaign would demonstrate the national will. And indeed, almost every social class endorsed the petition, which eventually attracted almost half a million signatures.

Well before the petition was presented to parliament in June 1861 and inevitably rejected, Sullivan had tried to capitalise on its mass mobilisation by proposing a new national political organisation. However, he was pre-empted by Thomas Neilson Underwood, a 31-year-old barrister from Tyrone, who had abandoned his London legal practice for a political career in Dublin. Announcing a banquet at the Rotunda on 17 March 1861, Underwood only gave Sullivan the minor role of replying to the toast. Many prominent constitutional nationalists attended the banquet, including The O'Donoghue, and most of the audience were moderate nationalists sick of parliamentary politics but opposed to physical force. However, on a pedestal on the podium sat the figure of a large phoenix bird with extended wings rising above the ashes. And a cohort of spectators repeatedly hissed mentions of William Smith O'Brien. Underwood proposed a new patriotic organisation called the National Brotherhood of St Patrick, whose nebulous principles included 'the union of all Irishmen for the achievement of Ireland's independence'. The sole qualification for membership was a belief that no foreign power could make laws for the Irish people. A show of hands endorsed Underwood's proposal.[7]

Sullivan branded the NBSP a Fenian conspiracy, especially after IRB leaders like O'Donovan Rossa attended similar banquets in Belfast, Carrick-on-Suir and Cork. In fact, almost certainly Stephens had no prior knowledge of Underwood's intentions, but it suited him very well that the NBSP showed Irish nationalism was stirring once again. Moreover, the IRB's young Dublin militants immediately began infiltrating the NBSP, making it both a front organisation and a recruiting ground for Fenianism. Denieffe boasted that 'as it was an open institution, we all became members and maintained a controlling influence'.[8]

However, in 1861 the new organisation was essentially a sideshow to a greater reality. By then sluggish recruitment, waning morale and a sense of drift had brought Fenianism in America and Ireland to such a low ebb that O'Mahony claimed the Fenian Brotherhood was often on the verge of extinction. Little was it realised that a new dynamic was coming in the form of the mortal remains of Terence Bellew McManus.

The Two Burials of Terence Bellew McManus

Probably few Fenians knew or had even heard of Terence Bellew McManus, a dead man who was never one of them. Yet, an IRB leader later recalled McManus's Dublin funeral in November 1861 as 'the great national event of the period'[1] and A.M. Sullivan claimed that it stirred 'such deep emotions that the proceedings assumed a magnitude and a solemnity which astonished and startled everyone'.[2]

Originally from Co. Fermanagh, McManus had worked as a draper in Dublin before shifting in his thirties to Liverpool, where he became a prosperous shipping agent and Young Ireland revolutionary.[3] In 1848, McManus returned to Ireland for the rising and he was wounded at Ballingarry. Condemned to be hung, drawn and quartered, his sentence was commuted to transportation for life in Australia. However, in March 1851, McManus, along with his fellow captive Thomas Meagher, escaped on a ship bound for California, and on 5 June he arrived in San Francisco to a hero's welcome. At the Union Hotel, prominent citizens hosted him a rousing reception that ended prematurely when a floor collapsed and everyone tumbled into the basement, a portent of McManus's new life in America, where his dreams crashed and he plummeted to rock bottom. Now middle-aged, McManus struggled for nearly a decade to rebuild his career, first as a shipping agent and then briefly as a rancher, but on 15 January 1861 he died poverty-stricken after a drunken fall. Few mourners bothered to attend his funeral in San Francisco's Calvary Cemetery.

A washed-up failure like McManus was an improbable candidate for political resurrection and fame – except that, as John O'Leary shrewdly observed, he had 'one all-redeeming merit in the eyes of his countrymen that he had risked his life and lost his liberty for Ireland. The heart of the country always goes out to the man who lives and dies an unrepentant rebel.'[4] As a tribute, San Francisco's Irish societies initially planned to erect a monument, but in May local Fenians persuaded them to re-inter McManus in Ireland. Ostensibly, this was simply about returning him to his birthplace, but secretly they intended exploiting a re-burial in order to boost the Fenian Brotherhood's standing in America. Despite remaining a Young Irelander to the last, McManus was also a committed revolutionary who shared with Fenians what one of them called an 'unrelenting hostility to English rule and the implacable determination to get rid of it'.[5] For a Fenian Brotherhood in the doldrums, McManus could not have died at a better time.

There was a certain grandeur about the concept of guiding McManus's corpse home to Ireland. Only once before, in 1840, had such a mighty journey been accomplished, when Napoleon Bonaparte's remains were returned to France from the South Atlantic island of St Helena – and only across half the distance envisaged for McManus. Strapped for cash, San Francisco Fenians appealed in March 1861 to their New York headquarters for help. As O'Mahony was still in Ireland, Michael Doheny established a fundraising committee, intuitively sensing, as he did, that by transforming McManus into a nationalist icon, he could achieve a great political coup for the Fenian Brotherhood. Furthermore, Doheny had accepted at face value Stephens's assurances about huge IRB strength and that Ireland was ripe for revolution. Accordingly, he visualised McManus's re-burial as a great opportunity to engineer another Irish rebellion, telling a cheering New York audience that, 'The idea of transferring McManus was in itself a resurrection, which he hoped would inaugurate another resurrection – the resurrection of Ireland from the foreign grave in which she had lain for centuries.'[6] Doheny planned to accompany McManus's remains to Ireland and have them carried from town to town, gathering recruits, until eventually 100,000 men rallied at somewhere like Tipperary's iconic mountain, Slievenamon, to commence a nationwide rising – probably led by himself.

However, on 29 May 1861, O'Mahony returned from Ireland and disclosed that Stephens had grossly exaggerated the IRB's size, influence and military capability, a report that persuaded Doheny to reluctantly abandon his revolutionary ambitions and settle for a massive New York commemoration of McManus's life.[7] Even this, though, would involve months of organising, which ultimately might still not succeed. Furthermore, as railways had not yet connected America's east and west coasts, the first leg of McManus's journey from San Francisco to New York would entail two lengthy sea voyages and a crossing of Panama. And everything depended on stirring the imagination of Irish nationalists on two continents. But there were signs from California that this might just happen. On 19 August 1861, McManus's body was finally exhumed, placed in a metal coffin, and enclosed inside a silver-embossed rosewood casket. Next day, thousands packed St Mary's Cathedral for a Requiem High Mass, after which Fenian delegations from California, Washington and Oregon formed an 1,800-strong procession that escorted McManus's casket through San Francisco streets lined with 25,000 mourners. At the city pier, local Fenian leaders, Captain Michael Smith and Jeremiah Kavanagh, carried the body on board a steamer that then sailed south to Panama, where a train transported McManus's remains overland to the Gulf of Mexico.

As the journey's ripple effect reached New York, excitement mounted among Irish-Americans and 'the longest wake in Irish history'[8] gathered momentum. During these early months of the American Civil War, Fenian propaganda had cleverly fused McManus and the Union cause by depicting him as a heroic soldier battling against his country's enslavement. Strong Irish-American support for the Union war effort further enhanced their community's standing, especially after an Irish infantry company participated in the Civil War's first great battle, at Bull Run on 21 July 1861. Moreover, Thomas Meagher – McManus's fellow escapee – had obtained Archbishop Hughes's permission for O'Mahony and Doheny to use religious trappings in their forthcoming extravaganza. On 13 September, Captain Smith and Kavanagh escorted McManus's coffin into New York Harbour. Four days later, the remains entered St Patrick's Cathedral in midtown Manhattan to lie in state, surrounded by a military guard of honour. Meagher joined columns of mourners filing past but broke down while paying homage to his fallen comrade. On Monday, 18 September, Archbishop Hughes presided at a packed Requiem High Mass and delivered a sermon that meditated on McManus's life, his patriotism and the Catholic doctrine of lawful resistance to oppressive temporal authority, one that Fenians regarded as a justification for a future Irish rising.[9]

On 18 October 1861, O'Mahony and Doheny staged a pageant whose solemnity and spectacle would linger long in New Yorkers' memories. On 23rd Street, 1½ miles from St Patrick's Cathedral, awaited a vast multitude that included Fenian delegations from across America, Irish organisations, thirty-two pall bearers, a military escort and numerous bands. From Ireland had come Miss Isabella McManus, Terence's sister and sole surviving family. Surrounding streets were a sea of colour, bedecked with countless banners and Irish and American flags. At mid-morning, when a hearse brought McManus's coffin from a nearby cemetery vault, Grand Marshal O'Mahony and his eight deputies led off one of the largest processions in New York history. The *New York Times* described mourners marching down Broadway, along with 'one great silent army on either sidewalk, keeping slow step to mournful dirges'.[10] From windows and building tops, more people watched as crowds emerged from side streets and joined the procession. Finally, at the North River pier, McManus's coffin was carried through dense crowds and put on board the *City of Washington* steamship. According to one historian, the New York commemoration was 'designed to be an awe-inspiring occasion and to garner as much publicity as possible for the Fenians. It succeeded in both respects'.[11] O'Mahony and Doheny had achieved their first propaganda triumph, jolting a semi-comatose organisation into renewed life and sparking a membership surge. Moreover, as financial contributions rolled in, O'Mahony sent $3,000 to Ireland for McManus's re-burial. New York's spectacle would be a hard act to follow. On 19 October, the *City of Washington* sailed for Ireland. Doheny led a Fenian-dominated eight-man delegation that included Michael Cavanagh, Captain Smith, Jeremiah Kavanagh and Captain Walley of the Fenian Brotherhood's military wing.

Irish newspapers had announced McManus's death on 23 February 1861, and three months later Stephens learned of American plans to re-inter him in Ireland. Initially, he dismissed McManus as a minor historical figure and opposed the IRB going public with an elaborate commemoration. But at the end of May, young activists from Luby's 'new' Dublin IRB who held dual membership of the National Brotherhood of St Patrick seized the initiative, and at the NBSP's rooms in Marlborough Street they established a National Obsequies Committee to arrange McManus's re-burial. Although this committee operated under a veil of secrecy, the IRB contingent dominated it from the start.[12] Consequently, Luby recalled that Stephens's attitude changed significantly. 'At first, if not indifferent exactly, he had little or no sympathy with the young men's action. He might, I fancy, have even discouraged it, if he thought such a course safe and practical. However, he attempted no opposition to it.'[13] However, Stephens and Luby 'gradually grew interested about making a success of the intended procession and ceremony. And Jim especially became an able adviser of his young men. Finally, he boldly assumed a sort of outside or secret direction of the whole business and became Grand Wire-puller General!'[14] Stephens never actually joined the Obsequies Committee, preferring to manipulate it from a distance, and Luby attended only one last-minute emergency meeting. But despite a majority of the Obsequies Committee being mainstream nationalists, under this façade of inclusivity and respectability a disciplined IRB cohort usually held sway, a grip that Stephens insisted they must never let go.

Yet, Stephens struggled to retain control of the Dublin funeral. Right at the start a dispute arose over McManus's final resting place in Ireland. California's Irish societies wanted him buried over Robert Emmet's grave in the grounds of the Royal Hospital, Kilmainham, but Doheny and Fenian Brotherhood headquarters preferred McManus interred beside Wolfe Tone in Bodenstown cemetery, Co Kildare.[15] However, Stephens insisted successfully on Dublin's Glasnevin cemetery, which since Daniel O'Connell's burial in 1847 had become a platform for political propaganda and a site of nationalist pilgrimage.[16] Stephens was determined that McManus's funeral would consolidate this tradition.

Perhaps surprisingly, Stephens's first adversaries were fellow Fenians. Luby recalled that O'Mahony's secretary, Michael Cavanagh, had alerted Stephens about Doheny's plan for 'a mad, harum-scarum premature insurrection. We were thus forewarned and so forearmed. In turn, Jim had put his merry men on their guard.'[17] Stephens and Luby now realised Doheny was dangerous, someone who had only reluctantly endorsed McManus's peaceful re-burial and might not stay in line.

Stephens also had to contend with Young Ireland leaders William Smith O'Brien, John Blake Dillon and John Martin, politicians whom he now reviled. Stephens felt a special personal animus for Dillon, who had dismissed him as his sons' tutor and whom Stephens blamed for sabotaging his American mission three years earlier by rejecting his request for a letter of recommendation to the Irish Directory in New York. But Stephens still needed their authority to make McManus's funeral a success.

However, as Stephens's greater ambition was for the IRB to supersede Young Ireland, any co-operation with them was entirely a one-way street. On Stephens's part, this was an exercise in cynical manipulation as the only role he envisaged for O'Brien, Dillon and Martin was ceremonial window dressing. Having embraced constitutional politics, the Young Ireland leaders were wary of Stephens: O'Brien had expressed suspicions about 'professional revolutionists' exploiting McManus's funeral to promote another rebellion. But once Stephens began smearing potential absentees from the funeral as an enemy of the dead, O'Brien, Dillon and Martin were trapped; opting out would only provoke accusations of betrayal. The relationship between these former comrades had descended into poisonous rivalry – one that might have set McManus spinning in his grave, had he actually been in it.

The IRB also suffered under relentless press criticism. Apart from the *Irishman,* every Catholic daily newspaper and journal backed the Young Ireland leaders – including an increasingly influential *Freeman's Journal.* A.M. Sullivan called the struggle over McManus's funeral a 'war between the secret organisation and the non-Fenian or anti-Fenian Nationalists'. The Roman Catholic Church also weighed in against Stephens. Archbishop Cullen of Dublin considered Fenianism a foreign ideological bacillus that could poison the entire Irish body politic. This conservative prelate's uncle had been executed after the 1798 rebellion, instilling in him a lifelong abhorrence of secret societies and rebellion.[18] Cullen's animosity had deepened in 1848, when as Rector of Rome's Irish College, he had witnessed Italian revolutionaries temporarily expel Pope Leo X111 from his Papal States. Politically, Cullen believed that a burgeoning Catholic middle class could only progress by acknowledging British rule in Ireland as legitimate, and that insurrection was not just contrary to God's law, but certain to provoke British repression and reverse decades of Catholic advance. Moreover, Cullen was convinced that Fenianism threatened the Roman Catholic Church's religious and political authority in Ireland, not just because it supported the separation of Church and State, but because it rejected the Church's claim to be the sole true guardian of the interests of the Irish people. Suspecting correctly that McManus's funeral was a Fenian project to boost revolutionary elements in Ireland, Cullen denied McManus's coffin entry into the Pro-Cathedral in Marlborough Street, refused him a High Mass, and ordered his priests to boycott the funeral. Neither an Obsequies

Committee delegation nor two written appeals from Isabella McManus could change Cullen's mind.

Stephens also needed to avoid provoking Dublin Castle. Political parades had been illegal for over a decade, and although McManus's re-burial would ostensibly be a religious occasion, Stephens wanted his funeral procession to become a massive defiance of British rule in Ireland. Luckily for him, the Irish government still knew little about the Fenian Brotherhood or the IRB, and Stephens himself stayed in the shadows. He was not on the Obsequies Committee, never visited its rooms in Marlborough Street, would absent himself from the reception parties for McManus's coffin in Cork and Dublin, and did not join the funeral procession. Nor did he attend the graveside oration. Luby was made responsible for making the funeral procession unlike a conventional political parade. He would ensure bands did not play party tunes and that stewards prevented drunkenness, brawls, chanting and attacks on the police. Indeed, on the day itself, silence would be the most effective battle cry of all. Luby would prove himself a phenomenal organiser. Mastering a multitude of details, he selected the funeral route, appointed stewards, marshals and pall bearers, recruited bands, purchased a cemetery plot and chose the graveside speaker. Fortunately for Luby, he had at least six months to plan before McManus's body reached Ireland.

During October 1861, the rival factions in Ireland vied for control of McManus's remains, like body snatchers fighting over a cadaver. Stephens dispatched O'Donovan Rossa and a cohort of armed Fenians to Cork in case Young Irelanders tried to take possession of McManus's coffin when it landed from New York. Stephens followed them soon afterwards but discreetly kept his distance. On Wednesday, 29 October, the *City of Washington* sailed into Queenstown. McManus's body went to a local church where mourners streamed past the coffin, at whose foot sat Isabella McManus. Next afternoon a steamer brought it and the American delegation 12 miles to Cork. Its bishop, Dr Delany, had banned McManus's remains from his churches, refused him a High Mass and ordered his priests to boycott any commemoration. However, Bishop William Keane of the adjoining diocese of Cloyne let the coffin rest in the Sisters of Mercy's hospital chapel. Finally, on Sunday, 2 November, in Cork twenty bands playing solemn music led a huge funeral procession that included 2,000 local farmers on horseback. Large crowds lined pavements – a striking repudiation of Bishop

Delany's authority and proof that vast interest in McManus had migrated from continent to continent. Finally, McManus's coffin reached Cork railway station and was put on board a train that at 10 p.m. left for Dublin.

Stephens and the American delegation occupied a compartment next to the wagon containing McManus's coffin. Rossa and his sharpshooters sat nearby, primed like armed guards in the American West to repel any marauding bandits. At Limerick Junction, silent IRB members knelt on the station platform in honour of McManus, but also nearby was a tumultuous crowd of more IRB members whose leaders Doheny had told months earlier about his plans for a rising – though not his later abandonment. Excitedly, they shouted for the 'Colonel' and became unrulier when Doheny did not appear. Fearing that Doheny might relapse and rush out and to join them, Stephens acted swiftly. When the departure bell rang, he ordered the crowd to kneel in prayer for the dead man as the train rolled away from the station. At 3 a.m. on Monday, 3 November 1861, McManus's remains reached journey's end at Kingsbridge railway station. Several thousand marchers escorted them to the Mechanics Institute in Abbey Street and placed the coffin on a platform in a black-draped and darkened lecture room. At the head stood a silver crucifix and two tall candles burned at either end, their dim lighting creating a rather macabre effect.

Initially, the American delegation and Miss McManus stayed at Carey's in Lower Bridge Street, a hotel much favoured by Fenian out-of-towners. But only a day later, after complaining about its shabbiness, they shifted to the luxurious Shelbourne on St Stephen's Green, where their abrasive behaviour alienated many guests. Moreover, Smith O'Brien also took a room at the Shelbourne, which became a hub of intrigue as the warring factions battled for control of McManus's funeral. Likened by one historian to 'a soap opera of internal strife',[19] the Shelbourne certainly boasted more prima donnas than an Italian operatic company. As Doheny grandstanded and held court, his coterie swaggered around like VIPs, boastful behaviour that Luby recalled left Young Ireland leaders like O'Brien 'haunted by an insane dread that the funeral would end in a rash, popular outbreak, sure to be crushed in blood and massacre'.[20] They believed that only by wresting control from such dangerous fanatics could Ireland be saved from catastrophe.

Luby spent the week before McManus's funeral defusing successive crises. Repeatedly, he rushed to pacify an agitated Isabella McManus, fleetingly the most influential woman in Ireland and for whose favour the rival factions competed. Possibly for the first time in her life, this forty-something-lady – whom Luby rather unkindly called an aged spinster – had men clambering over each other to catch her eye. Plucked from obscurity and ill-equipped to star in a great drama, Isabella was simultaneously in over her head and completely out of her depth. Furthermore, the IRB's enemies preyed on her devout religiosity by warning that heathens were exploiting Terence's funeral. Luby recalled a bizarre incident in which:

> some incense (why I don't exactly know) was constantly burned round the coffin. This was seized upon by the slavish priest-ridden press as an apt occasion to maunder about 'the strange pagan ceremonies' we indulged in. Of course, we were incessantly spoken of as a hellish horde of godless infidels and would-be lawless Jacobin cut-throats.[21]

Isabella might have been a simple countrywoman, but as last of the McManus line she wielded considerable symbolic power and the IRB needed her. Reluctantly, the Protestant Luby became Isabella's spiritual comforter. Another time, after Captain Michael Smith was chosen for the graveside oration, Isabella was told that speeches by civilians at funerals were satanic rituals that only red republicans practised. Like a fast-talking salesman, Luby frantically conjured up every possible argument, true or not, to soothe her furrowed brow until finally in 'a masterly display of the art of rigmarole' Luby restored Isabella 'to a desirable state of equanimity and amiability'.

But Luby's most vexing problem was entirely self-inflicted. For the graveside oration, he had chosen Father John Kenyon, a turbulent parish priest from Tipperary who had been a radical Young Irelander in the 1840s when he befriended fellow revolutionaries like Martin, Dillon, Luby, Meagher, Stephens and McManus himself. Luby admired Kenyon's passionate oratory and his willingness to defy the Roman Catholic hierarchy, but he did not realise that Kenyon's support for revolution had dimmed over time, nor that his invincible self-confidence meant that he was ultimately beyond control. On Monday, 4 November, Luby collected Kenyon from Kingsbridge railway station and was surprised when the priest outlined a graveside speech that contained little fiery rhetoric. After being put up at Luby's mother's house, Kenyon ventured into town, promising to return for dinner with Stephens. When he failed to appear, Luby searched Dublin city centre and eventually discovered Kenyon in Carey's hotel, basking in his celebrity status as he regaled Doheny's coterie, who in rapid time Luby had come to despise as bombastic freeloaders. Later, over dinner and whiskey, Kenyon ran through a draft of his oration, which was not the call to arms Stephens and Luby wanted but rather a vague aspiration to Ireland's eventual freedom. Privately dismissing it as 'do-nothing cant', Luby now realised his mistake but thought it was too late to change the funeral arrangements, even after Stephens privately expressed himself disappointed.

Next morning, after Kenyon shifted to the Shelbourne, Luby visited Stephens, who announced that the priest was out; Captain Smith was in. The stakes were too high for diplomatic niceties, and since Luby had chosen Kenyon, he could break the bad news. Later in the city centre, Luby accidentally encountered Kenyon, who remained composed, professed himself content and said Smith was the better choice. But, in reality, he was not willing to go quietly: behind a mask of sanguine acceptance Kenyon was furious at his humiliation and now regarded Stephens and Luby as arch-villains, Judas Iscariots who had betrayed a good Christian man. Henceforth, Kenyon's mission was to wreck a commemoration that was vital to the IRB's future.

On Wednesday, 6 November, Luby encountered Kenyon again at the Shelbourne, but despite a superficial politeness, Luby became suspicious when the priest and John Martin entered William Smith O'Brien's room. Although he never discovered what transpired, Kenyon thereafter sided with Young Irelanders on the Obsequies Committee. Disillusioned, Luby now loathed Kenyon with a vengeance.

After ditching Kenyon, Stephens himself began crafting for Captain Smith a Fenian message that would echo down through the ages. But Luby recalled that, during an all-night session, Stephens's chronic writer's block left him floundering.[22] Despite unlimited coffee and occasional nips of whiskey, Stephens eked out only a few paragraphs before grinding to a halt. Desperate, he summoned Luby, who eventually dragged him over the finishing line. Luby recalled Stephens asking Captain Smith, '"How do you like it?" "Sir", replied Smith, "it is a masterpiece." I need hardly add that the other enthusiastic admirer was Jim himself.'

But Stephens and Luby still feared that Young Irelanders might stage a last-minute coup, and after Luby had a premonition on 9 November, he warned Stephens that they intended capturing the Obsequies Committee. Stephens then directed Luby to attend the Committee's final meeting and he ran all the way to its rooms in Marlborough Street. Arriving just in time, Luby planted himself down beside Kenyon and, feigning innocence, he began winding the priest up. Kenyon, for his part, was spoiling for a fight, and when Maurice O'Donoghue, an IRB centre, was elected chairman, he erupted, proposing The O'Donoghue (Daniel O'Donoghue MP) instead.[23] Pandemonium ensued but a disciplined IRB contingent ensured that Maurice stayed in the chair.

Undeterred, Kenyon ploughed on. Without a sliver of embarrassment, he opposed Captain Smith's nomination as graveside orator because a speech was unnecessary. 'The funeral procession itself ought to speak to the people's minds with sufficient eloquence.' But Kenyon's abusive behaviour and self-pity had alienated a meeting that overwhelmingly ratified Smith's appointment. Defeated, Kenyon stormed out, shouting, 'You shall have no funeral. I'll take the body from you,' prompting the Obsequies Committee to install an all-night guard over McManus's coffin. Racing straight to the Shelbourne, Kenyon implored Miss McManus to remove the American delegation as guardians of her brother's remains, but she rebuffed him, perhaps because Isabella already knew about Kenyon's undignified performance, but possibly she just dreaded Terence's funeral ending in fiasco if the Americans walked away.

Although Luby was confident now that McManus's funeral would proceed, he doubted many mourners would actually attend. But the Dublin Metropolitan Police (DMP) had assigned 100 constables to crowd control, another 400 were held in reserve at nearby police stations, and over a dozen plainclothes detectives were to march in the procession. Sunday morning's weather was dismal. A thick mist hung over the capital, whose streets were ankle-deep in slush after a night of heavy sleet and rain. Luby feared 'a dismal, disastrous failure'[24] but from early on, thousands streamed into the city centre, trains from towns across Ireland disgorged official delegations, and travellers from England, Scotland and America also arrived. By noon, 40,000 people were packed in and around Abbey Street. Luby remembered that 'as far as the eye could reach nothing was to be seen in the long line of streetway looking east or west but vast silent crowds'.[25] McManus's funeral had become the largest in Ireland since Daniel O'Connell's fourteen years earlier, and for a single day British power seemingly vanished from the streets of Dublin.

Luby had arranged for horsemen in semi-military tunics to precede the cortege, stewards with white wands to control the vast crowds, and placards to direct mourners to assembly points along the route. Just before one o'clock, McManus's coffin was brought from the Mechanics' Institute, placed on a horse-drawn hearse and bands played solemn music as the funeral procession departed. The front carriages contained Miss McManus, Father Kenyon and the Obsequies Committee. Next came official delegations and deputations from many Dublin trades. Luby and a Father Patrick Lavelle walked in the main body of mourners. Rather than travel directly to Glasnevin, the procession went on a circuitous 5-mile journey that lasted almost four hours. After turning from Gardiner Street into Great Britain (now Parnell Street), Luby glanced back for the first time and was spellbound: 'the whole length of Gardiner Street with dense masses of men and fresh masses endlessly as it seemed, still defiling into it. I gasped and felt my chest heave; I could have sobbed and cried.'[26] A hundred and fifty thousand people, some of them crammed at the windows of every building, watched the long black marching column. During the afternoon many spectators joined the procession, which eventually swelled to 30,000. Luby recalled a sea of humanity, with 'fresh files of men seemingly interminable, issuing from side streets'.[27] Eventually the cortege crossed the Liffey, and at 3 p.m. it entered Thomas Street in the old heart of Dublin.

Stephens and Luby had deliberately designed a funeral route that passed places of historical importance, locating McManus in a long tradition of rebels who sacrificed themselves for Irish freedom. On Thomas Street, mourners spontaneously uncovered their heads outside a house in which the United Irishmen leader, Lord Edward Fitzgerald, was mortally wounded just before the 1798 Rebellion. Slightly further on, they did so again at the place outside St Catherine's Church, where in 1803 Robert Emmet was executed. Watching from a nearby window, Stephens gloated at the discomfiture of Young Ireland leaders whom he had sidelined but who dared not stay away.[28] On the High Street, the procession halted at a house where Wolfe Tone's remains had lain prior to burial, before marching silently past Dublin Castle, along Dame Street and College Green, down Westmorland Street, over Carlisle Bridge and into Sackville Street, the capital's main thoroughfare. As dusk approached, Luby ordered horsemen at the front to pick up the pace so that Smith could deliver his graveside oration before darkness fell.[29]

At 5 p.m. the procession finally approached Glasnevin, where Luby saw a tremendous crowd milling around. 'I was for several minutes in terror, lest someone should be hurt. The horses of our mounted men were getting restive, whirling about among the men, women and children.'[30] Although a pile-up was narrowly averted, daylight was fading fast and Luby improvised brown paper torches to light up the graveside.[31] After Father Lavelle recited prayers, Captain Smith delivered a speech that ended with a prediction that 'the day for which our fathers yearned, struggled, fought and suffered cannot be very far off'.

Visually and emotionally McManus's funeral was a triumph, one that Luby and not an establishment elite had brilliantly choreographed into something akin to a state funeral. Luby himself believed that what 'made it even more striking was the admirable behaviour of our people on that day. Vast as the crowd was, no accident occurred; neither man nor women nor child was hurt. The whole affair was singularly grave, serious, decorous, and impressive.'[32]

Yet ironically the funeral had never really been about McManus. Fenians knew him little and cared less. Moreover, far from McManus's grave becoming a place of pilgrimage, it soon fell into neglect after a poorly subscribed monument fund petered out, and not until 1933 was a stone figure finally erected over the grave. John O'Leary candidly admitted that 'the cause was all' and McManus's funeral was 'from first to last a great Fenian demonstration'.[33]

Nor, almost certainly, did most mourners share McManus's revolutionary politics. Some had come to behold a great public spectacle, others out of curiosity or just to meet friends on a memorable day. A.M. Sullivan thought, 'Most of the masses who lined the route probably had no political persuasions but were there simply to pay tribute to a brave man.'[34] Luby accepted that many mourners 'had no sympathy with our principles or aims'.[35] More irreverently, John O'Leary declared that, 'The rebel can reckon upon nothing in life; he is sure to be calumniated, he is likely to be robbed and may even be murdered, but let him go out of life and he is sure of a fine funeral.'[36] And less than nine months afterwards, Archbishop Cullen amassed even larger crowds at Drumcondra to celebrate the laying of a foundation stone for the new Catholic University.[37]

Nevertheless, contemporaries agreed that the IRB harvested most political capital from McManus's funeral. A.M. Sullivan declared, 'That day gave the Fenian chiefs a command of Ireland which they had never been able to command before. They henceforth assumed a boldness of action and language never previously attempted.'[38] Luby claimed that IRB membership doubled within six months after the funeral and even created a rather exaggerated notion of its strength.[39] Provincial and Dublin members had mingled together and united in a belief that their movement was transforming Irish history. Almost overnight, the IRB had become an influential player in Irish politics.

The IRB also realised that funerals could be unarmed but powerful propaganda against British rule in Ireland, creating a cult of martyrs that made Glasnevin cemetery a place of pilgrimage. Over time, as more funeral processions wound their way there, Fenians perfected their talent for theatrical propaganda.[40] McManus's funeral had in effect been a trial run. In 1877, 70,000 mourners watched as a 4,000-strong procession escorted John O'Mahony's remains to Glasnevin for interment alongside McManus. On another Sunday, 1 August 1915, an IRB leader, Tom Clarke, organised the greatest Fenian funeral of all. Using McManus's as his template, Clarke arranged for O'Donovan Rossa to lie in state at the City Hall, co-ordinated a great procession that also passed sites of historical significance to Irish nationalists, and had Patrick Pearse deliver a memorable graveside oration. Much shorter but far more memorable than Captain Smith's, Pearse's five-minute *tour de force* electrified onlookers and his closing peroration connected 1916 with 1861:

> They think they have pacified Ireland. They think that they purchased half of it and intimidated the other half. They think they have foreseen, think that they have provided against everything but the fools, the fools, the fools! – they have left us our Fenian dead and while Ireland holds these graves, Ireland unfree shall never be at peace.

McManus's funeral also strengthened Stephens's leadership of the IRB. Initially powerless to impose his will on young Dublin IRB activists, he then showed a rare flexibility by giving them their head. Even then, Stephens contributed less than Luby, who ruefully recalled that Stephens took the lion's share of credit. Afterwards, Stephens, with characteristic self-pity, declared that he had worked himself close to death masterminding everything from Cork to Glasnevin, and boasted of having thwarted a 'clique' of Young Irelanders who tried to hijack McManus's funeral.[41]

By shamelessly misappropriating all the glory for himself, Stephens attained complete ascendancy over the IRB, a dominance that increased when the American delegation returned home with a glowing report that nullified O'Mahony's only six months earlier. As Stephen's prestige soared, Fenians increasingly saw him as an effective leader who had withstood every attack and now posed a real threat to British rule. Apparently, as rank-and-file morale soared, the IRB needed only American funding, arms and officers to speedily liberate Ireland. Soon that money began to flow. From the IRB's foundation, Stephens had argued that a secret revolutionary society must be organised on military lines with officers and men obedient to a single commander at the top. Now James Stephens was that man.

4

Stephens and the IRB: 1861–65

After seizing the political initiative in Ireland during 1860–61, Stephens was determined to crush constitutional nationalism, now led by The O'Donoghue MP and 32-year-old A.M. (Alexander Martin) Sullivan, the powerful press magnate who now owned four newspapers: the *Nation,* the *Morning News, Evening News* and *Weekly News.* This battle for the hearts and minds of the Irish people would be long and brutal.

Ambitious to establish a new constitutional political party, Sullivan invited William Smith O'Brien to become its leader. But O'Brien had settled permanently for semi-retirement. Furthermore, the death of his wife Lucy in June 1861 had devastated O'Brien, who now longed only to lie beside her in the grave. As Martin and Blake Dillon had also become wasting assets, by a process of elimination, Sullivan and The O'Donoghue, MP, assumed leadership roles. But Sullivan was soon fighting for his political life after he realised that revolutionary nationalism had not disappeared.[1]

Sullivan appreciated his mistake when Stephens effortlessly outfoxed constitutional nationalists over the National Brotherhood of St Patrick and the McManus funeral. There now existed, Sullivan declared, a war between Fenian and non-Fenian Nationalists, but it was also a deeply personal struggle in which Stephens denounced Sullivan as the devil incarnate and whose life he intended making a living hell. Furthermore, Stephens opportunistically used Sullivan as a convenient scapegoat for every IRB setback. Sullivan recalled a relentless campaign of Fenian persecution and psychological warfare designed to destroy him. He and The O'Donoghue fought back, but the former's newspapers and the latter's oratory were not enough to save them. Irish politicians now needed a mass movement to succeed and they had none. Moreover, both men lacked experience in the snake pit of Irish politics. The embodiment of middle-class fastidiousness, both men adhered to Marquess of Queensberry rules; Stephens fought dirty and hit below the belt.

Constitutional nationalism's chance of regaining the political ascendancy came sooner than expected. On 8 November 1861 – two days before McManus's re-burial – an American naval vessel intercepted a British mail packet in the Atlantic and arrested two Confederate diplomats on a mission to seek diplomatic recognition from England and France. Lord Palmerston's government regarded this as piracy, which risked an Anglo–American war.[2] Sullivan responded by calling for a new national organisation that would keep Ireland out of any conflict as well as siding with Lincoln and the Union. Accordingly, he announced a public meeting at the Rotunda for 5 December 1861, and maintained a veneer of bipartisanship by inviting both moderate and advanced nationalists like Luby and Underwood. Secretly, though, the meeting was a political smokescreen to assimilate the National Brotherhood of St Patrick into his new organisation. However, the plan backfired. Naively, Sullivan believed he could out-manoeuvre Stephens, but as a conspirator he was out of his depth as Stephens had immediately realised his intentions and devised countermeasures. Moreover, complacently assuming that personality and oratory would suffice at the Rotunda, Sullivan relied on appointing The O'Donoghue as conference chairman.

On 5 December, hundreds of well-drilled IRB members attended the Rotunda meeting.[3] Directed from the platform by Luby, they helped pass a resolution supporting the North in the Civil War but fought a resolution proposing a new national political organisation. Instead, Stephens had primed Jeremiah Kavanagh – an American delegate at McManus's funeral – to recommend that a committee should consider if such an organisation was necessary. As Kavanagh's resolution was debated, Luby tried splitting The O'Donoghue from Sullivan by asking him to meet Stephens. Then, Luby produced a slate of nominees for Kavanagh's committee, which included The O'Donoghue and other constitutional nationalists, telling The O'Donoghue that everyone on the committee would defer to him. This was empty flattery intended to bamboozle: the list was pure window dressing that concealed a radical majority. John O'Leary gleefully recalled Kavanagh's resolution passing:

> amid a whirlwind of acclamations. The names of the Committee appointed by us – both the fogies well known in Dublin, and myself, and the long roll of our boys, all but utterly unknown quantities to the public, were received with echoing plaudits. This was the excruciatingly funny part of the performance. The majority present, led by the nose, actually believed the meeting to be a most harmonious proceeding; a very model of united action. So probably next day did the general public.[4]

With military precision, Luby had crushed Sullivan's constitutional nationalists, especially as Kavanagh's committee never met. Routed once again, Sullivan recalled battling a phantom, attempting unsuccessfully through newspaper articles and editorials to defeat a secret enemy that shunned public debate. At least, though, Sullivan did not lose The O'Donoghue to the IRB. When, he met Stephens, The O'Donoghue seemed open to an accommodation and agreed to serve on Kavanagh's committee. But, after receiving admonishing letters from William Smith O'Brien, he severed contact with Stephens. Sullivan claimed The O'Donoghue had only wobbled and always believed that Fenians might 'bathe Ireland in blood'. Moreover, Stephens never seriously wanted to recruit such a dangerous rival. Despite losing at the Rotunda, Sullivan soldiered on, but it would be almost three years before he again took on Stephens and the IRB.

At the start of 1862, Stephens sent organisers across Ireland to expand the IRB, but without money to subsidise them these young men relied on their own meagre finances and lived off the land.[5] Before McManus's funeral the IRB had barely existed outside parts of Munster and Leinster, but afterwards the Dublin organisation attracted more recruits from large drapery establishments and trade unions. By early 1862, Dublin's fifteen circles had between 8,000 and 10,000 members; the largest with over 1,200 members, mostly builders like its centre Hugh Brophy. Small circles also existed in north and south Co. Dublin. The Dublin IRB also financed Stephens and Luby on a successful recruiting drive in Kildare, Carlow and Kilkenny. Stephens called this 'the tour of tours; to compare it with any former one would be more than absurd. My expectations are in every way exceeded.'[6]

Invariably Stephens and Luby first swore in a prominent local person whose social standing won over others. At Leixlip in north-east Kildare, this was William Francis Roantree, a veteran of the Nicaraguan war who had himself photographed in military costume holding a Bowie knife in one hand and a revolver in the other. Eventually, his circle expanded to 2,000 members – among the IRB's largest. In Newbridge, another small Co. Kildare town 11 miles west of Dublin, a chimney sweep, Owen Sullivan, single-handedly built up a circle of over 200 members, 95 per cent of Newbridge's adult male population.[7]

Carlow was organised by Andrew Nolan, a travelling agent for a Dublin hardware shop whose job was ideal cover for extending the IRB into Kilkenny and adjoining counties. In late 1862, Stephens instructed John Devoy to establish the IRB in Naas and surrounding townlands, including Kill (Devoy's native parish) and the Bog of Allen. Devoy's cover was an office job with Watkins Brewery and he proved himself a cautious but skilled recruiter. Sometimes, Devoy led a 12-mile route march into Dublin. Passing Kill's Catholic church, his men attended Mass before continuing their journey. At times, IRB expansion was so rapid and uncoordinated that Stephens and Luby knew nothing about it. Before leaving Dublin for Naas, Devoy discovered several hundred unreported members in the Glencullen district. Then he attended a funeral at Stratford, Co. Wicklow, and learned there were 1,500 Fenians in the district. 'When I told this to Stephens on my next visit to Dublin, I found he had never heard of it. I have no doubt there were other such cases.'[8] Devoy was right. Luby recorded that in one Wicklow area, 1,500 men had joined the IRB without Stephens's knowledge.[9]

In Connaught, many mourners returned from the McManus funeral as Fenians and Edward Duffy soon followed them to the province. Already Stephens's confidant, he worked at Cannock and White's Mary Street drapery store until early 1862, when Stephens sent him to organise Connaught and Cavan, Longford and Westmeath as well. After becoming foreman at the same dry goods business in Castlebar where he had served an apprenticeship, Duffy travelled throughout Connaught on business while secretly organising IRB circles. But regular fasting and sleep deprivation taxed Duffy's health, and when racing to a meeting in late 1862, he fell off his horse. After lying helpless in a dyke for hours, Duffy was finally rescued but a severe cold affected his lungs and he developed consumption. Despite this life-threatening condition Duffy, remained active in the IRB.[10]

Although the IRB had established a foothold in Mayo, Sligo, Roscommon and Leitrim, Duffy still needed to overcome Connaught's deeply entrenched Ribbonism. Historically, this secret agrarian Roman Catholic society had battled Protestant Orangemen and violently defended tenant farmers against landlords. Historian Dr Kerron O Luain has claimed that its 'primary outlook was anti-Orangeism. By extension it was infused with Catholic nationalism. Within the Ribbon mentality the folk memory of dispossession intertwined with a hazy nationalism and vestiges of 1790s Republicanism. Above all it carried forward a sense of grievance towards Protestant ascendancy and English governance.'[11] However, by the 1860s Ribbonism had morphed into essentially an urban mutual-aid organisation and its insurrectionary phase was over. Many Ribbon leaders had prospered as publicans and shopkeepers who helped their ambitious working-class members get jobs, as well as those in economic difficulty or who wanted to emigrate. However, when necessary, Ribbonmen still resorted to strong-arm tactics and forcefully resisted rival societies encroaching on their territory. But although they often fought Fenians at fairs and markets, Duffy ignored advice to crush them because, despite Ribbonmens' sectarianism and blinkered political vision, he admired their rugged qualities and willingness to do battle.[12] Instead, Duffy set about absorbing them into the IRB, and he succeeded after recruiting James Hyland, a former Ribbonman who induced many comrades to defect. By employing Irish-speakers as recruiters in Ireland's most Gaelic-speaking province, Duffy also overcame his inability to speak the language, completing his takeover after the Ribbon Society split and Hyland persuaded even more members to join the IRB. In 1863, Stephens ordered Duffy to organise Connaught's expanding circles full-time, and by December 1864 the province had an estimated 3,764 members. During 1864 and 1865, O'Donovan Rossa, another language enthusiast, spent time in Connaught helping Duffy; Devoy considered both men the best IRB recruiters in Ireland.

In Munster, Cork remained an IRB stronghold with Rossa and the two Moynahan brothers, Mortimer and Michael, its most active organisers. Devoy described Skibbereen as 'a hotbed of Fenianism' and claimed that in 1866 Mountjoy Gaol held more prisoners from the town than anywhere else in Ireland.[13] The IRB spread throughout Ulster after John Nolan's large drapery house employer in Dublin transferred him to Belfast. Although Devoy regarded Nolan as rather unsophisticated, he was prodigiously energetic and made good progress. In Newtownards, Co. Down, Nolan recruited a Presbyterian linen manufacturer as centre of a circle comprised equally of Catholics, Presbyterians and Episcopalians – a lingering expression of the town's United Irishmen tradition.[14]

Nevertheless, despite the IRB's growth, Luby recalled the late spring and summer of 1862 as 'formidable and depressing days of trial' with revolutionary activity at a low ebb and American funding much diminished after Michael Doheny died of fever in April 1862.[15] James O'Connor also noticed Stephens's increasing indolence, a lethargy he traced to the leader's budding romance with his future wife, 20-year-old Jane Hopper.[16] Prominent Fenians feared their relationship was distracting Stephens from the IRB and revolution. Infatuated, Stephens rented a small cottage that Jane visited regularly, but although their love bloomed, his detractors thought Stephens himself was going to seed. A man who once easily walked 26 miles a day piled on the pounds and developed a paunch. O'Leary recalled that Stephens's sluggish but expensive lifestyle was 'distasteful to his followers as they knew that the work of the organisation was more or less at a standstill for want of money'.[17] O'Connor claimed that irritated Dublin centres demanded 'manly exertion instead of childish antics and senile devotion to a young girl'.[18] Initially, they tried 'gentle remonstrance' but Stephens always made excuses, blaming his inactivity on 'idiots' like O'Mahony for starving him of funds or the police's constant surveillance. Yet, Stephens never directly faced down his critics. In the summer of 1862, another remittance from O'Mahony meant Stephens could begin a new tour, but he missed the train. Despite promising Luby he would leave next day, Stephens then claimed he required the money to smuggle out of Ireland an informer set to testify at the trial of a Kilkenny centre. Finally, sensing his followers' waning confidence, Stephens jolted into action, and when another American remittance arrived, he and Luby headed for Kilkenny, Clonmel and Cork.[19]

An enigmatic politician, James Stephens puzzled even close associates, despite them acknowledging his towering political ability. Luby insisted that 'In spite of all his blemishes, I must sincerely admire the Captain. He was a born conspirator and without him it is doubtful there would have been a Fenian movement.'[20] Even his fiercest IRB critics never doubted Stephens's revolutionary devotion; O'Connor described him as a fearless patriot and rejected accusations that he was a charlatan who systematically fleeced the IRB. On the contrary, O'Connor claimed that Stephens cared nothing for money and never enriched himself, despite often using it injudiciously or for a different purpose than was intended.

In some respects, Stephens was an unlikely leader, and certainly not a charismatic Pied Piper. Standing only 5ft 7in tall, stoutly built and broad shouldered, he was bald on top and had small hands and feet. Nor, handicapped by a shrill voice, was Stephens a spellbinding demagogue capable of swaying the masses. Yet many Fenians worshipped him almost as a demi-god and he dominated Irish revolutionary politics for almost a decade. Undoubtedly, Stephens was a born conspirator. Even A.M. Sullivan acknowledged him as 'one of the ablest, most skilful and dangerous revolutionists of our time'.[21] He was also a brilliant organiser who seemingly created from nothing IRB circles in Ireland and Fenian Brotherhood branches in America. Furthermore, Stephens was endowed with great willpower, immense energy and boundless self-belief. O'Leary said:

> It was at all times part of his nature to be confident of the future; and such a measure of success as he obtained in his projects – and I think that success was considerable – was doubtless largely due to that hopeful temperament he undoubtedly possessed. He believed implicitly in, and had certainly an almost mesmeric power of infusing his own feelings and ideas into the breasts of others. His sublime confidence in himself I admired then and notwithstanding the shortcomings of his after career, I admire it still.[22]

Stephens also had an excellent memory, a prodigious work ethic and a genius for political manoeuvring that enabled him constantly to play his critics off against each other.

Stephens's conviction that he had a special historical mission to liberate Ireland endowed him with the inner strength to withstand every setback, and maintain both his grip on power and the trust of his followers. Furthermore, Stephens had the ability to detect and exploit his opponents' weaknesses as a prelude to destroying them, but also the charm and persuasiveness to win people over to his side. During 1862 he genially hosted at his Camden Street lodgings 'porter bottle nights' for lower-ranking Fenians, and on these social occasions Stephens beguiled his guests, dispensing bottles of Guinness, playing cards and joining in sing-songs. Luby recalled that if anyone expressed pessimism about the IRB's future, Stephens literally lubricated the wheels of friendship: 'He would quietly uncork an additional bottle and set it up for the despondent one.'[23] Finally, Stephens was actually helped by the fact that he lacked eloquence and could not move mass audiences, as flamboyant oratory would have aroused suspicions in the IRB that Stephens harboured Napoleonic ambitions.

However, gradually Stephen's leadership flaws became apparent, especially as his supreme self-confidence morphed into overweening arrogance and grandiosity. Considering himself an outstanding general and a great playwright, he began comparing himself to Caesar and Shakespeare, while James O'Connor claimed that Stephens regarded himself as Moses, Washington and William Tell, all rolled into one. 'He had full faith in his power to accomplish anything; that he was superior to every man living, a genius without a peer or a rival in this century and that all other men were smaller than himself in mental stature.'[24] Ultimately, Stephens resented any criticism and even mild dissent. Luby recalled challenging 'His Eminence' at a party for Dublin centres. Afterwards, Stephens warned Luby never again to criticise him in front of others. Incensed, Luby refused: 'Need I say that I at once indignantly repudiated any such insulting claim on his part to infallibility. I must add that he never afterwards treated me to a dose of any such arbitrary stuff.'[25] James O'Connor witnessed the same unyielding quality in Stephens: 'He was irritable under contradiction, impatient of the slightest opposition to his views. If any man attempted to expose his pretensions to universal knowledge – down with him. Show him a rival and he showed no mercy.'[26] Few stood their ground against Stephens's imperiousness, a cowardice that O'Connor thought reflected badly on both sides:

> There always existed among the Centres a feeling akin to fear of Stephens; yet it was not fear altogether but some quality composed of an old personal regard, dislike of divisions and a sense of having to surrender to his frowns and indignation. There was too little of that honest manly interchange of views between the 'boss' and his lieutenants which should have existed.[27]

Instead, Stephens became increasingly vain. Even his porter bottle nights were really occasions for him to flaunt his genius before what Luby called 'admiring disciples', but for whose opinions he actually cared nothing.

Progressively, Stephens preferred monologues to conversations, seemingly infatuated with his own voice. O'Connor recollected that:

> It would be no easy task to count the number of times I heard him talking of himself for hours. He knew (his own words) sixteen languages and was master of them all, whereas he had not mastered three. All the sciences were at his fingertips; the circle of human knowledge was in the palm of his hand.[28]

Stephens's narcissism reflected a lack of human sensibilities, an absence of empathy, compassion and emotional warmth. Incapable of connecting with people, there was at his core a coldness, an absence of charity and humility that left him with few genuine friends. Totally manipulative in his relations with others, an all-consuming love of autocratic power meant more to Stephens than people ever did. Time and again, he jettisoned in a heartbeat even long-time comrades like O'Mahony and Doheny when it advanced his political ambitions. Stephens also lacked a genuine sense of humour and certainly never laughed at himself – though he often gloated at others' misfortunes. Implacably, Stephens exacted vengeance on his political enemies, smeared and verbally intimidated them, and even had some assaulted. For Stephens politics really was war by other means and this made him a venomous hater, a specialist in violent, abusive language. A.M. Sullivan called him 'intolerant, unscrupulous and relentless',[29] a snarling verbal sledgehammer who battered into submission everyone who stood in his way.

An inflated ego convinced Stephens that his ever-restless mind constantly fermented ideas upon which he had to act before his next stroke of genius materialised. Luby recalled Stephens once interrupting an important conversation and rushing to the garden to rearrange flowerpots. Upon returning, he pretentiously claimed a new layout of colours had suddenly flashed into his mind. A vainglorious and theatrical streak also ran through Stephens's personality. Prior to being captured in November 1865 – without a shot being fired – he had melodramatically promised Luby that 'before he suffered himself to be arrested, he'd blow off the skulls of the audacious ones coming to lay their paws on him'.[30] Stephens also presented himself as a highly cultured person, even a renaissance man. During the McManus funeral he asked Luby for a chronicle of events that he intended incorporating into a great history of Fenianism. Stephens then shamelessly recited

Luby's memoir to IRB audiences as his own creation, and not a word of Stephens's own *magnum opus* ever appeared. Sometimes, Stephens's tenuous relationship with truth became outright make-believe. O'Leary found 'it often impossible to disentangle fact from fantasy in his talk. You often could not in the least believe what he said, but you mostly felt that he believed it himself and could seldom or ever know that he didn't.'[31] While still undecided many years later about whether Stephens was consciously dishonest, O'Leary thought this master of deception was best at deceiving himself. Never doubting his infallibility, Stephens believed he could always extricate himself from any predicament and constantly made promises he could not always keep, sure that something would always turn up.

Despite everything, 1862 ended quite favourably for Stephens as dissatisfaction with his leadership was confined to the Dublin IRB. O'Connor recalled that provincial members admired him as much as ever and never dreamt 'that months and months had been frittered away. The remnant of the year passed over our heads dully enough but we had stood firm against all shocks.'[32] Despite his occasional mockery of the 'Great Sultan', Luby's admiration for Stephens's political ability never wavered and he applauded 'the Captain's skilful methods of holding's men together unshaken during the trials and temptations of this most dreary year'.[33]

Luby recalled early 1863 as 'almost as gloomy and unpromising for the Fenian movement as the previous twelve months'.[34] Lacking American money, Stephens blasted O'Mahony for sending $1,000 to tenant farmers in the west of Ireland who were suffering from an agricultural depression. Incandescent, he questioned whether O'Mahony led a revolutionary society or a charitable institution. By now Stephens's relationship with O'Mahony was toxic, and in February 1863 he dispatched Luby to New York to investigate diminished American funding and, if necessary, suspend or even depose O'Mahony. O'Mahony gave Luby just over £70 and failed to arrange a meaningful programme of events for him. More positively, in four and a half months Luby travelled through nine states and Washington DC, addressing circles and laying the foundations for future growth. But although Luby saw that Fenianism had been losing ground, he never contemplated removing O'Mahony, whom he admired as an iconic figure.

Almost penniless, Luby left America on 5 July 1863 and contracted severe bronchitis during the voyage home. Reaching Dublin three weeks later, he handed over O'Mahony's remittance to Stephens as well as some cash from New York friends – a grand total of under $100. Stephens derided the collection as pitiable. After describing the IRB's condition as very unsatisfactory, Stephens whispered that 'to tell you the truth I would not care much if I were out of the business altogether'.[35] Luby was 'slopdologorised' at him, even hinting that he wanted out, but concluded that he was only expressing a fleeting despondency though at the time it sickened Luby. Stephens then surprised Luby again by announcing that he planned to publish an IRB newspaper, something that he had always opposed.

Next day, Stephens began another recruiting tour of the South. Bedridden, Luby was still besieged by Dublin centres complaining about Stephens's leadership and warning him that 'things were going to the devil'.[36] But when Luby informed Stephens of the discontent, he received a glowing account of the tour and IRB circles welcoming the newspaper project. Luby persuaded the dissidents to hold fire by declaring that the IRB would collapse if they undermined the leader's authority. Startled, the delegation insisted that Stephens continue his tour. However, surprisingly, after Luby updated him on 3 September 1863, Stephens returned immediately and convened a conference of IRB leaders. Possibly Stephens wanted to smoke out any remaining dissidents, confident now that he held all the cards as Limerick, Tipperary, Waterford and Cork had endorsed his leadership. At the meeting, Stephens displayed his tactical brilliance and skills as an actor. Apparently conciliatory, he regretted the recent discontent and asked for reform proposals, a request designed to divide critics who had not united around a common programme. Eventually it was proposed to create an IRB treasury department and a council to help Stephens expand Fenianism throughout Ireland. But Stephens insisted that he must have complete freedom of action and, recalled Luby, told the dissidents to put up or shut up: 'They should dispense with his services altogether. Or have him as he would be – responsible to no man – subject to no control – aided by none – bound to nobody.'[37] Suddenly. Bernard O'Connor, an artist with an artistic temperament, accused Stephens of infernal arrogance, an intervention that provoked sympathy for Stephens, who assumed a pose of patient dignity. Suddenly, drama descended into farce as:

O'Connor realised he was making a fool of himself, grabbed his hat, only to dart back and forth for several minutes shouting abuse at Stephens. This he kept doing for several minutes, till in the end the indignation of the meeting changed to uproarious laughter, in which 'The Captain' of course heartily joined.[38]

As the audience acquiesced in his hard-line stance Stephens rode a tide of goodwill, and apparently made a major concession by appointing Luby 'Lieutenant of Dublin'. This showy but vacuous title annoyed Luby, who afterwards encountered Stephens surrounded by an adoring clique 'sitting mute and obedient, metaphorically if not literally at the feet of their leader, who was quite exultant and triumphant'.[39] Stephens chided Luby for overreacting. 'The men all love me. They were only a little vexed at not seeing me more oftener of late. There was no real disaffection.' Stephens's overweening complacency flabbergasted Luby, who spurned his new title. The discontent, though, never came close to a coup. Nobody wanted to overthrow Stephens or even to wound him: frustrated at his lacklustre performance and the IRB's stagnation, they only wanted their old leader back. Stephens should have learned that even a provisional dictator needed to constantly replenish his support, but untrammelled power and unceasing adulation had detached him from reality, leaving him, said Luby, 'fatally open to the arts of sycophants. That was his weak point.'[40]

During late 1863, Stephens and O'Mahony grew further apart. Stephens claimed that O'Mahony's meagre remittances and financial mismanagement had compelled him to start a newspaper. Feeling scapegoated, O'Mahony denounced Stephens as 'selfishly arrogant and unscrupulous as to his means of success. He is a compound of fanaticism and vain glory, nor will he make many mouths at a lie, when he thinks it will help him along. To me personally, he has been shamelessly ungrateful.'[41] Besides their personal antagonism and an ongoing power struggle, both men differed fundamentally over the future direction of Fenianism. Stephens represented the radical 'Men of Action' who wanted to strike against England at the earliest opportunity. But O'Mahony clung to his cautious 'drag chain' policy of only striking after the Fenian Brotherhood and IRB had accumulated sufficient military resources and discipline to strike at England. Otherwise, the Irish side should bide its time.

By late 1863, O'Mahony had tired of Stephens's 'dictatorial arrogance', and on 3 November he declared his independence. Convening the Fenian Brotherhood's first national convention in Chicago, O'Mahony announced that although they would remain allies, he was no longer accountable to

Stephens. Under a new constitution, O'Mahony was elected Head Centre with a five-member Central Council as his Cabinet. O'Mahony's drag chain policy was approved and a secret resolution appointed Stephens as Chief Organiser of the Irish Republic – in effect, making Stephens and the IRB almost subsidiary to the American organisation. As an early Christmas present, O'Mahony sent Stephens a copy of the resolution.

But although O'Mahony had outmanoeuvred Stephens, he was now an elected official and vulnerable to internal dissent. At future national conventions a majority could depose him. Indeed, there were already murmurings about his leadership that radiated from Michael Scanlan and Henry Clarence McCarthy of Chicago, and James Gibbons of Philadelphia, ambitious Men of Action promoting a radical agenda inside the Fenian Brotherhood. Just like Stephens, they wanted to topple O'Mahony before proceeding rapidly to war against England, and so immediately after the Chicago convention they and Stephens began conspiring against him.

However, Stephens's immediate priority was launching an IRB newspaper that he hoped would provide a reliable revenue stream and end his dependence on fitful American funding.[42] Stephens also envisaged it reaching out to the general public and fostering popular support for armed resistance to British rule. It might even help him vanquish A.M. Sullivan and constitutional nationalism. Sullivan owned *The Nation*, Ireland's best-selling publication, but Stephens aspired to an even higher circulation, and if Sullivan was a brilliant leader writer, then in Stephens's mind he was best of all. The *Irish People* was in part Stephens's vanity project.

For premises Stephens rented a former apothecary shop at 12 Parliament Street, a thoroughfare that led from the Liffey quays to the front of the City Hall, on either side of which were the main entrances to Dublin Castle. As the seat of British power, the Castle was about to have a centre of sedition not far away. Carpenters swiftly renovated the building, creating offices and a printing room in the basement. Stephens wanted Luby, Kickham and O'Leary as joint editors, a division, O'Leary believed, that meant he would ultimately retain power in his own hands. O'Donovan Rossa became business manager, with James O'Connor as his assistant and bookkeeper. Selling at 3p in Ireland, England and Scotland, the *Irish People* was a sixteen-page tabloid whose first four pages consisted of news extracted from foreign publications and extensively covered the Fenian Brotherhood. The centre pages carried editorials, leading articles and replies to readers' letters. A literary section contained articles on literature and poetry as well as book reviews. The remaining pages consisted of items from provincial Irish newspapers and items on the arts.

For the *Irish People*'s launch on 28 November 1863, Stephens promised a major editorial, a *tour de force* called 'Isle, Race and Doom'. But after suffering writer's block, he needed Luby to act as 'midwife', nursing him through a difficult birth with copious supplies of brandy, coffee and tobacco. Even then Stephens went right to the wire. On deadline morning a messenger collecting the article found him still writing. However, on publication day, Stephens jubilantly claimed that the IRB had a runaway success on its hands as he bestowed praise on everyone involved. Inordinately proud of his own contribution, Stephens later boasted that it had inspired everything that subsequently appeared in the paper. Not everyone agreed; O'Connor called it a stinker.

But within weeks both Stephens and the *Irish People* were struggling. He had promised Luby that his third editorial would 'flatten all his enemies on their arses' and strike them dumb for eternity. But journalism's unceasing treadmill had burned him out. Citing an unspecified illness, Stephens retreated to bed. O'Connor witnessed symptoms of indigestion but others were sceptical. O'Leary joked that Stephens had 'collapsed into silence' and Luby said his brain had given way. Almost certainly, Stephens knew that the *Irish People* had encountered possibly insurmountable problems. Inexperienced in the highly competitive world of Irish newspapers, his naive optimism and serious miscalculations had left the *Irish People* facing insolvency and liquidation.

Whereas new publications usually required years of careful advance planning, Stephens had condensed the process into five hurried months. Furthermore, his management structure made no sense. Although Stephens retained ultimate control, a three-man editorial committee violated the fundamental journalistic principle that a single editor must be all-powerful. But the IRB had room for only one provisional dictator. Instead, Stephens's structure crumbled on first contact with reality. After Stephens ceased writing for the paper, O'Leary became sole editor. Assisted for a while by Luby as sub-editor, he learned on the job and kept the paper going. Overriding anyone who stood in his way, O'Leary closely supervised every article, made the correspondence column an attractive feature and the literary section more varied than was usual in the Irish press.

Initially, Stephens believed that in the paper he had discovered a magic money tree, but far from making a profit, the *Irish People* teetered permanently on the edge of collapse. O'Leary believed Stephens had started it with incredibly small financial reserves and subscriptions, advertisements and occasional American funding never covered costs. O'Connor knew the figures and claimed Stephens's southern tour had garnered less than a quarter of anticipated advance subscriptions. Conserving limited resources and driving down expenditure required a talented business manager, but Rossa had only ever run a Skibbereen shop and Luby ridiculed his 'managerial mismanagement'. Yet Rossa's grandiosity soon resembled that of a Fleet Street proprietor: his letters habitually began, 'My clerks inform me.' Amazingly, he paid compositors the highest wages of any Irish newspaper. Lightly worked already, they returned his generosity with complete ingratitude. O'Connor considered them crooks and was unsurprised when they disrupted production and blackmailed Rossa into paying them even more money.

Remarkably, Rossa was frequently absent for prolonged periods because Stephens still used him as an IRB recruiter, messenger and all-round troubleshooter. In October 1864, the twice-widowed Rossa married Mary Jane Irwin, whom he had met at a wake, and when Stephens ordered him to Britain on IRB business, Rossa took his new wife on a month-long 'honeymoon conspiracy tour'. Later, in July 1865, Stephens sent Rossa to America on another lengthy mission. During Rossa's absences an even less experienced 27-year-old O'Connor supervised commercial operations. But Rossa did at least keep the *Irish People* going when even O'Leary's shoestring budget ran out by chipping in his late wife's insurance policy. O'Leary sacrificed his own meagre salary and surrendered his private savings. In desperation, Stephens pawned some of his and Jane's clothes, meaning that the *Irish People* literally did cost him the shirt off his back. At one low point O'Leary, Luby and Rossa met the convalescing Stephens to discuss temporarily suspending publication, but eventually everybody agreed with him that risked destroying IRB morale.[43]

The property at 12 Parliament Street itself was a major problem. Luby claimed a sharp lawyer had inveigled Stephens into paying an exorbitant rent, while A.M. Sullivan's brother T.D. said of the location that, 'Of all the places in Dublin, a shop-fronted house in a busy street, within a stone-throw of Dublin Castle where government officials, soldiers and police are constantly

moving about.'[44] This action was either calculated defiance of British authority or typical of the IRB's then casualness. Also casual were Stephens's security
precautions once the *Irish People* offices came under police surveillance. A
few weeks after recovering from illness, Stephens resumed visiting them, frequently strolling openly through Dublin city centre. By Christmas 1863, the
Irish People's dire finances had ended Stephens's early hopes of winning a circulation war with the *Nation*. O'Connor saw his despondency. Having invested
his prestige in the paper, he now faced failure and reputational damage. And
yet the *Irish People* endured. Its survival was emblematic of the staff's – and,
indeed, the IRB'S – resilience, blind faith and sheer willpower. By early 1864
the newspaper had hit its stride, and until suppressed in September 1865 it
achieved an unbroken run of ninety-five issues.

A committed core of journalists like Kickham, O'Leary and Luby
contributed the majority of articles and reviews, making the *Irish People*
resemble an IRB in-house magazine preaching to the converted. But despite
this limiting its popular appeal, the paper vigorously propagated IRB policy
on major issues, including religious freedom and land ownership – even
when this alienated powerful interests like the Roman Catholic Church.
IRB members liked the paper's radical policies. Moreover, by attracting
disillusioned nationalists and enjoying increased recruitment, the *Irish People*
helped the IRB emerge from its nadir at the end of 1863. Luby asserted that
it was 'after the founding of the Irish People that the movement became
really strong in Connaught and Ulster and got considerably increased
strength elsewhere in Ireland. But also, we had no movement in England
and Scotland until after the Irish People had appeared.'[45] A.M. Sullivan
acknowledged that although the *Irish People* never threatened his newspaper's dominance in Ireland, 'it swept all before it among the Irish in England
and Scotland'. Above all, the paper repeatedly condemned constitutional
nationalism and piecemeal reform as futile. It insisted that only revolution
could free Ireland, and any cost in bloodshed would be insignificant compared to the millions who had died or emigrated during the Great Famine.

But during 1864, Stephens and the IRB once again faced a possible
resurgence of constitutional nationalism. First, John Martin and The
O'Donoghue decided to confront Fenianism through a National League
that would campaign for Repeal of the Union. But the League stumbled
right at the start when Martin's former Young Ireland comrades stood aside.
William Smith O'Brien was in terminal decline and died on 18 June. John

Blake Dillon acerbically rejected 'the possibility of repealing the Union by anything else than round shot and rifle bullets'.[46] Politically rusty, even Martin himself was sceptical and soon expressed doubts about the wisdom of returning to front-line politics. Right from the start, Stephens was determined to crush Martin's project and he ordered IRB militants to sabotage League meetings in a campaign of intimidation designed to frighten off potential supporters. Even The O'Donoghue quickly deserted Martin and began his long farewell to Irish nationalism itself. Martin carried on virtually alone, but Stephens's roughhouse tactics gradually wore him down, and although the League survived until 1866 this was merely a lingering death. That constitutional nationalism in the mid-1860s still looked for leadership to men like Martin, O'Brien and Dillon denoted stagnation and a critical lack of new blood that compared unfavourably to the IRB.

However, to Stephens's fury A.M. Sullivan also resurfaced in February 1864. After a committee of Dubliners requested the Corporation's permission to erect on College Green a statue of the late Prince Albert, Sullivan – recently elected to the Corporation – led an opposition campaign as nationalists had long wanted a statue of Henry Grattan on the site. But a majority on the Corporation feared accusations of disloyalty to the Crown and sanctioned the royal statue. Sullivan responded by calling a protest meeting on Monday, 22 February, at the Rotunda to demand the decision be rescinded. Stephens immediately decided to derail Sullivan's demonstration, as Grattan embodied constitutional nationalism and he suspected that Sullivan would broaden any victory into an anti-Fenian campaign. Accordingly, Stephens ordered his Dublin circles to flood the Rotunda.

Fenians in the densely packed hall barracked The O'Donoghue's opening speech, which complimented Sullivan, while spectators at the front produced sticks and stormed the platform. Amidst the mayhem, Rossa and a team of wreckers jumped barriers, shoved aside everyone standing terrified in their way and screamed as they overturned seats, chairs and tables. A sympathiser hustled Sullivan to an exit, where he and The O'Donoghue stumbled into the street. Inside, Rossa and his storming party smashed everything they could before marching triumphantly down Sackville Street. At Stephens's lodgings, James O'Connor watched an elated Stephens gloating over Sullivan's humiliation: 'Mr Luby was demonstrative in his admiration. Shaking Stephens warmly by the hand he said – "You are great. I'll never doubt you again."'[47]

However, when Sullivan called for another meeting at the Rotunda on 29 February, rumours circulated that Stephens intended mobilising 1,000 armed Fenians to crush him. Sullivan's friends begged him to cancel but he was determined to defend free speech against Fenian tyranny. 'I felt that it was a trial of strength between Mr Stephens and myself.'[48] On the day, 200 so-called National Volunteers recruited by The O'Donoghue guarded entrances, and when the Rotunda's doors opened, Sullivan's supporters ran a gauntlet of abuse from thousands of Fenians protesters. But when Rossa and his crew arrived an hour later, guards blocked them. A mass brawl ensued but the guards stood firm and the meeting went ahead. Sullivan claimed victory, but winning at the Rotunda did not mean defeating the IRB. Once again, he failed to create a new political organisation and continued to rely on newspaper editorials. By contrast, Stephens had assembled thousands of sympathisers and hundreds of assailants at the Rotunda – proof of a growing and vibrant IRB network in Dublin. A political sea change was under way, at least in the capital. By scattering his constitutional enemies, Stephens had also sated the Dublin IRB's craving for action and boosted morale. O'Leary believed that in Ireland disaffection was deepening day by day, that Fenians could build on their recent successes, and the IRB's most difficult days were behind it.

In fact, 1864 and 1865 were halcyon days for an IRB that grew in size and expanded geographically, thriving on a new political landscape in which a traumatised nation slowly emerged from its prolonged political coma. Repeated attempts to revive constitutional nationalism had failed, partly because British governments treated Irish MPs as expendable pawns and refused to enact significant reforms in Ireland. Moreover, constitutional nationalist leaders were either past their prime like O'Brien, Martin and Dillon, uncharismatic political mediocrities like A.M. Sullivan, or hollow men like The O'Donoghue. After the National League folded, The O'Donoghue gravitated entirely into the Liberal camp and broke with Sullivan. Demoralised and bereft of his once devoted supporters, he eventually went bankrupt – an ignominious fate that mirrored the decline of constitutional nationalism itself. Moreover, no new blood had replaced an older, fading generation.

A brilliant account of the Dublin IRB has shown that in the 1860s, British industrial imports devastated traditional crafts, increased unemployment and fuelled political discontent.[49] Furthermore, higher bread prices and an

English financial crisis that staunched capital flowing into Ireland increased economic hardship. Mass circulation newspapers and a new national school system that had over 800,000 literate pupils also assisted the IRB's rise. In Dublin especially, Fenianism appealed to a relatively well-educated social strata, particularly shop assistants and artisans who comprised almost three-quarters of the capital's Fenians. The *Irish People* circulated widely in pubs and barbershops, where its argument that British rule in Ireland caused emigration, poverty and unemployment was very effective. The IRB's political and historical lectures which preached revolution, especially at Dublin's Mechanics Institute, also raised political consciousness. Moreover, radical ideas percolated back from America to Ireland through letters home and returning migrants.

Dublin Fenianism also flourished among clusters of working-class tenements, workshops, trade unions and leisure activities, an enclosed world in which a code of silence protected the IRB from informers and police. Adult males who did not conform risked social exclusion, persecution and forced migration, pressure that extended into factories, workshops and emporiums whose Fenian foremen, overseers and clerks often recruited for the IRB. Socially, the IRB attracted ambitious young men, keen to enhance their self-esteem through an organisation that evoked respect and fear. The Dublin IRB also integrated into urban society new arrivals from the provinces – many of them drapers' assistants employed in large department stores. During leisure hours, newcomers and existing IRB members could fraternise in pubs whose warmth, light and relative comfort contrasted with the squalid, unsanitary and overcrowded conditions of their tenement homes. Drilling in the evenings and on Sundays also created a sense of camaraderie.

Stephens also refined and expanded the IRB by effectively abolishing the National Brotherhood of St Patrick. After initially thriving, this organisation came under sustained attack from Cardinal Cullen in Ireland and from English bishops, who regarded it as a rival for the allegiance of the Roman Catholics. In 1863, the English Synod of Bishops specifically condemned it by name as a secret society. In the same year, *The Irishman*, which functioned as its unofficial newspaper, was sold to a rival, and although the new editor covered the Brotherhood's activities, he made it clear that he did not support the organisation. Consequently, Devoy asserted that Stephens concluded he had no further use for it as a front organisation and ordered every Fenian member to leave.[50] As a result, the National Brotherhood dwindled rapidly, though it limped on for several months. As its meetings ceased, the more radical members were incorporated into the IRB.

During 1864 and 1865, the IRB expanded into new territory. Hitherto in Leinster, it was concentrated in Dublin and Kilkenny, while in Munster Fenianism existed mainly in Cork and Kerry. This stagnation was caused primarily by a chronic dearth of money that kept Stephens, Luby and their small staff living just above starvation level. They had difficulty reimbursing agents' expenses, which in turn hindered organising and recruiting that consequently was done mostly by IRB volunteers, whose poorly paid jobs limited their activity to Sundays in neighbouring districts. Breaking new ground far from Dublin, Cork and other population centres was especially challenging, and although Stephens's and Luby's tours helped, they were intermittent.

Nevertheless, from early 1864 the IRB grew rapidly in Ireland, England and Scotland. O'Leary gave credit especially to Edward Duffy in Connaught, which became as well organised as Munster and superior to Leinster and Ulster. Besides, increasing in membership, the IRB attracted a better calibre of recruit, both socially and educationally. Shopkeepers and shop assistants, builders, farmers and farmers' sons had long predominated in the rank and file, but now increasingly middle-class university graduates joined. O'Leary cited three O'Donovan brothers, Edmund, John and William, the sons of John senior, a great Gaelic scholar and professor of Celtic Languages at Queen's College, Belfast. At Trinity College Dublin, Edmund became the centre of a Fenian circle, and he later extended the IRB into Co. Clare, wrote a manual on rifle use and ran a quasi-military school for the Dublin IRB. In later life, Edmund became a famous war correspondent and brilliant linguist who reported from the Balkans and central Asia, where he learned Arabic and Tartar. In 1883, Edmund accompanied a British military expedition in the Sudan that became trapped and ran out of bullets. After a last bayonet charge, he and everyone else were slaughtered by soldiers of the Mahdi – whose cause, ironically, Edmund supported. Uniquely for a Fenian, he was honoured with a commemorative plaque in St Paul's Cathedral.

During 1864 and 1865, Fenianism also expanded by infiltrating the British Army in Ireland.[51] Previously, Stephens had opposed recruiting soldiers because England's much-vaunted intelligence system might unmask the IRB as a serious threat. But infiltration of the army had actually begun unofficially in 1863 when IRB centres in garrison towns initiated soldiers, and some IRB members deliberately enlisted to gain military experience. Rossa swore in two Skibbereen teachers called Sullivan and Driscoll, who had joined the 12th Regiment of Foot, and on their own initiative they recruited hundreds of men. Later that year, Sullivan and Driscoll encountered Devoy in Phoenix Park and predicted they could win over most Irish soldiers to the IRB, but without Stephens's authorisation, this initial breakthrough stalled.

Organised infiltration of the British Army was only instigated in early 1864 by 39-year-old Patrick 'Pagan' O'Leary. Originally from Co. Cork, he had migrated to America and initially studied for the priesthood, before defecting to fight in the Mexican War of 1846. But a head wound imbued O'Leary with religious mania and a fanatical hatred of Christianity. Blaming St Patrick for bringing Roman Catholicism to Ireland and rendering its inhabitants unwarlike, he changed his forename and insisted that Ireland must return to the old paganism. After joining the Fenian Brotherhood, O'Leary returned to Ireland in 1863. John O'Leary called his namesake a very peculiar character, and Devoy considered him a 'queer, unbalanced man, who was more like a survival of the fifth century that a modern Irishman'.[52] Certainly, 'Pagan's' behaviour was unconventional. Sporting a black frock coat, silk hat and long beard, he ostentatiously shunned tobacco, liquor and coffee on which duty was paid to England. At the *Irish People* office, O'Leary spent almost all his time casting bullets and sleeping overnight.

Recruiting Irish soldiers to the IRB obsessed 'Pagan', who envisaged many of the British garrison's 26,000 troops spearheading rebels in a future rising, O'Leary constantly – and unsuccessfully – badgered Stephens to allow recruiting, and the IRB leader finally relented only after O'Leary threatened to leave for America and accused him of undermining resistance to England. Only someone not quite right in the head would have dared blackmail Stephens in this way. But, despite making 'Pagan' chief organiser for the British Army, Stephens gave him no help; O'Leary would work alone and return only occasionally to apprise Stephens of his progress. Clearly, Stephens expected that his roving commission would result in O'Leary roving far away, thereby insulating himself from any damage when 'Pagan' surely failed. Stephens could never have anticipated O'Leary lasting long; more likely was his speedy arrest. Hopefully the police would suspect not a conspiracy but only a visibly damaged and possibly deranged individual. And even if put on trial, 'Pagan' might well be found 'guilty but insane'. What Stephens never expected was O'Leary's mission lasting nine months, his recruiting career being a glittering success, IRB members lauding him as a great Fenian, and Stephens appointing him hailed as a stroke of genius!

O'Leary's recruiting plan was simplicity itself. In pubs and private houses, on country roads and even at sentry boxes, he cultivated Irish soldiers as potential recruits, ingratiating himself with tales of his military exploits and sympathy for their exploitation by England. Very few of them, O'Leary predicted, would ever see a pension after twenty-one years of service, and even then, they would most likely end up as beggars or crippled veterans. Seemingly O'Leary's pitch persuaded thousands of soldiers to join the IRB, a success that Luby attributed to his 'wonderful zeal and energy' and his willingness to risk everything:

> No doubt, he was fearfully incautious in the way he carried on his work. But in this extreme recklessness probably lay the very secret of his rapid and widespread success. A cautious man dealing with British soldiers would not have achieved one-tenth of what he did in the same brief time.[53]

In mid-November 1864, O'Leary's luck finally ran out on the Bridge of Athlone. When he asked a potential recruit to take the IRB oath, the soldier immediately summoned policemen who blocked both ends of the bridge. Arrested as 'John Murphy', O'Leary stood trial at Mullingar in March 1865 on a charge of spreading disloyalty among soldiers. After the jury deadlocked, he was convicted at a retrial in July 1865 and sentenced to seven years' penal servitude, making him the first IRB member to wear prison grey. Devoy acknowledged that despite his mental defects, 'Pagan' had 'brought into existence the element in Fenianism that was most really dangerous to England'.[54]

'Pagan' O'Leary had certainly ridden his luck, but the British Army high command's complacency also facilitated his success. GOC, Sir George Brown was a 75-year-old Crimean War veteran widely seen as an inept bungler, who regarded Ireland as a relaxing pre-retirement backwater, 'the best position where an old officer can be placed'. Despite knowing Fenians were active in the army, Brown denied they were a serious threat: instead, he concentrated on preparing for the Prince of Wales' opening of the Dublin Exhibition in May 1865. On 10 March, Brown declared that 'we have not yet been able to establish any case of tampering with the troops'. He did not take O'Leary's conviction seriously, derided the idea of a widespread conspiracy among his soldiers, and said of a disquieting police report of April 1865 that 'the only thing to do is to keep an eye on these fellows'. A historian has described Brown's negligence as incredible, made explicable only by his ill health, imminent retirement and a belief that his soldiers could not possibly be treasonous. Acting with 'characteristic disdain', Brown dismissed concern about O'Leary's activities as police exaggeration.[55]

After O'Leary's arrest, Stephens acted swiftly to build on his achievements, though more methodically than 'Pagan's' rather slapdash *modus operandi*. As successor, Stephens chose William Roantree, the excellent organiser from Kildare who had been assisting O'Leary. Until his arrest in September 1865, Roantree systematised the IRB's network inside the British Army and extended it rapidly to barracks in Dublin, Cork, Limerick, Waterford, Fermoy, Athlone, Mullingar, Dundalk, Belfast, Londonderry, Enniskillen and the Curragh. As he recruited more soldiers, Roantree's work became increasingly hazardous, as many never hid their Fenian sympathies and some even sang rebel songs on the march.

During 1864, Stephens consolidated his relationship with the American Men of Action conspiring to weaken O'Mahony's leadership. McCarthy, Scanlan and Dunne had chipped away at O'Mahony's authority through constant criticism and calculated insubordination. Completely ignoring him, they organised in Chicago a great Fenian Fair to raise funds.[56] Ostensibly to acquire exhibits, McCarthy travelled to Ireland and invited Stephens to the Fair, but really to formalise an anti-O'Mahony alliance. McCarthy returned to America with a collection of what has been called ethic junk[56] and some of the finest examples of early Irish kitsch, which included a baby's cradle made from goose eggshell.[57] Before departing for America, Stephens placated his critics by giving Luby, O'Leary and Kickham a document appointing them as an Executive Committee of the IRB during his absence. It was all window dressing. The trio never made a single important decision and the committee was wound up after Stephens returned. However, the document itself would later haunt Stephens when G Division detectives captured Luby's copy.

Between 28 March and 3 April 1864, Stephens attended an immensely successful Chicago Fair that raised $50,000. At the same time, behind O'Mahony's back, he and the Men of Action formally united – not just against O'Mahony but his gradualist drag chain policy as well. To get a slice of the Fair's proceeds, Stephens toured American cities, promising Fenian circles that soon the IRB would ether fight or disband; to O'Mahony's dismay, Stephens's cry of 'War or Dissolution in '65' resonated with American Fenians. O'Mahony tried to counter Stephens without completely alienating the Men of Action and creating a schism, but his appeasement gradually wore O'Mahony down and only emboldened his radical enemies.

Despite arranging for O'Mahony's political assassination, Stephens shamelessly exploited a letter of introduction from him to Union armies. Stephens's 'War or Dissolution in '65' slogan certainly excited Irish-American soldiers, but his repeated declarations committed him unequivocally to an imminent Irish revolution.

Prior to leaving America on 2 August, Stephens forced O'Mahony to appoint Henry McCarthy as Deputy Head Centre of the Fenian Brotherhood and create at state level paid full-time organisers whose loyalty would be to the Men of Action. O'Mahony had reluctantly agreed in the hope of persuading Stephens and his allies to call off the dogs. But he little knew that they planned to destroy him through a silent coup that would establish a parallel power structure inside the Fenian Brotherhood – one that at best would leave O'Mahony a helpless figurehead and McCarthy as the real leader. Naively, O'Mahony recalled sanctioning McCarthy's appointment as Deputy Head Centre after he lied about sharing O'Mahony's beliefs and denounced Stephens.[58] Soon afterwards, Stephens left for Ireland, well satisfied that he had crushed O'Mahony and once again led Fenianism on both sides of the Atlantic.

5

Stephens, O'Mahony, the IRB and the Fenian Brotherhood: August 1864–September 1865

Soon after Stephens returned to Ireland in August 1864, a prominent Chicago Fenian warned O'Mahony that the IRB leader, Henry McCarthy, Michael Scanlan and P.W. Dunne were conspiring 'to stab me in the back'.[1] Believing a split with the Men of Action was now inevitable, O'Mahony decided to resign as Head Centre – only not yet. Fearing that a schism would destroy the Fenian Brotherhood, he clung on as his authority was whittled away, all the while hoping for something to turn up and rescue him from his predicament. O'Mahony then sent an envoy, Captain Phillip Coyne, to Ireland, probably hoping for a report that IRB preparations for a rising were inadequate and 'War or Dissolution in '65' was impractical.[2] But after a four-month investigation, Coyne returned in time for a Fenian Brotherhood convention at Cincinnati on 17 January 1865 with a positive report that concluded the masses desired revolution, and although the middle classes feared a rising, they would still side with the patriots. Even so, O'Mahony refused to issue the final call, delaying tactics that stoked more resentment against him, and despite being re-elected Head Centre, his enemies McCarthy, Scanlan and Dunne dominated the new Central Council and intended destroying him.

At a Central Council session in February 1865, O'Mahony's power dwindled further when McCarthy swore into the Brotherhood

Patrick J. Meehan, editor of the *Irish American*.[3] Hitherto a bitter enemy of Fenianism, Meehan had only joined the Brotherhood to stop it establishing a rival newspaper. Even more provocatively, McCarthy immediately co-opted Meehan on to the Central Council – but once again O'Mahony silently acquiesced. The Council also co-opted William Randall Roberts, an ambitious, wealthy 35-year-old New York businessman who planned to exploit the Fenian Brotherhood and rise high in American politics. As O'Mahony stood in his way, Roberts immediately joined the Men of Action. To discover if IRB preparations for a rising had progressed since Coyne's mission, the Council appointed yet another envoy: 33-year-old Captain Thomas J. Kelly. Originally from Mount Bellew, Co. Galway, Kelly had worked as a printer in New York before joining the Union Army. Severely wounded in the Civil War and discharged, Kelly devoted himself to the Fenian Brotherhood. O'Mahony then sent him to Ireland for three months to report on the feasibility of a rising. As O'Mahony suspected that Stephens had manipulated previous investigations in favour of rebellion, he warned Kelly to keep his distance from the IRB leader. Surprisingly, only a month after Kelly left America on 25 March 1865, O'Mahony and the Central Council dispatched yet another envoy, Colonel Francis Frederick Millen.[4] A soldier of fortune, Millen had once been a general in the Mexican army, before turning up at the Fenian Brotherhood's New York headquarters in October 1864 and putting his military expertise at O'Mahony's disposal. The Head Centre almost certainly sent Millen to Ireland as an insurance policy in case Kelly disappointed, ensuring there would at least be one adverse report about IRB readiness.

If O'Mahony had told Stephens about Kelly's assignment, he kept quiet about its purpose and the IRB leader sent him a blistering twenty-eight-page rebuke:[5] 'You cannot possibly conceive what I felt on learning the real nature of his mission. I consider Captain K's mission the deadliest blow ever aimed against us.' Stephens claimed that he had nothing against Kelly personally but believed his mission was an 'inquisition'. He was especially amazed that Kelly's report would decide whether O'Mahony supported a rising. Moreover, wasting another three months would rule out a rising in 1865 and nullify Stephens's repeated promises. In which case, Stephens declared, the cause would be lost. Furthermore, he warned that Kelly's mission was unsettling the IRB; 100 men from one circle had left for England and America.

Stephens believed that O'Mahony was using Kelly to destabilise him – just as he was undermining O'Mahony. But in Stephens's world loyalty went only one way. However, he could reasonably complain about O'Mahony's behaviour, as Stephens believed that the question of a rising in 1865 had already been settled the previous year when American audiences had rapturously cheered his pledge to rise before the year's end. And the Cincinnati convention had unequivocally endorsed a decision to meet again in Ireland during the following year, thereby implicitly sanctioning a rising in 1865. Nevertheless, in O'Mahony Stephens now had his scapegoat if anything went wrong.

Despite O'Mahony's instructions, Kelly fell completely under the spell of Stephens, who shepherded him to staged encounters with IRB centres. Indeed, Stephens himself could have written Kelly's report of 21 June, which likened IRB's growth to a rolling snowball.[6] Kelly extolled the IRB's high morale and numerical strength; Cork City and County had reported over 36,000 members. Fenians everywhere eagerly anticipated a rising before year's end and accepted Stephens's claim that O'Mahony had promised American aid. Postponement would devastate them: 'There will be such another exodus as was never seen since the time of Moses, putting the present immense emigration entirely in the shade. The organisation cannot otherwise survive the month of December.'[7] IRB centres had assured Kelly that all they needed was proper leadership and substantial military equipment. Accordingly, they had men watching British armouries from which weapons and supplies could be seized at the start of a rising. Furthermore, sixty new centres recruited in England could launch diversionary attacks and delay British reinforcements from reaching Ireland. The Fenian Brotherhood should immediately furnish the IRB with arms or provide it funds to purchase them, as well as supply experienced officers to whip IRB volunteers into shape.

Millen sailed from New York on 14 April 1865, and in early May he reached Dublin. By staying at a hotel near the Four Courts and living in plain sight, Millen successfully evaded G Division detectives, and on 25 May he finally met Stephens, who had just returned from a tour of IRB circles in Great Britain. As he later recalled, Millen was not overly impressed:

Though pleased with his intellectual countenance and gentlemanly deportment, he did not yet come up to my ideas of what should be the beau-ideal of a revolutionary leader. As our acquaintance progressed I came to like him better in some respects, and now can concede him to be possessed of considerable fanaticism generally, and some determination of purpose, but at the same time know him to be so self-opinionated and dogmatical in his character and ideas, that even when he knows himself to be in the wrong he would not admit it, and would prefer to see any project ruined in which he might be engaged, rather than have the views of others adopted, though perhaps much better than his own and though the party advancing them might be more capable than himself of executing such project.[8]

Testily, Stephens criticised American Fenian leaders for behaving like schoolboys playing games rather than serious revolutionaries; from a safe distance they continually made extravagant promises to him on which they never delivered. But a moment of truth was fast approaching when they would have to fulfil them or be exposed as frauds. However, although Coyne's report should have ended any doubts about IRB preparedness, Stephens promised to assist Millen's investigation. Later, the IRB leader boasted he had 100,000 men ready to rebel and warned Millen that a rising before December 1865 was imperative; otherwise, the IRB would disintegrate. Indeed, time was slipping away and ideally an insurrection should start in August; if Millen's report only reached America in October, he would abandon the whole enterprise.

Initially, Stephens's pressure left Millen unmoved. He questioned an inflexible commitment to rising by a particular date, and whether or not the Fenian Brotherhood and IRB were at peak readiness. Echoing O'Mahony, Millen preferred waiting – even for years – until England was embroiled in a major war; otherwise, the enemy's 'colossal power' would crush any rebellion. Millen was also astounded at Stephens's grandiose projects, which included a Dublin cannon factory that he boasted the British would never discover. Millen also came to suspect that Stephens was giving him the run-around. Often evading Millen for five or six days, Stephens would explain that he was busy meeting Kelly, centres and IRB representatives from Ireland and Britain – all the while going sleepless for two or three days in a row. Instead, Stephens gave Millen displacement activity like estimating the cost of equipping an army of 50,000 men, a task that wasted eight days and utterly frustrated Millen. Stephens also asked for a drawing of this army marshalled in a line of battle with its artillery ready for a campaign, something Millen knew no experienced military officer would ever request. Still, once again, he reluctantly complied.[9]

Then, in late June 1865, Stephens and Kelly suddenly blindsided Millen. Insisting that the same messenger should convey his and Kelly's reports to America for O'Mahony and the Central Council to compare, they demanded that Millen complete his submission within forty-eight hours. Their shock therapy worked. With little time and only limited knowledge of the IRB, Millen's report of 24 June resembled Kelly's in tone and content, expressed the same fears, and made similar recommendations.[10] Declaring himself satisfied with IRB preparations, Millen insisted that three-quarters of the population was patriotic and eager to rebel, as Ireland was sinking into despair and their only choice was between emigration and revolution. Unless a rising happened in 1865 or early 1866, Millen predicted an almost apocalyptic exodus from the country would commence:

> We are running a race with emigration and if we do not move soon, we will have no men to move with. Should it be whispered among our friends here that we will not be prepared for action this year or early next spring I fear that such of them as could leave the country would emigrate en masse and leave Ireland at last, literally a grazing ground for English beeves.[11]

Despite his private doubts about Stephens, Millen praised his judgement and integrity, while warning that sending any more envoys would only undermine IRB confidence in its leader. Finally, while Millen was a bringer of war, he also desired to make peace. Deploring recent bickering, he rather naively urged O'Mahony and Stephens to settle their differences face-to-face at a conference in some neutral location like Paris, before uniting around a common Fenian programme.

Interestingly, neither Kelly nor Millen mentioned – perhaps had never detected – any IRB disquiet about Stephens's leadership. But John Devoy's disillusion stretched back to August 1864, when Stephens told everyone that 1865 would be the year of action. Devoy recalled Stephens breezily pacing the *Irish People* office and reiterating that rebellion was definitely coming. Knowing the IRB was bereft of weapons, Devoy asked what would it fight with?

He paused in his walk, turned to me and replied: 'Oh, we'll get all the arms we need from America. We'll have more than 100,000 rifles and a good supply of artillery.' I asked: 'what about officers?' And he assured me there would be plenty, including several Generals and quite a number of Colonels, all of them veterans. 'We'll get 3000 officers in Chicago', he added. This was too much for me and I said: 'why, there can't be 3000 officers in all the Chicago regiments.' He saw that I was a doubting Thomas and he explained that he meant the Chicago District which included the whole West. His habit of exaggeration was incurable.[12]

For weeks afterwards, Stephens toured circles in a kind of victory lap, meeting centres and radiating optimism. As drilling intensified, Devoy witnessed preparations of all kinds – except procuring arms.

Throughout 1865, Joseph Denieffe recalled an undercurrent of insubordination as Irish soldiers criticised Stephens's reluctance to rise immediately.[13] Denieffe shared their impatience, convinced as he was that the time to strike had come. There was also IRB dissatisfaction with Stephens – at the top, among ordinary members and Irish-American officers as well. Some feared Stephens had not prepared the IRB well for an insurrection, while others suspected he did not intend fighting at all. Yet when rumours spread of a coup to install a more aggressive successor, Luby and Denieffe circulated a document endorsing Stephens's leadership that twenty-five high-ranking IRB members signed. But privately, Denieffe's despair mounted: 'The dilly-dallying was kept up while there was no actual revolution in sight.'[14]

James O'Connor also claimed Stephens brushed off appeals for weapons. Stephens had established some engineering schools and recruited a pike maker whose weapons would have been useless against rifles. O'Connor recalled that for at least twelve months prior to September 1865, Stephens had been urged to intensify arming the IRB, but he had procrastinated. 'Stephens was without plan or preparations. He did not mean to fight that year, notwithstanding his imprudent notices, for he was unready then as he had been five years previously.'[15]

On 9 April 1865, the American Civil War ended, and soon afterwards Union and Confederate armies demobilised. Many Irish-American officers joined the Fenian Brotherhood and some went straight to Ireland at their own expense. In May, at the Central Council, William Roberts presided in place of a terminally ill McCarthy, and after he read out urgent letters from Stephens, Kelly and Millen, the Council assigned Col. William G. Halpin to IRB headquarters in Dublin and instructed Millen to stay on as a militarily adviser. Between June and September, it also dispatched 150 experienced army officers to Ireland. Millen described many as talented and efficient, but a large minority were 'as worthless a set of scamps as ever faced the sun. Fellows who lived by loafing around the bar-rooms and gin houses of New York and other large cities in the Union.'[16] Frequently drunk and in debt, they were as ready to cut a throat as a deck of cards.

Although the Central Council's next session scrutinised Kelly's and Millen's favourable reports, it resisted crossing the Rubicon. O'Mahony and a hesitant minority still opposed an immediate rising and they stood firm even after an appeal from O'Donovan Rossa, whom Stephens had sent to trigger military action. Instead, the Council appointed two members to conduct an absolutely final investigation of IRB strength, weaponry, discipline and morale. Hopefully, the emissaries would also restore transatlantic harmony.[17] From the Men of Action, O'Mahony nominated P.W. Dunne, but balanced him with Patrick J. Meehan, who had assured O'Mahony that he would only support an insurrection if the Fenian Brotherhood and IRB were both completely ready. O'Mahony even entrusted Meehan with a set of documents that included his and Dunne's credentials, a draft for £570, and a request that Rossa represent the IRB at Fenian Brotherhood headquarters in New York. But Meehan was no counterweight to Dunne. He had duped O'Mahony, whose overthrow he wanted. The famously slippery Meehan was already in Roberts's camp.

On 22 July, Dunne, Meehan, Rossa and Halpin landed in Ireland. Even Stephens was not told in advance about the mission, and Denieffe only learned when Dunne entered his shop and requested that he and Meehan meet the IRB leader. Denieffe was surprised, because in New York he knew about Meehan's hostility to Fenianism. Millen was also puzzled; for years rumours had circulated that Meehan had once been a Fenian but was expelled as a suspected spy. Even Dunne had his doubts. He wanted to see Stephens alone first, so that he could explain the situation in New York. Accordingly, Denieffe arranged that Dunne and Stephens meet first at his house, followed an hour later by Meehan. Yet, astonishingly, soon after Stephens and his entourage arrived, Dunne brought an agitated Meehan, who confessed to losing O'Mahony's documents. Knowing Meehan's history, Denieffe, Brophy and Duffy suspected treachery and vowed that unless he produced the papers, he would not leave the room alive. Terror-stricken, Meehan said he had concealed them inside his trousers' waistband, from which they must have fallen after he left his Kingstown hotel and travelled by train into Dublin. Stephens dispatched Denieffe and Millen, who vainly searched Kingstown railway station, Meehan's train and finally his hotel.

Millen recalled that after he returned:

Stephens did not say much but Brophy, Duffy and Denieffe was so enraged that but for the interference of the Boss they would have taken Meehan's life on the spot. Meehan went on his knees and in the most solemn manner called God to witness that he had lost his papers accidentally and unknown to himself.[18]

Stephens protected Meehan from harm, not out of charity but because Meehan was now more pliable, desperate to prove his loyalty. Superficially, Stephens was also more generous and accommodating. As O'Mahony had instructed Dunne and Millen to restore good relations with the IRB, the IRB leader announced an advisory council consisting of O'Leary, Kickham, Rossa and Millen that would henceforth act as his Cabinet. But it was a charade. Stephens delegated the quartet almost no powers and, claimed Millen, he continued doing 'exactly what he pleased and the Council was always sure to endorse his action whatever it might be'.[19] Yet, within days of meeting some hastily assembled centres from Dublin and nearby counties at the end of July, Meehan and Dunne sent a report to America that confirmed IRB preparations were complete, urged the Central Council to send 300 experienced officers to Ireland, and recommended that O'Mahony issue the Final Call. They then embarked on a lengthy tour of selected areas, which proved they had glossed over considerable deficiencies in the IRB. But it was too late for them to row back on a report that had now reached New York. Meehan and Dunne were already committed to a rising in Ireland.

O'Mahony knew that accepting Dunne's and Meehan's recommendations was hazardous, especially as England was not involved in a major war. But having run out of excuses for delay, he reluctantly issued the Final Call on 5 August. O'Mahony felt that 'the Fenian Organisation was about to barter a system of action, which promised certain victory in the future for what was almost forlorn hope in the present. The odds were then fearfully against the success of any attempt at an immediate uprising in Ireland.'[20] He then turned to fitting out a naval expedition whose landing in Ireland would coincide with the rising. Upon completion, O'Mahony intended to resign as Head Centre and join the expedition as an ordinary volunteer.

6

Lord Wodehouse and Ireland:
November 1864–September 1865

When Lord Derby's Conservative government fell in June 1859, Lord Naas left Dublin Castle, and the new Liberal prime minster Lord Palmerston appointed Lord Carlisle as Viceroy and Sir Robert Peel, the former prime minister's son, became Chief Secretary. Carlisle revelled in his ceremonial role and left administration to Peel, until in September 1864 the Viceroy became terminally ill and resigned. His successor was 38-year-old Lord Wodehouse, the scion of a prosperous Norfolk family and an Oxford graduate with a first-class degree in classics, who was knowledgeable in European history and fluent in Italian and French.[1] Ambitious, conciliatory, honest, diligent and high-minded, Wodehouse was an instinctively liberal supporter of free trade, mass education and colonial self-determination. Hoping eventually for Cabinet office, he insisted on running the Irish government, and especially its Fenian policy; much to the chagrin of Peel, with whom relations were difficult from the start. Palmerston trusted Wodehouse and sometimes allowed him to take major decisions without his and the Cabinet's prior approval.

Wodehouse's attitude to Ireland and its people was complex and ambivalent. He strongly disliked Roman Catholicism and so did his wife Florence, a daughter of the zealously evangelical Earl of Clare. Furthermore, Wodehouse believed races progressed at different speeds and that the Irish were backward compared to their English rulers, an opinion he sometimes expressed in hot-headed language that he would later regret: 'What a miserable spectacle Ireland presents. Is there a nation in the world so generally odious? Wretched weakness in action, contemptible vapouring in speech and cowardly assassinations seem to be the chief characteristics of the native Irishman. I had forgotten – slavish bigotry which is another pleasing trait.'[2] But Wodehouse also blamed Ireland's arrested development on an unhappy history of conquest, rebellion, religious antagonism and agrarian crime. Paternalistically, he thought that if Ireland enjoyed peace and good government it could eventually become an advanced European state – although the process would take time. 'The results of the misgovernment and fierce religious hatred of centuries cannot be undone in a generation. A century is not too long.'[3] Wanting to give Ireland space for development, Wodehouse hoped, especially, to avoid introducing draconian repression.

An efficient administrator, Wodehouse travelled extensively, read official memoranda meticulously and worked harmoniously with Under-Secretary Sir Thomas Larcom, a superb mandarin whom Wodehouse called 'a keen-witted, thorough-paced permanent official. I never met better.'[4] But Chief Secretary Peel resented being demoted and constantly undermined the Viceroy. Despite sharing his great father's name and title, the son was temperamentally a polar opposite. Daniel O'Connell had memorably likened prime minister Peel's chilly reserved face to a silver platter on a coffin lid, but the Chief Secretary simply could not control his emotions. Excitable and abrasive, he had a gift for offending people. After he scoffed at 'the cabbage garden heroes of 1848', William Smith O'Brien challenged Peel to a duel, but as these were no longer acceptable, a newspaper suggested they fight it out instead with cabbage stalks in the widow's garden. Wodehouse soon realised what a heavy Irish cross he had to bear. When Peel clashed with Chancellor of the Exchequer Gladstone, he seriously embarrassed the Viceroy, as Gladstone was his political patron and the prime-minister-in-waiting. It was a fight Peel could not possibly win, and Wodehouse said he had to pour 'a can of oil on the troubled waters'.[5] But Peel was constantly fighting with people high and low. Once, Wodehouse noted wearily that, 'Peel has got into a foolish fracas with a Mr Gray in a railway carriage. A most trumpery affair, but a rowdy Chief Secretary is a discredit to the Govt.'[6] Yet the Chief Secretary never learned; time and again his tantrums and erratic public behaviour mortified the Viceroy.

In July 1865, Wodehouse had a new commander-in-chief, 66-year-old Sir Hugh Rose. After ruthlessly suppressing the Indian Mutiny in 1857, he had acquired a fearsome reputation and his staff stood in awe of this harsh disciplinarian. An Irish observer said Rose cut 'a curious figure, long and lanky, with a very strange, lean and very pitiless face. To his officers he was reported to be repelling and harsh. But with the ladies he was the most engaging old dandy in the world.'⁷ Among the idiosyncrasies that Rose's aide-de-camp, Col. Frederick Wellesley, memorably recalled was his routinely changing clothes three or four times a day:

> He would appear at breakfast in a black velvet jacket with perhaps bright yellow trousers. This dress he would change for luncheon at which he would appear in uniform. After luncheon he would again exchange his uniform for some other fantastic dress. He was tall and thin, with extremely long hands, on one of which he always wore a magnificent single sapphire. In speech he was almost effeminate, and had a trick when talking of constantly drawing his sleeves back from his cuffs to draw attention to his clothes. If one ever rendered him a service, however trivial, his invariable reply was, 'Thanks – a thousand thanks.'⁸

Time and again, Rose invited people to dinner but he never appeared and, as a bachelor, dined out alone. Once, his entire staff and their wives waited until very late, but Rose never turned up. Wellesley attributed this rudeness to forgetfulness, but possibly he sadistically enjoyed exploiting his authority by playing cruel practical jokes on subordinates who never dreamt of absenting themselves. Certainly, Rose was a stern taskmaster who saw his mission in Ireland as crushing Fenianism. Wellesley recalled that his staff had all heard that:

> one day during the Indian mutiny, he was sitting in his tent when an officer entered it to report that he had arrived with a batch of prisoners. Having heard what the officer had to say, he made a sign that implied the prisoners were to be taken to the execution ground to be blown from guns. As the officer left the tent he told him to report again when his orders had been carried out – and when he did so he merely remarked, 'Thanks, a thousand thanks. Have a glass of sherry?'⁹

After living mostly abroad on military and diplomatic service, Rose's mindset was emphatically colonialist; Irish Catholics, he said, were like Indians:

credulous, impulsive, imaginative and clever, but lacking an aptitude for self-government. Pompous and smug, he had acted in India as a co-equal of the Viceroy, and accordingly was unlikely to welcome orders from the younger Wodehouse, whose only experience of gunfire was shooting pheasants on his friends' estates.

Initially, Wodehouse was satisfied at conditions in Ireland:

> The Fenians are undoubtedly active in propagating their treasonable views. The government here keeps a vigilant watch upon their movements through the police which is very necessary for although the Fenian movement may be almost treated as ridiculous and is certainly not in the least dangerous it is always prudent to neglect no precaution against mischief.[10]

For some years Dublin Castle had received reports on Fenianism from America and police officers in Ireland, but no official had fashioned this information into a coherent narrative of the conspiracy. Likewise, the British government had remained indifferent. In November 1864, Palmerston – himself an Irish peer – dismissed as a joke an anonymous letter describing the revolutionary ambitions of Irish-America.[11] Sharing his scepticism, Wodehouse predicted that, 'This movement will come to nothing but it keeps alive the embers of disaffection. The police keep a quiet but sharp watch upon them.'[12] Furthermore, he claimed – mistakenly – that the Fenians had completely failed to sabotage the army and police.

Quite rapidly from early 1865, the Irish government's relative uncon-cern about Fenianism gave way to mounting anxiety. After the British ambassador in America claimed that Fenians were sending arms, money and men to Ireland, G Division increased its monitoring of the IRB. On 3 March, Wodehouse warned Home Secretary Sir George Grey that Fenian activities were causing uneasiness in some parts of the country and that American weapons flowing into disaffected counties had to be stopped. He also thought Co. Cork should be proclaimed, and three days later sent Attorney-General Lawson to get the prime minister's approval. Palmerston believed the Viceroy was attributing to the Fenian movement an impor-tance it did not deserve. If Wodehouse insisted on proclamation as a matter of immediate necessity, he would reluctantly consent – but not otherwise. The Viceroy himself was reluctant to push harder as Fenianism was still attracting little attention in England. However, he warned Grey that 'the Fenians mean serious business and it would be a mistake to treat them with more ridicule'.[13]

To strengthen his case, Wodehouse asked G Division for more intelligence on the conspiracy and Superintendent Ryan had two star detectives, Smollen and Doyle, surveil the *Irish People* offices. Joseph Denieffe recalled 'detectives hovering around like birds of prey. The Castle birds were known to all.'[14] Gradually, Ryan concluded that the paper's premises were a hotbed of disaffection and seditious propaganda. On 21 March, Wodehouse warned Foreign Secretary Clarendon that reports to him from all Ireland left no doubt about increasing Fenian disaffection, that agents from America and England were in the country, that the conspiracy was collecting arms, recruiting soldiers and secretly drilling. Especially concerning was that, unlike previous Irish plots, it was sustained by foreign money. Cork was the most disaffected county.

Then, in April 1864, G Division made a big intelligence breakthrough when an informer, Pierce Nagle, provided a copy of the IRB oath, disclosed the *Irish People*'s real purpose and identified James Stephens as the movement's leader.

A former schoolmaster from Clonmel, Co. Tipperary, Nagle had met Stephens in 1863 before migrating to New York, where O'Mahony employed him at the Fenian Brotherhood headquarters. But Nagle's obnoxious personality alienated O'Mahony, who fired him and said he could pay his own way back to Ireland. Nagle retaliated by approaching the British consul in New York and agreed that, for a return ticket, he would spy on Stephens and the IRB. In Dublin, Nagle worked for a builder whose foreman, Denis Cromien, was an IRB centre and regularly visited the *Irish People* offices. In March 1864, Cromien got Nagle a job there folding copies, and he quickly told G Division that Stephens was the IRB leader and he frequently appeared at the *Irish People* offices. James O'Connor described Nagle as 'an ill-shaped man, sinister-looking, crooked in eye and crooked in form. He had a glutinous mouth, a guilty expression, a sneaking manner and a small voice for a big man.'[15] Once again, his repulsiveness got Nagle sacked, but Luby took him back and soon Stephens – who had a weakness for ingratiating sycophants – was using Nagle as a messenger. Nagle now informed G Division that secret drilling with arms and pikes was happening across Ireland, and that American money, weapons and several thousand military officers had secretly bolstered the conspiracy. Moreover, 'Pagan' O'Leary was recruiting Irish soldiers for the IRB and casting bullets at the *Irish People* offices.

Concern at Dublin Castle rose further after a detective, Talbot, infiltrated the IRB in Tipperary and claimed there were 120,000 drilled Fenians in Ireland and that IRB weapons were being stored in Dublin timber yards. Also, with the American Civil War over, detectives observed many former army officers arriving in Ireland. By midsummer, the police reported that Fenianism was spreading rapidly across Ireland and preparing for a rising soon after harvest time. In Kilkenny, Cork and Waterford over half the male population were said to be enthusiastic Fenians. James O'Connor recollected 'preparations on both sides' for an imminent rising. 'We felt that the time was approaching; that something should be done by us or the Government. It was a question of who would take the initiative.'[16] Luby believed that 'the crisis of our fate was drawing near. Detectives were now constantly watching the office. Each day indeed they seemed to grow more vigilant than ever.'[17] Yet, despite proclaiming 1865 as the year of action, Stephens seemed inert; he refused to buy arms and even stopped IRB members from purchasing their own weapons. O'Connor also claimed that delay was demoralising a rank and file that craved action, and that the IRB was slowly disintegrating. He speculated that if the British government had only displayed more patience, Stephens would have been ousted as leader, and even had Fenians rebelled, the rising would have been brief and feeble.

But Dublin Castle was unaware of IRB dissension and instead feared that a Fenian insurrection was imminent. On 3 September 1865, Wodehouse told Sir George Grey: 'The newspapers are so full of rumours of Fenian plots. There is a striking agreement between the reports of our spies in the United States and our spies here as to the intention of the Fenians to attempt some outbreak early this autumn.'[18] Reportedly, many Irish-American officers were on their way to Ireland, soon to be followed by vessels carrying arms and ammunition. The *Irish People* was 'openly treasonable' and, by constantly inflaming public opinion, doing 'infinite mischief'. As its editorials became increasingly menacing, the paper warned on 12 August that landlords were doomed and that the spilling of blood was inevitable in any successful insurrection.

On 5 September, Cork's Lord Lieutenant, Baron Fermoy, warned Wodehouse that for too long Fenianism had been derided as a harmless craze, but now the conspiracy was penetrating every county town and the surrounding countryside. Tipperary's Lord Lieutenant, Lord Lismore, claimed that disaffection pervaded the entire county and a rising was imminent. Wodehouse insisted that the army and police would ensure that any outbreak was minor in scale, but privately he worried about an Irish Constabulary that was 500 men under strength and suffering from sluggish recruitment. And the Viceroy was also concerned about alarmist rumours damaging public confidence, telling Grey on 12 September that 'the public mind begins to be much disturbed to hear about the Fenians and there is a vague expectation prevalent in the South of Ireland of an immediate rising. It is difficult to believe people capable of such an egregious folly but the matter must be treated as serious.'[19] Farmers in some parts of Ireland were selling their produce only for gold, one gentleman had told the Viceroy that he has sent all his plate to England, and another was debating the practicality of defending his house from Fenian attackers.

Despite his confidence about defeating any rising, Wodehouse feared that public disquiet might suddenly slide into uncontrolled hysteria: he noted 'a tendency to unreasoning panic amongst the upper and middle classes which it is very desirable to check'.[20] However, in early September the Viceroy was still focused on short-term panaceas like increasing Constabulary pay and drafting in troop reinforcements during the winter. He did, though, tell foreign minister Russell that the Irish situation was potentially danger-ous. 'The Fenians are not to be despised. They mean mischief and if they get arms and leaders from America may attempt an outbreak which would cause bloodshed and confusion.'[21] Consequently, if an opportunity arose, Wodehouse contemplated introducing more drastic measures earlier, such as arresting Fenian leaders. His great problem was that, as late as 12 September 1865, he still believed that legal proof that would stand up in court was nec-essary before he authorised mass arrests. Failing that, Wodehouse favoured closing and prosecuting the *Irish People,* though even then the operation would probably scoop up only minor front men. And Dublin juries were notoriously reluctant to convict in newspaper cases. But, Wodehouse still believed he had enough time to reach a considered decision.

Then, in mid-September, police told the Viceroy that Fenian prepara-tions for insurrection were now all but complete.[22] The conspiracy had hundreds of circles, centres in every town, tens of thousands of men drill-ing, hundreds of Irish-American officers across the country, and funds flowing in from America. Fenians confidently anticipated a rising: one believed 'the Irish Government was sitting on a mine'.[23] Rumours were rife about an America naval expedition once a rebellion began in Ireland, the British consul in Philadelphia even claimed a Fenian Regiment had already embarked in early September.

Informers like Nagle insisted a rising was imminent and urged the Irish government to strike before it was too late. One IRB informer, John Warner, declared that the IRB had 4,000 members in Co. Cork and was recruiting heavily inside the British Army. And for the first time, Warner provided an exact – if inaccurate – date for the insurrection. On 20 September, the anniversary of Robert Emmet's execution, bodies of 200 men would attack police barracks across Ireland, slaughter policemen, seize arms and massacre everyone who refused to take the Fenian oath. Cork's Resident Magistrate, Mr Cronin, warned of a looming catastrophe. Rumours of impending rebellion were causing farmers to withdraw money from banks, while Dublin Castle believed that 'many of the militia, military, coast guard, Dublin Fire Brigade and even some of the police had sworn an adherence to the conspiracy'.[24]

Assuming he now had only days to prevent a nationwide rising, Wodehouse performed a policy somersault and opted for a simultaneous pre-emptive strike in Dublin and Cork. Except for suspending Habeas Corpus, he intended using the traditional instruments by which the Irish government suppressed subversion – mass arrests, special commission trials, newspaper closures and the proclamation of entire counties. By striking first, the Viceroy hoped to regain the initiative, end a seemingly endless Fenian agitation, and present Stephens with a stark choice: fight or flight. On 14 September, at a hurriedly summoned conference in the Vice-regal Lodge, Attorney General Lawson authorised Wodehouse, Peel, Rose and Larcom to arrest suspects in Dublin and Cork on the following evening, suppress the *Irish People*, and proclaim Co. Cork. The short time before acting would minimise the risk of a leak that might allow targets to evade arrest or destroy incriminating documents. Wodehouse later told Home Secretary Grey that: 'We were obliged to observe the strictest secrecy as to our intentions, as the disaffected have spies in all directions, watching the movements of the police.'[25] Such was the speed of events, Wodehouse claimed afterwards, that he did not even have time to tell Prime Minister Palmerston and Grey about the operation beforehand.

The Struggle Between Dublin Castle and the IRB: 15 September 1865–December 1865

Lulling Fenians into a false sense of security, Dublin Castle created a smokescreen for the morning and afternoon of Friday, 15 September, when Wodehouse travelled 9 miles to Howth and spent the day exploring nearby Lambay Island, while Superintendent Ryan secretly planned to catch his targets off guard with night-time raids on the *Irish People* premises and the homes of prominent IRB suspects. Before he led detectives and police parties out at 9 p.m., Ryan alerted police and army barracks across Dublin, and stationed constables at Dublin's telegraph offices to prevent news of the clampdown spreading across the country.

The raids took Fenians completely by surprise. At 9.30 p.m., Ryan's party found the *Irish People* premises in darkness and the doors locked, forced entry, destroyed the printing presses and seized papers, books and a revolver. James O'Connor and O'Donovan Rossa heard the news while in a Dame Street pub, just before Rossa sailed next day to America carrying messages from Stephens, but they decided to stay 'and face the storm'.[1] But as Rossa walked home to destroy an important document, detectives pounced on him. O'Connor managed to hire a cab and went to an IRB meeting at James Flood's house, where he alerted Stephens. As the IRB leader slipped into hiding at Fairfield House, Sandymount, O'Connor returned to Parliament Street and watched police flashlights circulating around the *Irish People* building. He then strolled through surrounding streets where Ryan, detective Smollen and six policemen arrested him.[2] Smollen had already detained Nagle, who had left Flood's house early and was on his way to Dublin Castle with news of Stephens's location. Smollen ignored Nagle's protests that he was a government agent delivering vital information.

Oblivious to the government's pre-emptive strike, some prominent Fenians were caught at home. Luby was asleep at his mother's cottage in Dolphin's Barn. Detectives politely let him dress and eat breakfast as they located incriminating documents that he had removed earlier from the *Irish People* offices but not hidden away. Most significant was Stephens's document appointing Luby, O'Leary and Kickham as an Executive Committee during his American trip.[3] Ryan had also ordered raids on brothels in central Dublin. One Irish-American officer found in bed with a prostitute was a perfect gentleman, who defended her honour and fulminated at scoundrels who had defiled a lady's boudoir. By morning, 16 September, G Division had arrested twenty-one Dublin Fenians, but apart from Luby, Rossa, O'Connor and O'Leary, most were minor figures and Nagle was a government informer. Stephens, Kickham, Brophy and Duffy were on the run.

Later that day Wodehouse returned from Howth, proclaimed Cork city and county, and issued a £200 reward for the capture of Stephens. Initially, he believed the operation was a success. Some of the most important Fenian leaders were in custody and Attorney General Lawson was examining captured papers and correspondence that the Viceroy claimed corroborated police reports:

> I am convinced that we could not safely have put off any longer striking a blow against this conspiracy, which was rapidly assuming a more dangerous character. If not checked now, it would have become really dangerous to the peace of the country and would not have ended without bloodshed and plunder.[4]

Wodehouse told Peel that 'the disaffected are in a panic everywhere, expecting he will be the next arrested'.[5] Palmerston congratulated the Viceroy on peacefully smashing 'a nest of Fenians' without a shot fired.[6] And Wodehouse was pleased that no landed proprietor, barrister, leading manufacturer or tradesman had been arrested; proof, he said, that the government had on its side all the country's wealth and higher intelligence.

Some Fenians had been eager for battle. But next day, Stephens ordered Dublin centres to avoid violence until December, a command that IRB messengers carried to Cork, Limerick, Sligo, Waterford and Belfast and then all over Ireland.

Besides Dublin and Cork, police made arrests throughout the country and in Britain, so that by early October there were 179 Fenian prisoners in Ireland – 41 of them in Dublin – and 8 in England. Delighted, Rose told Wodehouse that 15 September was an historical watershed and that henceforth Ireland would quietly submit to the law.[7] The jubilation did not last long. Stephens, Kickham, Duffy and Brophy had escaped, only three of fifteen Dublin centres were in custody, and Devoy insisted that IRB recruiting actually increased. A prominent Fenian declared that 'a state of feeling recalling the feverish days of '48 but on a much larger scale was visible throughout the land'.[8] The arrests gave the IRB publicity on a scale previously unknown in nationalist politics, and police photographs of suspects put faces on men who hitherto were known only by reputation. Moreover, major newspapers carried extensive reports of the seizure of the Irish People and turned the clampdown into a publicity coup for the IRB. Nor did the *Irish People*'s suppression crush the IRB's journalistic crusade against constitutional nationalism. It simply switched to *The Irishman*, whose owner, Richard Piggott, ran his paper on the same lines as the *Irish People*.

Wodehouse now sensed that Dublin Castle was in for the long haul. As early as 27 September, he gloomily admitted that:

A very bad feeling is reported among the peasantry in many parts of the south, and I should not be surprised if there were to be some partial outbreak, notwithstanding the panic which our measures at first caused among the rebellious. The support which the movement receives from America will prevent it from soon dying away.[9]

Despite reassuring newspaper headlines, Wodehouse believed public confidence was waning in a government that had apparently watched subversion grow unchecked until dramatic action became necessary. Within a fortnight, Wodehouse admitted that the loyalist gentry were very alarmed, especially in Cork, and interrogated Fenian prisoners had disclosed 'most atrocious designs on the part of the confederacy against persons and property'.[10] Irish-American officers remained a threat: 'These despera-does really intended an outbreak this autumn and whilst Stephens (the soul of the plot in Ireland, a really clever conspirator) is at large, I don't feel sure they may not even now commit some folly.'[11] On 1 October, Wodehouse warned that 'a handful of determined men, well-armed, land-ing on the Irish coast would throw the whole country into confusion'.[12] A week later, less than a fortnight before Palmerston's death, Wodehouse warned him that 'the demeanour of the people is in many parts sullen and discontented'.[13]

Conflicting pressures buffeted Wodehouse. While newspapers demanded intensified repression, Rose insisted that Fenianism had been crushed. He persuaded the Viceroy that dramatic gestures, designed to satisfy public opinion, might actually alarm a civilian population that had been repeat-edly assured the crisis was over. So, Wodehouse rejected pleas from Lord Lieutenants to proclaim entire counties, though he could not completely ignore loyalist demands and, on 29 September, proclaimed five baronies in Tipperary, two in Waterford and one in Limerick. Wodehouse admitted that 'this might all seem very vacillating', but it might prevent panic in those disaffected areas.[14]

Dublin Castle believed that only Stephens's capture would restore public confidence, especially as it thought he still intended a rising. But the Irish government knew nothing of his whereabouts and a £200 reward had elicited only rumours and uncorroborated sightings. Supposedly, Stephens was masquerading as a disabled beggar, criss-crossing Dublin, sloping past unsuspecting policemen and collecting coins from sympathetic passers-by. In fact, said James O'Connor, 'Stephens was not in the habit of disguising himself and he never did assume any of the shapes attributed to him by persons of fertile imagination. During his organising days he never even altered the fashion of his remarkable beard.'[15] Instead, Stephens, his wife and sister-in-law lived at Fairfield House in Sandymount, a mainly loyalist Dublin suburb along whose seafront he sauntered on fine mornings like a gentleman of means. After Kickham, Duffy and Brophy joined him, they mounted round-the-clock counter-surveillance. Equipped with binoculars and a loaded revolver, each man did two three-hour shifts a day, positioned at windows that commanded approaches to the residence.

However, far from planning an early rising, Stephens isolated himself from his Dublin and provincial centres. He contacted the former through

John Nolan, but even he did not know about Fairfield House as Stephens's orders came via Duffy and Brophy. Kickham, Duffy and Brophy liaised with provincial centres, ensuring that Stephens alone had the whole picture. Immediately after 15 September 1865, Stephens established a Central Military Council, whose seven American officers included Millen as president and three colonels, Daly, Michael Kerwin and Halpin. Stephens controlled the Council by transmitting orders through the only civilian member, John Nolan. Besides, it was mainly concerned with supporting about 150 Irish-American officers distributed throughout Ireland. Although O'Mahony had promised them a rising would begin soon after they reached Ireland, they became increasingly depressed after 15 September. Those living in Dublin hotels and boarding houses had endless time on their hands and optimism waned as they exhausted funds from O'Mahony and the small change that Stephens doled out. As their dream adventure rapidly became a nightmare, former Union officers' hopes of smiting England with their terrible swift sword faded, while former Confederates feared going down with yet another lost cause. They wanted an immediate insurrection, but when Stephens refused even to meet them, these Irish-American officers concluded that he was simply stringing them along.

Stephens scorned the dissenters as 'grumblers', and even Millen himself despised some as 'a very worthless lot of men',[16] freeloading reprobates enjoying an extended period of rest and recreation as they ran up debts in bars and restaurants, scammed sympathetic locals and frequented Dublin pot-houses. Eventually, their curiosity satisfied and unwilling to endure material suffering any longer, let alone risk their lives, they wanted to go home. But Millen still admired most Irish-American officers' commitment and resented Stephens's demeaning attitude towards them. On 10 November 1865, Stephens summarily rejected a new scheme of organisation devised by Millen that the Central Military Council had ratified. Increasingly, Millen felt that Stephens was deliberately sabotaging anyone attempting to improve the IRB's effectiveness.[17]

During October and November 1865, the 'grumblers' became convinced that Stephens was deliberately freezing them out. Col. Daly had had enough and left for America. Pressured by the Military Council, the dissidents agreed to stay until New Year's Day 1866, but after Stephens's arrest in November they reneged and decamped to Glasgow, and then returned to America with damaging accounts of a hopeless state of affairs in Ireland.

On 16 September 1865, Fenian prisoners appeared at the police office court in Lower Castle Yard, when Nagle made his public debut as a government spy. Confounded, defendants like Rossa and O'Connor watched their former comrade describe secret IRB drilling, American money and arms sent to Ireland, and allege that several thousand American army officers were in the country. After Justice Stronge remanded the prisoners for a week, their charges were raised to High Treason, a capital offence. But O'Leary recalled that the mood lightened when one man exclaimed, "'High thrasyson, bedad", evidently being much impressed with the seemingly dignified position in which he stood.'[18] At Richmond Gaol, the prisoners appointed John Lawless, a Fenian sympathiser, as their solicitor and they were secretly helped by a warder, John Breslin, who although not a Fenian was a committed nationalist, all of whose brothers bar one were in the IRB. Breslin accompanied the prison doctor on his daily rounds and could pass on information and newspaper cuttings. But what Fenian prisoners yearned most for was a rising and yet as time passed uneventfully, no word came from Stephens.

Stephens was in a quandary, caught between two deeply unappealing courses of action. Either he postponed the revolution and faced his followers' wrath, or he pressed ahead with a rising for which he believed the IRB was woefully unprepared. Crippled by doubt, Stephens temporised but, at some point, he would have to choose. He was saved in the early hours of Saturday, 11 November 1865, when a police party arrived outside Fairfield House.

How Superintendent Ryan located Stephens has never been satisfactorily explained. Ryan himself reported that on 9 November a man from Sandymount visited G Division and told Acting Inspector Hughes of his suspicions about a Mr Herbert of Fairfield House, whom he had once seen standing in the *Irish People*'s doorway.[19] After 15 September 1865, Mr Herbert had dramatically changed his daily routine and become virtually a recluse. And Ryan thought this informer's description of the suspect and his wife strongly resembled Mr and Mrs Stephens. In another version, police recognised Mrs Stephens shopping in central Dublin on Friday, 10 November, and tailed her back to Fairfield House.[20]

Just before 6 a.m. on Saturday, 11 November, DMP Assistant Commissioner Col. Henry Lake and Superintendent Ryan led six detectives and thirty police constables into the grounds of a darkened Fairfield House. The heavily armed party scaled garden walls and surrounded the building without incident as its occupants had retired after a drinks party. When Acting Inspector Hughes knocked on the back door it was some time before Stephens himself came downstairs. From behind the door Stephens stalled, claiming he was in his nightshirt, but Hughes made him open up immediately, chased Stephens upstairs to his bedroom and arrested him. According to the *Mail*, 'Mrs Stephens stared out of the bed, alarmed at seeing the police and said, "Are you going to take my husband from me?"'[21] In adjoining bedrooms, Lake's men arrested Kickham, Brophy and Duffy before discovering four loaded revolvers hidden under pillows. As the captives dressed, police constables searched wardrobes and collected documents that included the names and ranks of Irish-American officers and centres, as well as many letters. These allowed G Division to build a much better picture of the IRB. Outside Fairfield House the four detainees were put in separate cabs and brought to Dublin Castle. Wodehouse was euphoric at the coup, proclaiming it 'a greater blow to the conspirators than all that we have done hitherto'.[22]

Within hours, newspapers began trashing Stephens's reputation, contrasting his supposed high life with the suffering of Fenian prisoners. One described Fairfield House as an Aladdin's cave stuffed with fine furniture, Brussels carpets and plentiful wine, situated inside immaculately maintained grounds: 'There can be no doubt that Mr Stephens took remarkably good care of himself.'[23] This character assassination with its insinuation that Stephens luxuriated in the trappings of power, resonated with some Fenians. Millen complained about Stephens's wife and sister-in-law's frequent shopping expeditions at a time when many Irish-American officers were virtually starving.

At Dublin Castle, police immediately charged the four men with plotting war against the Queen, and at the Police Commissioner's Court, Justice Stronge remanded them to Richmond prison. On Tuesday, 14 November, they returned to Dublin Castle for arraignment, their prison van escorted by cavalry with sabres drawn and policemen armed with revolvers and cutlasses. Along the route patrols stood ready to prevent a rescue attempt. This time, the Castle's small courtroom was thronged with government luminaries, including Sir Hugh Rose, Chief Secretary Peel, DMP Assistant Commissioner Colonel Henry Lake and Wodehouse's private secretary.[24] All eyes were fixed on Public Enemy Number One Stephens, the creature who had caused them years of misery. Probably the only sympathiser was John

Lawless, the solicitor who was already representing those Dublin Fenians arrested two months earlier. Around a table at the front sat Stephens and his fellow accused, encircled by six detectives carrying revolvers. Lawless noticed how the IRB leader had already aged, that his face was thinner and careworn and he seemed in the throes of 'silent agony'. The lines around Stephens's mouth were drawn deeper while his skin was 'pallid as marble' and drained of colour. Yet, although Stephens faced lengthy imprisonment, transportation and possibly even execution, Lawless thought he still radiated pride and defiance. Kickham and Brophy also displayed a 'wonderful equanimity', though Duffy was downcast and sullen.[25]

Superintendent Hughes and Fairfield House's landlord, Mr Halbert, testified for two days, but Nagle was the Crown's main witness. Lawless called him a 'slimy-looking individual' with 'perfidy and treason indelibly branded on every feature of his countenance', 'a compound of deceit, cunning, avarice and pusillanimity'. 'How any Fenian could for an instant have trusted him it was very difficult for me to explain.'[26] Already the most reviled man in Ireland, Nagle's face flushed as he tremulously identified Stephens, who responded with 'a single glance of cool, indifferent contempt'. Justice Stronge weighed in to strengthen the prosecution's case, reciting various captured documents that included Stephens's claim that 'our preparations are perfected; the flag of the Irish Republic must be raised this year'.

On Wednesday, Stephens flared momentarily when Stronge implied that the £600 seized at Fairfield House had been skimmed from the IRB. As Lawless recalled, 'The effect of this upon Stephens was perfectly terrible. His face became scarlet with passion, his lips worked convulsively and his eyes fiercely blazed. This however was but for an instant after which he became cool and collected and passionless as stone.'[27] Eventually, Stronge committed the four men for trial before a special commission that would start on 27 November. Throughout, Stephens's demeanour had swung between indifference and belligerence, but now he rose slowly, folded his arms and emphatically denounced the proceedings as a farce. Having refused to employ a solicitor or even enter a plea, Stephens now repudiated as corrupt the entire British legal system and denied its right to judge and punish him. Duffy said nothing and neither did Kickham, whose extreme deafness meant he could barely follow proceedings anyway. Brophy began speaking but stopped at a signal from Stephens.

The four accused were now returned to Richmond Gaol, a large male convict prison on the South Circular Road, above whose massive gateway was inscribed a warning that inmates should 'cease to do evil: learn to do well'. Subsequently, a myth circulated – strongly promoted by Stephens himself – that he began devising an escape plan immediately after his arrest. In fact, neither Stephens nor the IRB had initially contemplated a break-out from Richmond, supposedly one of the strongest gaols in Ireland. The governor Dominick Marques had successfully contained prisoners after the 1848 rising but his career was now in freefall. After being diagnosed with exhaustion in late August 1865, he was sent on indefinite leave, only to be prematurely recalled on 16 September as Fenian prisoners inundated his under-staffed gaol. Tightening security, Marques located Stephens on the main building's top storey, had all letters to Fenian inmates opened, food and clothing searched, and he also planted in the cell between Stephens and Kickham a young habitual offender called McLeod. Promised leniency on a jewellery theft and a £20 bonus for spying on Stephens, McLeod, in an emergency, was to pull a wire in his cell that would trigger a large gong in the corridor at whose end was a door, outside which at night sat a policeman. The DMP also drafted in twenty-five constables as guards, but Marques distrusted a police force purportedly riddled with Fenians and soon had most transferred out. His Board of Superintendents had also pressed Marques to scale back the police presence in order to reduce the cost to ratepayers. But, crucially, Marques told neither Dublin Castle nor the two Inspectors-General of Prisons about these changes, which left only four policemen dispersed throughout the prison. Accordingly, the authorities did not use military guards from Portobello barracks, less than a mile away. Disastrously, Marques also decided to contain Stephens by minimising his human contact, especially at night, when the prisoner was isolated almost completely. Consequently, Stephens's confinement depended not on guards but massive iron bars, heavy closed doors and complicated locks, a quarantine that ironically facilitated an escape.

Whether Stephens actually wanted to escape is debatable. Certainly, he initiated no steps to regain his freedom, perhaps preferring captivity for at least a while to IRB infighting, transatlantic quarrels and unceasing pressure for a rising. And a trial would cast Stephens in a heroic role, a martyr sacrificing himself for his country. Furthermore, as he rejected visitors and communicated with the outside solely through Lawless, only a prison insider could set an escape plan in motion. By chance, the hospital steward, John Breslin, wanted to help Stephens. He knew Richmond's layout and daily routine and the escape plan was his entirely. Initially, Breslin enrolled his brother, Niall, a Fenian who persuaded Kelly to rescue Stephens, especially as his capture had shaken IRB morale. Devoy recalled that: 'It spread dismay among the rank and file of the Fenians. While this feeling was not shared by the leaders still at large they could not help recognise the fact that their followers were much discouraged by the blow.'[28]

Time was short. As Stephens's trial was scheduled for 27 November, planning began immediately. Breslin's second brother, Michael – a clerk in the Police Superintendent's office – acted as intermediary between Kelly and the prison, where his visits never aroused suspicion. Kelly also instructed John Breslin to liaise with another warder, Daniel Byrne, a long-time Fenian who had racked up an appalling disciplinary record and been reduced to night watchman. Embittered and keen on revenge, he could assist an escape because every second night Byrne was the only watchman on duty, circulating alone through a silent prison. Moreover, John Breslin's daily tour with the prison doctor meant he could inform Stephens about the rescue plan's progress. Whatever private reservations Stephens might have had about escaping, he could not have backed out without destroying his reputation in the Fenian movement.

The plan was for Breslin to release Stephens from his cell, lead him through a series of heavy locked doors, and down flights of stairs into a courtyard that surrounded the main building. Breslin and Byrne would then guide Stephens across open ground to the outer prison wall. Using beeswax impressions of the keys for entering Stephens's corridor and opening his cell door, Breslin had a Fenian optician, Michael Lambert, make duplicates. Concealed outside Richmond, Kelly's rescue party would help Stephens scale the prison wall and escort him to safety. In case of resistance from prison authorities, Devoy had selected a dozen courageous Dublin IRB men for the mission. Most had military experience, including Michael Cody, an ex-Dublin Militia man; John Harrison, who had served in the Royal Navy; Dennis Duggan, formerly of the English Volunteers; and John Millen, who had served with the Royal and American navies. The rescue was timed for 24 November, partly because Byrne superstitiously claimed that nearly all his strokes of good fortune had befallen him on that day of the month.

Freeing every Fenian prisoner would have been a tremendous propaganda coup, but Kelly decided to rescue only Stephens. He was racing against time and organising a mass break-out would have been prohibitively complex. Moreover, although the duplicate key for Stephens's cell door would have also freed Kickham and Brophy on the same floor, Kickham's near deafness might have ruined everything. Lawless was adamant that, 'The great thing was to get out Stephens, the man whom the organisation most wanted and the man who was most likely, after having got out, to remain out. To this end all efforts were directed.'[29] Above all, involving more people would have greatly increased the danger of a leak. Even concentrating on Stephens alone carried risks. When Kelly informed his inner circle about the mission, they promptly told family and friends, until eventually word spread to about 200 Dublin Fenians. Furthermore, information did reach the British authorities. After Thomas Duggan, a National schoolteacher and Fenian centre, returned to his home village, Ballincollig in Co. Cork,[30] he began recruiting members from the 4th Royal Irish Dragoon Guards. On 22 November, two soldiers told their commanding officer that Duggan was boasting 'there were five Fenian warders at Richmond Prison and that these five could let Stephens out at any moment they liked'. The officer transmitted this information to Dublin Castle.[31]

On the night of Thursday, 23 November, Devoy's scouts confirmed that the British authorities still knew nothing. Portobello Barracks was quiet and both the South Circular Road and Love Lane close to Richmond Gaol were almost deserted, as vile weather kept Dubliners indoors. Devoy recalled that 'the night was dark and wet and a few policemen on duty in the lonely neighbourhood of the prison kept as much as possible under shelter.'[32] More dramatically, Denieffe remembered how 'the rain came down in torrents, the wind blew great guns, Heaven's artillery boomed and reverberated through the deeps of the dark, impenetrable sky and the daring Fenians only saw each other's faces in momentary glimpses by the lightning flashes.'[33] Scouts encountered a policeman huddling under an elm tree on the canal bank, and another sheltering in a hallway on the South Circular road, 'but a little conversation enlivened by a swing from a flask of whiskey revealed the fact that not a single extra man was out and that nothing startling was expected'.[34] Kelly's party gathered at a Camden Street pub not far from the prison, but the person responsible for bringing revolvers arrived empty-handed. Furious, Devoy hired a cab and toured the city rounding up weapons. In three groups, the rescuers walked by different routes to Richmond Gaol, where some positioned themselves on the other side of the Circular Road opposite the prison wall, others stood under the shadow of a hedge directly opposite the prison gate, and more were stationed in a dark nook at the western end of the prison wall.

Waiting patiently for a signal to move – a rescuer imitating the quacking of a duck – Kelly's party was briefly confused by that of a real duck in a neighbouring garden. Finally, when the prison clock struck 1 a.m., Breslin left his quarters and slipped quietly through two doors into Stephens's corridor, moving carefully to avoid alerting McLeod and the policeman stationed outside a door at the other end. In the darkness, Stephens – fully dressed and ready – heard a key turn in his cell door, slid from a hammock in stockinged feet, took a loaded revolver from Breslin, and followed him quietly through more doors and down various flights of stairs. McLeod had heard everything and seen a lantern shadow on the wall, but he did nothing. The key for Stephens's cell also fitted his door and McLeod confessed later to being 'afraid of my life to ring the cord lest they might shoot me or rip me open'.[35] Almost certainly Breslin would not have risked the sound of gunfire, but silently slitting McLeod's throat was another matter. When Stephens stepped into the prison yard, he still had to climb a very high interior wall studded with broken glass and then cross the governor's garden before reaching the outer wall. But when Byrne appeared, Breslin realised he had not tested the ladder normally used to light lamps, and Breslin realised it was too short for even a tall person to scramble over the first wall. Concealing Stephens inside an unoccupied sentry box and ordering him to shoot anyone who interfered, Breslin and Byrne fetched from the lunatics' dining room two long tables on which to position the ladder. Clambering over the wall, an out-of-condition Stephens landed on a tool shed, slid to the ground, and walked across to the outer wall, over which he flung some gravel to alert his rescuers. Kelly's men now crossed the South Circular Road and tossed a rope end over the 18ft wall. As four men held the rope steady, Stephens clambered up the other side and eventually appeared at the top, sweating and panting. Peering down, he vainly tried hitching the rope between two stones on the parapet in order to descend. Finally taking advice from below, Stephens jumped down and was caught safely. Stephens was quickly secreted less than a mile away in the house of Mrs Boland, whose brother carried messages for Stephens. To conceal the fact that Stephens had received outside help, Devoy pulled the rope back from over the wall. On the other side, Breslin had left the tables and ladder in place and keys in locks. Breslin returned to his room, wiped soil from his clothes and shoes, went to bed and pretended to be fast asleep. Byrne, meanwhile, carried on with his rounds, giving Kelly time to spirit Stephens away. Only at 4.20 a.m. – feigning astonishment – did he tell Marques about finding the tables and ladder.

Concerned, Marques summoned every available warder and immediately sent a search party to Stephens's cell. Eventually it returned and reported that Stephens's cell door was open, a padlock and key lay in the corridor, and the Fenian leader had vanished. When Marques informed Dublin Castle, a mortified Wodehouse told Russell that 'the exultation of the Fenians knows no bounds, and I fear they will give more trouble than ever. I fear there is but small hope of Stephens's recapture.'[36] Telegrams alerted London and police stations throughout Ireland, where constables scoured roads, lanes and fields. In Dublin, a huge dragnet operation began across the capital's south side and police watched the country's harbours. The government now offered a £1,000 reward for Stephens's recapture, and offered to pardon anyone involved in the escape who came forward. Stephens's description was posted on the front door of every police barrack and railway station, detectives and informers scrutinised every passenger. Wodehouse suspected immediately that Stephens's escape was an inside job. 'We have always been told that the Fenians boasted they had they had confederates everywhere. They have now given us striking proof that they did not boast in vain.'[37] Later that morning, McLeod was hauled before Marques and corroborated the Viceroy's suspicions. By claiming Stephens's cell had opened at 1 a.m., McLeod immediately implicated Byrne, who had waited over three hours before raising the alarm. A raid on his quarters discovered a copy of the Fenian oath in Byrnes's handwriting and other documents proving that for three years he had been an IRB captain. Byrne was immediately arrested and charged with aiding Stephens's escape. McLeod's claim of hearing single footsteps implied that Byrne was the only suspect, allowing Breslin for the moment to remain undetected. Wodehouse was sceptical and demanded to know if there was reason to suspect other warders. But even convicting Byrne proved impossible, as two trials resulted in hung juries.

The hunt for Stephens also petered out. Detectives, policemen, coast-guards and informers turned up nothing and left the British intelligence system in Ireland – supposedly the best in the world – literally clueless. Larcom reported many supposed sightings of the fugitive, 'half of them only intended to mislead', but he regarded as 'more or less reliable' information that Stephens was still in Dublin masquerading as a woman.[38] Deliberately perpetuating the legend of Stephens as a master of disguise, Lawless had him posing as a German traveller infiltrating Athlone Castle and sketching its military defences. Another rumour had Stephens still in Richmond, hiding so deep in its bowels that only a massive search could flush him out. Failing to recapture Stephens only heaped more public and press opprobrium on the Irish government, and Wodehouse ordered Larcom to prepare for press attacks on both of them. Their strategy was to stonewall, cover up, pass the buck. Accordingly, the Viceroy rejected demands for an independent public inquiry that might ask embarrassing questions about the lack of military and DMP guards at Richmond. Wodehouse also concealed a serious intelligence lapse. Soon after Stephens's escape, police arrested Thomas Duggan of Ballincollig, the IRB centre who had boasted about Fenian wardens being prepared to free Stephens. At his trial the prosecution claimed that a military report on Duggan only reached Dublin two hours after Stephens had escaped, an assertion that just coincidentally cleared the Irish administration of negligence. But this was entirely false. Wodehouse privately admitted that the report – which he said clearly indicated a rescue attempt – had arrived on 23 November. 'It is certainly a very awkward circumstance that no special precautions were taken on the receipt of such striking information to prevent Stephens' escape.'[39] Dodging culpability, Dublin Castle instead blamed the Board of Superintendents, which promptly said prison staff were at fault. Meeting at Richmond Gaol on 2 December, the Board suspended Head Warder Meagher and soon afterwards dismissed Marques – the man who had dutifully carried out its advice to remove DMP constables. Both the Board and Dublin Castle needed a fall guy and Marques was a perfect fit. The Inspectors-General of Prisons presented a damning report that he had presided over a chaotic regime and buckled under the strain. Marques, they declared, was suffering from 'infirmity of mind' and 'had proved his entire incompetency to meet the present emergency and has exhibited a want of judgement and even of common sense'.[40] This damning verdict allowed Wodehouse to remove Marques from office and, on 22 December, the governor applied for retirement.

Public reaction to Stephens's escape varied considerably. One newspaper claimed, 'It has thrown Dublin into an almost unprecedented pitch of excitement. The Government is dismayed and confounded, the Fenians are exultant with equally good cause. "What next?" is on every lip.'[41] Fearing an immediate rebellion, many loyalists panicked and petitioned Dublin for military reinforcements. Despairing that 'all our work is undone', Wodehouse recorded 'rumours today of an outbreak in Dublin. I don't believe them, but I have written to Rose that we must omit no precaution.'[42] On 27 November, he spoke of 'abundant proof that there is a widespread sympathy amongst the lower classes of Irishmen and they will yet give us much trouble'.[43] Larcom asked Sir Henry Lake, DMP Assistant Chief Commissioner, to examine the Castle's defences and reinforce its guards at every gate.[44]

For the first time, the *Irish People* arrests focussed national attention on Fenianism, while Stephens's dramatic escape transformed him into a major political figure, celebrated by nationalists and loathed by loyalists like no man since Daniel O'Connell. Devoy said, 'His word was law to an organisation numbering fully 80,000 men. The Irish in America regarded him as the predestined leader of a revolution.'[45] Many nationalists elevated Stephens to an almost mythical status, a Scarlet Pimpernel who had eluded every trap and embodied an indestructible national resistance. But Devoy believed the acclaim turned his head, and O'Connor claimed the adulation inflated Stephens's 'enormous egotism and overpowering vanity'.[46]

Many Fenians regretted Stephens's imprisonment, but IRB militants saw it as an opportunity to precipitate the rising that he had denied them. To fill the power vacuum, Kelly convened an emergency meeting of centres and the Military Council at which Devoy, on behalf of the dissidents, proposed Millen as Stephenss' temporary replacement. They actually knew little about Millen, but assumed that a Fenian general would immediately press ahead with a rising. This manoeuvre was in effect a silent coup that would leave Stephens nominally IRB leader, but strip him of real power and transfer it to revolutionary extremists. However, the plan backfired spectacularly. Instead of routinely backing their president, every Military Council member – bar Millen himself – opposed Devoy's motion. Devoy recalled that 'they said nothing against Millen but it was quite evident that they had no confidence in him. They pleaded for delay and that no hasty action be taken. Halpin spoke very plausibly against taking any action until

Stephens was released (a thing we all expected.)'[47] Kelly predicted that Stephens would soon resume the IRB leadership.

Even in prison, Stephens never relinquished the reins of power, and when Kelly sent news about Devoy's motion, he was determined to take Millen down and banish this dangerous rival. As a pretext, Stephens ordered Millen to assume command in America of a Fenian naval expedition to Ireland, ostensibly an important promotion. But Millen was not deceived. He boycotted another Military Council meeting and sent a letter protesting at Stephens's order and announcing that he was leaving for Belgium to purchase weapons. After Kelly hinted that Millen was really absconding with IRB funds, the Council rescinded Millen's appointment as president.

Millen's departure still left the matter of a rising unresolved. Many Fenians believed that Stephens had escaped to lead an insurrection, and throughout December more American officers arrived in Ireland. James O'Connor recalled that, 'If ever a nation was excited for war, it was the Ireland of 1865.'[48] And despite his demotion, Millen anticipated returning soon in command of an American invasion fleet. However, a split in the Fenian Brotherhood shattered his expectations.

After the Final Call in August 1865, O'Mahony worked frantically to raise the necessary supplies for a rising, a burden that only increased after the *Irish People* arrests. On 16 September, Stephens asked O'Mahony for £5,000 and a naval expedition before Christmas. Six days later, O'Mahony sent £1,000, and a week later, another £6,500. Then things fell apart.[49] After William Roberts succeeded McCarthy as leader of the Men of Action, he, Scanlan and Dunne set about ousting O'Mahony. Furthermore, despite acting as Stephens's ally, the wealthy and steely Roberts had a different political and military agenda from an IRB leader whom he had never met and whose minion, or even co-conspirator, he would never be. Strongly influenced by General Thomas Sweeny, a one-armed Civil War hero, Roberts repudiated a naval expedition to Ireland in favour of a Canadian invasion that would annex a territorial base for the Irish Republic and possibly trigger an Anglo–American conflict. Roberts's coup against O'Mahony began on 22 September when the Central Council summoned a convention in Chicago for 16 October, despite O'Mahony's furious objections that he was in the midst of implementing the Final Call. On 6 October from Dublin, Halpin warned O'Mahony that many penniless Irish-American officers were begging to be sent home on a free passage. A week later, an envoy of Stephens's,

Captain James Murphy, pleaded with O'Mahony for officers and military equipment immediately. On 22 September, O'Mahony sent £1,000, followed a week later by another £6,500. Although the Chicago convention endorsed Stephens's demands, the likelihood of them ever materialising was vanishingly small. The convention seriously diminished O'Mahony's authority by replacing the post of Head Centre with a weak presidency, and creating a fifteen-man Senate headed by Roberts that superseded the Central Council and could veto presidential decisions. O'Mahony was tempted to refuse the presidency but once again he stayed on, defeated and emotionally drained. Privately, O'Mahony lashed out at Roberts as a half-educated shopkeeper who declaimed flatulent nothings, yet, unlike him, Roberts was a gifted political intriguer who rapidly installed General Thomas Sweeny as Fenian Secretary of War. With his unerring ability to misread people, O'Mahony ratified Sweeny's appointment, naively assuming he could trust a distinguished officer and gentleman.

Allocated $50,000 dollars for arms and authorised to plan military operations, Sweeny recruited an Army of the Irish Republic. In late November, he revealed his true intentions by demanding $50,000 from Bernard Killian, the Fenian treasurer, for a Canadian invasion. On 26 November, O'Mahony and Killian confronted Sweeny with a letter from Stephens confirming that the IRB would rise at the end of December, but Sweeny dismissed the idea of a successful Irish rising and even offered to travel to Ireland and prevent an outbreak. Confident of Roberts's backing, Sweeny instead demanded control of the Fenian treasury and refused henceforth to obey O'Mahony's orders. Outraged, O'Mahony severed Sweeny's funding but still hesitated to publicly confront his enemies until after he issued the Irish Republic bonds. However, the bond agent, Patrick Keenoberts, resigned on 27 November, thereby putting the bond issue in limbo since only the Senate could appoint a new agent. Cornered and desperate, O'Mahony went ahead anyway and signed the bonds himself, an action that finally split the Fenian Brotherhood.

On 4 December 1865, the Senate summoned O'Mahony to a political court martial but he retaliated by denouncing it as an illegal assembly and banning Sweeny from Fenian Brotherhood headquarters. O'Mahony also called another Fenian convention in New York for 2 January 1866 to pass judgement on the warring parties. On 18 December the Senate expelled O'Mahony and Killian from the Fenian Brotherhood. Amidst this political chaos, Millen arrived in New York on 15 December only to discover that no invasion fleet existed – indeed, not a single vessel had been fitted out. To make up lost ground, O'Mahony appointed Millen to prepare a naval expedition, but only weeks later 'special orders' from Stephens forced him reluctantly to ask for Millen's resignation.[50] Clearly Stephens had dispatched Millen to America on a pretext, prior to squeezing him out entirely. Furious, Millen would not go quietly into the night. Three months later he approached the British consul in New York and like Nagle before him became an informer.

Soon after Millen left for New York, Stephens sent pilots to navigate the Fenian invasion fleet to Ireland. They had imagined American preparations as far advanced and their disappointment at not sailing immediately crushed O'Mahony.[51] He needed to stop them going home and exposing the Fenian Brotherhood's disarray, so they languished in New York while O'Mahony struggled to raise enough money to equip a single ship. Subsidising the pilots drained a Fenian treasury that was down to its last $10,000 at the same time as O'Mahony was caring for an influx of refugees, many of them IRB centres who had fled Ireland after Stephens's arrest. None of them sought work and instead they hung around Fenian headquarters collecting subsistence allowances. By contrast, many Irish-American officers in Ireland had stood their ground, despite enduring considerable hardship and danger.

During early December 1865, IRB expectations of a rising reached new heights. The Military Council ordered circles in Ireland, England, Scotland and Wales to prepare for an imminent rebellion and Devoy estimated that several thousand Fenians came to Ireland from Britain, mainly young, unmarried men, highly motivated and eager for action. Their arrival in Ireland only intensified an already feverish political atmosphere. Devoy recalled that:

> The men were keyed up to the highest pitch of excitement. It was the same with the soldiers. The swearing in of new members went on more briskly than at any previous time. Up to the last week in December Kelly's orders all indicated a fight at an early day. We were to 'keep the steam up' and have our men ready for action at a moment's notice.[52]

However, in early December, O'Mahony warned that Fenian Brotherhood tensions were imperilling American aid. Stephens responded immediately by sending General Halpin to reconcile the warring factions, but upon reaching America on 20 December, Halpin realised this was an impossible mission. He sided with O'Mahony and denounced Roberts. Meanwhile, on about 22 December, Stephens learned – not from O'Mahony – that the dispute had become an open rift and there was no invasion fleet. Stephens could justifiably accuse O'Mahony of misleading him about American preparedness when the IRB members regarded a rising as inevitable. The timing could not have been worse.

Stephens now realised that the Fenian Brotherhood dissidents had rejected not just O'Mahony, but him as well, and that Roberts was beyond his control. Devoy noticed just how much the American schism depressed Stephens and claimed this led him to commit the worst blunder of his career and at the worst possible moment. Whereas he could always use the brittle O'Mahony as a punchbag, Roberts was unyielding and he would soon turn off the money tap. On 22 December, Stephens switched his allegiance back to O'Mahony, and in a letter vilified 'rascally blunderers' who did not see that if Canada fell to a Fenian invasion, England would simply redeploy its troops to Ireland. 'Only a fool or a traitor could entertain such a nation.'[53] O'Mahony had begged Stephens to come to America immediately, assume leadership of the Fenian Brotherhood, and act as 'supreme arbiter' in ending the schism. Instead, he had gone on the offensive and urged O'Mahony to 'cut and hack the rotten branches around you without pity. Lash them from you like so many dogs.' Perhaps, as Devoy believed, stress had warped Stephens's political judgement, or possibly he overestimated his popularity in America and assumed that many of Roberts's supporters would defect. In fact, the publication of Stephens's diatribe completely alienated the Senate wing, which vowed never again to assist the IRB as long as Stephens remained its leader. In Devoy's damning verdict, the crisis was 'a fair test of Stephens's capacity for leadership – the first real test – and it found him wanting. It widened the breach and made it irreparable.'[54]

Yet paradoxically, the American split was a perfect pretext for Stephens to extricate himself from the morass into which his revolutionary bluster had driven him. Forced at last to pronounce on a rising, Stephens summoned Dublin centres to Col Kelly's Grantham Street lodgings on 29 December, when they assumed he would give them final orders for an insurrection. But, beforehand, Stephens consulted the Military Council. By a single vote it favoured postponing the rising due to a shortage of weapons and the Fenian Brotherhood split. At almost literally the last moment Stephens had shown his hand, but he still needed to win over the IRB. Stephens first met the Dublin centres, who were brought to Grantham Street in relays.[55] Acting as a lookout, Devoy dismissed this as a fix, designed to divide potential opposition and stop it uniting against Stephens. Instead, he told each group that the American schism had reduced the funds to buy weapons and he needed time to heal it. Accordingly, Stephens recommended postponing the insurrection for three weeks to a month, but if the schism was not healed soon the rising would still proceed. The centre realised this was a fait accompli, that Stephens had made up his mind, and everyone acquiesced – consoling themselves that at least a fight would definitely commence in the not-too-distant future. A day or so later, Stephens met provincial centres at the City Mansion Hotel in Bridge Street and told them Dublin centres had already consented to a delay. More easily than in Grantham Street, Stephens won approval. Devoy was disgusted at Stephens's stage-managed consultation:

> Had all the Centres been present at the same time, a discussion could not have been avoided and probably a vote would have been taken. Considering the confident spirit then prevailing, it would have put Stephens' persuasive powers to the test – and he was not an orator – to prevent a vote in favour of fighting at once.[56]

Disappointment and confusion consumed the IRB. O'Mahony claimed that: 'Stephens experienced a very great difficulty in getting it postponed and his popularity suffered considerably thereby and with none more than the Dublin centres.'[57] Months later, many Irish centres who had fled to New York told O'Mahony that they wanted to fight in December 1865, even without American support. Most warlike were Irish-American officers, who insisted that Dublin could have been taken in a sudden, well-coordinated attack, using captured British Army weapons. Probably only someone with Stephens's authority could have survived the setback. Arguably, if Stephens believed England's vastly superior military resources meant catastrophic defeat, he had acted responsibly and saved many lives – without destroying the IRB. But it was Stephens who had taken his followers to the brink in the first place by recklessly inflating their expectations, even though by December 1865, IRB preparations were no more advanced than six months earlier, when Stephens could have more easily backtracked. Instead, he carried on towards a rising in which he had no faith. Haunted, perhaps, by the premature rising of 1848, Stephens's fatal flaw as a revolutionary leader was that he seemed only to contemplate fighting when virtually guaranteed victory in advance. But successful revolutionaries are daring risk-takers ready to stake everything on achieving victory against great odds. In 1865, many Fenians relished the prospect of action. Stephens was not dragging them reluctantly to war: they knew the risks, and many believed they could still win or at least put up a good fight. If the IRB bandwagon came to a screeching halt on 29 November 1865 and trust in Stephens faltered, then he had only himself to blame.

8

Dublin Castle: From Stephens's Escape to the Suspension of Habeas Corpus: February 1866

Despite Wodehouse's early optimism that the government had vanquished the *Irish People* and Fenianism, he soon resigned himself to a long war of attrition. Beyond the immediate failure to recapture Stephens, Wodehouse sensed that the IRB could survive indefinitely by feeding off nationalism's historic grievances, and that 'The old hatred of English rule fomented by the Irish in America burns too strongly for any measures to cure under a long time. It can only die out slowly; and will I fear survive the present century whatever we may do.'[1] A recent murder attempt on two detectives quite near the Castle gates might have been literally the opening shots in a Fenian assassination campaign against government officials. Superintendent Ryan of G Division claimed that an IRB Vigilance Committee controlled a 'shooting circle' – an assassination squad – and had its own detectives conducting counter-surveillance and unmasking informers. As a siege mentality enveloped Dublin Castle, Larcom laboured long weary days evaluating intelligence reports, chairing conferences and supervising civil servants and the police. He and a jittery Viceroy also fretted about the Castle's vulnerability to Fenian assault. On 19 November, Wodehouse confronted 'a Yankee looking fellow passing about the Castle yard after church this morning and directed the police to him. He was evidently taking "bearers" or I am mistaken.'[2] A few days later, Larcom asked General Cunnyngham, the Dublin army commander, to ensure maximum vigilance at the Castle:

'I don't think our enemies will take courage to "meet us in the gate" but we must take care not to give them a chance.' On 26 November 1865, Larcom instructed DMP Assistant Commissioner Lake to reinforce guards at the Castle's wall and three gates.

A newspaper vividly recorded the fraught situation, especially a welter of rumours about strange ships seen in Dublin Bay that were supposedly Fenian privateers swarming with Irish-American officers about to land, and that a date for a rising had been set and the prisons were to be stormed.[3] A spate of poison pen letters threatening death unnerved public figures like Superintendent Ryan, Justice Stronge and Justice Keogh. A newspaper observed that, 'a perfect shower of threatening letters has fallen',[4] while the Viceroy witnessed Keogh 'in a perfect panic about the Fenians; talked wildly about the decline of British power etc. I never met such a coward.'[5] On 15 November, Wodehouse was warned that magistrates, detectives and news-paper editors were doomed. Usually, he remained composed when himself in danger, even when told once that he would die before Christmas. The Viceroy especially enjoyed recounting one warning: 'My Lord, Tomorrow, we intend to kill you at the corner of Kildare Street, but we would like you to know that there is nothing personal in it.'[6] Wodehouse, though, was con-cerned about Fenians attacking and even murdering those informers due to testify at the Special Commission trials, one of whom, George Gilles, was so terrified of retribution that he retracted his evidence in the witness box and was sentenced to penal servitude.[7] Promising 'the most vigilant precautions to put them out of the way of the Fenians', Wodehouse kept informers – especially Nagle – in protective custody throughout the trials. Occasionally, the tension caused even this urbane politician to lash out sarcastically at 'a pleasant and inviting country! No wonder Irish men who have anything to lose, would rather live anywhere than in Ireland, and that Englishmen despise a race whose chief weapon is the assassin's bullet.'[8] But such outbursts were rare and contrition always followed quickly.

The difficult security situation perplexed Sir Hugh Rose, especially after Stephens's escape, when Dublin Castle requisitioned troops for guard duty at Irish prisons. He believed correctly that Stephens had received inside help at Richmond and that Fenians had infiltrated other civil service departments, like a clerk in the Crown Solicitor's Office who was caught with 'a most elaborate plan' to attack Dublin's army barracks.[9] The Irish government also suspected treachery among coastguards, customs officers and railway workers. Wodehouse and Larcom increased security at Dublin Castle, by using ciphers to safeguard communications with England and locked boxes to prevent Fenians in the post and telegraphic departments tampering with correspondence.[10] They also pressured government departments to suspend or reassign employees suspected of Fenianism. There is some evidence of Fenians infiltrating the police, though not G Division. Nagle accused some employees at the Irish Constabulary depot of treason, and he claimed that Devoy intended recruiting many policemen – though apparently with little success. Although Michael Breslin was not a policeman or Fenian, as a clerk in the DMP superintendent's office he helped his brother John organise Stephens's escape. A hackney carriage driver who conveyed messengers from the Upper Castle Yard was a Fenian sympathiser, while Fenians also supposedly worked at the Castle's ordnance office. Eventually something like paranoia gripped Dublin Castle, and when heavy snow brought down its telegraph wires in January 1866, sabotage was initially blamed.[11]

The Inspector-General of the Irish Constabulary and the DMP Commissioner repeatedly warned Wodehouse that Stephens's arrest and the heavy presence of Irish-American officers in Dublin presaged a rising before or during the Special Commission trials. They recommended proclaiming the City and County of Dublin, but the Viceroy doubted he could justify such a radical measure, especially as 'the bark of the Fenians has hitherto not been accompanied by any bite'.[12] However, Wodehouse needed the Special Commission to go smoothly because Dublin abounded with rumours of another sensational Fenian rescue. Supposedly, Stephens intended to attack Green Street Courthouse, rout the soldiers on guard, liberate every prisoner, and raise his rebel standard. John Lawless, the Fenian solicitor, recalled that, 'However highly coloured were these reports, they found numerous believers; and the liquor stores, street-corners, and places of public resort were filled all day with excited partisans.'[13] The Viceroy demanded high security at the courthouse, particularly to prevent Fenians assassinating Judge Keogh. 'We have most fears for Judge Keogh and it is thought there may be men desperate enough to shoot him on the Bench. It is impossible to feel confident that these fears are altogether unfounded.'[14]

From early morning on Monday, 27 November, British forces in Dublin were on high alert. Thousands of troops stood ready in their barracks, Rose had posted officers and soldiers at Mountjoy and Kilmainham gaols, and numerous police constables walked the streets. Six hundred armed soldiers also occupied buildings adjoining Green Street courthouse. Located in the north inner city, near the Four Courts, it was situated amongst tenements, lodging houses, dingy lanes and narrow streets. Facing the courthouse was the grim visage of Newgate Prison with its black stone walls, corner towers and facilities for public hangings. For republicans this was political holy ground. Robert Emmet and John Mitchel had been tried in Green Street, and Wolfe Tone had died at Newgate from a self-inflicted wound. Luby, O'Leary, Rossa and the rest could not have wished for a more historic setting.

Outside the courthouse a cordon of police and troops held back a large crowd, and mounted police roamed the neighbourhood when the prisoners' van arrived from Richmond Bridewell. Dublin Castle claimed that only this heavy security deterred armed Fenians seen loitering in the halls of nearby lodging houses from liberating the defendants.[15] At the courthouse entrance, Lawless squeezed past nervous doorkeepers who 'seemed to imagine that everybody admitted was armed to the teeth, and carried a Fenian infernal machine in his pocket'.[16] In the crowded courtroom, defence and prosecution counsel sat at a large table directly facing the judges' bench and a few feet from the prisoners' dock. Two galleries contained candidates for jury service and members of the public. The wives and sisters of some defendants, like Luby, Rossa and O'Leary, were accommodated in the reporters' gallery. But the government was taking no chances: policemen and detectives made up at least three-quarters of the 400 spectators. In a subterranean holding room, O'Leary, Luby, Rossa, Kickham and Mulcahy chatted and listened to legal advice and political information from Lawless, whom they had hired after being charged with High Treason. He described their demeanour as relaxed but quietly reserved.

Just before the Special Commission began, Dublin Castle realised that executing men for a rising that had never materialised would be hard to justify and downgraded the main charge to Treason-Felony. Renouncing the death penalty also made convictions easier to secure, as it no longer required two witnesses to corroborate state evidence. Moreover, juries now knew that guilty verdicts would not result in executions. The Irish government tilted the odds further in its favour by selecting William Keogh and John D. Fitzgerald as presiding judges. A decade earlier, nationalists had accused Keogh of betraying Ireland, hostility that left him embittered and short-tempered. In their different ways nationalists and unionists expected Keogh to show the defendants no mercy. As Keogh continued living at home, troops guarded his spacious suburban residence and detectives shadowed him daily to and from the local railway station. It was also widely anticipated that Fitzgerald would deliver convictions. He had attended the Privy Council meeting that approved the *Irish People* arrests – a conflict of interest that seemingly troubled him not.

When the Special Commission opened on 27 November, Lawless spied Keogh looking 'well-pleased with himself. A full sensuous, long red face, long nose, keen, piercing eyes, wide mouth and round head set on a stout, fleshy frame.'[17] Fitzgerald was 'a thin, sharp-looking gentleman, whose slight proportions contrasted oddly with the burly frame of the bon vivant beside him'.[18] After a grand jury speedily issued true bills against Luby, O'Leary and Rossa, Luby's trial began first next day. Despite his confiscated documents being powerful prosecution evidence, he pleaded not guilty. Lawless considered Attorney-General Lawson lacked gravitas, speaking ability and high legal expertise, but he scored by reading incendiary passages from the *Irish People* – for which Luby was legally responsible. Lawson also implicated Luby by producing Stephens's executive letter that temporarily entrusted the IRB to Luby, O'Leary and Kickham during his American tour. A detective also swore to hearing Luby and O'Leary discuss a landing place on the west coast of Ireland for an American expedition.

On Wednesday, 29 November, Nagle made his long-awaited appearance. Lawless excoriated him as a 'loathsome reptile', 'a professional trader in the blood of his companions' and 'a black-hearted dog' but he sensed immediately that Nagle had been well coached. 'He looked boldly around the court on entering and took his seat in the witness-chair with perfect confidence and an appearance of self-possession.' Under Solicitor-General Sullivan's gentle questioning, Nagle relaxed and reinforced an already strong case against Luby. Lawless had retained Isaac Butt, a brilliant, charismatic lawyer, a Protestant, an Orangeman, and a former Conservative MP. A reckless spendthrift and philanderer, Butt was at the lowest point of his life and believed the trials offered him a chance to regain national prominence and resume a lucrative legal career. Lawless fully expected Butt's relentless cross-examination to crush Nagle, but he was astonished when the lawyer hardly landed a blow. 'Nagle had evidently been instructed how to comport himself by the prosecuting solicitors; for he sat still and unmoved in his chair while question after question was roared at him by Mr Butt in the voice of a lion.'[19] Swatting away Butt's efforts to trip him up, elicit damaging admissions and vilify his character, Nagle blandly denied ever being a swindler or embezzler and only became agitated when he blamed Fenians for ruining the life of an idealistic young schoolmaster serving his community – himself.

In a passionate closing speech that ignored the damning evidence, Butt warned the jury against convicting Luby just for his radical political beliefs. It was all in vain. After Keogh's summing-up on 1 December 1865, the trial's fourth and final day, Luby's jury needed only two hours to find him guilty. Addressing the court before sentencing, Luby admitting being technically guilty 'in accordance with British law' – though in his mind no doubt 'guilty and proud of it'. He was confident that 'the majority of my countrymen would pronounce that I am not a criminal, but that I have deserved well of my country'. After Keogh sentenced Luby to twenty years' penal servitude, soldiers and police immediately escorted him to Mountjoy Prison.

Next day, Saturday, 2 December, O'Leary's trial began. Dressed in his habitual dark clothes, he struck a compelling figure, especially to his many adoring lady friends. Slight but tall and charismatic with an angular face that radiated intellectual energy and determination, O'Leary was described by an observer as standing in the dock with his eyes flashing hatred and contempt towards judges, prosecution and jury. After Luby conformed to British legal norms and still went down, O'Leary flouted courtroom etiquette from the start. Argumentative and disrespectful, he retorted when asked to enter a plea that it was the government, prosecutors and Nagle who were guilty. Contemptuous of the judges, he derided Fitzgerald as 'a mere time-server' and Keogh 'a renegade ruffian'.

The prosecution case, strong though not overwhelming, proved O'Leary had worked at the *Irish People*, written articles for it and handled financial transactions between American and Irish Fenians. However, it did not establish definitively that O'Leary was actually in the IRB. Butt depicted him as a naive litterateur whose writings had accidentally associated him with revolutionaries and their newspaper, but for whose cause he had no sympathy. However, O'Leary refused to publicly abandon his comrades and overrode Butt's attempts to silence him, insisting that not for moment did he disown his connection with the *Irish People*.

As in Luby's case, the jury deliberated for only a couple of hours before returning a guilty verdict – in just enough time, said Lawless, to finish their brandies. He recalled O'Leary addressing the court in a voice 'burning with hate and defiance' as he compared Keogh and Fitzgerald to two infamous hanging judges: Lord Chief Justice Jeffreys, who had condemned 170 people to death at the notorious 'Bloody Assize', and Lord Norbury, who had sentenced Robert Emmet to be hung, drawn and quartered.

O'Donovan Rossa's trial began on 9 December. As 'a patriot-soldier in the hands of a foreign power', he denounced the Special Commission as a fraudulent farce, its judges corrupt and his conviction pre-determined. Accordingly, he was far less willing than Luby and even O'Leary to play the legal game, especially as the evidence against him was overwhelming. Rossa had already been identified as an IRB envoy and Nagle had placed him in Stephens's inner circle. So, rather than watch his lawyers vainly going through the motions, this political brawler went head-to-head with his accusers. Entertaining his courtroom supporters and amusing newspaper readers everywhere, Rossa mocked the judges, ridiculed the prosecution and humiliated the British legal system in Ireland. As he later admitted, Rossa was also partly motivated by vanity. Described by one historian as a 'revolutionary showman'[20] who loved being the centre of attention, his zest and playfulness would over time sour, turning him into a bitter and humourless man.

As his jury was being empanelled, Rossa suddenly declared the trial a legal farce, dismissed his startled lawyers and then, flouting the legal maxim about having a fool for a client, he decided to defend himself. No longer seeking an acquittal, Rossa had embraced the desperate lawyer's ploy that if you cannot pound the facts then pound the table. A spectator recalled Rossa's bravura performance as he 'cross-examined the informers in fierce fashion. He badgered the detectives, he questioned the police, he debated with the Crown lawyers, he argued with the judges, he fought with the Crown side all round.'[21] Unstoppable, Rossa repeatedly ignored warnings from the bench, called the judges and jury Crown puppets, and persistently insulted Keogh. However, his attempts to goad the judge came to naught. Journalist Samuel Rutherford wrote: 'The more the prisoner tried to excite or offend him, the more careful he seemed to be to exhibit towards the prisoner, dignity, generosity and forbearance.'[22] Perhaps Keogh derived secret satisfaction from himself goading Rossa. Finally, Rossa confronted

Nagle. A spectator recalled that: 'Both of the men looked a hell of hate into each other's eyes. Each put forth his best – the prisoner trying to entrap the informer; the latter doing his best to foil the effort, or better still, to turn it to the injury of the prisoner.'[23] Rossa managed to render Nagle momentarily speechless by asking if he felt guilty for sending to prison men who had once counted him a friend, but overall, they were evenly matched. Eventually their spat ground to a halt and Keogh ordered Nagle from the witness box.

Ending his cross-examination of witnesses on 12 December, Rossa brought judges and jury no relief as he immediately began reading into the court record every publication that had been used as evidence, including editions of the *Irish People* – though Rossa promised to leave out advertisements. A spectator recalled that 'horror set upon the faces of the judges, jurymen, sheriffs, lawyers and turn keys'. Defying Keogh's frequent interjections, Rossa ploughed on for eight and a half hours, marching everyone down a legal trail of tears in a deliberately monotonous voice that only worsened their misery. Nevertheless, they could still laugh when a juror cried out that Rossa's behaviour 'was enough to stir up an armed insurrection among the persons in court'.

Rossa wanted to drag out proceedings because on 14 December, Keogh and Fitzgerald were to convene a Special Commission in Cork. By speaking until the court adjourned at six o'clock, he intended to keep the judges in Dublin and prevent them leaving for Cork. When the gaslights came on, Rossa suggested halting for the day, but Keogh was wise to Rossa's strategy, saw his increasing tiredness and decided to let Rossa talk himself out. Eventually Rossa's pyrotechnics came to an end. Exhausted, he dropped the *Irish People* file on a table and exclaimed, 'let the law take its dirty course'. For probably for the first time in his life, Rossa had run out of words. Instead, Keogh had the last word. After the jury deliberated for an hour and found Rossa guilty, the judge sentenced him to penal servitude for life. Rossa replied insouciantly, 'All right My Lord.' Prison officers and policemen then escorted him from the dock, smiling and saluting friends in the gallery as he sauntered out of court.

Later that day, Keogh and Fitzgerald travelled to Cork without realising that a worried Irish government had protected them after reports that Fenians planned to attack their train.[24] A pilot engine was added to keep it moving, and soldiers and police were secreted at railway stations between Dublin and Cork where cavalry routinely escorted the judges to and from the courthouse. Troops guarded their lodgings round the clock. The Special Commission trials continued in Dublin and Cork until mid-February 1866. Of forty-one accused in Dublin, thirty-seven were convicted, three acquitted, and one trial ended in a hung jury. In Cork, eleven of fourteen defendants were convicted.

Devoy claimed that the Special Commission trials rebounded on Dublin Castle by putting IRB members on their mettle, stimulating recruiting and arousing public sympathy for the defendants. Extensive newspaper reports of their demeanour confirmed that, far from cowering in the dock or begging for mercy, they never faltered, even after receiving heavy prison sentences. Luby had maintained a dignified restraint, O'Leary exuded cold hatred and Rossa revelled in gleeful contempt of court. This turned the trials into a Fenian propaganda triumph: on the first day a crowd followed their van back to Richmond Bridewell and eventually swelled to 1,000 people, who rioted at the prison, raining stones down on police and shouting support for the Fenians. On the second day a regiment of Hussars with swords drawn escorted the van on its return journey, but crowds still cheered the prisoners. Many nationalists also believed that Dublin Castle had rigged the trial by selecting biased judges and packing juries. Almost certainly Keogh's and Fitzgerald's establishment backgrounds did predispose them to favour the prosecution, but their conduct was surprisingly restrained and balanced. Perhaps they believed there was no need to act otherwise: that the evidence against the defendants was persuasive and often overwhelming. Clearly Keogh and Fitzgerald were satisfied that the accused had already convicted themselves.

Convicted Fenians were held temporarily in Dublin's Mountjoy Prison. But Wodehouse doubted that any Irish gaol was secure and he wanted them swiftly removed to England. 'The sympathy with Fenianism is so widely spread amongst the class from whom warders, policemen and even soldiers are taken that treachery is to say the least not improbable wherever the prisoners are guarded, principally or exclusively by Irishmen.'[25] Furthermore, their continued detention in Ireland would only stoke more political agitation. The Viceroy favoured transferring them immediately to English gaols surreptitiously at night, as moving them openly through Dublin in daylight might provoke rioting or another escape fiasco. At 4 a.m. on Christmas Eve 1865, Luby, O'Leary, Rossa and others were suddenly awakened, chained together and put inside a black van guarded by six warders. For an hour they heard wheels rumbling over deserted city streets and cavalry galloping alongside before the horses finally stopped. Emerging into the December darkness, Rossa recognised Kingstown pier and saw a steamer ready to sail. Prisoners marched on board through two lines of armed soldiers, closely scrutinised by detectives who had arrested them three months earlier. From the Welsh port of Holyhead their train travelled to London's Pentonville prison. Taking no chances with such high-security convicts, its governor had already weeded out Irishmen from his prison guards and arranged for police parties to patrol the outside perimeter. Soon afterwards the Fenian prisoners were sent to Chatham and Portland gaols.

Wodehouse was delighted at the Special Commissions' high conviction rate and reports from Cork about rising loyalist morale. Momentarily, his hopes soared that the IRB was finally in retreat, but they rapidly subsided. Rose, on the other hand, remained supremely confident that Fenians would never dare rebel. 'It is hard to believe that the Fenians would be so insane as to attempt an outbreak so that Stephens would face a contest. I have always doubted Stephens's pluck; to have a rising would be the highest of rashness on his part.'[26] He eagerly swallowed a false report that Stephens had stolen IRB funds, deserted his tearful wife and fled to France with a lady friend. Commanding thousands of trained soldiers, artillery, cavalry and plentiful weapons, Rose was confident his military superiority made insurrection an act of insanity. On 26 November 1865, he boasted that, 'I have always written and said that the Fenians would not attempt a rising. Nothing could induce them to do so except the arrival and co-operation of iron-clads and an army from America and it was quite clear that such allies would never leave the American shores for Ireland.'[27] Wodehouse was more worried than Rose, especially after an American informant claimed that former Confederate soldiers were preparing a naval expedition to land at Dingle, Co. Kerry, on St Patrick's Day. 'The Confederates are devil-may-care men and there will be tough fighting if they show themselves in Ireland.'[28]

The logistical demands that Fenianism imposed on the British Army in Ireland vexed Wodehouse and Rose. After Stephens escaped from Richmond, they had agreed that dispatching troop reinforcements throughout Ireland would imply government panic, but soon the Viceroy was badgering the commander-in-chief to station soldiers in every latest trouble spot. In early December 1865 this was Galway, a county that had featured at Luby's trial as an ideal landing place for an American expedition.

Wodehouse also wanted more soldiers in Tralee, where police had reported rumours of an imminent rising. A policy of constantly rotating scarce military resources around Ireland irritated Rose, who had actually inspected Galway a month earlier and found the whole county peaceful. But the Viceroy kept up the pressure. On 10 December, as rumours circulated of a Fenian rising at Christmas, he asked Rose to devise plans for suppressing outbreaks in Dublin and Cork, and later that day told Home Secretary Grey that disaffection among the peasantry was rapidly increasing.[29]

Successive false alarms about a Fenian rising created a siege mentality in Dublin Castle, where a claustrophobic atmosphere enveloped civil servants. Senior officials sacrificed their holidays and remained in place for long periods. Wodehouse himself stayed in Dublin throughout Christmas 1865 and induced Rose to cancel his annual leave. By 21 December, Yuletide cheer was in short supply. The Viceroy knew that public opinion was brittle and confidence in the Irish government low:

> I find that 'uneasy lies the Crown' is true of Vice-regal as well as regal heads. I have really a very troublesome task on my hands. A foolish panic has seized many people and they imagine we are on the eve of a great rebellion. Xmas day is I am assured to be the signal for a general massacre. There is no satisfying these alarmists. If the people are riotous, they say 'here is the beginning of the rebellion' – If they are quiet, they say a silent rebel is the most dangerous plotter of all.[30]

Nevertheless, on 24 December, DMP Assistant Commissioner Lake asked Rose to post cavalry patrols along Dublin's North Circular Road on Christmas Day in case Fenian columns converged on the capital, an unprecedented proposal that Rose insisted would panic Dubliners. He and Wodehouse turned Lake down and instead kept troops in reserve ready to aid the police if necessary. Christmas Day and Boxing Day were not festive occasions at the Vice-regal Lodge. On 25 December, Wodehouse reported, 'Great alarm that there will be a rising tonight. The Govt is beset with applications for troops from the South of Ireland. At Dublin we are obliged to be on the watch. All as yet is quiet.'[31] But on 28 December, his nerves were still frayed. 'We have a number of American-Irish prowling about Dublin and the disaffected parts of the country. As long as I see them busily at work, I cannot feel easy, although I am far from sharing the exaggerated fears of some.'[32] Loyalist memories of past massacres and concern about Fenian hatred of landlords had also stoked fears of a 'Jacquerie', a peasants' revolt:

> If any serious outbreak occurred, I have no doubt it would quickly assume that form and that dreadful atrocities will be perpetrated. At the same time my firm belief is that no such outbreak will occur if all reasonable precautions are taken. Meantime the general distrust which prevails is doing incalculable harm to the country.[33]

But, amidst the gloom, Wodehouse was finally rid of his troublesome Chief Secretary. For over a year he had silently endured Peel's embarrassing public antics and inflated self-importance. In November, rumours about the new prime minister, Lord John Russell, promoting Peel to his Cabinet impelled Wodehouse to threaten resignation. Instead, on 18 November, a mortified Peel said he was resigning; Russell was not even reappointing him Chief Secretary. After rejecting the mostly honorific post of Chancellor of the Duchy of Lancaster, an irascible Peel remained a lame duck Chief Secretary until 7 December, when Russell replaced him with Chichester Fortescue, a Louth MP from an old Anglo-Irish family.

Next day, Peel left Ireland. Wodehouse noted that 'his departure is a great relief to me. His utter want of judgement and above all his "inconsequences" make him a very undesirable colleague. He is quick-witted, clever, and vigorous but will always be a source of weakness rather than strength to any Govt with which he allies himself.'[34] However, at their first meeting Fortescue floored Wodehouse by claiming the right to represent Ireland in the Cabinet. Having dispensed with one troublesome rival, the Viceroy would not brook another, especially as the Fenian threat required the Irish government to speak with one single voice. Wodehouse settled the matter by threatening to resign if Fortescue was promoted above him: if Russell had considered this, he backed away immediately and left Wodehouse supreme at Dublin Castle.

Although Stephens's promised year of action had come to naught, 1866 brought Dublin Castle little relief. A.M. Sullivan believed:

> every one could discern that the danger had by no means blown over. The Fenians, it was well known, were making strenuous

efforts to repair the gaps made in their ranks and to recover themselves for a strike in force. As fast as seizures swept off leaders, others stepped into the vacant posts. Court-houses, dock, prison vans were filled and emptied again and again. The deadly duel went on. It seemed interminable.[35]

On 1 January, Wodehouse bleakly recorded that 'the year which opens promises to be even more anxious. May His providence guide and protect me.' On the same day, a report that fourteen disillusioned Irish-American officers had returned home briefly raised the Viceroy's spirits, but a fortnight later he proclaimed the County and City of Dublin – a dramatic measure that Wodehouse had rejected only a few months earlier. Police seizures of pikes and bullets had changed his mind. But although police believed arms and ammunition were stored throughout Dublin, locating them in poorer areas sympathetic to Fenianism was proving difficult. On 17 January 1866, the DMP and Irish Constabulary claimed a rising was imminent and that 100 Fenians from England had arrived in Dublin to fight.[36] G Division estimated 2,000 Fenians from England were in Ireland – 500 of them living in Dublin lodging houses – and that the IRB had an estimated 80,000 trained members. Superintendent Ryan also asserted that Fenian morale was buoyant, American aid for a rising was expected and sympathisers in England planned to incinerate docks in London and Liverpool, as well as destroy railway and telegraph communications.[37]

   On 17 January, Wodehouse warned Grey that Fenians were more active than ever. 'I am convinced they really contemplate a rising.'[38] He was confident the army could suppress a rebellion but doubted there were enough military resources to prevent one, especially as the Irish Constabulary was almost 1,800 constables under strength. 'In spite of all my efforts to tranquillise the public mind a panic is creeping all over the country.'[39] Hoping public alarm would subside, the Viceroy rejected most applications for troop reinforcements, only to be inundated with even more requests. Giving ground, he had soldiers sent to remote areas of Kerry and proclaimed both Sligo and Carlow, but Wodehouse was sceptical this would break the downward spiral. From America, Doyle warned Dublin Castle to prepare for a coming storm: 'I believe these men are in earnest, that the danger is imminent and that time is short. I believe that blood will be spilt. Now is the time to prepare; it might be too late two months hence.'

By January and February 1866, the Irish government's locker of measures for combatting Fenianism was almost bare, as only suspending Habeas Corpus remained; for Wodehouse, it was a last roll of the dice. Just like the previous September, he wanted a pre-emptive strike that would catch Fenians by surprise and end the seemingly endless stand-off by bringing the crisis to a head. Either the Viceroy goaded Fenians into a rising when the government held the initiative and could crush them, or they tamely walked away. For Stephens it really would be fight or flight.

Having blindsided the Cabinet over the *Irish People* arrests, Wodehouse now prepared ministers for radical action in Ireland. He started by telling Grey that suspending Habeas Corpus would let the Irish government arrest Fenian agents and Irish-American officers. 'The remedy may appear sharp, but the disease is very serious, and I am convinced would yield to nothing but sharp treatment.'[40] Within days, Grey read Wodehouse's letter to the Cabinet, which immediately sent two more regiments to Ireland. Ministers might have asked Wodehouse – though, apparently, they did not – why, only months after the *Irish People* arrests, an even more draconian measure was necessary.

A day after 9 February 1866, when Wodehouse advised Grey that parliament should suspend Habeas Corpus, the Privy Council proclaimed Roscommon, Wicklow, Armagh and Wexford. Three days later, the Viceroy told Gladstone: 'I cannot undertake that we shall not have an outbreak in the course of the spring. I have no doubt they are preparing for it. It is a very serious state of things.'[41] Any insurrection would involve atrocities on the same scale as 1798 and devastation similar in kind to the American Civil War. Although Rose reassured Wodehouse there would be no organised rising, he speculated that frightening violence might erupt. If so, the British Army would act as a last line of defence against satanic Fenianism; civilisation might easily collapse and Ireland descend into barbarism. There was 'no devilry which Irish Fenians trained in the American Civil War are not prepared to undertake'.[42] They might use torpedoes and dynamite and burn down isolated police and army barracks. But even worse, Rose declared, was in store for civilians. On 14 February, Rose told Wodehouse that a month earlier an Irish-American colonel had addressed Fenian soldiers and enthusiastically conjured up a vision of pillage, rape and looting on a scale greater even than in 1641 and 1798. The officer especially extolled the systematic violation of women that he had practised in the American Civil War and fully intended re-enacting in Ireland. Such a rampage, he declared, was a wonderful reason for joining an insurrection.[43]

But Rose was more concerned that Fenianism was seriously stretching British Army resources, especially as a Viceroy desperate to maintain public morale was overriding his military assessments. On 15 February, Rose complained to Prince George, Duke of Cambridge about Wodehouse constantly requesting troops for troubled districts despite his worries about draining army reserves. Furthermore, Fenian agents were brazenly attempting to recruit his soldiers, and at Limerick three sergeants of the 73rd Regiment had been unmasked as Fenians. He accused some complacent commanders of resembling officers in India who were almost shot during the Mutiny by men they insisted were completely loyal. Similarly, in September 1865, almost every regiment had declared itself free of Fenianism. But subsequently an inspection revealed considerable laxity, such as an Irish-American officer slipping into a sergeants' mess without the commanding officer's knowledge.

However, Rose was averse to suspending Habeas Corpus; not on libertarian grounds, but because it had always been an unattractive and inefficient remedy. As a blunt instrument it would probably exacerbate an already dire situation by dividing British public opinion, damaging England's reputation abroad and engendering sympathy for Fenianism. Moreover, it would only remove dangerous men from society temporarily before they were freed to resume their revolutionary careers. Instead, Rose recommended expelling from Ireland Fenians suspected of serious offences and compulsorily resettling them in America.[44] Irish-American officers should be deported. However, Wodehouse believed he and the British government were already stretching their liberal principles to the limit. Accordingly, Rose settled for suspension rather than constantly reinforcing the Army in Ireland. 'No number of troops will quieten the alarm.'[45]

After consulting Fortescue, Wodehouse warned the Cabinet on 14 February that it was in a race against time.[46] IRB leaders expected suspension soon and were eager to strike the first blow, probably within two or three weeks, if not sooner. Rounding up prominent conspirators could yet avert catastrophe – though an abortive outbreak was still probable when suspension happened. The Viceroy wanted action by Monday, 19 February, at the latest. Home Secretary Grey and Foreign Secretary Lord Clarendon backed Wodehouse and the rest deferred to them. At 5.30 p.m. on Friday,

16 February 1866, Wodehouse learned that the government would rush a suspension bill through parliament immediately. Even before it became law, the Viceroy and Lord Chancellor decided to catch the principal Dublin conspirators by surprise, while provincial police simultaneously detained well-known IRB leaders. Wodehouse instructed Superintendent Ryan to organise raids in the capital and he worked throughout the night, compiling lists of targets – especially Irish-American officers – and places to raid. Simultaneously, police parties would conduct arms searches. At six o'clock on Saturday morning, six G Division detectives assembled secretly at Dublin Castle, and two hours later the operation began.

John Devoy watched as 'large bodies of police, accompanied by detectives, moved about the city, searching suspected residences, hotels, lodging houses and taprooms making arrests'.[47] Devoy claimed that some police parties contained Fenians whose tipoffs enabled many targets to escape. Some fled to England and America, but most went underground in Dublin, staying with friends or in lodging houses and frequently changing addresses to evade capture. Devoy claimed some Fenians used firearms to successfully fight their way out when cornered, and that many more would have resisted had Stephens not previously ordered that all revolvers be handed over and stored in depots. By noon, ninety-one men were in custody, ten Dubliners, thirty-five Americans – ten of them former Union officers – and thirty-eight from England. The rest said nothing, though Ryan noticed their military bearing. Five men captured in Dublin were from the provinces – one a former police constable from Mallow, Co. Cork. All thirty-eight suspects from England had recently arrived from London and Lancashire. Ninety men were lodged in Mountjoy and Kilmainham, while a 16-year-old youth was released. Four more arrests were made on Saturday evening. Rose congratulated Wodehouse on his 'capital bag' of Irish-Americans and hoped for numerous arrests outside Dublin.[48] On 19 February, Wodehouse boasted: 'I shall endeavour to strike injurious blows at the conspiracy whilst the impression produced by the suspension is strong.'[49] Between 17 February and 1 March 1866, the police arrested 165 men, 94 of them from England and 45 from America.

From the Suspension of Habeas Corpus to Lord Wodehouse's Departure: 17 February–16 July 1866

G Division never came close to catching Stephens, who briefly shifted with the Bolands to a safe house on Dublin's north side before joining a Mrs Butler at her Kildare Street residence.[1] Although secretly republican, this fashionable dressmaker catered mainly to the Ascendancy class and made an unlikely suspect to be harbouring Ireland's most wanted man. Just as unlikely as the idea of Stephens living opposite the loyalist Kildare Street Club, safely ensconced amidst numerous solicitors' offices and the homes of upper middle-class professionals.

However, within two days of suspension, Dublin detectives captured all but a dozen American officers.[2] Before the crackdown, police had already caught the two best Fenian soldiers in Dublin, John Boyle O'Reilly and Patrick Keating. Some IRB men fled to England and America, but many went on the run in Ireland. In the capital, they moved constantly between safe houses, keeping just one step ahead of detectives searching residences, hotels and boarding houses. Most fugitives hid out with friends or lodged in 'The Liberties,' a largely working-class area in the south inner city that was reasonably safe. Avoiding former haunts in South Great Georges Street, Lower Abbey Street and Ormond Quay – all of them now under constant police surveillance – they snatched cheap meals in cafes and occasionally relaxed in friendly pubs. But mostly, fugitives walked the streets and stayed close to each other for mutual protection. Devoy claimed some sympathetic DMP officers tipped the IRB off about imminent police raids, but when cornered, suspects offered little resistance. Stephens had ordered that revolvers be stored in depots.[3]

Devoy claimed that immediately after suspension most Fenians assumed Stephens would soon launch an insurrection. Hundreds stopped attending work and readied themselves for action. However, when the IRB leader procrastinated, some threatened mutiny. Two centres urged Devoy to 'pitch Stephens to the devil' and call out Fenian soldiers himself, but he refused as this would have split the movement throughout Ireland.[4] Then, on Monday 19 February 1866, Devoy, now Roantree's successor, learned that Fenian soldiers planned to seize Richmond barracks and start a rebellion. Although only a few hotheads were involved, Devoy acted quickly to quell the dissidents. In a borrowed army uniform and surrounded by friendly soldiers, he entered the barracks and ordered Fenians to stand down and await further instructions.

Devoy himself wanted a rising but only one that Stephens called, and by mid-February 1866 he believed that the IRB leader was finally ready to act. For some time, Devoy had reported in cipher to Stephens about Fenianism in the British Army, but in early February he was ordered to submit a weekly written memorandum. Devoy considered this useless and dangerous, but he reluctantly complied, even after going on the run. On Tuesday, 20 February, as he flitted between pub back rooms, guarded by vigilant lookouts, Devoy compiled what he intended to be his last report, warning that the IRB could not hold together much longer: either Stephens started the rising immediately or postponed it and let Fenian excitement subside.[5] But decisive action was imperative: otherwise, the IRB would become completely demoralised. In the late afternoon of 20 February, Colonel Kelly gave the report to Stephens. Much later, Devoy learned that Stephens had never paid much attention to his reports, and indeed, might not have read them at all. But the latest one prompted Kelly to emphasise its importance to Stephens, and within hours Devoy was summoned to Kildare Street for a high-level IRB conference – effectively a war cabinet – that would debate whether or not to rise.[6] Joining Stephens were Kelly, Halpin, Devoy, Mortimer Moynahan, David Murphy from Munster, John Nolan from Ulster and Edmund O'Donovan, who knew Dublin and Clare well. Only Edward Duffy from Munster was absent. Arrested with Stephens in November 1865 but terminally ill with consumption, Duffy had been bailed on compassionate grounds. Eschewing alcohol and tobacco, they debated well into early morning. Stephens astonished Devoy by admitting that until his latest report he had not realised how serious was the situation, but now Stephens wanted unity on a course of action. Devoy was incredulous at how isolated Stephens had become from his followers, that three days after suspension he still had no response to the latest British assault on Fenianism, indeed had apparently not thought much about it at all. Devoy now concluded that his reports had been nothing more than displacement activity intended by Stephens to create an illusion of momentum – all part, he suspected, of a wider pattern of deception.

Initially, debate focussed on the IRB itself, which everyone agreed was unbroken and would answer a call to arms – provided the necessary arms existed. In fact, the organisation had only about 2,000 rifles, a few thousand shotguns, 200 revolvers and a large number of pikes. Devoy countered that IRB raiding parties could seize more rifles from government arsenals. But once again the IRB leader was about to disappoint: 'The sentiment that night was all in favour of fight and I was satisfied that if a vote had been taken it would have been for immediate action. But it was plain to all of us that whilst Stephens said nothing positive, he was really in favour of another postponement.'[7] Just as he had in November and December 1865, Stephens avoided proposing an indefinite delay and argued instead for a short pause while he supposedly finalised arrangements for the rising. That was the most Stephens dared recommend because, Devoy recalled, 'The sentiment was so universal in favour of fighting that he seemed loath to ask for a long postponement.' Devoy was not fooled. Finally, at about 3 a.m. on 21 February, the meeting adjourned until eight o'clock that evening. While others rested, Kelly and Devoy attended a series of meetings and only snatched a few hours' sleep before returning bleary-eyed and exhausted to Kildare Street.

A final decision about a rising was now urgent. Devoy urged immediate action, convinced that revolutionary success depended more on willpower than military hardware, on the readiness to risk everything with confidence that the Irish people would answer a call to freedom. He believed that 'revolutions don't go by the rules of logic and reasoning. If they did there would never be a revolution in any country in the world.'[8] Nevertheless, Devoy sensed that the mood in Kildare Street had changed from belligerence to hesitation, perhaps because of Stephens's obvious doubts. Kelly and Halpin now recommended that, without sufficient rifles and effective help from America, the rising should be postponed until more favourable times. With police parties still making numerous arrests in Dublin, tightening the net around prominent Fenians and depleting the IRB as well as most American officers lodged in Mountjoy prison, a majority in Kildare Street saw no hope of success. 'Thus,' said Devoy, 'the last chance for a Rising in that year was thrown away, and the temporary disruption of the movement followed.'[9] Devoy considered postponement a failure of leadership and his ebbing faith in Stephens finally evaporated. Waiting for better times, he believed, was futile as the British would make further arrests, seize more weapons and steadily grind the IRB down. Having never succumbed to hero worship, Devoy now scorned a chief who constantly disappointed. Whereas Tone and Emmet led from the front and literally put their necks on the line, Stephens seemed to prefer retreat; apparently willing to fight only if virtually guaranteed victory in advance.

Furthermore, on Stephens's watch the Irish government had twice out-foxed Fenians. On 12 September 1865 and 17 February 1866, Dublin Castle had camouflaged its intentions, prepared offensives and struck pre-emp-tively, utterly confounding the IRB. While many Fenians thought it was almost miraculous that the IRB had withstood both hammer blows, Devoy believed a revolutionary movement must do more than simply survive, on the defensive and – just like many Fenians – on the run. Disenchanted with a leader who seemingly preferred flight to fight, Devoy might soon have broken with Stephens, but instead, he almost immediately landed in prison. On 8 February 1866, Patrick Foley – a soldier spy in the IRB – told Superintendent Ryan that Devoy was now organising Fenianism in the British Army. A day after the Kildare Street conference, while he met Fenian soldiers in the back room of Pilsworth's public house on James's Street, lookouts spotted two detectives outside. Instinctively Devoy reached for his revolver, but another lookout warned him not to fire because a large police and army raiding party was approaching. As he took his hand from his pocket, Devoy and the Fenian soldiers were quickly arrested.

Soon afterwards Stephens left Ireland for the United States, ostensibly to reunite American Fenianism and solicit funds, but he was also fleeing IRB squabbling and the relentless pressure for a rising. Moreover, prolonged confinement in Kildare Street had stifled him, so different was Mrs Butler's residence from the relaxing environment of Fairfield House. And he knew that if re-arrested, his revolutionary career was finished; the British would never allow him to escape again. On 12 March 1866, he and Col. Kelly rode by cab to the quays, where they met 31-year-old John Flood, a Fenian journalist who had been in Kelly's party that had rescued Stephens from Richmond Gaol. Flood had persuaded a childhood friend, Captain Nicholas Weldon, to smuggle the trio out of Ireland in his small collier brig. Stephens was undisguised as they strode past several policemen and boarded the vessel. After three days on the Irish Sea battling adverse winds, it reached Scotland, from where they travelled by mail train to London. After staying in a hotel opposite Buckingham Palace, they travelled to Dover and took a mail steamer to Calais. Sending Kelly ahead to America, Stephens spent five weeks in Paris, feted as a celebrity and mixing with high society. Finally, on April 1866, he departed for America and arrived in New York twelve days later.

From a distance, Stephens controlled the IRB by appointing ultra-loyal Edward Duffy as provisional leader. Terminally ill with consumption, Duffy was out on bail before his trial for treason-felony and constantly under police surveillance at the European Hotel in Bolton Street. Almost penniless, Duffy's straitened circumstances contrasted with Stephens's quite luxurious lifestyle at Fairfield House and even Kildare Street. Moreover, despite promising Duffy subsistence funds, a habitually stingy Stephens sent him nothing. Duffy's situation was made even more difficult by G Division detectives hunting down IRB centres who had evaded arrest, rumours about informers, and an American schism that had undermined morale. Despite some remission from consumption, Duffy suffered bouts of depression that occasionally made him appear lacklustre, when ironically it was his energy and enthusiasm that sustained Duffy for the rest of his short life. But unavoidably, Duffy's personal contact with IRB members was limited and he relied heavily on John O'Leary's sister Ellen, who also lived at the European Hotel as his executive assistant. She had also liquidated a mortgage to help Stephens's escape from Ireland and sat on a Ladies Committee of the IRB that raised funds for prisoners' families, visited prisoners in Irish and British gaols, and worked clandestinely to reconnect centres and circles with each other and Duffy as well.

Initially, Wodehouse hailed the Habeas Corpus suspension as a decisive victory over Fenianism and he boasted that: 'The town is perfectly quiet and the arrests cause general satisfaction amongst the loyal and respectable classes.'[10] With almost indecent haste, a once sceptical Rose congratulated Wodehouse on his 'capital bag' of Irish-Americans and hoped that he would capture just as many outside Dublin.[11] The DMP Commissioner also welcomed suspension, which he claimed had stopped a downward spiral just in time. Later he observed of the arrests that 'the effects were magical; Private Fenian meetings were given up, drilling ceased, and the menacing tone of Fenianism, so much heard in the streets and public houses were silent, the public alarm subsided, people resumed their ordinary pursuits'.[12] But suspension exacted a high toll on the Irish government. Since September 1865 it had been under severe pressure, which spiked again after 17 February 1866 as hundreds of detainees flowed into Irish gaols. Although Devoy's estimate of 3,000 inmates is grossly exaggerated, the prison system was quickly overwhelmed. Between suspension and 4 February 1867, 987 suspected Fenians were arrested – of whom 26 had previously been released and then re-arrested. Between suspension and September 1866, a weekly average of 550 Fenians were in custody, reaching a peak of 669 in the second week of April 1866.[13] Wodehouse examined every case and personally decided who remained in detention. On 25 February 1866, he recorded that, 'The whole of the past week incessantly engaged in determining against whom warrants should be issued. One of the hardest week's work I ever did.'[14] Two weeks later he was still at it. 'Overwhelmed with business connected with the arrests under the H.C.S. Act. I think Larcom will break down altogether.'[15] On 21 April he confessed, 'I am weary to death of this place and I should be only too glad of a decent pretext to get away.'[16] Disappointed, exhausted and suffering from influenza, Wodehouse lashed out at the Irish:

> No people but the Irish could be such egregious fools as to be led by such phantoms. On the whole I think there is no people on the face of the earth more unworthy of respect. They had always been despised by the Englishman and as a nation they have always deserved his contempt.[17]

But, as always, he swiftly regretted such an outburst: 'My remarks about Irishmen are unfair and unjust. They are excusable only on account of the bilious condition of my mind and body when I wrote them. I recant.'[18] The Irish were an unfortunate people whose tribulations were aggravated by British governments who mistakenly tried to rule Irishmen just like the English. However, 'This last folly will pass away, and there will be slow but certain improvement. That is my faith.'[19]

Devoy acknowledged that in the short term, suspension weakened the IRB. 'For the moment it broke the strength of the organisation, temporarily dislocated all communication, and created new and serious difficulties.'[20] However, Dublin Castle soon realised it had not destroyed Fenianism. On 7 March, Wodehouse warned the Admiralty to alert its coastal patrols for an American naval expedition that an intelligence report said would soon arrive in Dublin Bay. Subsequently, rumours circulated about a Fenian rising on St Patrick's Day, 17 March, and Wodehouse noted absentees from the preceding evening's St Patrick's Ball in Dublin Castle: 'There were foolish people, it is said, who stayed away for fear of the Fenians.'[21] On 23 March, he told Home Secretary Grey that 'the conspiracy is only checked here, not broken.'[22] When Stephens reached Paris, Wodehouse fretted at the DMP's failure to capture him in Ireland, that it was 'difficult to understand how Stephens (and other notorious Fenians also to my certain knowledge) can have gone about Dublin with impunity for so long. I have no doubt he will soon come back.'[23] On 28 May 1866, he was 'sorry to say there are still signs of life in this wretched conspiracy'.[24]

Although suspension temporarily reassured loyalists, it simultaneously alienated many nationalists. Superintendent Ryan reported that 'the feeling of a large and dangerous section of the people here is much against the existing Government'.[25] Extending far beyond Fenian ranks, this discontent had boosted IRB morale and helped explain 'the great hold it has taken on the community'. Even in England there was anger, not just among Irishmen but also radical artisans and businessmen. On 20 March 1866, the DMP Commissioners claimed Fenianism was flourishing in the manufacturing towns of northern England and Scotland, where many working men, despite not being in the IRB, sympathised with it. In England – and in Ireland – businessmen who warned employees that working men could never overthrow a government were being told that French workers had done that more than once. Within weeks of suspension, the DMP Commissioners reported that Fenianism had revived and that arrests, arms raids and police searches had not 'produced the least effect on the members of that body in repressing their spirit or apparently disturbing their organisation more than in a temporary way'.[26] Public fears of a rising had also returned. They attributed the Fenian renaissance mainly to Duffy, who had proved himself a surprisingly effective stand-in for Stephens and was a man of superior ability, directing the IRB with all the energy of a person in perfect health.

However, ironically, the Irish administration actually contributed more than Duffy to the IRB's resurgence. Within two months of mistakenly assuming that suspension had finally decimated Fenianism, it began releasing Fenian prisoners. Suspending Habeas Corpus had troubled the liberal Viceroy, as did the entire policy of repression he had pursued since September 1865. An enlightened politician who treasured the rule of law, press freedom and individual liberty, Wodehouse was mightily embarrassed at closing newspapers, imprisoning men without trial, establishing Special Commissions and authorising police raids. Increasingly this humane, fair-minded and not particularly thick-skinned man was portrayed as a tyrant and compared to odious European despots like the Tsar of Russia, who ruled by decree and arbitrarily imprisoned political opponents. To protect his reputation, Wodehouse began freeing detainees against whom evidence was inconclusive and reduced the number of detainees to a hard core of dangerous revolutionaries.

The Viceroy also had to consider English public opinion. Despite the Conservative party's strong support, a speech by the radical MP John Bright, in which he spoke of his shame and humiliation that between 5 and 6 million people in Ireland had been deprived of their personal freedom, resonated widely. Although press and people had instinctively rallied to the government's side, Wodehouse knew they might eventually come to share Bright's unease if suspension lasted indefinitely. Furthermore, the prison system had rapidly become overwhelmed. Dublin gaols were crammed and detainees had to be transferred to prisons in Belfast and Naas.

The Irish government was also under pressure from William West, the US Consul in Dublin. An Irishman who had become a naturalised American, he claimed thirty-eight of the first detainees were native-born or naturalised Americans who should be freed. West, in turn, was being hounded by prisoners' relatives, many of whom occupied his consulate on 18 February 1866 demanding his assistance. Next day, he listened sympathetically to them claiming that prisoners and their families were in Ireland for purely personal reasons such as purchasing property or recovering from ill health. Kate Burke described her devoted husband

Denis – a Military Council member – as a guardian angel watching over her as she recuperated from surgery. Indeed, in her telling, Ireland's almost miraculous healing powers rivalled the great European spas and perhaps even Lourdes itself. Suspension of Habeas Corpus also risked an Anglo–American diplomatic rift. Dublin Castle and the British government rejected West's repeated demands for access to American prisoners, insisting that Americans born in Ireland remained British subjects. West also complained about the harsh conditions in which prisoners were held. Somewhat unfairly, Wodehouse and Attorney General Lawson dismissed West as a Fenian dupe, when in fact he suspected that many American detainees were heavily implicated in subversion. Despite British intransigence, US Secretary of State Seward never formally complained about their treatment, even though by early March 1866 West had not secured a single prisoner release.[27]

Continued detention without trial inflamed nationalist opinion, provoked public disorder and made excellent Fenian propaganda. So did a harsh and monotonous prison regime of oakum picking, stone breaking, treadmill walking, unappetising food, small, badly lit cells and daily exercise of endlessly circling a courtyard. But most terrible was the perpetual silence that psychologically damaged many prisoners and reputedly drove one man insane. Anxious to avoid another escape fiasco, Wodehouse tightened prison security, reinforcing Fenian prisoners' cells at Mountjoy with iron sheeting whose sound would alert armed guards to an attempted break-out. Prisoners especially resented the zoo-like conditions that permitted 'respectable' visitors to peep into cells at supposedly semi-human barbarians who threatened their civilised world. On 14 June, Wodehouse inspected security arrangements at Mountjoy and 'saw the caged Fenians. The Governor said the men were not any of them of a superior class of society but sharp cunning villains, some of them. Those I saw in the exercising ground looked thorough Yankee rowdies.'[28]

Attempting to lower the political temperature, Dublin Castle shielded inmates from public and press scrutiny, especially during prison transfers. However, in Limerick on Tuesday, 1 May, police detachments entered the county gaol and mounted Lancers arrived at a nearby army barracks. As word spread that Fenian detainees were being shifted to Dublin's Mountjoy Prison, hundreds of relatives and friends flocked to the gaol, where guards forced twelve prisoners through a wailing crowd. Newspapers reported heart-rending scenes at the railway station, where two constables held each Fenian by the collar and led them to waiting carriages. Tearful wives and weeping children waved farewell as a train carrying their husbands and fathers receded into the distance. Portraying English rule in Ireland as a heartless engine of oppression made powerful Fenian propaganda and undoubtedly nudged Dublin Castle towards defusing the tensions that suspension had unleashed.[29]

As early as 13 April 1866, Wodehouse was 'endeavouring now to discharge as many prisoners as possible, only keeping in really dangerous men'.[30] Some colleagues opposed him and Chief Secretary Fortescue slowed down releases during the Viceroy's visits to England. But the process went on – even under Wodehouse's Conservative successor. Native Irishmen released on bail were allowed to remain in the country, though liable to re-arrest at any time. On 22 April, Attorney General Lawson announced that he would entertain applications from 'foreigners' who wanted to return home. At first, American prisoners insisted on unconditional release, but harsh prison life soon exacted a severe physical and mental toll. One called Kilmainham Gaol 'worse than death' and another claimed that sleep deprivation at Mountjoy had mentally destroyed him. Soon detainees began accepting release provided they left Ireland forever, and after they signed a guarantee, armed police escorted them to their port of embarkation. By 22 September, 114 detainees had gone to America, 108 to Great Britain, two to Australia and one – mystifyingly – to Archangel on the Arctic coast of Russia.[31]

Within weeks, Superintendent Ryan told Dublin Castle that suspension had over-stretched a DMP that now bore the brunt of Fenian antagonism. 'The bitter feeling against the Police remains undiminished and some very violent assaults have been committed on them and serious injuries inflicted during the last fortnight.'[32] However, doubts about the DMP's effectiveness – and even loyalty – soon permeated the Irish administration. On 16 May, Sir Hugh Rose complained to Wodehouse about G Division after two joint police and army raids had fallen through because, he claimed, the Fenian targets were warned in advance. In fact, one raid was botched because poor co-ordination had caused police and soldiers to arrive at different times. When Stephens arrived safely in Paris and boasted that he had moved freely around Dublin after escaping from Richmond Gaol, Wodehouse was badly shaken. 'I can't say much for our police. Stephens will come back again, and yet do harm.'[33] By mid-June, the Viceroy suspected that 'traitors in the camp' explained G Division's failure to crush Fenianism, but he rejected Fortescue's proposal to import Scotland Yard detectives to investigate their Dublin counterparts for treachery. Despite the relentless pressure under which he worked and too many exhausting days, Wodehouse's political judgement had not eroded; he warned Fortescue that his idea was repugnant and risked a serious political scandal, because if word leaked it would damage G Division morale and horrify public opinion.[34] It might also have triggered resignations in Dublin Castle and the DMP.

Even before Habeas Corpus suspension, Sir Hugh Rose had targeted Fenianism in the Irish garrison after he became commander-in-chief in July 1865. Convinced his predecessor Sir George Brown had exhibited the same complacency that had pervaded the British Army in India before the Mutiny, he decided to 'root out' disloyalty. Devoy saw in Rose a 'ruthless sternness that seemed to fit him best for the work of putting down the Fenians'.[35] Rose's steeliness dated from his tour of duty in Ireland during the 1820s, suppressing secret Ribbon societies and anti-tithe protests. He had concluded that 'the Irish bane of intimidation' had poisoned an entire legal system and forced magistrates to appease offenders. 'This intimidation is the fruit of two dark features of the Irish character, proverbial lawlessness and vindictiveness, both perpetually brought into play for the redress of political and private wrongs against the dominant race.'[36] Political and religious animosity as well as agrarian outrage had created cemeteries across Ireland, filled with the graves of judges, magistrates, jurymen, Protestant clergymen, land agents, tithe proctors and incoming tenants. Rose had even compiled 'a murder map of the South of Ireland, darkened with the red crosses, which are the sites of assassination'.[37] Yet magistrates and juries still meted out derisory sentences like the fortnight one Fenian served after he tried persuading soldiers to betray their oath – an offence punishable by death.

After becoming commander-in-chief, Rose made his commanding officers report on possible Fenian infiltration of their regiments, but they overwhelmingly denied any disloyalty existed. Rose then scrutinised G Division reports that accused Fenian agents of recruiting many soldiers and claimed that widespread disaffection permeated the Dublin garrison, not just among Irishmen and Catholics but anyone wanting to punish superiors who had ever disciplined them. One soldier had boasted that:

Sir Hugh Rose was not in India now where he could shoot men down in cold blood, that he was now where he would be shot himself, that Lord Wodehouse and he were 'booked for Chester' [i.e., assassination] and the first to be popped, that the date was not far off when they (meaning Fenian soldiers) would have revenge for the tyranny that has been practised on them.[38]

Another soldier claimed fifty determined men could capture the Royal Barracks with help from its Fenian soldiers, that the IRB had infiltrated regiments across the United Kingdom and the Rifle Volunteers of England contained hundreds of Fenians. Fenians in London had also tampered with the Guards: 'It would seem that no Regiment is clear of the Fenian contamination.'[39]

From early 1866, Rose began utilising reports from Ryan's informers and agents in the army to begin dismantling Devoy's soldier network. First to be arrested was 22-year-old John Boyle O'Reilly, a former journalist and poet whom Devoy had recruited in October 1865 and regarded as the most remarkable Fenian in the British Army. O'Reilly served in the 10th Hussars, a crack cavalry regiment stationed at Islandbridge Barracks in south-west Dublin, where he organised an IRB circle. He also carried despatches between Rose and Wodehouse, and he offered to let Devoy steam them open. But O'Reilly was arrested on 14 February and led across the barracks square, berated all the way by his furious commanding officer, Colonel Baker, who shook a fist and shouted, 'Damn you O'Reilly, you have ruined the finest regiment in Her Majesty's service.'

On 22 February 1866, Private Patrick Foley of the 5th Dragoon Guards, who had begun spying on the IRB a day after being recruited, tailed fellow Guards to a Fenian meeting at Pilsworth's public house in Dublin. He then tipped off the police, who immediately arrested the soldiers and Devoy as well. Another Fenian soldier, Sergeant McCarthy of the 53rd Regiment, and two comrades were also detained at Carrick-on-Suir in Co. Tipperary and immediately transferred to Richmond Gaol. Thomas Chambers, the 61st Regiment's IRB centre whom Devoy considered the most intelligent and best-educated Fenian soldier after O'Reilly, evaded arrest until he was accidentally caught at Pilsworth's. Flimsy evidence against some detainees compelled Rose to restrict the courts martial to thirty soldiers. Devoy recalled their devious prosecutor, Captain Whelan, going:

cell to cell in Arbour Hill Military Prison where the Fenian soldiers charged with Fenianism were on starvation diet, telling each man that the others had all turned informers and that I had supplied to the Castle a list of all the men I had sworn in. Several of the men broke down and he schooled and drilled them in the evidence.[40]

Rose claimed he was 'too good of a disciplinarian not to visit with instant and proper punishment treason in soldiers or anything approaching to it'.[41] He was especially angry that apparently McCarthy had plans of a 'diabolical, bloodthirsty nature' to commit atrocities.[42] These included killing a fellow sergeant and 'blowing out the brains of Corporal Kennedy in order to get the arms out of his possession and hand them over to the Fenians'.[43] Supposedly, McCarthy then intended murdering every soldier who refused to join a Fenian rebellion, and tying informers naked to trees before bayoneting them every fifteen minutes. He also planned to stuff sponges down the rifle barrels of loyalist soldiers and cripple their horses. On 31 May 1866, Rose told Wodehouse that McCarthy should be executed as a salutary reminder that 'soldiers are not at liberty to concoct schemes of mutiny with impunity'. It would also deter his fellow conspirators into becoming informers: 'We shall have civilians convicted on the evidence of soldiers and soldiers convicted on civilian evidence – and the mutual confidence will be shaken forever.' McCarthy's death would also end the dangerous public perception that Dublin Castle was afraid to enforce the law, in case this provoked the very rebellion it so desperately wanted to avoid. But Wodehouse refused to sanction the execution of someone for plotting a rebellion that did not actually happen.

Between February and August 1866, courts martial in Dublin, Cork, Limerick and Enniskillen acquitted a few defendants and sentenced the rest to between a year and life imprisonment. In October the convicted men, except for McCarthy and Chambers, were sent to Portland Prison in England before transportation to the penal colony of Western Australia. Devoy claimed that although the trials were intended to destroy the organisation in the British Army and strike terror into disgruntled soldiers, they did not succeed. But Devoy's oft-repeated assertion that his soldier network was only broken up after a panicked British government hurriedly moved Irish regiments to England is a myth. Rose kept the heavily infiltrated 5th Dragoon Guards in Dublin and used the 4th (Royal Irish) Dragoon Guards in disaffected areas.

During the first six months of 1866, murders and attempted murders of policemen and informers happened in Dublin. On 9 February, fellow Fenians shot George Clarke dead at Royal Canal Bank near the North Circular Road for betraying an IRB armoury. Superintendent Ryan rejected the accusation, but Devoy insisted conclusive proof came from Michael Breslin, a clerk in the Police Superintendent's Office who told the IRB about Clarke speaking to Superintendent Hughes just before detectives raided the arms dump.[44] An IRB court martial ordered Sam Cavanagh and a Dublin centre, Garret O'Shaughnessy, to execute Clarke, and afterwards they fled immediately to America. Next day, 10 February, an inform-ant told Superintendent Ryan that Col. Kelly had established a Vigilance Committee to unmask informers and a 'Shooting Circle' to assassinate them. Later, Henry Barton – nicknamed 'The German' – was killed, sup-posedly for causing the arrests of Devoy and Fenian soldiers at Pilsworth's public house.

Despite suspending Habeas Corpus and increasing troop levels, the Irish government seemed helpless to counter the violence. Ryan declared that Kelly was the heart and soul of the assassination movement. The assassina-tion campaign was symptomatic of an anger coursing through the IRB at the repeated setbacks it suffered in late 1865 and early 1866, from the *Irish People* arrests and the Special Commission trials to a postponed rising and Habeas Corpus suspension. Superintendent Ryan reported that the fail-ure of Fenians to respond effectively had fuelled a desire for retaliation, striking terror into enemy minds by cutting down anyone involved in sup-pressing Fenianism. The Shooting Circle was also called the Assassination Circle, the Black Bean Circle and the Committee of Public Safety. Its first leader, Michael Cody, was a boilerman in his early 20s, a revolutionary zealot who habitually punched policemen and had helped rescue Stephens from Richmond Gaol. On the run during the winter of 1865–66, Cody and Devoy had already discussed assassinating informers like Nagle, and although Devoy never joined the Vigilance Committee or Shooting Circle, he certainly knew much about their activities:

There were men killed for treason and there were propositions made to kill other men who were not killed; but those who suffered death were members of the IRB who beyond all reasonable doubt gave information to the government; and there never was a charge of treachery made, or a proposition to punish treachery that was not known to certain men in the organisation.[45]

On 8 April 1866, two detectives and a party of soldiers acted on information from a Private James Maher and arrested Cody in possession of two revolvers. Cody suspected Maher of treachery and vowed vengeance. A fortnight later, Maher was lured to Hoey's pub in Bridgefoot Street, shot three times and seriously wounded. On Sunday, 29 April, DMP constable Charles O'Neill was shot dead in Pill Lane in the north inner city. Then G Division detectives became targets. On 1 May, a young Irishman recently returned from America told Superintendent Ryan that New York Fenians wanted him and Acting Inspector Hughes dead, and if nobody in Dublin killed them, an assassin would be sent to Ireland.[46] Having previously dismissed such threats, Ryan now believed Fenians were ready to act on them. Informers had reported Fenians discussing his assassination and that of detectives Dawson and Smollen, whom the 'Shooting Circle' was shadowing.[47]

Then on Sunday, 20 May, the attempted assassination of an informer occurred in Howth.[48] Sixty-year-old John Warner, a former soldier become an IRB captain, had testified at Cork's Special Commission and helped convict many former comrades. Relocated to the Dublin suburb of Ballybough, Warner lived openly in what locals dubbed 'the informer's house', but his prodigious alcohol consumption frequently landed him in trouble. During a public house fracas, he drew a pistol, but patrons seized the weapon and pummelled him badly. Relocated again to Howth, Warner, his wife, six children and a minder, Constable Twomey, lived beside the police station. However, Warner's conduct did not improve and he was not a hard man to find. Three months later, as he and Twomey stood intoxicated against a cemetery wall, an 'Edward O'Connor' approached them and inquired about a place to eat. In fact, O'Connor was 26-year-old Patrick Tierney, a former soldier turned Fenian who had traced Warner to Howth and was there to kill him.

Assuming an American accent and posing as a former Confederate soldier, Tierney reeled Warner in as they strolled down memory lane and swapped wartime stories. After Warner invited Tierney back to his house, Twomey went straight to bed while the others drank porter. Eventually, the landlady offered Tierney a bed for the night, but before retiring Tierney asked to be shown to the yard, where he suddenly stabbed Warner in the neck. When Warner grabbed him, Tierney only escaped by wriggling out of his jacket, leaving behind the knife and a revolver before leaping over a wall. Bleeding profusely, Warner ran back inside and awakened a naked Twomey, who chased after Tierney. Badly wounded, Warner waited for a doctor, who bandaged him; the knife blade had missed his vital arteries and hit a vertebra. Meanwhile, Howth police had alerted neighbouring stations, and eventually Clontarf police caught Tierney walking on the road wearing only his shirt and trousers, carrying boots under his arms. In custody, Tierney at first stuck coolly to his cover story about being Edward O'Connor, recently returned to Ireland after eight years in America. Under questioning he eventually cracked and revealed his true identity. A daily return train ticket proved that Tierney had anticipated speedily finishing his business in Howth. On 14 June 1866, Tierney pleaded guilty to attempted murder and was sentenced to life imprisonment at Spike Island Prison in Cork.

Murders and attempted murders during 1866 shocked the Irish administration. Sir Hugh Rose complained about a series of attacks on his soldiers, including two artillerymen shot in Kilkenny. Although comparatively rare, such incidents created a climate of fear, especially frightening to soldiers who had provided intelligence on Fenianism. Rose transferred some soldiers to England or abroad for their own safety, but a fear of reprisal substantially curtailed the flow of information. He also criticised public displays of support for the killers. 'Although the assassinations or attempts at them have been committed in public not an individual has been arrested for them.'[49] Seemingly, a large Dublin garrison was no deterrent, and indeed, attacks had increased after he reinforced it. Superintendent Ryan claimed that the IRB's circle structure made it impossible to secure evidence – the very reason for which Habeas Corpus had been suspended.

Amidst the gloom, Wodehouse consoled himself that this time Fenianism really was disintegrating, that the attacks proved it could not fight on the open battlefield. Tierney's assault on Warner convinced the Viceroy that Fenianism was morally decomposing, descending into banditry and barbarism. 'Every such attempt puts another nail in the coffin of the conspiracy. When conspirators become assassins, they cease to be politically formidable.'[50] After Tierney's arrest, the attacks abruptly ceased and Wodehouse concluded that the government was regaining the upper hand.

Although the Vigilance Committee and Shooting Circle faded away, they left a legacy. Half a century later, Michael Collins, another Fenian leader steeped in Irish history, decided to complete the work begun fitfully in 1866. By creating an Irish Volunteers intelligence department and a squad that decimated G Division and eliminated informers, he crippled the British intelligence system in Ireland.[51]

By April 1866, Lord Russell's Liberal government – like Wodehouse himself – had run out of steam, and it was the prime minister who precipitated its fall. In attempting to crown his political career with a Reform Bill that enfranchised 400,000 new 'respectable' working-class voters, he alienated his more traditional MPs, and on 20 April, Russell's Commons majority fell to five. Sensing imminent collapse, Wodehouse asked Russell for a peerage and he quickly became the Earl of Kimberley, though fully aware that his time in Ireland would soon end – and on a note of failure. Three weeks earlier, the Cabinet had decided to renew the Habeas Corpus Suspension Act.

On 26 June, Russell finally resigned as prime minister and Lord Derby formed a Conservative government with Lord Abercorn as Viceroy, and Lord Naas as Chief Secretary. On 16 July, the new Earl Kimberley held a well-attended farewell levee at Dublin Castle, though a small crowd hissed and jeered him later when he passed the old *Irish People* office. Next day, Kimberley left for England.

10

Chief Secretary Lord Naas and Conservative Government Policy in Ireland: July–December 1866

Two Irishmen headed the new Conservative administration in Ireland: Viceroy Lord Abercorn and Chief Secretary Lord Naas, the courtesy title of 44-year-old Richard Southwell Bourke.[1]

From an Anglo-Irish family whose roots stretched back to the Norman Conquest of England, Naas was raised on a Co. Meath estate by strongly evangelical parents who taught him the vital importance of religion in Irish life. At Trinity College Dublin, an academically mediocre Naas became better known as a charming socialite, but after graduating he immersed himself in Russian history, visited the country in 1845, and later wrote a book about it. During the Famine, Naas's Christian sense of *noblesse oblige* led him into relief work, popular gratitude for which clinched his election in August 1847 as Tory MP for Co. Kildare. Despite his relative political obscurity, Naas became Chief Secretary for Ireland in 1852 when the Tories returned to power. Only 30 years old, his appointment surprised even himself, but the prime minister, Lord Derby, lacked competition to fill the post. Although the government lasted only nine months, Naas seized his opportunity and became Derby's Chief Secretary again between February 1858 and June 1859. Accordingly, in July 1866, he was the natural choice for the post again when, for a third time, Derby became prime minister.

From the start, Naas and Abercorn avoided the rivalries that had bedev-illed Dublin Castle under their Liberal predecessors. Abercorn gladly conceded political supremacy to the Chief Secretary, surrendering both his Cabinet seat and the government's Irish policy. A lazy political lightweight, stiff and conceited, Abercorn was memorably described by a contemporary as an empty man who 'passed his life in doing nothing but taking care of his hair'.[2] Another observer considered him a nonentity who enjoyed the trappings of office, his Phoenix Park lodge, the flunkies, levees, Castle balls, banquets and Royal visits. Abercorn radiated a lofty disdain for lesser mor-tals and 'always bore himself with a haughty but reserved condescension', looking down on people as if they were dirt on his shoes. 'His lady was a true grande dame and ever comported herself as such.'[3] By contrast, Naas relished power, possessed great stamina and, as a politically experienced Irishman, had Derby's trust.

In opposition, Naas had pursued a bipartisan Irish policy, supporting the previous Corpus, though privately he regarded Wodehouse as an irreso-lute Viceroy who had emboldened Fenians, alarmed loyalists and allowed security to deteriorate. And when finally forced to act, he had resorted to heavy-handed repression that filled the jails, still left loyalists feeling insecure, and alienated large swathes of moderate nationalism. Naas wanted to break this cycle of vacillation and coercion by radically overhauling the intelligence system in Ireland, Britain and America, before launching a secret war against Fenianism in which spies and informers would infiltrate the IRB and unmask its leaders.[4] Pre-emptive strikes could then cripple the conspiracy long before it organised a rising. Moreover, by convict-ing defendants in the ordinary courts, Dublin Castle could abandon the panoply of repressive measures that had alienated moderate nationalists and tarnished British rule in Ireland. Furthermore, draining the poison from Irish political life would eliminate its recurrent sense of crisis, restore a long-forgotten sense of normality, and make Ireland in fact as well as law another part of the United Kingdom. And if Naas's innovative policy succeeded, the Tories might prosper in Ireland, expanding beyond its tra-ditional base and attracting support from Irish Catholics.

But officials from the previous regime resisted Naas, including Under-Secretary Larcom, DMP Assistant Commissioner Lake, Superintendent Ryan of G Division, Inspector-General Wood of the Irish Constabulary and Sir Hugh Rose. Yet far from ousting Larcom, Naas had the 65-year-old defer his longed-for retirement. The Viceroy had worked with the Under-Secretary during his previous time in Dublin Castle and trusted him. He also needed Larcom to lighten his own heavy workload; the Chief Secretary was constantly shuttling between Dublin Castle and London, attending Cabinet, supervising the Irish Office and speaking in parliament. Naas had no choice but to retain Rose, who became Lord Strathnairn in July 1866 and considered himself superior to the Chief Secretary; less a general, more a proconsul. Imperious, fond of his own voice, brusque and humourless, Strathnairn thought politicians were prone to panic – especially when public opinion became roused – and hastily demand reinforcements and troop deployments in disaffected areas. However, unlike a usually deferential Wodehouse, Naas was more inclined to raise questions, while 65-year-old Strathnairn felt a barely concealed disdain for the younger Naas, whom he regarded as an inexperienced politician who apparently took Fenianism much too seriously. But, being responsible for the entire British government apparatus in Ireland, Naas believed he had the final say: Strathnairn worked for him, not vice versa. However, enforcing his will would never be easy, because while Naas had Derby and Disraeli on his side, Strathnairn was backed by Secretary for War Jonathan Peel and Prince George, Duke of Cambridge, Queen Victoria's cousin and commander-in-chief of the Forces. Moreover, Strathnairn's glittering reputation with the British public made him a dangerous man to cross.

By making intelligence gathering the centrepiece of his Fenian policy, Naas had a Herculean task reforming a ramshackle system in which no secret service existed to collect information, and which lacked an intelligence department to analyse it. There were confidential reports from the Irish police and the British Minister in Washington, but Larcom kept them in a locked cupboard. And although Naas needed a better understanding of how Fenianism had rapidly become a serious threat to British rule in Ireland, no official account of the conspiracy existed – except perhaps inside Larcom's head, and he was not long for the world of government. On Larcom's recommendation, the Chief Secretary commissioned a history of Fenianism from Robert Anderson, a 25-year-old barrister from a loyalist Scots Presbyterian family long domiciled in Londonderry. Robert's father was Crown Solicitor and his brother Samuel Lee worked in Dublin Castle's law department. Robert had embraced the Andersons' ardent Ulster Unionism, loathed Irish nationalism and equated republicanism with barbarism, and he now stood ready to battle the forces of darkness. With great forensic skill and perhaps surprising restraint, Anderson synthesised police and diplomatic reports, official letters and memoranda, Home Office and Scotland Yard communications, magistrates' submissions and captured Fenian papers into a masterly narrative. His two-volume account greatly enlightened the Chief Secretary and remains indispensable to every historian of Fenianism.

Naas also improved the system of photographing Fenian prisoners and suspects, creating literally a better picture of their movement. Images of Fenians sentenced to penal servitude had long been routinely taken, but after the *Irish People* was suppressed in September 1865 this practice was extended to prisoners remanded on Fenian-related charges. Then, after Habeas Corpus was suspended in February 1866, Fenian internees were photographed and their personal details recorded. This information was used for surveillance, facilitating the identification of prison escapees and men on the run or those who gave false names. It also helped detect Fenians released from internment on a promise to leave for England or America, but who secretly returned to Ireland. In early December 1866, Naas claimed that Fenian photographs were widely disseminated.[5]

Naas began galvanising the intelligence system by demanding regular summaries from the police and Dublin Castle's law department, and a new sense of urgency led to a proliferation of reports during the second half of 1866. He also sent another two detectives to America, though they soon returned after gaining little information and losing track of Stephens when he vanished from public view in November 1866. A short time later, Inspector Doyle followed them home. In Britain, Fenians had been sending men, weapons and money to Ireland, while Irish communities in Liverpool, Manchester and Glasgow sheltered newly arrived Irish-American officers and suspects fleeing from Ireland after Habeas Corpus was suspended. Yet intelligence gathering was a black hole in Britain, whose authorities had never taken Fenianism seriously, especially in the absence of outrages there. Naas was also hampered in Britain by significant bureaucratic resistance and he had little political leverage to compel co-operation from politicians and police chiefs, many of whom believed Fenianism was an Irish problem, Naas's problem. Nor did Home Secretary Spencer Walpole energise provincial police forces in case they demanded financial assistance from central government and help from an already overstretched London Metropolitan Police. Furthermore, for many British politicians, civil servants and police chiefs, employing undercover detectives, police agents and informers to infiltrate a subversive organisation was redolent of continental tyranny, a phenomenon that always inflamed English public opinion. In any case, the small detective branches of most British police forces lacked sufficient resources for such work: only later was a British counterpart to G Division created.

On 15 August 1866, Inspector-General Wood told Naas that while Habeas Corpus suspension had set back Fenianism in Ireland, he feared it was growing in British cities like Liverpool, Manchester and Glasgow.[6] Wood wanted forty-six detectives from British police forces stationed in these three places to establish whether Fenian agents were promoting the conspiracy. Unsurprisingly, nothing happened, and Naas had to rely on the Irish police for intelligence about Fenianism in England. Sometimes G Division obtained information from Dublin informants, but it was hardly high-grade material. Irish Constabulary police officers stationed in Glasgow, Liverpool and Manchester also conducted surveillance on Irish communities and transatlantic liners on which Irish-American officers and Fenian emissaries travelled. In August 1866, there were only two such officers in Liverpool, one in Manchester and one in Glasgow, while Walpole prevented Dublin Castle locating one in London. Later in August 1866, the Home Secretary rejected Naas's offer of six detectives to investigate Fenianism in the first three cities. Walpole then partially relented and had two London detectives, Inspector Williamson and Sergeant Mulvany, investigate whether Fenianism in Liverpool posed a serious threat. However, Liverpool's Chief Constable Major John James Greig resented any encroachment on his bailiwick, and regarded the idea that Fenianism even existed in it as a slur on his professional ability. After a fortnight, no doubt closely monitored by Greig, Williamson decided that 'although the Fenian spirit exists in Liverpool there is no extensive organisation, and no drilling or meetings of Fenians in numbers takes place. For some months past the Fenian cause has been in a depressed state in this town.'[7] He could not have been more wrong. Within weeks, Mulvany returned to Liverpool after the arrest of four men for guarding a stockpile of rifles, bayonets and phosphorus that were almost certainly stolen from military bases or handed over by sympathetic soldiers. By late 1866, Liverpool was in fact the epicentre of English Fenianism, yet there Naas had met only obstruction from Greig and a cursory inquiry by Williamson. Within months this recalcitrance would almost cause a disaster.

Frustrated by the British police, Naas welcomed an unusual offer to enhance his intelligence capability in England from Lieutenant Colonel W.H.A. Feilding, an Assistant Adjutant General attached to the army's Dublin Division.[8] Throughout 1865 and 1866, Feilding controlled a network of soldier spies that had helped smash Fenianism within the British Army in Ireland. Feilding clearly relished his role as spymaster, but by mid-1866 his agents had become wasted assets, because the courts martial of Fenian soldiers were being wound up and his agents' identities had become known to the IRB. But rather than discharge them – and put himself out of a job – Feilding proposed that Naas use his men to infiltrate civilian Fenianism in England. The Chief Secretary accepted, because if Feilding's spies repeated their previous success in Ireland, they would inflict considerable damage on the conspiracy.

Among the agents transferred to England was Private Maher, who had already survived a Fenian assassination attempt in Dublin. Feilding claimed Maher was familiar with Fenian machinations, an intelligent and well-educated man with a great memory for faces and names.[9] Another spy, Patrick Foley, had been responsible for Devoy's arrest in February 1866; many years later, Devoy claimed a DMP Inspector Doyle had tipped him off about Foley's treachery. Feilding sent Foley and a soldier called Abrahams to London, where they insinuated themselves into the IRB. Plucked from their military and geographical comfort zone, Feilding's agents were out of their element – and depth. One did report that American Fenians were conducting 'business', and that at the end of October or early November 1866 Fenian parties from all over England would travel secretly to Ireland, ready when Stephens arrived in late December to create 'a great stir'. However, this 'information' was hardly intelligence gold: commonplace in Fenian ranks, it was more often than not rumour and speculation.

Foley and Abrahams quickly aroused Fenian suspicions. In early September 1866, another soldier spy inside the East London IRB learned that their descriptions had been sent from Ireland and they were to be assassinated. Hurriedly, Feilding ordered Foley to Liverpool, there to ingratiate himself with local Fenians. But on 17 September, after hearing nothing from Foley for a week, Feilding told Naas, 'I fear that Foley has fallen into the hands of the Fenians.'[10] In fact, Foley soon resurfaced, by which time Feilding regarded him as overly at risk and terminated his espionage career with an annuity and free passage for him and his family to any British colony. When London Fenians exposed the agent who had saved Foley and Abrahams, Feilding was forced to extract him as well. In a very short time Feilding's embryonic intelligence network had crumbled, and Naas's hopes of a breakthrough in England ended.

Despite this disappointment Naas wanted to make swift political progress in Ireland, and in August 1866 he decided to let the Habeas Corpus Suspension Act lapse, a highly symbolic act he hoped would impress nationalists. However, Larcom, Inspector General Wood, DMP and Assistant Commissioner Lake argued that only suspension six months earlier had averted catastrophe. Although the country now seemed peaceful, they believed suspension had only peeled away Fenianism's soft outer layer, leaving an unrepentant hard core – in and out of jail. Opening prison gates unconditionally was a gamble that might simultaneously rejuvenate the IRB and make Dublin Castle look weak, possibly causing another collapse in public morale. Moreover, if Stephens fulfilled his promise to return by New Year 1867, hundreds of newly released prisoners would readily join his rebellion.[11]

Loath to override their unanimous opinion, Naas reluctantly renewed the Suspension Act. Instead of a grand gesture, he continued releasing prisoners piecemeal, starting with detainees from outside Ireland provided they left immediately for England or America. Another 266 prisoners followed, and by December only 73 remained in custody. Naas also authorised only seven arrest warrants under the Suspension Act. Uneasy police chiefs complained it was 'as if the Habeas Corpus Suspension Act had expired and it had not been renewed' and that Fenians might believe Dublin Castle had let down its guard.[12] The police chiefs warned that Fenianism was reviving, as many released prisoners returned immediately to the conspiracy. The problem with Naas's new departure was that success – if it came at all – required time for his intelligence reforms to work, let alone change historic attitudes and reconcile Irish nationalists to British rule. But time was a luxury that Naas lacked. From 2,000 miles away, Stephens was controlling the political narrative in Ireland through speeches, newspaper headlines and an oft-repeated promise to rise by the end of 1866. Politicians, newspapers, the public and Fenians had all became fixated on New Year's Day 1867, and as it drew closer official and civilian anxiety rose ever higher. Naas had devised a long-term strategy but increasingly he was transfixed by the immediate danger of insurrection.

Police suspicions that Habeas Corpus suspension had not crushed the IRB were correct. Despite the arrest of three Dublin Centres in February 1866 and others fleeing to Britain, Fenianism in the capital proved remarkably resilient, and by April 1866 it had filled the gaps. This necessitated more police swoops in April and May that detained another half dozen centres, temporarily depriving Dublin Fenianism of its vitality as drilling and public house meetings ceased.[13] Superficially, normality had returned to the capital, but the IRB had simply been driven further underground, becoming more secretive than ever and even less vulnerable to police infiltration. Despite lacking specific information, Superintendent Ryan believed that Fenian psychology was unchanged: 'It would be a mistake to suppose that arrest and imprisonment has had a beneficial effect on the persons arrested, the greater portion of whom are now at liberty.'[14] Moreover, steady prisoner releases and Stephens's repeated promises of a rising had sustained IRB morale, inspiring Fenians to dig in and wait for the fight to begin.

During late 1866, Fenianism revived swiftly, especially in the south and west. Superintendent Ryan declared that paid agents and emissaries from England and America were in Dublin, while Inspector-General Wood said Fenians were smuggling weapons into Ireland and raising funds through raffles, bogus charity collections for 'distressed families', and extorting protection money from shopkeepers and businessmen. Public lectures on history and politics were being used as cover for disseminating Fenian propaganda.[15] As usual, though, reports of a burgeoning Fenian threat left Strathnairn supremely unimpressed. On 30 September, Rose, now ennobled as Lord Strathnairn, boasted that 'Fenianism is put down in this country', as Habeas Corpus suspension forced Irish-American officers out of Ireland and stopped drilling.[16] Yet in mid-October 1866, Naas still opposed troop reductions as Stephens had repeatedly promised a rising by New Year, declarations that 'had an extraordinary influence upon the conspirators at home', especially as more Irish-American officers were arriving in Ireland.

In fact, official disquiet had been growing for weeks. On 10 August, New York's British consul had declared that 'Stephens must support his despotic rule by action this year as he promised or sink. If he is determined upon an expedition from this country this year the time is near at hand when he must be looked for in Ireland.'[17] Although during September and October Inspector Doyle described American Fenianism as penniless and directionless, thereafter he became more pessimistic and, on 23 November, he said Stephens's supporters expected 'fighting, early and fierce', for which New York centres had created an arms fund.[18] Amidst a welter of rumours, an American informer claimed Fenian emissaries were already in Ireland purchasing horses for the Fenian cavalry. Supposedly, the rebellion would begin with 30,000 Fenians storming Dublin Castle, taking hostage the Viceroy, Chief Secretary and important state officials. But the necks of lower-ranking civil servants were literally on the line: those who resisted would be hanged. Rebels were to capture police and army barracks and seize their weapons, sabotage telegraph and railway lines throughout Ireland, but spare the Atlantic cable – presumably so that news of Ireland's liberation could reach America quickly.[19]

On 7 November, *The Times* revealed that Dublin Castle had put some army barracks in readiness for street fighting. Another infantry regiment had been stationed in Cork and more ships, gunboats, sailors and marines had joined the naval force on the western coast. The number of policemen had been increased and civil servants reminded of their oath of loyalty. Rumours abounded that Irish-American officers had left to fight in an imminent rising. Bogus American newspaper reports claimed that on 28 November a clean-shaven Stephens and a large military staff had sailed from New York. Dublin Castle recorded that: 'A state of alarm almost amounting to a panic proceeded from one end of the country to the other.'[20]

Pessimistic police and diplomatic reports darkened Dublin Castle's already sombre mood, and even Abercorn awakened from his political coma. On 15 November 1866, Naas tried reassuring the Viceroy that he had sufficient resources to defeat a rebellion; rather than reactivate the Habeas Corpus Suspension Act and make widespread arrests, intelligence-led operations would eventually produce results.[21] Moreover, Naas claimed that letting American Fenians arrive in Ireland would enable police to seize their papers and plans – an intelligence bonanza. But almost immediately, the Chief Secretary received more reports about rising public alarm. The Cabinet was also concerned, and on 19 November, Foreign Secretary Lord Stanley told Larcom, 'I have no doubt Stephens is coming. After all he had said he can't help himself.'[22] Naas probably did not appreciate the irony that demands for draconian action to reassure the civilian population, despite the security situation not warranting it, was the same dilemma facing Wodehouse only months earlier. Indeed, events beyond Naas's control were also driving him reluctantly towards repression and he authorised officials to draw up precautionary measures. On 21 November, Dublin Castle's Constabulary Office instructed county inspectors to submit lists of prominent suspects, but the result was overkill as police recommended over 1,000 arrests. The Chief Secretary told Derby that 80 per cent were 'cases of a slight suspicion' that he 'absolutely refused to entertain'.[23] Eventually, Naas and Attorney General Morris pruned the list to forty men they believed were Fenian ringleaders.

But the commander-in-chief dismissed precautionary measures as unnecessary, and during November and December he rejected most of Naas's numerous requests for troop deployments in disturbed areas. He was confident that England's vast military superiority, Fenian weakness and Stephens's cowardice meant that Ireland was completely pacified. 'Despite their worst intentions, the Fenians have not been able to do anything. They have not fired a cartridge or raised a pike against the troops. I always said the Fenians would not attempt a rising.'[24] Strathnairn also assured anxious loyalists that they had nothing to fear from restless natives: 'They have neither arms, artillery, or organisation and it is impossible to imagine and it is preposterous to imagine a set of short-sighted, deluded, half-civilised lower orders crawling out of their huts to attack the moral and military power of England unembarrassed by a difficulty or an enemy abroad.'[25]

For some time, Naas had resisted draconian action, but in late November and early December public alarm reached a crescendo throughout the South, whose Lord Lieutenants warned of an imminent rebellion. Lord Fermoy claimed Co. Cork was 'imperilled'. Customs officers were seizing weapons and an influx of Irish-American officers was threatening to become a flood. At Cork on 28 November, two transatlantic liners had disgorged over seventy young men dressed in the Yankee style, carrying hardly any luggage and offering only vague reasons for visiting Ireland. Meticulous searches found nothing incriminating, and after police released them, detectives could only watch as they boarded trains and headed inland. Fermoy wanted conspirators rounded up, a speedy military display in Cork and more naval patrols with Marines on the coast. Dublin Castle noted, 'The general terror was increasing and, in some districts, amounted to a panic.'[26] Naas felt overwhelmed: 'If we have the whole British Army at our disposal, it might be possible to carry out the wishes of the enormous numbers of persons who are writing every day to demand military protection.' But if the government acceded to every request, 'there would not be a single man left in Dublin, at the Curragh or Cork'.[27]

On 27 November, Superintendent Ryan claimed 30,000 Dublin Fenians were ready to rise at a moment's notice, and Dublin Castle noted that fears of an insurrection had triggered bank runs. The grand sum of £11,000 had poured out of one Drogheda savings bank in a single day, and £5,000 in gold left another bank in a small Munster town over a three-day period. On 29 November, Superintendant Ryan predicted: 'irregular warfare and indiscriminate massacre. The Fenians would rise simultaneously all over Ireland; and the docks and warehouses, arsenals and magazines in England will be destroyed by means of liquid fire.'[28]

During the last week of November, both Naas and Strathnairn were in London, though keeping their distance from each other. Strathnairn spent weeks at the War Office chairing an Army Transport Committee, while Naas attended parliament, supervised the Irish Office and successfully went over the commander-in-chief's head to convince Prime Minister Derby that three infantry regiments should be immediately deployed in disaffected parts of Ireland. During their absence the nerves of some Dublin Castle officials had snapped. They concluded that the long-feared rising was imminent – just when the administration's political and military leaders were simultaneously out of the country. Attorney-General Morris warned Naas that 'Larcom and Wood are exceedingly alarmed about the state of affairs – you would be surprised at the panic which has seized the public mind.'[29] Soon afterwards, Morris pleaded for his immediate return, 'as I think Larcom is getting nervous and we want a strong man at the helm'.[30]

On 23 November 1866, Strathnairn learned about official anxiety but was unimpressed. 'It is hard to believe that the Fenians would be so insane as to attempt an outbreak or that Stephens would face a contest.'[31] He was also furious to learn that, behind his back, Naas had secured three more regiments. Soon afterwards, Dublin Castle asked him to return. Strathnairn thought politicians and civil servants had once again lost their minds and he initially refused, especially as his prolonged absence in London was public knowledge and a sudden, unexpected return would create public alarm. He stayed on in London for a few more days and then relented, fabricating a cover story about collecting more information in Dublin for the Transport Committee.

On his return, Strathnairn learned that the Irish government had induced his second-in-command to put army patrols on the streets of

Dublin, a role he believed was for the police. After Naas had blindsided him in London, Strathnairn saw this as insubordination by both his deputy and Dublin Castle. Exasperated that jittery politicians and civil servants were badgering him, Strathnairn decided to make them pay attention. Declaring that he would not risk his soldiers against rebels using incendiaries, Strathnairn asked Naas for heavy artillery to blast insurgents out of churchyards, gardens, public buildings, private houses and town squares.[32] Naas was duly shocked and awed, and turned him down flat. Inflicting immense devastation on the second city of the British Empire would cause uproar in parliament and probably bring down the government. By now Naas himself was being bombarded from all directions – politicians, press, loyalists, Lord Lieutenants and magistrates, and apart from bland assurances he had so little ammunition to return fire. But a disillusioned population had heard all this before; the public crisis of confidence deepened and the clamour for action grew louder.

Deciding that government infighting had to stop, Naas tried to mollify Strathnairn with a lengthy memorandum explaining his Fenian policy and the frequent requests for troops.[33] In a bitterly divided nation, many alienated poor would join an insurrection if it enjoyed early military success, while almost the entire middle and upper classes, prosperous tradesmen and large farmers would side with the government. Naas's main priority was keeping both sides apart to prevent a shot being fired. If Fenians unlashed the dogs of war, he foresaw Ireland becoming a grim wasteland akin to a civil war. 'All the old animosities of creed and race' would be released, causing damage that would last a generation. To avoid this catastrophe, the government had to end a serious crisis of public confidence that was bankrupting businesses and driving farmers to sell off livestock, before fleeing their homes to safety in the towns or even England.

Naas argued that only a military presence could guarantee security throughout Ireland, because even a small body of redcoats in a neighbourhood reminded everyone about the futility of revolution, especially as British troops were now better armed and military posts easier to defend. The British Army in Ireland was more superior than ever to its enemies. Furthermore, loyalists deserved a military presence in their districts, and so did 12,000 policemen scattered across Ireland, isolated as they were in small groups inside hard-to-defend barracks. Concentrating them in fewer places would simply panic loyalists and embolden Fenians. Naas did not want troops stationed indiscriminately all over the country but more military posts in some areas. For the Chief Secretary, political necessity trumped everything, even military logic. Inundated daily with demands for army protection, Naas insisted that Strathnairn should militarily occupy the most disloyal parts of the country, simultaneously raising civilian and police morale while making disorder impossible.

Irish government unity became vital when events between Friday, 30 November, and Monday, 3 December 1866, meant Naas could delay no longer. On Friday, 30 November, the Privy Council proclaimed County Mayo, and next day the three promised infantry regiments arrived. Signs of jumpiness was everywhere. More troops and a six-gun artillery battery were stationed in Dublin Castle, on whose approaches palisades were erected. Every DMP station was issued with oil lamps in case Fenians severed the gas supply. On 2 December, in South Great Georges Street, Dublin, Superintendent Ryan and a posse of G Division detectives pounced on Mr Walsh, a Stephens lookalike, and lodged him in Mountjoy Gaol.

On 3 December 1866, General Peel and Prince George Duke of Cambridge, established a committee to consider imposing martial law in Ireland and Naas finally authorised arrests under the Habeas Corpus Suspension Act.[34] But unlike September 1865 and February 1866, G Division could not launch one dramatic round-up as the Fenians were more on guard. Instead, arrests of one, two or three suspects continued right up to Christmas. Initially the authorities feared Fenian retaliation. On 8 December, Inspector-General Wood warned Naas that 'serious mischief is intended. An outbreak appears to be inevitable if the strongest possible measures are not at once taken.'[35] On that day an unfounded rumour swept the west of Ireland that a pitched battle had occurred during the night at Kilmallock, Co. Limerick, between Fenians and the Irish Constabulary, leaving six policemen and four insurgents dead.

But gradually the tension waned, until just under 100 suspects were in custody, half of them detained in Dublin, including eleven centres who had replaced men caught in February. This was a thinning of the ranks that the IRB could not sustain indefinitely. According to one historian, 'Fenians were in essence, as a date for rebellion approached, in the impossible position of having to find a third generation of battalion commander.'[36] On 23 December, Naas told Derby that Larcom had viewed the recent danger as possibly greater than Wodehouse had faced in February, but the

Fenians were now in retreat.[37] After declaring there would never be a rising, Strathnairn basked in self-satisfaction: unlike wobbling politicians, he had kept his nerve. Furthermore, he could celebrate apparent victory by denigrating his foe, Stephens: 'I have always doubted his pluck and I believe he will never venture to try his luck again in Ireland.'[38] On Christmas Day he circulated a rumour that, 'Stephens having pocketed a large amount of the sinews of war has eloped with a lady to Paris, Mrs Stephens being left without money or a husband and in tears.'[39]

Mrs Jane Stephens and her husband James Stephens, head centre and provisional dictator of the Irish Republican Brotherhood.

Thomas Clarke Luby. Stephens's closest associate until his arrest in 1865.

Charles J. Kickham, the near-blind Fenian who was a talented writer, poet and journalist.

Left: John Devoy. Organised IRB
infiltration of the British Army in Ireland.

Right: Jeremiah O'Donovan Rossa.
The firebrand Fenian from Cork.

John O'Leary. Editor of the Irish People
and historian of the Fenian movement.

Edward Duffy. Fenian leader in
Connaught who backed out of the 1867
rising at the last moment.

John O'Mahony. The head centre in America of the Fenian Brotherhood and a long-time friend of Stephens, who became completely disillusioned with the IRB leader.

Thomas Kelly. The former confidant of Stephens who overthrew him, organised the Fenian rising in March 1867, and was later rescued from police custody in Manchester.

Gustave Paul Cluseret. The Frenchman who was appointed to lead the Fenian rising in Ireland but defected at the last moment.

Octave Fariola. The Belgian army officer whom Stephens recruited to help lead the Fenian rising.

Thomas McCafferty. The former confederate officer who led the raid on Chester in February 1867.

A print of Lord Wodehouse, later ennobled as Lord Kimberley. Liberal Viceroy of Ireland, 1864–66.

Sir Hugh Rose, later ennobled as Lord Strathnairn. Commander-in-chief of the British Army in Ireland, 1865–70.

Lord Naas, later ennobled as Lord Mayo.
Conservative Chief Secretary of Ireland, 1866–68.

Depiction of the rescue of Kelly and Deasy in Manchester on 18 September 1867.

Depiction of Fenian prisoners being marched after the
rising from the lower castle yard to Mountjoy Prison.

The Cuba Five after their release from Chatham Prison and exile to America.

11

Stephens in America:
May 1866–January 1867

Stephens intended his American mission to heal a Fenian Brotherhood schism that had only deepened during the winter of 1865–66. On 2 January 1866 in New York, a Fenian Brotherhood convention readopted the 1863 constitution, appointed O'Mahony Head Centre once again, abolished the Senate, expelled Roberts and ten other senators and rejected their Canadian strategy. Afterwards, more Irish-American officers sailed for Ireland. On the convention's last day, Captain O'Brien returned from Ireland with letters from Stephens that denounced Roberts and appointed O'Mahony as the IRB's American representative. O'Mahony's shrunken political base and his diminished stature meant he was once more subordinate to the IRB leader. O'Mahony recalled: 'I was, in fact, but the agent of James Stephens on this continent, and my sole business was to act as his Commissary General and to furnish him with more material and men.'[1]

Soon afterwards, the Senate wing held its own convention in Pittsburgh, Pennsylvania, and General Sweeny presented a Canadian invasion plan that appealed to many wavering Fenians. O'Mahony then received complaints about his delay in commencing hostilities against England, and within weeks he pre-empted the Senate wing by authorising the seizure of Campo Bello, an island near the Maine–New Brunswick border that both Canada and the United States claimed. O'Mahony believed that capturing Campo Bello would be a limited, inexpensive operation, whereas the Senate wing planned a full-scale and probably doomed invasion of Canada. Furthermore, a military victory would also shore up his political authority before Stephens arrived in New York. Accordingly, several hundred unarmed Fenians in civilian clothing began assembling at Eastport, Maine, but the operation took much longer than Killian had anticipated, and only on 17 April did a Fenian ship arrive with arms and ammunition. Two days later it was all over without a shot fired, when the American government suddenly sent troops into Eastport and seized the weapons – a fiasco that largely curtailed the sale of republican bonds and discredited O'Mahony as well. Changing course, he now tried to reunite the Fenian Brotherhood and, through Col. Halpin, put out peace feelers to Roberts. However, with his enemy on the ropes and scenting complete victory, Roberts rejected O'Mahony's overtures.

On 10 May, Stephens reached New York, where enthusiastic Fenians escorted his carriage to Manhattan's Metropolitan Hotel. Next day, he castigated O'Mahony for the Campo Bello debacle. Accepting the inevitable, O'Mahony resigned his leadership in favour of Stephens, who appointed Thomas Kelly as his deputy. Stephens now set about reconciling the Fenian Brotherhood's warring factions, a diplomatic endeavour that would have tested Talleyrand himself. But Stephens mistakenly assumed his mere presence on American soil would suffice and that Roberts would bend to his will. However, the Senate leader's meteoric rise and his prickly personality should have forewarned Stephens that he was a heavyweight who required tactful handling. Instead, Stephens forgot that he came burdened with considerable political baggage, having only months earlier tried to destroy Roberts. The Senate leader must have regarded him as the last person to act as an honest broker. But rather than carefully prepare the ground for mediation, Stephens effectively summoned Roberts to the Metropolitan and escorted him immediately to a conference room, where he saw O'Mahony relaxing at a window, casually puffing on a cigar. Furious at being blindsided, Roberts turned and strode away, swearing never again to enter his rival's presence. New York's British consul, D. Thomas, was having Stephens shadowed and reported that his arrogance was alienating people: 'The friends of Stephens are getting quite disgusted at his arbitrary, egotistical and tyrannical conduct and are falling from him like snow from a ditch.'[2] Dublin Castle was delighted at the political damage Stephens's behaviour was causing in America: 'His idea of unity seemed to be the subservience of all to himself.' Just when Stephens needed to focus entirely on Ireland and the Irish situation, he became mired in the schism that had torn American Fenianism apart. Soon the Senate wing began smearing him as a British spy. Moreover, Stephens was singularly ill-equipped to replace O'Mahony as Fenian Brotherhood leader. In Ireland he led an illegal secret society, lived in the shadows, avoided public addresses and rarely met the IRB rank and file. Whereas in America, the Fenian Brotherhood was an open and legal organisation that organised rallies whose crowds expected from their leader charisma and inspiring oratory. Stephens, though, was no rabble-rouser, but rather a mediocre speaker who lacked eloquence, passion and dramatic flair. Now, relatively late in life, he was thrust reluctantly onto the public stage in front of audiences that eagerly awaited an almost mythical leader.

Stephens was on the boards as early as 15 May, trying to boost Fenian morale and raise funds. He began a speaking tour of New England with a rally at Jones's Wood in New York, but his turgid lectures disappointed spectators craving the old-time religion about smashing the British Empire and liberating Ireland from the Saxon foe. Their muted response compelled Stephens to fire up his rhetoric by promising that 'the day for which we have yearned and toiled through many years is imminent and inevitable. The men at home have resolved to fight this year and fight they will.' Stephens claimed he had 200,000 fighting men in Ireland, 50,000 of them drilled and ready for action at a moment's notice.

However, Roberts's Senate wing still shunned Stephens, and it finally invaded Canada. On 1 June, Brigadier General John O'Neill led a ragtag army of 1,500 Fenians across the Niagara River, but after an initial victory at the town of Ridgeway, heavy British reinforcements drove them back into the United States. After this debacle, Stephens ratcheted up pressure on the Senate wing. During another speaking tour in July and August he called Roberts a traitor, and urged his disillusioned supporters to defect to himself. On 10 July in Boston, Stephens boasted that by year's end he would be in Ireland, there to triumph or die, a pledge he constantly repeated. But this only exposed a fatal contradiction between Stephens's leadership in America and Ireland, because by publicly promising a rising no later than 1 January 1867, he had forewarned Dublin Castle and given it ample time to organise countermeasures. Although thousands of miles separated Ireland from America, Stephens might as well have tipped off G Division himself, especially as Irish newspapers dutifully recycled his American speeches. Furthermore, D. Thomas perceptively recognised that Stephens's fiery oratory and his commitment to an early revolution left him no line of retreat: 'Stephens must support his despotic rule by action this year as he promised or sink. If he is determined upon an expedition from this country this year the time is near at home when he should be looked for in Ireland.'[3]

To prove his seriousness about a rising, Stephens began recruiting professional military officers. The first, 43-year-old Frenchman Gustave Paul Cluseret, was a turbulent character, said always to be in search of a revolution.[4] After serving in the French Army during the Crimean War, he had been rapidly promoted to brigadier general. Increasingly liberal, republican and anti-clerical, Cluseret had also acquired a reputation for shiftiness and treachery, nicknamed 'Captain Tin Can' after he confiscated his soldiers' meat and bread rations. Then he resigned suddenly after military stores went missing. Later, Cluseret managed an Algerian estate until an entire flock of sheep mysteriously disappeared. In 1860 he fought with Garibaldi's Sicilian Expedition in Italy, before joining the Union Army when the American Civil War commenced. Although motivated partly by a hatred of slavery, Cluseret's tyrannical behaviour and rudimentary English alienated his officers, and in May 1863 he relinquished his command. Cash-strapped and desperate, Cluseret was rescued by his friend Claude Pelletier, a French socialist, political refugee and wealthy manufacturer prominent in New York's French community. Pelletier appointed Cluseret as editor of a political journal.

Thomas Kelly also knew Pelletier and introduced him to Stephens as a potential political patron. When Pelletier showed Cluseret a photograph of Stephens he disliked his 'little, furtive, blinking eyes', but after meeting him, Cluseret concluded he was a clever politician and born organiser, though vain and overbearing as well. Stephens boasted of many thousands of followers in Ireland and a huge arsenal of arms and ammunition, which Cluseret suspected existed in his imagination. Nevertheless, in a chequered life of endless reinvention, Cluseret always identified with subject peoples struggling to overthrow foreign domination, and so he embraced the Irish cause. Moreover, humdrum civilian life irked Cluseret, who missed the exhilaration of battle, and he leapt at Stephens's offer to command the Fenian army. Stephens predicted that for the first ninety days of a rising, rebels would face only 30,000 British soldiers and that 10,000 Fenians could seize every major port, road and railway in Ireland. As popular support grew, he claimed rebel forces would overwhelm the enemy before reinforcements arrived. On that basis Cluseret drafted a plan of campaign.

Beginning in New York on 21 August, Cluseret joined Stephens at Fenian rallies in cities like Cleveland, Ohio and St Louis. He said that although Stephens was neither a writer or an orator, his message clearly resonated and that 'the enthusiasm of the people was kept at a white heat'. This was especially true as spectators imbibed rivers of firewater. 'The amount of whiskey that was drunk is inconceivable. What fortunes in liquor then disappeared into the stomachs of Irish men.'[5] On 28 October, Stephens's tour ended with a monster rally at Jones's Wood, a resort on Manhattan Island that was popular with working-class New Yorkers. Fenians had pulled out all the stops for Stephens, advertising the event as a last chance to see him before he left for his date with destiny. The result was one of the greatest political gatherings in New York history. From seven o'clock on a pleasant morning, men, women and children disembarked from excursion steamers, travelled by horse-car or walked to Jones's Wood, choking the avenues leading to its entrance gates. Inside, 50,000 exuberant spectators crowded hills and platforms that overlooked the East River and the lawns surrounding the Jones's Wood Hotel.

At 2 p.m. Stephens finally appeared, to a deafening welcome. In a dark suit, blue overcoat and a broad-brimmed velvet hat, he and prominent Fenians had spent an hour inside the hotel before Stephens proceeded to a grandstand, smiling and waving as he strode through parting crowds. A journalist for the *New York Herald* reported an excited atmosphere:

> From one hillside to the other and beyond was one swelling, swarming mass of faces, crowded almost to suffocation. When their bonnets were crushed in the jam the women tore them off and catching them by the strings, whirled them in the air, shouting and cheering like the rest.[6]

When he began speaking, Stephens initially struggled to make himself heard over cheering, a continuous buzz of conversation, some shouting and – surprisingly – occasional heckling. Exasperated, he seemed at times about to give up. Once, when the crowd surged forward, Stephens berated stewards. But he kept going, and more than once Stephens gave his audience the call to arms for which it longed. Asserting that 50,000 trained men in

Ireland awaited the final battle for freedom, Stephens cried that 'within the next two months will be determined the great question of Irish independence. We mean what we say. We shall be fighting on Irish soil before the first of January and I shall be there by the side of my countrymen.'

Jones's Wood was the triumphant pinnacle of Stephens's career, but it also foreshadowed his rapid downfall. Before tens of thousands of people, he had given cast-iron commitments and utterly committed himself to a rising, raising Fenian expectations to great heights and making retreat unimaginable. After years of equivocation, Stephens had finally run of road; reneging now would unleash a tidal wave of anger that would likely sweep him into political oblivion.

Afterwards, Stephens recuperated at the Metropolitan Hotel, where Cluseret introduced an old Union Army friend, 27-year-old Octave Fariola.[7] Another soldier of fortune peddling fanciful tales about himself, Fariola posed as a Swiss citizen and the nephew of a Roman Catholic bishop. In fact, he was from the Belgian city of Liege, the son of an army paymaster and a graduate of Brussel's Royal Military Academy. After serving as a cavalry regiment lieutenant, Fariola brought his family to America, where as a liberal, anti-slavery republican he fought with the Union Army in the Civil War. Masquerading as a European aristocrat, he was promoted to lieutenant colonel, though a lofty, condescending manner alienated his troops. Later, Fariola farmed in Louisiana until August 1866, when a letter from Cluseret invited him to become Chief of Staff in a Fenian revolutionary army. Excited at the prospect of war, Fariola left behind his family and business in early November 1866 and went to New York, where Cluseret assured him that the Fenian leader Stephens was a political titan 'of large brain and prodigious ability, honest and disinterested, possessing mighty influence in Ireland and America'.[8]

When Fariola visited the Metropolitan Hotel, a week after Jones's Wood, Stephens was in bed. Fariola later regretted not obeying his first instinct and heading straight back to Louisiana, but Stephens was a masterly storyteller and his tales gradually won Fariola over, promising that together they would create an independent, democratic Irish Republic. Furthermore, he claimed 200,000 well-armed followers in Ireland, and a large expeditionary force of Irish-American officers ready to embark in steamers that would eventually scour the Atlantic and use torpedoes to sink British merchantmen. Stephens also expounded at length about the support he enjoyed from Irish peasants, Irish-America, European newspapers and thousands of Fenian soldiers in the British Army. Fariola recalled that:

> The whole of the statement was so extraordinary that I came to the conclusion that if he was not telling the truth he must be a fool or a scoundrel of the worst character and as his sanity appeared above doubt and his honesty was vouched for by Kelly, I could not do otherwise than believe him.[9]

In fact, Stephens's boasts were mostly gross exaggerations and, in some cases, outright fantasy. There were no torpedoes and the only Fenian steamer lay idle in Brooklyn Harbour while Kelly tried selling it to raise desperately needed funds. Still, reassured, Fariola accepted the post of Chief of Staff.

On Fariola's advice, Cluseret also recruited 40-year-old Victor Vifquain, whom he had known in Belgium and also America, where Vifquain had served in the Illinois State Militia. After the Civil War – in which he was awarded the Congressional Medal of Honor for bravery – Vifquain became a prosperous farmer in Nebraska, but after Fariola wrote to him Vifquain agreed to serve.

Fariola, though, still had unanswered questions, especially about why Stephens appointed Cluseret and him rather than well-qualified Irish-American Civil War veterans. His supposition was that Stephens needed them to attract professional European officers, but he later suspected they were being used as window dressing to allay the doubts of prominent Fenians about his own military ability. But at the time, the idea that the IRB leader had created an impressive façade behind which lay nothing seemed too fantastic for Fariola to contemplate.

Fariola envisaged a rising evolving gradually as rebels gained in confidence and a provisional government established a base in which to prepare an army for regular warfare. Galway, Sligo and Limerick would be occupied, with the latter serving as the rebel capital. In the countryside, insurgents were to sever railway and telegraph lines and attack smaller police barracks, while weapons would be sent to the east in order to deceive the British that Dublin was their principal target. The IRB in England was to stand ready to retaliate with dynamite if captured insurgents in Ireland were not treated as prisoners of war. Fariola was given to understand that docks and important buildings, like the *Times* newspaper in London, would be incinerated. As the provisional government began functioning, British troops would exhaust themselves hunting small bands of guerrillas everywhere and become vulnerable to counter-attack. Then, regular warfare could begin.

However, Fariola was stunned when Cluseret told him that Stephens intended to pass over the first phase, land in Ireland with an expeditionary force, immediately surround Dublin Castle with 30,000 armed men and compel the Irish government to surrender unconditionally. Fariola regarded Stephens's strategy as absurd and was puzzled that Cluseret had accepted command of a Fenian army without a guarantee that it could definitely be created. But Cluseret was not prepared to question the leader's judgement, and Stephens slapped Fariola down: 'Mr Stephens gave me to understand that he was alone to judge and to know whether he could give us the army we wanted and that, he repeated, he would do to a certainty and before New Year's Day.' In view of Stephens's absolute self-assurance, Fariola let the matter drop. 'I could not for a moment take Mr Stephens for a mad man neither could I for a moment think that he was deceiving us.'[10] Fariola thought that Stephens must have sensitive information that he could not share with anyone, but he never ascertained the reason.

Tensions over military strategy strained relations between Stephens, Cluseret and Fariola, three men with inflated egos and a tenuous connection to truth. Cluseret patronised Fariola as a gallant officer flawed by 'insatiable ambition'; Stephens was a smooth raconteur but 'as regards action he was worth nothing'. Fariola regarded Cluseret as a brave soldier who vastly overestimated his political ability and yet shrank from challenging Stephens. Stephens was an organising genius, but his arrogance made him resent criticism. Moreover, he surrounded himself with men of inferior ability who would never become rivals. Militarily, Fariola dismissed Stephens as 'worse than incompetent' and felt his vanity was his Achilles heel: 'He is satisfied that he excels all military men in the art of war, as he excels all political economists in the art of governing society, and all conspirators in that of conspiring.'[11] Stephens disliked Fariola for questioning his military ability and Cluseret for grumbling about poor remuneration. These personality clashes reflected a wider unease at Fenian headquarters about Stephens's lethargic preparations for a rising, a lacklustre demeanour that hardly represented a commander galvanising himself for the greatest challenge of his life. Cluseret recalled that:

Stephens began to blow cold as he had hitherto blown hot. So long as it was a matter of going onwards, the American-Irish were tolerably obedient to the despotic requirements of their Head Centre; but the moment they imagined they saw symptoms of coldness in him, and as month succeeded month and the end of the year approached and yet no announcement had been made of the campaign, they became indignant and enraged.[12]

Possibly responding to such murmurings, Stephens suddenly quit the Metropolitan Hotel in mid-November 1866 and shifted to a slightly less expensive apartment on 13th Street, telling only trusted subordinates about the new location and posting guards in surrounding streets.

Stephens's promise to rise by 1 January 1867 left Fariola only six weeks to design a structure for the Fenian army, draw up military regulations, study Ireland's topography and scrutinise British forces in Ireland. Moreover, soon after Fariola became chief of staff, Stephens ordered him to France, where he was to recruit foreign officers and prepare them to leave for Ireland after Christmas 1866. Just before departing America in mid-November, Fariola visited Fenian HQ to collect his travel funds and final instructions, but he was kept waiting all day while Stephens conducted minor business. Finally, Cluseret and Col. Kelly appeared with a bag of gold for Fariola's expenses, only for Stephens to snatch it away, claiming that Fariola would lose commission on the gold in Paris. Instead, a Fenian agent in the French capital would pay him directly. Fariola acquiesced, even when Stephens handed him just enough money for his boat ticket and £7 subsistence allowance. Stephens did invite Fariola to dinner, but only Cluseret bade Fariola farewell when his ship embarked. Still, Fariola's departure must have convinced Stephens's closest associates that this time there really was no turning back.

No longer able to temporise, Stephens now steeled himself to make crucial decisions that would decide his fate and that of the Fenian revolution. Months earlier, when he had promised to rise, New Year must have seemed far distant, and probably Stephens had anticipated something turning up to extricate himself from his seemingly unbreakable commitment. Possibly, England would become embroiled in a prolonged foreign war. However, the European conflict that actually occurred between Austria and Prussia lasted just seven weeks in June and July 1866. Furthermore, despite his Jones's Wood success, Stephens's American mission had not been a financial success. During seven months he had raised only $57,000 and allocated just $22,000 to revolutionary activity at a time when heavy expenditure was draining the Fenian treasury of funds for arms and ammunition. Moreover, Fenian prisoners in Canada needed money for their legal defence, while emissaries travelling constantly between America and Ireland had to cover their expenses. Yet Stephens himself was part of the problem. Accustomed now to the finer things in life, he lived for months on end at the Metropolitan Hotel in sumptuous quarters, all the while attired in smart suits, fine shirts and expensive shoes.

By mid-November 1866, as time ran out, Stephens finally decided that the rebellion – for which the Fenians were completely unprepared – must not happen. However, as a sudden *volte face* risked his downfall, Stephens was finally compelled to tell his inner circle about the dire situation and hopefully persuade it to delay the rising. Stephens might then just be able to contain the shock waves he would send coursing through the Fenian movement.

To succeed, Stephens needed Kelly as his human shield, someone who could swing fellow radicals behind postponement. But this necessitated Stephens coming clean with Kelly and convincing him that a rising would end in calamitous failure. Stephens could then plausibly argue that he had to accept the military advice of Civil War veterans. Even better, if it was Kelly who first publicly favoured delay, then he might become the scapegoat for delivering bad news. To allow Kelly time and space to absorb the bad news, Stephens gave him the books and immediately departed New York for a tour of major cities, ostensibly to meet local Fenian leaders and donors. Stephens left Kelly in absolute control of affairs – an extraordinary if temporary relinquishing of power on the part of Stephens.

During a four-week absence, Stephens claimed that fragile health confined him mostly to hotel bedrooms, where visitors found a man apparently not long for this world. In fact, despite his frequent intimations of mortality, Stephens managed to survive for another thirty-five years. But although he exaggerated his plight, Stephens was certainly stressed and acting strangely. Bizarrely, after the Fenian officer Col. Godfrey Massey arranged for him to meet President Andrew Johnson, Stephens refused to enter the White House as they were late. Disgusted, Massey walked away. In darkened hotel rooms, Stephens passed day after long day in a state of suspended animation, all the time hoping that once again Kelly would rescue him. At times Stephens must have contemplated skipping out on America, just as he had silently left Ireland seven months earlier. But to where and what end? Returning to Ireland meant either renewed hiding, possible capture and execution, or launching a doomed rising. Self-imposed exile in France would incur disgrace and political oblivion. But going back to New York involved confronting angry men packing revolvers; postponing the rebellion might literally be for Stephens a matter of life and death.

On 14 December 1866, Stephens arrived back in New York, but any hope that Kelly would save him was soon confounded. Time and again Kelly had indeed stood by Stephens, who misinterpreted this as proof of unconditional fidelity when actually Kelly's highest loyalty was to the Fenian revolution. Kelly had consistently supported Stephens as the person best equipped to deliver it, but should Stephens betray his trust, Kelly would abandon him in a heartbeat. Now, like an auditor examining the company accounts, Kelly had concluded that for years his boss had fiddled the books, deceiving everyone through sleight of hand, vainglorious boasts and bogus promises. For Kelly such irresponsibility was a damning indictment of Stephens's eight-year leadership, and probably he regretted not letting him rot in prison. Far from delaying the rising, Kelly now believed Stephens must be deposed so it could go ahead.

On 15 December, Stephens met Kelly and other Fenian leaders.[13] Disingenuously, he expressed surprise when Kelly revealed that preparations for an insurrection were in a desperate state: 'I found that matters were even worse than my apprehension – we had nothing like what I promised and expected, and the little we had we could not forward.'[14] But others were outraged when Stephens revealed he had accumulated only 4,000 weapons, a seventh of the minimum necessary, and finally admitted that he could not fulfil his oft-repeated pledge of a rising. After requesting yet another postponement, Stephens said he was honour bound to be in Ireland by 1 January 1867, and offered to leave on the next boat – even though he expected to be captured and executed. Everyone turned him down and the meeting broke up without a decision on postponement. Next evening, Stephens met Fenian army officers and asked them to accompany him to Ireland, though they would only reinforce Irish-American officers already there. Initially a majority gave Stephens the benefit of the doubt, but when some officers wavered, the mood became tense. Suddenly, Kelly's verbal onslaught turned the tide. Stephens recalled being accused of defeatism, abandoning the cause 'in despair or through cowardice shrank from struggle; frightened by the powers I had created'.[15]

Stephens characterised Kelly's behaviour as the 'mad and criminal action' of 'a far more treacherous or insane man than I wish to believe'.[16] Stephens identified a plot to replace him with Kelly, and he was not wrong – though blind as ever to his own faults, he simply could not see that they had every reason to cast him aside, and probably regretted not doing so long before. For almost a fortnight Stephens struggled to reach an accommodation with his enemies. But Kelly kept his distance while he mobilised General William Halpin, Colonel Thomas F. Burke, Captain Thomas McCafferty and Colonel Godfrey Massey for a final showdown. Unlike Stephens, they lived by a military code of honour in which promises made were promises kept, and retreat was unimaginable. Otherwise, history's verdict on them would be damning. Now, their strategy was to commence an insurrection and hope that the Irish people would turn it into a full-blown revolution. This was indeed a leap in the dark, but Kelly and his fellow radicals were gamblers whose best hope now was that against all odds they would land on their feet.

On either 31 December 1866 or 1 January 1867, in West Eleventh Street, Stephens and Kelly met again for the last time at a conference of Fenian army officers. The tension was electric as everyone present realised that Stephens was no longer the peerless leader they had for years followed blindly. Men whom, Stephens recalled, had once been 'my most obsequious admirers',[17] now hated the very sight of him. Finally, Stephens instigated a rebellion, just not the one he had for so long promised. Accusing Stephens of treason, McCafferty drew his pistol to literally give it to him with both barrels, before Kelly physically intervened and saved Stephens's life – though only to prevent the public relations disaster of a leader's assassination. Finally, the co-ordinated attack pummelled – or frightened – Stephens into submission. Isolated, vulnerable and with some men acting as if Kelly had already ousted him, Stephens relinquished control of the Fenian Brotherhood.

Stephens claimed that in a show of public unity, Kelly let him retain the title of COIR (Chief Organiser of the Irish Republic) responsible for civil affairs while Kelly readied Fenianism for a rising. But the Rubicon had been crossed. Stephens said they parted in anger and any pretence of harmony soon vanished. On 7 January 1867, Kelly addressed a Fenian rally in New York and delivered the coup de grace, telling an astounded audience that Stephens had been unmasked as a common thief. Just in time, Kelly himself had prevented Stephens looting the Fenian treasury and fritter-ing away their hard-earned money in the fleshpots of Paris. After Kelly scorned Stephens as literally a coward, the entire audience instantaneously endorsed Kelly's deposition of their former hero and Brigadier General Gleeson replaced Stephens as COIR, Head of the Fenian Brotherhood in America. As news of Stephens's overthrow spread, Roberts's faction glee-fully claimed he had intended spending his plunder on fast horses and faster women. In one day, Stephens had suffered a mighty fall. At daybreak on 7 January 1867, he was still, publicly, leader of Fenianism in America and Ireland; by nightfall Stephens stood vanquished and alone, the prelude to decades of disgrace, exile and obscurity.

Stephens recalled that he was to join Kelly's party when they embarked for France on Saturday, 12 January 1867, but that 'the boat sailed two hours sooner than I thought and I was left behind'.[18] Certainly, it was a convenient misunderstanding. Stripped of all moral authority, Stephens would have suffered excruciating embarrassment in the company of men who now loathed him; possibly he was also petrified at the thought of ending up 'lost at sea'. For their part, his former subordinates become deadly enemies who regarded Stephens's absence as a perfect metaphor for his career as Fenian leader: time and again he had missed the boat. Not that his fate concerned them much. In their eyes Stephens was already history, a bad but rapidly fading memory.

During January 1867 the political mood in Ireland changed dramatically, as an all-pervasive tension rapidly faded. A.M. Sullivan recalled that:

Then indeed the British Government stood to arms. Then indeed did alarm once more paralyse all minds. It seemed as if the worst reality would be less painful than this prolonged uncertainty and recurring panic. War steamers cruised around the island. Every harbour and landing place was watched. Every fishing-boat was searched. Every passenger was scrutinised. Each morning people scanned the papers eagerly to learn if the Rebel Chief had yet been discovered. As the last week of 1866 approached the public apprehension became almost unbearable. Until the great clock of the General Post Office had chimed midnight on the 31st of December and Christ Church bells rang in the New Year the belief that an explosion was at hand could not be shaken.[19]

When no rising materialised, Loyalist relief quickly became ridicule. 'A general chorus of felicitation was raised in the press over this really final disappearance of the Fenian spectre.'[20]

For their part, Fenians were dismayed at Stephens reneging on his promised rebellion and humiliated at the scorn heaped upon them. Sullivan declared that: 'The shouts of derision which arose over this Stephens fiasco cut like daggers to the hearts of the men in Ireland and America who clung with invincible tenacity to the fatal purpose of an armed struggle.'[21] However, both sides knew nothing about Stephens's recent deposition. Remarkably, British intelligence on the conspiracy during December 1866 and January 1867 was almost non-existent. Dublin Castle considered G Division reports singularly wanting, while in late December an important informer in Liverpool, John Corydon, had blemished his credibility by mistakenly claiming that Stephens and many Irish-American officers had left New York for Ireland. Corydon then fell off the grid completely, losing contact with his police handlers entirely during January 1867. This intelligence vacuum misled the British government into believing that Fenianism was on the wane, unaware – like IRB centres in Ireland – that in Kelly it had a new leader whom Larcom soon perceived as reckless and determined as Stephens was vacillating and timid. On 17 January 1867, the DMP and Irish Constabulary claimed a rising was imminent and that 100 Fenians from England had arrived in Dublin to fight.[22] Indeed, Kelly rapidly accelerated military preparations for a rising. When acting for Stephens in November and December 1866, he had familiarised himself with Cluseret and Fariola's war plans, as well as membership returns that Fenian couriers brought from Ireland. Now, at Fenian headquarters in New York, Kelly began preparing an insurrection by establishing a military planning group of eighteen officers that included Halpin, Burke, McCafferty and Massey.

Fenians considered 26-year-old McCafferty a legendary figure, though possibly he had manufactured the legend himself. McCafferty claimed to have fought heroically during the American Civil War with Morgan's Raiders, Confederate cavalry raiders who terrorised Kentucky, Indiana and Ohio. Afterwards, McCafferty became a paid Fenian organiser in Detroit, Michigan, where he impressed O'Mahony, Stephens and Kelly. Tall, muscular, bronzed with grey eyes and jet-black hair flowing over the shoulders, McCafferty was undoubtedly a charismatic figure. His forceful, laconic manner, low voice and an aura of deadly seriousness intimidated everyone, including Devoy, who called him 'the most desperate man in the movement who never made idle threats, essentially a man of action, very chary of words and his manner was cold'.[23] Convinced of his destiny and with an impressive military reputation, McCafferty habitually bent other men to his will.

Godfrey Massey was actually Patrick Condon. Born in Limerick, the illegitimate son of Protestant William Massey and Catholic Mary Condon, he had served with the British Army in the Crimean War. Migrating to America in 1856, Massey fought for the Confederacy during the Civil War and was promoted to colonel. Afterwards, Massey worked for a New Orleans commercial house and became a Fenian, displaying in both capacities his considerable organising ability. In October 1866, Massey shifted to New York and worked at Fenian headquarters, cultivating first O'Mahony and later Stephens. Some people regarded Massey as a shady character, but most found him plausible. When a New Orleans Fenian warned Stephens about Massey's sudden appearance in the city out of nowhere and lying about his military record, he refused to investigate further.[24] Kelly was similarly credulous: Massey, after all, had sided with him against Stephens.

After reassuring the IRB that a rising had only been delayed, Kelly funnelled officers to Ireland and Britain. McCafferty was dispatched to London, and on 11 January 1867, Massey sailed from New York with orders from Kelly to inform American officers in which Irish district they would fight during the rebellion. To avoid incriminating written evidence, Massey memorised names, places and dates. Kelly also gave him £500 in gold to distribute among IRB leaders. On 28 January 1867, Massey reached Liverpool and met its Fenian leaders, two Irish-American officers called Austin Gibbons and Michael O'Rorke. Next day, he travelled to London.[25]

Meanwhile, Fariola had been in Paris since early December 1866. Almost penniless, he pawned a watch and borrowed money from his wife's family. Isolated from Fenian affairs, Fariola went on preparing for a rising and recruited European officers. However, on 20 January 1867 – when he assumed that Stephens, Kelly and Cluseret had left America – he learned about a schism among Irish-American officers in London, some of whom knew he was in Paris and requested his mediation. This was an unfamiliar role for Fariola, who usually started arguments, but such discord imperilled the rebellion and so he set off to heal the rift. Fenianism in England now moved centre stage.

Fenianism in England and the Descent on Chester: January–February 1867

For centuries, Irish traders, travellers and seasonal farmworkers had travelled to Britain, but during the early nineteenth century the scale and pace of settled migration increased rapidly as booming factories attracted cheap, unskilled labour from Ireland.[1] By 1841, 419,000 Irish men and women lived in Britain, an influx that accelerated after the Famine when 2.1 million people left Ireland in a decade. Most migrated to America, but about 200,000 settled permanently in Britain, which by 1861 had 806,000 ethnic Irish, mostly young and living in the industrial towns of South Wales, the Midlands, south Lancashire, North-East England and Scotland. The four largest concentrations were in Glasgow, London, Liverpool and Manchester, although Edinburgh, Dundee, Leeds and Birmingham were also heavily settled. Religious discrimination, poverty, poor housing, bad health and a high death rate intensified many Irish migrants' sense of alienation, and Fenianism appealed especially to a younger generation, who wanted vengeance for a homeland many had never seen.

By the 1860s the epicentre of Fenianism in Britain was Liverpool, a booming metropolis situated on the eastern bank of the River Mersey.[2] Over a fifth of its 443,000 inhabitants were Catholic Irish, making Liverpool the largest such concentration in England. And after the American Civil War ended in May 1865, Fenianism in the town grew significantly as Irish-American officers made it their British base of operations. Local police responded by collecting intelligence on the IRB and assisting Martin Meagher, Richard McHale and Michael Clear, three Irish Constabulary detectives whom Dublin Castle had stationed in Liverpool. However, Chief Constable Major John Greig, a 60-year-old former army officer and prickly martinet, regarded the trio as meddling outsiders. He insisted Fenianism could never thrive on his patch and dismissed incontrovertible evidence that in fact the IRB had hundreds of members and thousands of hard-core sympathisers. Even in late 1865, Greig scorned reports – all true – that Fenian leaders in America and Ireland were using Liverpool to ship arms to Dublin and send emissaries across northern England to recruit members and raise funds. Greig also denied that Liverpool was the 'great hotbed' of Fenianism in England, and claimed very few people shared that opinion.[3] Moreover, he accused the three Irish detectives of heightening official concern by reporting every incident related to the conspiracy, however trifling. Furthermore, Greig feared that heavy-handed policing might provoke serious disorder in Liverpool – a political and religious melting pot with a history of sectarian rioting. Accordingly, he adopted a light-touch policy of 'vigilant moderation' towards Fenianism.

Despite Greig's disdain, Meagher, McHale and Clear remained active during 1865 and 1866, making themselves highly visible to potential informers among Irish-American officers who had descended into poverty and boredom. Lodging in pubs and dingy boarding houses, destitute and near starvation, many subsisted on intermittent handouts as the prospect of a rising receded. Eventually, one of them took the bait. John Joseph Corydon was a former Union medical officer in the American Civil War, who later acted as a transatlantic courier for O'Mahony. In April 1866, he transferred to Liverpool and entered an IRB inner circle that included two American officers, Austin Gibbons and Captain Beecher. Gibbons's pub in the Vauxhall district was a favourite Fenian rendezvous, where he also provided fellow American officers bed and board, advanced them money and supplied free food and drink. Beecher was really 26-year-old Michael O'Rorke. He had fought in the Union Army alongside his father until the Battle of Spotsylvania in March 1864, when a Confederate sniper mortally wounded the father, who died in Michael's arms. In June 1865, O'Mahony sent O'Rorke to Ireland, where he cared for officers who had evaded arrest after Habeas Corpus was suspended in February 1866. Before Stephens left for America in March 1866, he ordered O'Rorke to transfer these officers to Britain. Based in Liverpool, O'Rorke acted as their paymaster, met IRB circles throughout England, and during monthly visits to Dublin he gained considerable influence over the IRB in Ireland.

For six months Corydon had lodged with Gibbons, who treated him well, but the interminable wait for a rising encouraged him to become an informer. And he was good at it. In September 1866, Corydon sent Liverpool police to O'Rorke's house, but he had left for Dublin a day earlier. Suspecting treachery, O'Rorke shifted immediately to a new house that Corydon never located. However, he did have three Fenians guarding a cache of rifles arrested, and later identified Liverpool's chief IRB centres and Fenian meeting places.

The Irish detectives in Liverpool shared their prize asset with Greig but the Chief Constable dismissed Corydon as an unimpressive Irish Yankee. On 15 September 1866, Corydon warned that Fenians planned military action in England to divert attention from the coming rebellion, and that Fenian agents in Aldershot and elsewhere had 'worked up' army regiments bound for Ireland. Frustratingly, though, Corydon only provided a broad outline of Fenian strategy, not specific details about places and dates. At the end of 1866, Greig believed his scepticism about the informer was vindicated when Corydon reported IRB funds running low, morale sagging and Liverpool Fenianism in a depressed state.[4]

At the same time, Fenianism in London was in turmoil. When Fariola reached the capital in late January 1867, he discovered many Irish-American officers penniless and demoralised at Stephens's failure to launch a rising. Instead, Stephens had ordered them to take civilian jobs, but they unanimously refused. Fariola recalled that: 'The fact was that all had become disgusted with their inaction. When I found them, they were reduced almost to starvation, being without news from America for a month. They had no idea of what to do.'[5] Also in London were some IRB leaders from Ireland who had fled after the suspension of Habeas Corpus, joined there by John Flood, whom Stephens had appointed Head Centre for England and Scotland. But Flood became disgusted when Stephens's funds dried up and the rising never materialised. O'Rorke recollected that at the end of 1866, a minority of Irish-American officers disillusioned with Stephens concluded that without a rising 'the Organisation would fall to pieces – a calamity which all agreed could not be repaired for an entire generation'.[6] Accordingly, this dissident minority established a fifteen-man Directory comprised of radicals like Flood, O'Rorke, General Halpin and John Nolan, the former IRB organiser in Ulster. Severing its links with America, this Directory decided to start the fight in Ireland alone, and its military credibility was enhanced by recruiting the newly arrived McCafferty. Why McCafferty defected to the Directory is a mystery; perhaps he wanted to leapfrog Kelly and lead the rebellion himself. Together, McCafferty and Flood quickly became the Directory's driving force.

When most American officers in London recoiled at the schism, the Directory threatened to starve them out; a potent weapon, as Massey was still on his way to England with Kelly's funds. Moreover, a Directory member called Newman, who was the conduit for Stephens's subsidies, refused to distribute remittances to Fenian opponents. Eventually the American holdouts offered to submit, provided the Directory showed them its plans for a rising. But the Directory feared a leak and declined, offering them only a single seat. Even then, their representative had to accept every majority decision. When the Directory continued starving them out, the American officers turned to Fariola as their last best hope. Despite having never met him, they knew his military reputation and assumed he was in Europe to finally launch the rising. But in London, Fariola quickly realised that healing the split was impossible. Meanwhile, news of Stephens's overthrow reached the English capital and persuaded the Directory to wait until Kelly himself arrived. Before returning to Paris to consult Kelly, Fariola discovered that McCafferty had visited Liverpool and established ties with its IRB leaders.

When Fariola reached Paris on Friday, 25 January 1867, he discovered that Kelly, Cluseret and Vifquain had arrived but without Stephens.[7] Kelly told him that Stephens had been deposed and then feigned illness to hide his cowardice. Kelly ordered Fariola to remain in post while he went to Ireland and secured IRB approval for Stephens's overthrow. On Sunday, 27 January, Kelly sent Cluseret and Fariola to London to await him there, and told them that they should make another attempt to end the Fenian schism. As money was short, Fariola had to leave behind in Paris those European officers he had recruited for the rising. Clearly this was revolution on a shoestring budget. Kelly had also sent £800 to the London Directory, unaware that it was separately planning dramatic military action, and he told Cluseret and Fariola that O'Rorke was already in Ireland on behalf of the Directory, inviting IRB leaders to London for consultations about an insurrection.

In London, Cluseret – as Fariola had already – stumbled metaphorically into a nest of vipers:

> Alas! How little I knew of the Irish character when I accepted this mission. On my arrival I was literally overwhelmed with complaints, recriminations, accusations etc. etc. Everybody came to me with their personal grievances – but with nothing else.[8]

Realising that Irish-American officers were still abysmally unprepared for rebellion, Cluseret refused to lead them into battle against regular British troops. 'The most effective arms possessed by the insurgents were shillelaghs with a pike at the end of them.'[9] When the Directory demanded an immediate meeting with Kelly, Cluseret telegraphed him in Paris to hurry to London. Massey also warned Kelly that the Directory was running out of patience. Scrapping his Irish visit, Kelly travelled incognito to London. Although many American officers recognised him as Chief Executive of the Irish Republic, the Directory refused to acknowledge Kelly's supremacy. Instead, it offered him a seat, provided he accepted every majority decision – effectively a demand for his almost complete surrender. But Kelly had been dealt a weak hand. Unlike the Directory, he lacked important connections in Ireland and London's IRB centres had pledged allegiance to the Directory. Furthermore, Kelly desperately wanted to avoid a rift with the Directory, whose military ambitions might wreck his own plans for a rising. Consequently, he and the Directory agreed that a rising should commence on 12 February 1867.

However, by the second week of February 1867 further negotiations between Kelly and the Directory had reached stalemate, and the Fenian schism became a power struggle between Kelly, who advocated methodically preparing for a rising in the near future, and radicals like McCafferty, who demanded immediate military action. In one sense it was a quarrel about timing, as only weeks divided them: O'Rorke himself admitted that 'the idea of putting off the project never entered the heads of either party. The only question was as to the time.'[10] But the relationship had become toxic. Kelly's counsel of delay reminded the Directory of Stephens's procrastination, while Kelly believed an extremist Directory was imperilling the entire revolutionary enterprise. And while Kelly loathed McCafferty for (in his eyes) betraying him, McCafferty cared only about the revolution, not Kelly's wounded pride. Also, both sides differed strongly over how the insurrection should begin. While Kelly favoured careful planning that culminated in co-ordinated attacks across Ireland, McCafferty preferred to start with an unorthodox military operation that struck at the heart of the British Empire, demonstrating that Fenians could overcome great odds and in the process capturing the Irish people's imagination. Although O'Rorke disliked acting independently of Kelly, he sided with the Directory majority.

Confident the Directory now held the whip hand over Kelly, McCafferty and Flood revealed their military strategy to Fariola. Fifteen hundred Fenians from across northern England would flock to Chester in the north-west and, led by McCafferty, seize 30,000 rifles and a million rounds of ball cartridge from the Castle armoury. Transported by horse and cart 1½ miles to the railway station, they would be put on a commandeered train and driven 85 miles west to the Welsh port of Holyhead. Telegraph wires and railway lines would be severed to delay any pursuit. From Holyhead, a captured ferry would convey the haul to Ireland (probably on the coast of Kerry), its landing coinciding with the nationwide rebellion planned for 12 February 1867. Armed with the Chester weapons, 2,000 Fenians would fight a guerrilla war in Ireland, one that the Directory believed McCafferty – formerly of Morgan's Raiders – was well equipped to command.

As Fariola pondered this astounding revelation, Kelly entered the room. Fariola recalled that upon learning about the Chester operation, 'Kelly considered their plan as perfectly mad and certain to prevent the execution of the plans of the Brotherhood entrusted to him. They told him in answer that their plan was the better on account of its very madness.'[11] Clearly each side interpreted madness very differently. Whereas Kelly regarded McCafferty and Flood's project as insane, an act of folly certain to end in disaster, they believed it was audacious and inspired. Furthermore, McCafferty and Flood thought that while it might just succeed, Kelly's strategy stood not a ghost of a chance, that the Irish people would not rally behind a discredited Fenian leadership that had accumulated less than 1,000 rifles. Moreover, the Directory considered McCafferty a winner. Supposedly, at the siege of Vicksburg in 1863, he had accomplished an equally daring exploit when McCafferty and fellow Morgan's Raiders had penetrated behind Federal lines and captured large amounts of weaponry, which they transported by steamer down the Mississippi under heavy fire from Union batteries. Fenians also knew that in 1848 Terence Bellew McManus had planned to seize weapons from Chester Castle and take them by steamer to Ireland. And, Fariola was less sceptical than Kelly. He believed McCafferty's plan was 'bold almost to insanity but it might succeed and then result in arming a body of 1,200 or 1,500 men with whom to commence a guerrilla warfare, the only one in the speaker's mind that could have a chance of ultimate success'.[12]

Clearly, the gulf between both sides had become unbridgeable. Kelly seemed helpless, but just in time he was rescued when, around 10 February, a high-powered IRB delegation from Ireland suddenly arrived in London. It consisted of Dominic Mahony, the Head Centre of Cork, William Harbison from Belfast and Edward Byrne from Dublin. They hoped to get some of Kelly's money and normalise relations between America and Ireland now that Stephens had gone. The trio affirmed that their men were ready for war, but expressed fears that bellicose Fenians in Ireland and England might precipitate a premature rising. Accordingly, they sought to reassert control by joining with Kelly in establishing a Provisional Government. Rather invidiously, it also included Michael O'Rorke, who now sat on two bodies pursuing different military strategies. The Provisional Government then elected Kelly as chairman, ratified Cluseret and Fariola's appointments, and drew up a proclamation of an Irish Republic that would be promulgated when the rising began. Then, in a somersault (which baffled Fariola), Mahony, Byrne and Harbison delegated their powers to Kelly and returned to Ireland – having each pocketed £30 of Kelly's money.

At this moment Edward Duffy arrived in London from Connaught. Increasingly disillusioned and in worsening health, he had been on the brink of migrating to America with his widowed mother and five siblings, before learning at the last moment that £300 would finance the escape of Fenian prisoners from Portland Gaol in Devon.[13] Feeling honour bound to free imprisoned comrades, Duffy appointed a new IRB leader in Connaught, sent a sister on a successful fundraising tour of the west of Ireland, and brought the money to London. But the Directory rejected a breakout from Portland and stuck with its even more spectacular Chester operation. The Provisional Government also told Duffy of its own plan for an early insurrection. Although strongly opposed to a rising, Duffy felt he could not desert comrades about to risk their own lives. O'Rorke recalled that 'poor

Ned Duffy was not in favour; but when all the other delegates declared that they could hold their own for a given time, he nobly pledged himself to attempt his part. The decision was then unanimous.'[14] Above all, Duffy could not abandon his loyal followers in Connaught, especially as his successor there had almost immediately resigned. Despairingly, Duffy sent a message to Devoy in Mountjoy Gaol: 'The fight will be in three weeks but we'll be badly beaten. Plead guilty, so as to get a short sentence, so you can remain in Ireland and help to reorganise the movement.'[15] Cancelling his departure for America, Duffy returned to Connaught and awaited the call to arms. Meanwhile, Kelly's new alliance with the IRB in Ireland allowed him to wrest power back from the Directory, and he immediately postponed the rising planned for 12 February 1867 – without setting a new date. This unilateral action forced the Directory to either acknowledge Kelly's newfound authority or break with him entirely. Just possibly, Kelly had intended provoking them into a hopeless insurrection. This would eliminate a dangerous splinter group while simultaneously lulling Dublin Castle into believing it had defeated the long-expected rebellion – a perfect smokescreen for Kelly's own rising.

Convinced that Kelly had been stringing it along, the Directory reacted furiously. Cluseret tried unsuccessfully to mediate, but the Directory refused to recognise Kelly, whom it now regarded as another Stephens, someone destined always to falter at the moment of truth. Fariola recollected that 'McCafferty and Flood spoke very bitterly of Kelly and said that he was all humbug.'[16] O'Rorke claimed a Directory majority, accused Kelly of creating a supreme crisis, and decided to proceed immediately with the Chester raid. 'The Directory, being pledged to a certain time could not well wait for the completion of the arrangements of the Provisional Government. Although I disapproved of this precipitate action at the time, I deferred to the opinion of the majority.'[17] Fariola recalled the Directory's fierce determination not to retreat, as that would 'make them the subject of sneering contempt from the world'.[18] Cluseret recalled Stephens had constantly mocked 'spouters', only himself to baulk at the critical moment, but that his usurpers refused to meekly fade away. When he said there was not one chance in a hundred of success, they retorted: 'My dear general. We are not under the smallest illusion as to what awaits us; but the word of an Irishman, once given is sacred.'[19] Like Emmet, they thought it unmanly to go down without a fight. After leaving London,

McCafferty and Flood booked into Chester's King's Hotel under aliases for 9 and 10 February 1867.

Knowing for some weeks that a significant military operation was imminent, Liverpool's IRB leaders had warned centres throughout Lancashire and Yorkshire to prepare for action. On 1 February, Corydon resurfaced, told his police handlers that he had been ill, and reported Kelly's recent presence in Paris and the existence of a London Directory, which McHale informed Dublin Castle was bound to launch a rising soon or it would disintegrate. On 10 February, McCafferty travelled from Chester to Liverpool and addressed American officers and IRB centres about the next day's raid on Chester, which he said would involve 2,500 men and was the prelude to a rising in Ireland. After McCafferty distributed money for train tickets to Chester, he had the code word 'Chester' telegraphed to IRB centres in Manchester, Leeds, Stafford, Birmingham, Wolverhampton and other towns across northern and central England. To prevent a leak, McCafferty let only this small inner circle know the arrangements, but Corydon was in the audience.[20]

As the Chester operation was to begin at seven o'clock on the evening of 11 February and he was expected in the city at lunchtime, Corydon hurriedly tipped off McHale and Major Greig's deputy, Superintendent Ride. McHale rushed to Liverpool's General Post Office and telegraphed Dublin Castle.[21] Ride attended his Chief Constable's house at 9.15 p.m. Greig was incredulous, but Ride presented comprehensive written notes about an imminent Fenian attack on Chester Castle. And Corydon had warned that this was just the prelude to a rising in Ireland. Greig had to decide almost instantly about his course of action. If he warned Chester and no Fenian raid occurred, Greig would damage his professional reputation; but if he ignored Corydon's warning and an Irish rebellion ensued, Greig would become the scapegoat for a national humiliation. Whatever he did carried risks, but Greig calculated that action was preferable to doing nothing.

Greig now 'intuitively felt that there was not a moment to be lost as the first batches of Fenians were on their way'.[22] He decided against telegraphing a warning to the Mayor of Chester, William Johnston, at that time of night. It was just as well. Johnston lived 5 miles outside Chester in the village of Broughton, and a message would not have reached his house until the following morning. Besides, the mayor was actually away visiting Flintshire in north Wales. Instead, Greig decided that senior Liverpool police officers should personally tell Chester's blissfully ignorant authorities about the danger they faced and the necessity of immediate countermeasures. So, at 10 p.m., Ride and an Inspector Carlisle left by night ferry, crossed the River Mersey to Rock Ferry landing, and caught a train. Fifty minutes later, they were in Chester.

A walled city of 36,000 inhabitants in north-west England, Chester was a port on the River Dee and the county seat of Cheshire.[23] In the Middle Ages, Chester had functioned as a gateway to Wales and a barrier against Irish invasions, but by 1867 its Norman castle contained only a nominal garrison. Having missed out on the canal, turnpike and industrial revolution, Chester itself was long past its glory days, eclipsed as a port by Liverpool and reduced to a provincial backwater. Politically and socially tranquil, the city was unlike Liverpool and Birkenhead just over 20 miles away. Its long-established Irish community had grown to about 2,000 after the Famine, but except for the working-class district of Boughton, most were dispersed throughout the city and well-integrated. Crime was low, there was no history of sectarian rioting and no organised Fenian movement. Accordingly, there was no need for close police surveillance in Chester, and anyway, its three-dozen constabulary was ineffective, riddled with absenteeism, drunkenness and insubordination. A well-executed descent might well achieve total surprise and meet little or no resistance.

Ride and Carlisle quickly convinced Chief Constable Fenwick and Deputy Mayor Williams that Chester was in imminent danger, and they immediately warned Captain Edwards, who commanded the Castle's sixty-strong garrison. Shortly after 3 a.m., the four men entered Chester railway station intending to telegraph Manchester for military reinforcements. However, a small group of strangers was pacing the platform, nervous and watchful, while another fifteen men occupied the first-class waiting room, deep in conversation and wearing haversacks. Two of them shadowed the official party to the telegraph office, and when Deputy Mayor Williams entered the waiting room everyone fell silent. Everything about the strangers – their suspicious behaviour, sullenness and military-style attire – suggested Fenians, and indeed McCafferty was present to see that the operation was going to plan. Clearly unconcerned at the sudden appearance of Ride's party, McCafferty soon afterwards went back to his hotel, where he and Flood had booked lunch for 2 p.m. Even when station manager Binger told Ride and Carlisle that the men's leader – McCafferty – had returned to the King's Hotel and groups of Irishmen were assembling in the nearby Boughton district, both policemen considered their mission accomplished. Claiming they needed to brief Greig, Ride and Carlisle had Binger improvise a special train on which they left for Liverpool. Chester was on its own.

In Birkenhead, Ride and Carlisle instructed a plainclothes policeman to keep watch at Rock Ferry for any strangers entering the railway station and warn the Chester authorities that Fenians were coming. Upon reaching Liverpool at 6 a.m., Ride and Carlisle updated Greig on the situation in Chester, and a race now developed between Fenians and the British authorities as both sides drafted more men into Chester. At 2.30 a.m. on Monday, 11 February, thirty men arrived by train from Manchester, joined the waiting room contingent, and then marched off towards the Boughton district. The *Chester Record* disparaged them as 'for the most part a low-looking body of men, most of them bearing a half-starved look, although others were great lumps but nearly all meanly clad'.[24] Although many Fenians came on foot, a concentrated influx by rail occurred between 8 a.m. and 2 p.m. Almost 200 came from Crewe, another 100 from Manchester, and 30 men from Birkenhead. Between 3.30 and 4.30 in the afternoon, a series of trains deposited 100 more Fenians at Chester station. Up for the fight, they belted out 'When Johnny Comes Marching Home' and 'The Lakes of Killarney'. By 5 p.m., Chief Constable Fenwick estimated 1,300 Fenians were in Chester, while stationmaster Binger reported more trains arriving. The *Chester Record* described many Birkenhead men wearing slouch hats or sporting a goatee as Yankees or seafarers, though others resembled the 'dockyard loafer'. Perhaps surprisingly, given that early February was hardly the height of the tourist season, this sudden invasion of strangers excited remarkably little interest, and certainly no panic among the local population. This was partly due to the Fenians' restrained behaviour even as the clock counted down to military action. The *Chester Record* declared that, 'Although they were a body of men looking "fit for anything" they kept the peace, interfering with no-one and avoided the society of anyone who asked questions, returned evasive and curt replies to every attempt to draw them into conversation.'[25] However, another newspaper explained Chester's relative tranquillity differently: 'Indeed, the excitement seemed to be welcomed by many as an agreeable relief to the oppressive monotony of ordinary Chester life.'[26]

Simultaneously, the British authorities prepared for action. By daybreak on 11 February, Fenwick and Williams had alerted Major Humberston of the Volunteers, Captain Wright of the Militia and Captain John Smith, Chief Constable of the Cheshire County police, whose headquarters were also in Chester. Smith summoned to the Castle 100 police constables from all over the county and issued them sidearms. Humberston also transferred 500 stands of rifles into the Castle, where, by 1 p.m., 120 uniformed Volunteers had mustered, a figure that rose during the afternoon to 231. The Volunteer Artillery also moved their two .32 pounder guns to the Inner barrack. Shortly after 7 p.m., the Deputy Mayor convened a town meeting and swore in many special constables. Military reinforcements had also poured in from Manchester, increasing the Castle garrison to 122 soldiers, while a battalion of Scots Guards was on its way from London. However, at 3.45 p.m., Greig rejected a telegram appeal from Chester's authorities for 200 policemen. Having covered his back, Greig was more concerned about possible trouble in Liverpool itself and he only sent an officer to Chester on a fact-finding mission, the time-honoured excuse for doing nothing.

Despite Greig's failure to act, by Monday afternoon Chester authorities had enough resources to repel even a determined attack on the Castle. This McCafferty and Flood realised when they left their hotel at mid-morning for a leisurely stroll. With their plans unravelling, McCafferty now had to display his reputed military prowess, perhaps by ordering an immediate attack on the Castle. But in more senses than one McCafferty was in unfamiliar territory. Having never exercised leadership, let alone commanded hundreds of men, he was horribly exposed in a rapidly deteriorating situation that required a cool head. Instead, McCafferty lost his nerve and buckled. Overwhelmed by a sudden, unexpected setback, he floundered, especially after realising that someone must have forewarned the British.

With a surprise attack on the Castle forestalled and British reinforcements on the way to Chester, Fenians now risked being encircled and trapped inside the city. Hurriedly, Fenian leaders gathered at the King's Hotel and concluded that if they tried to attack the Castle, their line of retreat would be severed and everyone captured.[27] To prevent this disaster, McCafferty ordered an immediate evacuation. Soon afterwards, he was spotted at the railway station shouting, 'the affair is sold' and telling Fenians to leave the city. Then, McCafferty himself disappeared. Many Fenians regarded McCafferty as a magician, but few had suspected that a vanishing act was part of his repertoire. In groups of ten, twenty and thirty, men began leaving, some by train but most on foot. Although angry and confused, they went peacefully, throwing their weapons and ammunition into the Chester Canal. Meanwhile, Austin Gibbons had dashed to Birkenhead railway station, where hundreds of Fenians were about to depart for Chester. Shortly afterwards, McCafferty was nowhere to be seen. Amidst a milling crowd at Birkenhead railway station, Corydon was buying his ticket when Gibbons leapt from an incoming train, shouted, 'the thing was sold' by 'a traitor in the camp' and told everyone to return home.[28] But many Fenians had already departed for Chester.

Overnight, the Castle garrison, Volunteers, Cheshire County police reinforcements and city fire brigade remained on duty, especially as rumours circulated that Fenians intended firebombing buildings, or at least Chester's prestigious jewellery shops. Nothing happened. Instead, many Fenians must have slept in pubs or outside on park benches and in doorways. Some of the last departed on the 10.20 a.m. train for Birkenhead, as crowds at the station jeered them. Forty minutes later, 500 Fusilier Guards finally arrived after an eight-hour overnight journey from London. Like a Biblical visitation, the mysterious strangers had come and gone without firing a shot, or even breaking a windowpane.

Historians have long debated whether McCafferty's plan had any chance of success. Some have argued that it was entirely feasible and only miscarried through Corydon's treachery. Indeed, one has claimed that no attack on the Castle was intended, because Fenian troops in the garrison were, under cover of darkness, to admit through an unguarded back door a small group that would overpower the front gate sentries and admit the main rebel body.[29] Chief Constable Fenwick asserted later that many of Chester's Irish sympathised with and had raised funds for the IRB, and would have joined the raid had it proceeded.[30] If Fenwick was right, then the Fenians, on leaving the railway station for the Castle, had only to turn left at the end of City Road to be among their own people in Boughton. Returning, they would again pass through friendly territory, developing sufficient momentum to reach Holyhead and then sail for Ireland.

However, other historians contend that even without Corydon's betrayal, the Chester operation was fatally flawed.[31] Drafting 1,500 men gradually into Chester in order to avoid alarming the authorities meant that over fifteen hours would pass between the first and last Fenians arriving – a staggered process that would have given Chester's authorities time to initiate countermeasures. The Fenians' numerical strength, then, was really a weakness. And, if the Fenians had no help, then Humberston's prompt action of the morning of 11 February left them no alternative but to assault a reinforced Castle that was very easy to defend. Even had Fenians seized the Castle weapons, transferring them to the railway station would have been difficult. Much of Chester's population lived along the route and would have resisted strangers laden down with stolen rifles. Moreover, the odds against commandeering a train and a cross-channel ferry before successfully reaching Ireland were colossal. Corydon's information only ensured that Fenian failure at Chester was total.

Crucially, Fenians in Chester experienced a complete vacuum of leadership. Liverpool's IRB leaders did not even reach the city after learning from Gibbons that the operation was off. And, once the authorities began taking countermeasures, McCafferty should have acted decisively to regain the initiative, but instead his performance was woefully inept. Yet, remarkably, McCafferty evaded responsibility for the debacle, partly because it was quickly overshadowed by the greater failure of the rising itself. Indeed, McCafferty's subsequent imprisonment actually made him a political martyr and he long remained silent about the Chester affair. Only seven years later did he tell Devoy that on 11 February he had travelled to London for last-minute consultations with the Directory, and during the return journey his train had been shunted into a siding to let through Fusilier Guards on their way to Chester.[32] But McCafferty's sequence of events made no sense, as the Guards did not leave London until 2 a.m. on the night of 11–12 February, hours after the Castle raid was supposed to have begun. Moreover, McCafferty had no plausible reason for a last-minute trip to London – a dereliction of duty in itself – and his explanation was really a fabrication designed to camouflage his inglorious performance. Furthermore, Chief Constable Fenwick's diary recorded McCafferty's presence at the railway station, while King's Hotel staff later confirmed that he was in Chester throughout 11 February.[33] A journalist also recognised him walking among the Fenians wearing a Kossuth (slouch) hat.[34]

After fleeing Chester, McCafferty and Flood hid in Liverpool until 18 February, when they left for Whitehaven on the Cumbrian coast. But police had been tipped off – undoubtedly by Corydon – and shadowed them. After staying overnight in an hotel, they left on a collier that on 23 February reached Dublin Bay. Waiting detectives watched them transfer to an oyster boat being rowed by three men, gave chase in a ferry boat, and arrested the pair as they boarded another collier. Despite giving false names, McCafferty and Flood were identified at Mountjoy Prison. Returning to Liverpool, Corydon attended an angry meeting that tried unsuccessfully to identify a traitor who was 'worse than Nagle'. But Corydon was shocked when a local newspaper reported that the Chester raid had been betrayed by a Liverpool Fenian who had held a commission in the Union Army. However, Corydon held his nerve and was never suspected.

After Fenians retreated from Chester, honours and votes of thanks rained down on saviours like Fenwick, who was awarded a salary increase. But the big winner was Major Greig, lauded as the man who had averted revolution in Ireland. Showered with gifts and congratulatory letters, Greig was also feted by politicians, press and the public. Queen Victoria made him a Companion of the Bath. Effectively Chief Constable for life, he remained in office until 1881, when illness forced a 75-year-old Greig to finally retire. Still, privately, Major Greig must have reflected on how close he had come to his own professional Waterloo, and that it was indeed a damned close-run thing. Luck had played an important role in the final outcome; none came the Fenians' way and all went to the British.

News of the Chester setback did not reach Kerry in time for its Fenian military leader, John James O'Connor, to stand his men down.[35] Twenty-three-year-old O'Connor had returned to his native county in the autumn of 1865, after serving in the Union Army during the Civil War. Promoted to captain, he had fought at the battles of Bull Run, Antietam, Spotsylvania and Petersburg. After Habeas Corpus was suspended in February 1866, O'Connor went underground until 12 February 1867, when he resurfaced in Cahirciveen. That morning, O'Connor sent Captain Mortimer Moriarty by mail train to Killarney, where he instructed the town's IRB centre to prepare for O'Connor's arrival. Totally isolated and unaware that the rising was cancelled in the evening, O'Connor mobilised followers in Cahirciveen, ready to march them to Killarney. However, an informer had already told the British authorities about the intended rising and Moriarty's mission to Killarney. When police stopped the mail train outside the town, they arrested Moriarty and sent mounted messengers to warn police in Killorglin and Cahirciveen, who immediately reinforced their barracks.

O'Connor had intended capturing weapons from Cahirciveen police station but his small force – some carrying only pitchforks – dared not risk attacking the reinforced building. Instead, they marched along the coast road towards Glenbeigh, planning to link up with other rebel groups in Killorglin or Killarney. Early on 13 February, O'Connor's party encountered a messenger, Constable William Duggan, riding from Killorglin to Cahirciveen. When he refused to stop, they shot and severely wounded him. From the captured dispatch, O'Connor realised the authorities knew everything. After capturing some arms from a coastguard station, O'Connor advanced on Glenbeigh, where the mail train driver told him about Moriarty's arrest and that there was no rising in Killarney or Killorglin. To evade capture, O'Connor turned his party towards Glencar and vanished into the mountains. The Kerry rising had petered out after just fifteen hours. Even so, exaggerated rumours had spread like wildfire throughout the county about telegraph wires being cut, mounted dispatch carriers murdered, coastguard stations and police barracks attacked and rebels swarming everywhere. Panicked local gentry flooded into Killarney with their wives, children, savings, gold, jewels and other valuables. Huddling in the Railway Hotel, they helped army officers and policemen fortify the premises, brought in provisions, piled sand-filled canvas bags at windows, distributed arms and posed sentries. Scouts were sent out and urgent appeals for aid telegraphed to Dublin Castle. Soon military reinforcements hastened by train to Killarney from the Curragh, Cork and Limerick.

Naas and Rose were lucky that the Kerry rising never developed into a full-blown 'Fenian Panic' and full-scale rebellion, because they were both out of the country at the time. The Viceroy was attending Cabinet and parliament in London, but the commander-in-chief was relaxing at Kimbolton Castle in Huntingdonshire. Having avoided immense political embarrassment, they returned hurriedly to Ireland.

13

The Countdown
to the Rising

Cluseret's refusal to leave for Ireland until the rising developed into regular warfare forced Kelly to appoint a temporary commander-in-chief. He finally settled on Godfrey Massey, but Mahony, Harbison and Byrne hesitated, doubting his leadership ability. Massey then manipulated Cluseret into endorsing him by pretending that Kelly had secured the Provisional Government's approval, and when Cluseret nominated Massey, Mahony, Harbison and Byrne ratified his appointment. Later, two of them told Cluseret of their doubts about Massey and that they had only relented out of deference to the general.[1] On 11 February 1867, Massey left for Ireland to consult IRB leaders and inspect their preparations for a rising. While in Dublin, he and Byrne met eleven centres, who claimed 14,000 members. On 13 and 14 February, Massey spent two days in Castlebar and Westport, Co. Mayo, reconnoitring areas suitable for military operations. Afterwards, thirty Cork centres reported that they had 20,000 members but only 1,500 weapons, most of them pikes: clearly Fenians were seriously ill-equipped for an insurrection that was possibly only weeks away. Finally, Massey surveyed the Tipperary countryside and returned to Dublin.[2]

After the Chester fiasco and McCafferty and Flood's subsequent arrest, the Directory disintegrated, ending the IRB schism in London and leaving Kelly supreme as Fenian leader. Kelly's position strengthened further when O'Rorke and Halpin came over to his side. O'Rorke had opposed the Chester raid, while Halpin and Kelly had been friends since 1865, when they were allies of Stephens in Dublin. Besides, Kelly's revolution was now the only one Fenians had left. However, new fissures soon emerged between Kelly, Cluseret and Fariola. During Massey's absence in Ireland, London Fenians and IRB circles in Ireland had responded to the Chester failure by forcing Kelly to set the rising for 5 March. Cluseret was furious at Kelly apparently allowing political pressure to override military considerations at a time when Fenians were still not equipped to fight the British Army in Ireland. Disillusioned after weeks of mediating between Kelly and the London Directory, Cluseret's confidence sank further when Kelly expressed pessimism about the rising's chances of success. Then Kelly urged him to fiddle the figures and reduce from 10,000 to 5,000 the number of insurgents needed at the start of hostilities.[3] Although he reluctantly agreed, Cluseret still refused to assume command in Ireland from the outset. His relationship with Fariola had also become toxic. Cluseret accused the Belgian of lacking deference and an 'insatiable ambition' to become commander-in-chief. For his part, Fariola resented Cluseret for summarily evicting him from his Great Portland Street lodgings and occupying the rooms himself.

Brimming with confidence, Massey returned to London on 24 February 1867 and assured Kelly that every district was organised, IRB leaders were ready, and the rank and file awaited only a signal to rise. After informing Massey that the insurrection was fixed for 5 March, Kelly ordered him straight back to Ireland to notify IRB leaders and remain to lead the rebel army. At Massey's behest, Kelly asked Fariola to become his deputy in Ireland, but behind Massey's back Kelly also wanted Fariola to monitor Massey's conduct and rectify any mistakes that he made – hardly a vote of confidence in someone Kelly had only recently promoted. When Fariola blanched at shackling himself to someone he now considered a self-promoting glory hunter, Kelly insinuated cowardice and suggested Fariola return to Paris and 'eat my Fenian pay', while brave Fenians risked their lives in Ireland. The taunt goaded Fariola into changing his mind.[4] Kelly himself, though, would not be joining him. Despite his previous insistence on fighting with the Fenian army, he now claimed the Provisional Government wanted London to be his base of operations. Waspishly, Fariola observed that Kelly's role was to 'manage the Irish Republic from London in full safety'.[5] Cluseret then recalled accidentally stumbling upon Massey just before he left for Ireland, helplessly drunk in a gutter, smoking expensive cigars and waving banknotes in the air. Cluseret claimed he wanted Massey fired but could not find Kelly in time, though Robert Anderson insisted this was because Cluseret was also inebriated.[6] While Massey clearly still had money, Fariola left England with just enough cash for his boat ticket and a cab fare.[7] For a disillusioned Cluseret, Massey's abysmal performance was the last straw, and soon afterwards he retreated to Paris, ostensibly to await the call from Ireland to assume command of the rebel army. Kelly was not deceived. Canny as ever, Cluseret had extracted three months' advance salary from him before they left New York. Scornfully, Kelly suggested that Cluseret should at least contribute some novel exhibits to the forthcoming Paris International Exposition.[8] Neither was Vifquain up for the fight. After he complained that shortage of cash was keeping him in Brussels, Kelly sent him money, which Vifquain promptly pocketed without budging.

During the last weeks of February 1867, American officers in Britain left for Ireland. On 18 February at Liverpool's Zoological Gardens, Michael O'Rorke informed Corydon and others that the rebellion would begin soon, assigned them to districts in Ireland, and distributed money.[9] Two hundred Fenians had already travelled ahead after the Chester raid on ferries from Liverpool and Holyhead, but on 16 February they were arrested at Dublin's North Wall Quay and taken to Sackville Street police station. Since none carried weapons, Naas released them, provided they left for England immediately.[10] On 20 February, Corydon and his fellow American officers sailed from Liverpool in a buoyant mood.

For some weeks, Dublin Castle had feared a serious crisis was imminent. By early February 1867, it knew about Stephens's downfall and Superintendent Ryan reported that Kelly was in England planning a rising. On 19 February, Ryan claimed that Fenians were still determined on a general rising in the near future.[11] Supposedly, they intended seizing livestock to feed the rebel army, capture police barracks, and perhaps even the Castle itself. On 22 February, Ryan reiterated that Fenians planned to rise, helped by 150 men from the Chester raid who were now in Dublin, well-disguised and eager for action.[12] However, discovering the rising's exact date was still proving elusive. On 25 February, Ryan reported large numbers of Irish-American officers in the country, many about to leave Dublin and assume command of rebels in districts throughout Ireland. They had cut off their beards and otherwise disguised themselves.[13]

On 25 February, Dublin Castle's intelligence about the rising expanded significantly after Massey returned to Dublin from London. At a house near the Grand Canal, he and Edward Duffy told Dublin centres and American officers (including Corydon) that the insurrection would begin on the night of 5 March, when railway lines, bridges and telegraph wires across Ireland would be destroyed. Massey designated Corydon to inform Cork's IRB leaders. Over the following two days, Corydon secretly met Assistant Inspector General Brownrigg of the Irish Constabulary – proof that Dublin Castle now considered Corydon a valuable asset. Hitherto, Brownrigg had only known the informer through McHale's written reports and even thought he might be a Fenian double agent. But seeing him in the flesh dispelled his doubts: Corydon was the real deal. Corydon never attempted to ferret out any sensitive information and agreed with Brownrigg's assessment that a rising was 'the scheme of a lot of insane persons. Unless I thought so too you would not have had me.' Corydon described IRB leaders as reckless adventurers doomed to fail, and despite being in great danger, he promised to stop them. 'As he had taken up the business, he was determined to see it out.'[14]

Corydon told Brownrigg the rising would commence on 5 March, with Massey initially commanding the rebel forces. There would be widespread destruction as Fenians supposedly planned to plunder aristocrats' homes – though their owners' lives would be spared provided they cooperated. Prominent public officials would be made hostages. Violence against women was forbidden: rapists would be executed. Military action in Ulster was ruled out, 'as it was considered to be perfectly useless to try it'. The central highlands would become Massey's base of operations, while Fenians would drive cattle and sheep into an unnamed town that would serve as a temporary capital. Corydon reported 'great mystery' about what would happen in Dublin, which he claimed contained an estimated 7,000 Fenians – 4,000 of them armed. The Dublin rising would commence a day or two after that in the countryside, with some areas of the capital being incinerated. Col. Kelly was in London and he planned military action throughout England. Corydon agreed with Brownrigg that many people in Ireland were Fenian sympathisers, and had indeed contracted a rebel virus. Brownrigg believed that:

> The great majority of the lower classes are deeply disloyal and that the apparent indifference of many of them arises from fundamental nature for if I may speak metaphorically disease lurks in the blood and is likely to break out if any exciting cause disturbs the system and

perhaps at a time when the constitution is not in a condition to resist the attack.[15]

The quality of police intelligence also improved suddenly. During the weekend before the rising, a Head Constable Talbot reported from Carrick-on-Suir that orders had been issued for an insurrection 'next Tuesday night', 5 March. Dublin Fenians would assemble near the Grand Canal at midnight, and 'under the command of a man called Halpin' march on Dublin simultaneously with men from Dundalk, Mullingar and Meath.[16]

Possibly Brownrigg kept Superintendent Ryan out of the loop, because it was only days before the rising that the latter's reports corroborated Corydon's information. On 28 February, an informer told Ryan that Fenians would rise in the following week and that Irish-American officers were especially resolute.[17] However, Fenian leaders were keeping the exact day secret until the last moment in order to prevent a leak to the British authorities. The military strategy entailed Dublin Fenians joining columns from Wicklow and Wexford, before descending on the capital. An American officer had told Fenians in Dalkey village, 9 miles south of Dublin, to be ready on Tuesday night, 5 March, to move towards Wicklow, luring British troops out of Dublin and enabling Fenians in the capital to overwhelm a weakened army garrison. On Sunday, 3 March, Ryan was told that Fenians from Kingstown and outlying districts would move towards the hills of Tallaght and join over 5,000 Dublin Fenians, drawing troops away from the capital and enabling 10,000 rebels in the capital to commence operations. Ryan also reported that Edward Duffy had passed through Dublin on his way to the west of Ireland, accompanied by American officers who would lead the Connaught rising.[18]

Amidst mounting official concern, Commander-in-Chief Strathnairn was an oasis of calm. Contemptuous as ever of Fenianism, he declared on 25 February that: 'As to the intentions of the Fenians I am of the opinion that I always have been that they will do nothing.'[19]

On 1 March 1867, Massey booked into Cork's Neeham's Hotel, while Fariola stayed at the Italian Hotel. Massey told the city's IRB Head Centre Dominic Mahony to have his men ready for 5 March and seize weapons from gun shops when the rising began. However, over the next three days relations between Fariola and Massey disintegrated. Fariola recalled Massey's imperious behaviour and his posturing as an all-conquering generalissimo. When a local IRB leader suddenly entered a room unannounced:

Massey turned round in his chair and regarded the incomer haughtily. 'How dare you, sir, come into a room where your betters are without knocking beforehand? Where were you brought up?' I looked at Massey in astonishment. Was this the way to address a brother on the eve of a deadly enterprise? The visitor blushed fiery red, bit his lips and left the room.[20]

Another Cork IRB officer recounted a tawdry encounter when a broke Massey tapped him up for £10: 'He was a very fine working man, about 6 feet high and well-proportioned, curly black hair and grand black moustache. But – "handsome is as handsome does" – and judged by this rule, Massey was no better than a poltroon.'[21]

In London, Fariola had lectured American officers – including Massey – on the importance of effecting a gradual transition from the first phase of guerrilla warfare and avoiding defeats in big battles until regular warfare commenced. Kelly had insisted that the top priority was holding out until the rebellion achieved diplomatic recognition or an American naval expedition arrived. Yet in Cork, Fariola realised that Massey had disregarded just about everything he was told. During his preliminary tour of Ireland between 11 and 23 February, Massey had transferred American officers to new districts and denuded Connaught of its military leadership. Even worse, despite his scarce resources, he now wanted to achieve a rapid knock-out victory over the main British forces in Ireland, gambling everything on an immediate battle of annihilation that would liberate both Limerick and Cork within a week. Fariola was incredulous. To him, Massey seemed unhinged, gripped by grandiose delusions. Fariola recalled that he 'requested him in the name of the Provisional Government to stop all future proceedings and told him he had ruined the cause. But the thing could not be stopped: Massey would not; he did no longer recognise the P.G. except Kelly and declined to comply with my advice.'[22] Fariola messaged Kelly in London that Massey was beyond all reason and restraint, but as the rising was imminent, he was told Massey could not be deposed without the rebellion imploding before it even began. Hubris personified, Massey careered unstoppably down his highway to glory.

Such was the shambles that Massey created that Fariola suspected him of calculated treachery:

For in his preliminary tour over the island he had taken care to disor-
ganise and derange all our plans, he had given orders directly opposite
to his line of instructions, and it must have been for the sole purpose
of making the assurance of our discomfiture and of his own security
in his treachery double sure. The being was a liar.[23]

In fact, Massey did not betray Fenianism or deliberately sabotage the rising
before 5 March 1867. Dublin Castle records contain no evidence that he
was a British spy. The chaos he engendered was rooted in Massey's vainglorious personality, his lust for historical greatness, and a wilful refusal to
obey orders. Massey envisaged the rising as a golden opportunity to fulfil
his destiny and become Ireland's Napoleon, Washington and Garibaldi all
rolled into one. He had even recruited William Stephens, a *New York Herald*
reporter, to chronicle his victorious military campaign. Astonishingly,
Massey had already revealed his strategy for the insurrection to Stephens
and named his closest collaborators. However, Massey's erratic behaviour, his constantly changing plans, transferring officers from one place to
another and the public humiliation of subordinates reflected an insecure
person hiding behind a thin facade of confidence and decisiveness, but over-
promoted, out of his depth and dreading exposure.

After Edward Duffy had his sister Ellen warn Massey that his men would
not rise except under a prestigious foreign officer, Massey asked Fariola to
assume military command in Connaught. But Fariola refused to accept an
inferior post.[24] Fariola then learned that on the night of 4 March, Massey
intended rendezvousing with 8,000 Fenians near Limerick Junction railway station before launching his campaign next day. For posterity, Massey
wanted William Stephens to record ecstatic Fenians welcoming their liberator, and so, early on 4 March, Stephens and Fariola travelled ahead to the
Junction. Unable to afford his hotel bill, Fariola surrendered his luggage
as surety. Forewarned by Corydon, Dublin Castle had already dispatched
troops to Tipperary Town and the Junction, where Fariola noticed a
detachment of Guards. 'This was not reassuring. I strolled to the one hotel.
It was occupied by the officers in charge.' Posing as a journalist for a Paris
newspaper, Fariola awaited Massey's arrival:

I lit a cigar and strolled into the open air. Everything was quiet. I
rambled on the roads in the vicinity, making short tours in every

direction. My ear was on the strain, and such was the effect of imagination that I fancied more than once I heard the tramp of the coming insurgents borne to me on the wind. But no insurgents came and the night was waning.[25]

On 4 March, Massey rode the midnight train to Limerick Junction without realising that Corydon had betrayed everything. A few days earlier, at Millstreet in north-west Co. Cork, Corydon gave local Fenians the date of the rising, but he failed to contact John James O'Connor, who was still on the run after leading the recent Kerry rising. On 2 March, he vainly searched for O'Connor in Cork city, whose IRB centre, Dominic Mahony, told Corydon that Edward Duffy had aborted the rising in Kerry and ordered him to assume command of the insurrection at Midleton, Co. Cork.[26] Corydon was also to attend Coveney's pub in North Main Street that evening and confer with Fenian officers, including Captain Patrick Condon, who was to lead the rising in Cork. Condon and Corydon had actually served together in the same regiment during the American Civil War, when Condon swore Corydon into the Fenian Brotherhood. After reuniting in Coveney's, Condon left at 9 p.m. to meet IRB members in a nearby pub. But Corydon followed him and saw Condon issuing orders to about fifty men. By chance, local police suspected the pub was violating licensing hours and raided the premises just after the 11 p.m. closing time, capturing Condon as he bolted upstairs. But Condon gave a false name, and police did not realise his importance until Corydon secretly told them. On the eve of the rising, the IRB command structure in Cork had been decapitated.

Corydon remained in Cork until Monday morning, 4 March, when he travelled to Midleton about 15 miles east of Cork. On the train he encountered a Fenian messenger, who revealed that Massey would reach Limerick Junction at midnight. Catching the next train to Dublin, Corydon arrived at the Castle by mid-afternoon.[27] The Irish government could hardly believe its luck; truly Corydon was the gift that kept on giving. Deputy Inspector General Brownrigg and a police party left immediately by train for Limerick Junction. Upon reaching the station, Massey metaphorically hit the buffers; when Brownrigg arrested him, the rebel commander-in-chief fainted and collapsed on the platform. Simultaneously, police detained prominent Fenians in Limerick City, news of which also spread through

Tipperary, shattering rebel morale and causing some columns heading to the Junction to turn back.

Escorted immediately to Dublin and lodged in Mountjoy Gaol, Massey's arrest was a coup for the Irish administration. Attorney General Hedges Chatterton claimed that it happened just in time; otherwise the country would have been swimming in blood.[28] But at the time, Fariola actually felt liberated and more optimistic about success: 'The timber was not in him. He was an encumbrance. I'm freer to act now.'[29] As acting commander-in-chief, Fariola set out early on 5 March to hopefully locate a Fenian army encamped nearby. After walking 2 miles, a mounted policeman challenged him and chased Fariola when he turned and fled. Repeatedly firing his carbine, the pursuer eventually cornered Fariola, who shot him in the face: 'To this moment I cannot tell if the policeman was killed. Perhaps he was more frightened than hurt. As I did not stop to see, I presume I shall never know.'[30] Muddy and bedraggled, Fariola reached his hotel just as morning broke and British Army buglers sounded *reveille*. After learning that the insurrection had failed, a penniless Fariola skipped out, left behind his luggage and an unpaid bill, caught the night mail train to Dublin, and fled back to England with literally only the clothes on his back.

The Fenian Rising

For days before 5 March 1867, Dublin had teemed with rumours that a Fenian rebellion would soon begin in the mountainous districts between Dublin, Wicklow and Kildare. But such speculation had been rife during previous months and the latest spate was widely discounted. However, this time was different. Dublin Castle and G Division had kept British Army headquarters at the Royal Hospital, Kilmainham, apprised of Fenian plans, and especially about rebels mobilising at Tallaght, a location of symbolic importance as a place of rebellion in 1798. On 5 March, Dublin Castle told Strathnairn about an 'intended general rising in Dublin and throughout the greater part of the country'.[1]

Sixteen months earlier, after Larcom asked Strathnairn for measures to suppress a Fenian uprising in the capital, his report had emphasised that Dublin's topography facilitated the defeat of rebels: the River Liffey divided Dublin and enabled security forces to occupy bridges and prevent insurgents from either linking up or retreating from one part of the city to another. Control of the broad circular road that surrounded Dublin and the Liffey quays also meant that troops could move rapidly along them. Furthermore, Strathnairn recommended bolstering the defences of prestigious and politically important buildings. These included Dublin Castle, the Four Courts and Custom House, as well as Broadstone and Amiens Street railway stations, while cavalry should patrol Phoenix Park to protect the Vice-regal Lodge. Army commanders across Dublin were to institute emergency measures if a heavy field gun outside the Royal Hospital fired three times.[2] Additionally, Strathnairn now decided that two columns of soldiers were to descend on Tallaght and envelop rebels in a pincer movement. The first, under a Major Greene, would travel by train from Newbridge military barracks in Co. Kildare, 20 miles north-east, to the railway station near Tallaght and attack insurgents on their left flank. Another column from Portobello Barracks, under a Major Curzon, would surprise them front and right. Defeating Fenians in open countryside actually suited Strathnairn, as it prevented his soldiers engaging in urban warfare, possibly causing massive casualties and physical damage.

The rebel commander in Dublin was 42-year-old William Halpin, who held the Fenian rank of general. Originally from Co. Meath, he had fought with the Union Army in many Civil War battles, including the siege of Atlanta, and was promoted to lieutenant colonel. In early 1865, O'Mahony sent him to Ireland, where Halpin sat on the Military Council and became close to Stephens and Kelly, though he later helped overthrow the IRB leader. In January 1867, Halpin arrived in London and joined the Directory, though he never broke with Kelly, who valued his military expertise and excellent knowledge of Dublin. As probably the most militarily distinguished Irish-American officer, Halpin was an obvious choice to lead Fenians in the capital, and in early February 1867 Kelly sent him to Dublin. On 26 February, Halpin attended the meeting at which Massey outlined his strategy, and during late February and early March he fleshed out the proposed Dublin rising.

It can be inferred that Halpin adhered to his instructions from Kelly, Cluseret and Fariola. In the first phase, Fenians were to engage in guerrilla warfare, gathering strength, cohesion, weapons and public support. Military activity should be confined primarily to attacks on isolated police barracks and raids on homes for arms. Above all, Halpin should avoid pitched battles against superior British forces – especially the army. Accordingly, the mustering of rebels at Tallaght was almost certainly a giant bluff, designed to lure British soldiers out of the capital, after which Fenians would melt away into the Dublin and Wicklow hills, enticing the enemy into exhausting pursuits. Simultaneously, in a city denuded of troops, Dublin Fenians would rise and attack key targets, possibly even occupying the capital itself. In the days preceding 5 March, Halpin reconnoitred police barracks on the outskirts. Among them were Stepaside and Glencullen, which guarded roads along which Fenians would march to Tallaght.[3] On 4 March, he convened a leadership conference at the Bleeding Horse pub in Camden Street, and ordered Joseph Denieffe to remain in the capital until events at Tallaght were under way. Halpin would then send him a message for Dublin Fenians to rise.[4]

The Irish government suspected that a Fenian concentration at Tallaght was a trap, designed in part to leave the capital exposed to attack from within. Larcom warned Strathnairn that:

> The Dublin Fenians are to assemble at Tallaght, the Green Hills, leaving a certain chosen number to plunder etc., as soon as the troops are withdrawn to deal with those outside. But the troops will not be withdrawn. We will get upon their rear.[5]

On 5 March, a peculiar atmosphere prevailed in Dublin. A.M. Sullivan recollected: 'Catholic churches crowded by the youth of the country, making spiritual preparations for what they believed would be a struggle in which many would fall and few survive.'[6] During the afternoon, Col. Frederick Wellesley carried dispatches for Strathnairn through an eerie capital and was 'surprised to see the town absolutely deserted. It seemed like a city of the dead; not a soul did I meet, man, woman or child.'[7] Shortly afterwards, Fenians began leaving the capital on foot for Tallaght Hill.

Nowadays part of a densely populated extension of Dublin, Tallaght then was a country village, 9 miles from the city centre. Fenians marched there along two routes a few miles apart: one that ran through the villages of Crumlin, Walkinstown and Green Hills, while another went via Rathmines, Rathgar and Roundtown. Many rebels carried bundles containing bread and a change of clothing, but they had also concealed pike-heads inside their coats. The DMP planned to disrupt this mobilisation and prevent men, weapons and ammunition leaving Dublin by establishing a cordon around the inner city and using mounted patrols to watch Fenians on the march. At Kilmainham, police caught thirty-three Fenians with five rifles, and another seven at Rathmines in possession of a rifle, revolver and 500 rounds of ball cartridges. Ten more Fenians were arrested on the bridges leading to Rathmines, another six on the Chapelizod Road, and five near Donnybrook police station. Police search parties also combed Dublin for weapons and explosives. At Halston Street in the north inner city they seized a large haul that included 249 pikes, 21 rifles and bayonets, mechanical appliances for making ball cartridges and gunpowder. Nevertheless, many Fenians evaded the cordon and reached Tallaght. Between 10.45 p.m. on Tuesday, 5 March, and 2 a.m. on Wednesday, 6 March, police in E Division, a rural district bordering Tallaght, watched as several thousand men proceeded towards the hills, mostly in small groups but sometimes entire IRB circles. Near Crumlin between 500 and 600 armed Fenians encountered a DMP sergeant and two constables, who dashed through rebel lines to safety.[8]

Kelly probably hoped that by delaying the rising for three weeks he had reduced the risk of bad weather, but conditions on the night of 5 March 1867 were atrocious. From his cell in Mountjoy Prison, Devoy watched as 'rain, sleet and snow followed each other in quick succession'.[9] More graphically, Joseph Denieffe recollected the weather as:

> extremely cold and tempestuous, which caused much suffering to the men who went out. Of all the nights that have passed over my head that memorable night was the most furious that I remember. The wind blew a hurricane, accompanied by sleet and rain, the streets were deserted, save by an occasional car passing now and then and the only sounds heard were those of wind and rain falling in torrents.[10]

Fighting began 5 miles east of Tallaght, when a marauding Dublin IRB circle under their centre, John Kirwan, attacked police barracks in the Wicklow Hills, apparently hoping to divert British forces away from Tallaght Hill. At midnight, they assaulted Dundrum police barrack, but its defenders held firm, returned fire and severely wounded Kirwan. Command of about 1,000 insurgents now fell to Patrick Lennon, who led them to Stepaside police station. When its five policemen rejected surrender, a battle erupted that lasted until Lennon had straw pushed through shattered windows and the building set alight. After its defenders gave up, Lennon's party marched them towards Bray, but halted after scouts reported that its police barracks was impregnable. Upon learning that British troops and cavalry were approaching, Lennon circled back to attack police stations across the Dublin Hills.

At 1 a. m. on Wednesday, 6 March, 4 miles beyond Tallaght police station, rockets lit up the sky and guided many Fenians to Tallaght Hill, although police and newspaper estimates varied considerably between 2,000–8,000 men. Rebels had successfully avoided Tallaght police station and its fifteen officers under Sub-Inspector Burke, but an undisciplined circle led by Stephen O'Donoghue ignored orders and attacked the barracks. Despite having only twenty rifles, they were spoiling for a fight – especially some headstrong teenagers. However, when police return fire fatally wounded O'Donoghue, the younger rebels scattered first. When they eventually reached Tallaght Hill with the bad news, unease immediately rippled through Fenian ranks – just as British soldiers appeared in the distance.

At seven o'clock on Tuesday evening, Colonel Wellesley was strolling in the Royal Hospital grounds when a DMP messenger raced up the avenue and breathlessly blurted out that Fenians had risen, attacked a police barrack between Dublin and Tallaght, and massacred an entire garrison.[11] After Strathnairn was told, he had the field gun outside Kilmainham Hospital fired three times to alert commanders across the capital. Soon, army officers flooded telegraph offices with messages for garrisons throughout the country. A journalist reported that, 'the activity of the military authorities all night was extraordinary. At all barracks troops were held in readiness and orderlies were galloping through the streets during the night with messages and orders.'[12] Greene at Newbridge and Curzon at Portobello then set off with their columns for Tallaght, though an accident to Greene's special train delayed his column.

Originally, Strathnairn had intended remaining at Kilmainham to maintain order in the capital, but now he decided to command British forces at Tallaght. First, Strathnairn ordered Wellesley to bring from Richmond Barracks a column of infantry, lancers and two heavy guns, with which he intended to personally crush the rebels at Tallaght. Strathnairn could justify his presence there as being necessary to impress upon soldiers the importance of their task, but possibly the victor of India also wanted to crown a glittering career as the saviour of Ireland. However, first, he needed to visit Dublin Castle and get Naas and Larcom's permission to leave the capital, even with only a small body of troops. Wellesley believed this cost vital time and that it was also undignified for a field marshal to lead out little more than a handful of soldiers.[13] But Strathnairn's military secretary, Owen Tudor Burne, saw that his blood was up and, 'like an old war-horse sniffing at the bridle',[14] he relished again putting down restless natives.

At ten o'clock, the Royal Hospital gates swung open, and in complete darkness Strathnairn led out his tiny column. Almost immediately, an advance guard apprehended a civilian with a loaded revolver. Despite his furious protests that he worked in the Chief Secretary's Office, troops brought him to the rear, where he truculently refused to walk and flung himself to the ground. Wellesley recalled that:

> There was nothing to do but have him tied to a gun. When it advanced, he again threw himself down and was consequently dragged along like a minnow at the end of a trolling line. The gun plan was, however, completely successful, as the little creature soon found that walking was after all the best means of locomotion.[15]

Leaving the suburbs behind, the column captured many Fenians returning to Dublin, an indication that something significant had occurred in the hills. Almost certainly these rebels were from the bands that had attacked Stepaside, Glencullen and Tallaght police stations. Still hoping to crush the rebels himself, Strathnairn became exasperated when Wellesley sought permission to strengthen the detail at the rear guarding an increasing number of prisoners, as he was reluctant to diminish an already small fighting force. But after Wellesley warned him that so many prisoners could easily escape into the darkness, Strathnairn ingeniously ordered that captives' belts and braces be removed and buttons cut off their trousers, which were then split down the back. Wellesley fondly recalled that:

> This somewhat comical operation was carried out to the letter, much to the indignation of the prisoners. Their ludicrous position was not noticeable at night-time, but when morning dawned, it was indescribably amusing to see these men, some of them respectable drapers' assistants with high hats and overcoats with velvet collars, marching along holding up their trousers.[16]

As Strathnairn's column suffered repeated delays, he was obviously not leading a forced march. First, he diverted troops to search every wayside cottage, but all they found were old women in bed, some of them calmly smoking clay pipes. Strathnairn also sent soldiers far out of their way to retake police barracks that had supposedly fallen to the rebels, only to discover constables safely barricaded inside unscathed walls.[17] Then the field guns took a wrong turn in the darkness and temporarily separated from the main column. While Strathnairn waited for them to return, his troops captured even more Fenians, as well as six carts driven by old women that were full of weapons and ammunition concealed under bales of hay.[18] Passing the carts, Strathnairn's horsed stepped on a loaded revolver, which went off but caused no injuries.[19] Shortly before dawn, Strathnairn sent an officer ahead to investigate the situation at Tallaght. But when he reported that police defenders at Tallaght barracks had repulsed Fenian attackers and captured over sixty prisoners, the general immediately led his column there. Wellesley could:

> not remember a more touching spectacle that that which awaited us on approaching this little isolated barracks, a tiny whitewashed building. In front of it, drawn up in line, were six of the Constabulary men in command of an old white-haired sergeant; they presented arms to Lord Strathnairn as he approached.[20]

The sergeant was actually sub-inspector Burke, who wanted to display his haul of prisoners locked up inside and a wounded man (i.e. Stephen O'Donoghue) whom he had placed on a bed in the cellar. Wellesley recalled that:

> The office was so full of people that it was next to impossible to get in, especially as the door opened inwards. I managed to just get my head in, but it did not remain there long, as the smell of Fenian human-ity was too much for me. The man in the cellar died while we were there.[21]

Strathnairn was having the time of his life.

By now the sun had risen and Strathnairn's column resumed its march to Tallaght Hill. Passing along a 6ft-high wall, Strathnairn noticed half a dozen Fenians in the fields beyond and ordered Wellesley to capture them. As there was no gate in the wall and the rebels had a considerable head start, Wellesley stood on his horse's saddle and clambered over, followed by his soldiers. But their pursuit was hopeless as the rebels faded into distance. Suddenly, as Wellesley stood in a ditch, he heard a cry, 'Look out!' and ducked his head just in time as Strathnairn's favourite jumper flew over him and landed safely. After catching the fugitives, the general drove them back like an old sheepdog rounding up strays and returning them to their pen. Wellesley recollected that 'we soon afterwards arrived at the end of our journey but alas there was no one to fight'.[22]

Tallaght Hill was deserted, as rebels there had experienced a complete vacuum of leadership. Most Fenians had left Dublin poorly armed after learning about a rising only on the day itself from circle leaders who told them nothing, and then incredibly themselves failed to turn up. Even Halpin went missing before action. Astonishingly, instead of being present at Tallaght from the start, he decided to lead a large body of men there from Killakee demesne, 4 miles south-east of Tallaght. After Halpin and fifty lightly armed volunteers assembled, they waited a long time, but the main group of reinforcements never materialised. Halpin then vanished, an inglorious performance eerily reminiscent of McCafferty's disappearing act at Chester. Later, Denieffe denied accusations about Halpin being drunk at the Bleeding Horse pub a day earlier and that his nerves were shot: 'I never saw him more cool, calm and rational than he was on that night.'[23] But Halpin never satisfactorily explained where he went. Denieffe recalled that he resurfaced next day in Dublin, a broken man, depressed in mind and body. Conducted to a safe house, Halpin was eventually smuggled to England.

Bereft of leadership and stranded in the cold darkness, thousands of wet, shivering Fenians waited aimlessly at Tallaght Hill for someone to turn up and assume command. As their rudimentary communications system disintegrated, remnants of Stephen O'Donoghue's circle arrived to report their defeat at Tallaght police station. Almost simultaneously, soldiers from Major Greene's column and Strathnairn's advance guard approached from opposite directions. Disorientated, demoralised rebels discarded their weapons and fled. The decisive battle that Strathnairn craved never happened. Instead, there was a stampede as insurgents scattered in every direction. The so-called Battle of Tallaght was literally a bloodless victory in which British soldiers never fired a shot. During mopping-up operations, they captured dozens of rebels, but most had escaped in the darkness and made their way back into Dublin. There, police pickets caught some on the Grand Canal bridges, but others reportedly swam across to safety. The haul of arms and ammunition recovered in the fields was so large that the latter was thrown into a wet ditch and the weapons were taken back to Dublin in requisitioned carts, along with 193 dispirited prisoners.

Many exhausted captives could barely drag their feet along as their column snaked through the streets of a capital lined with spectators. Upon finally reaching the Upper Castle Yard at about two o'clock in the afternoon, some men fainted and collapsed. Eventually, soldiers marched them to the parade ground of the police barracks in the Lower Castle Yard, where curious high-ranking dignitaries scrutinised those whom they despised as creatures who had caused them so much misery. They included Viceroy Lord Abercorn, DMP Commissioner of Police O'Ferrell, Assistant Commissioner Colonel Lake, Superintendent Ryan and Samuel Lee Anderson. Meanwhile, detectives circulated, taking names and searching for prominent suspects. Embarrassingly, the argumentative man whom Strathnairn's advance guard had arrested at the start and dragged to Tallaght and back actually was a civil servant in Naas's office. Discreetly released, he was sent on his way. Perhaps surprisingly, police considerately handed bowls of water through their barracks' windows to thirsty detainees, and allowed them to lie down on straw provided for that purpose. Nearby stood carts piled high with captured weapons. A strong detachment of Coldstream Guards under a Captain Hall watched over the prisoners as Colonel Lake charged them with high treason. Wellesley remembered the look of terror in their eyes when Hall ordered his soldiers to load their rifles, assuming as many did that they were about to be executed without even a drumhead court martial.[24] In fact, Hall was only guarding against escape attempts by famished prisoners as they were marched off to Kilmainham Gaol. Significantly, large crowds gathered outside Dublin Castle cheered the captives loudly. Having gone hungry since dinner on the previous day, Strathnairn and Wellesley lunched at the Castle, a meal that Wellesley remembered as the most enjoyable in his life.[25]

Normality returned swiftly to the capital. On 8 March, Strathnairn hosted a ball for Dublin's high society, a victory dance at which he rather shamelessly basked in adoration, when the real British hero at Tallaght had been sub-Inspector Burke. Everyone present must have breathed a collective sigh of relief that the long-dreaded political earthquake had been only a mild tremor. In the end nothing had changed, the old order had prevailed, and apparently all was well again with the world.

On the other side of the country, attention was initially focussed on the strategically important Limerick Junction railway station. Located at the heart of Ireland's most disaffected districts – Tipperary, Cork and Limerick – it was to be the centre of military operations in the South. From there rebels could disrupt the entire Great Southern and Western Railway network and prevent British troops from leaving their bases at Limerick, Clonmel and Waterford on one side, and Buttevant, Fermoy and Cork on

the other. On Monday, 4 March, rumours circulated of an imminent outbreak at the Junction just as troops, cavalry and artillery flooded the area
and the British Army requisitioned accommodation locally. Prominent
families in the area were also advised to move to hotels or the houses
of friends in nearby towns. Some went to Nenagh, the county town of
Tipperary, others preferred Limerick, and a few preferred Dublin. Within
hours, news of Massey's arrest spread rapidly throughout Munster, and
mustering groups of rebels dispersed while columns marching towards
the Junction turned back.

Although Dublin and Tallaght dominated newspaper headlines, the most
serious warfare and destruction occurred in Co. Cork, where rebels fought
police and army, severed railway and telegraph lines, and attacked Irish
Constabulary barracks.[26] Cork city itself was initially to remain quiescent,
while Captain Patrick Condon led a rising in East Cork – a region that
loyalists regarded as a hotbed of treason. But his arrest on 2 March disrupted
the local IRB, especially as Condon had not acquainted subordinates with
his plans. Two days later, police arrested the IRB centre of Midleton, James
O'Sullivan and other prominent Fenians. But three prominent militarists
– John McClure, Peter O'Neill Crowley and John Edward Kelly – were
determined to fight.

Twenty-year-old McClure was an Irish-American who had fought for
the Union in the Civil War, and afterwards joined the Fenian Brotherhood.
In mid-December 1865, he sailed to Ireland with his brother-in-law
Condon, and during January and February 1867, they organised East Cork
for rebellion. McClure stayed in Ballymacoda with 34-year-old Crowley,
a well-to-do farmer and the centre of his local IRB circle.[27] Crowley's
grand-uncle, Father Peter O'Neill, had been flogged for his role in the 1798
rebellion, a punishment that permanently embittered the Crowley family.
Amnestied after five years in Botany Bay, O'Neill befriended Peter when his
parents died, imbuing him with intense nationalism and religious fervour.
Crowley always wore a large bronze crucifix around his neck, had taken a
vow of celibacy, and abstained from alcohol. Standing 6ft 2in tall, broad-
shouldered, deep-chested and powerfully built, his charismatic, driven
personality made Crowley a natural leader, whose entire 100-strong circle
would follow him into the rising.

Known as the Protestant Fenian, 27-year-old Kelly's parents had
migrated from Kinsale, Co. Cork to America, where young John became

apprenticed to a printer. In early 1860 he joined the Fenian Brotherhood in New York, and a year later he returned to Ireland, where he worked as a compositor for the *Cork Herald*. Kelly also secretly conducted military training for the IRB and supported Irish-American officers based in the county. Soon 'Kelly's Men' became known as his 'daredevils'. On Saturday, 2 March 1867, Kelly met Crowley in Cork City and described his own plans for military action. Even Crowley thought them rash, but he agreed to help if no rising materialised. The trio knew about the IRB's critical shortage of weaponry: Crowley's circle possessed only one rifle (his own), some old shotguns and a few pikes, while McClure had just a revolver. Accordingly, they decided first to raid police stations and coastguard stations in the Midleton, Knockadoon and Castlemartyr triangle for arms and ammunition, before coalescing with other raiding parties into a large strike force.

The night of 5 March in Co. Cork was Skellig Night, a time of folk festivities, music, dancing, drinking and fireworks when civilians partied and policemen relaxed – ideal camouflage for catching British forces by surprise. East Cork's rising began in Midleton, where a local carpenter, Timothy Daly, had succeeded James O'Sullivan as IRB centre a day after the latter's arrest. In the darkness Daly led about forty Fenians armed with pikes and a few guns down Main Street and past puzzled revellers, who mistook them for policemen. A four-man police patrol had uneventfully circled the town centre, until both sides collided at the southern end of Main Street. Then, Daly's men trapped the policemen against a high wall and ordered them to surrender. Daly tried to capture a Constable O'Donnell's rifle by jamming a revolver against his head and firing. But just in time, O'Donnell pushed Daly away and he was only grazed. Simultaneously, a volley from Daly's men wounded a Constable Sheedy, who ran a short distance, collapsed, and bled to death as his colleagues fled amidst a hail of bullets. Surprisingly, the Fenians did not attack Midleton police station. Instead, after seizing Sheedy and O'Donnell's weapons, they set out on a 6-mile march to Castlemartyr.[28]

Meanwhile, Crowley and McClure led a well-planned surprise attack on Knockadoon coastguard station, situated 13 miles south of Youghal at the end of a long road running to a remote strand. Although nominally Crowley's superior officer, McClure deferred to the older man, who commanded a circle. After suddenly and silently overwhelming the station without firing a shot, the rebels stripped Chief Boatman Robert Hoyle and his men of their weapons, and were about to force-march them away from Knockadoon when a coastguard's wife successfully appealed for her husband's release. Fenians and prisoners then proceeded back through Ballymacoda to Killeagh, where Crowley and McClure waited for various raiding parties operating in East Cork. Soon afterwards Kelly arrived from Youghal, but with only ten men. However, a large rebel band expected from Castlemartyr never turned up. Daly's Midleton party had arrived in Castlemartyr and combined with local Fenians to attack the police station, but its six well-trained and armed defenders had already closed its shutters and fortified the building. When they opened fire and killed Daly, the shaken and leaderless attackers melted away.

Realising that reinforcements were not coming from Midleton and Castlemartyr, Crowley and McClure dismissed every unarmed man and set out to discover what had gone wrong. Soon after 6 a.m. they reached the outskirts of Castlemartyr, where McClure acceded to the coastguards' pleas and released them. They went into Castlemartyr and immediately alerted its police barracks to the rebels' presence. While Crowley's men rested, a scout, 'Bowler' Cullinan, reconnoitred ahead, but as he passed the police barracks Chief Boatman Hoyle had him arrested. Shortly afterwards, Crowley and McClure learned from a local resident about the abortive attack on Castlemartyr police station and Daly's death.

At 1 p.m. the rebels watched forlornly as a train from Youghal pulled into nearby Mogeely railway halt and disgorged over 100 soldiers on their way to garrison Castlemartyr and scour the surrounding countryside. In less than a day the East Cork rising had come and gone. However, Crowley, McClure and Kelly brimmed with a no-surrender mentality. After dismissing most of their band, they led a small group north-west, intending to join rebels still holding out around Mallow and Limerick Junction. For three weeks soldiers and police pursued them, attempting to extinguish this last flicker of resistance. Only their capture or death would allow the Irish government to officially proclaim the rising over.

After manoeuvring around Mallow, Crowley's party halted near Darragh Hill in the Cork/Limerick border country. On Thursday, 28 March, Crowley went disguised into Cork City and learned that the rising had collapsed everywhere. Even now, he could have escaped to America or France, but to Crowley flight was anathema: for him it really was do or die. On Saturday, he, McClure and Kelly slept overnight in a friendly house, but an informer had spotted locals giving them food and told Mitchelstown police, who in turn summoned the Waterford Flying Column.[29] On Saturday night a Major Bell and Resident Magistrate Henry E. Redmond arrived with 100 soldiers and thirty cavalrymen, for whom ten policemen would act as guides. Early on Sunday morning, 31 March, Crowley, McClure and Kelly left their hiding place and moved south, but after only half a mile they heard soldiers of the Flying Column sweeping the area. Major Bell intended surrounding nearby Kilclooney Wood, a 10-acre concentration of fir trees on the banks of the Ahaphoucha River, about 8 miles west of Mitchelstown. Simultaneously, Redmond and other soldiers conducted house-to-house searches. Crouching behind a hedge, the three fugitives crept cautiously over a ditch but were spotted breaking cover. Fleeing in the darkness, Crowley and McClure lost contact with Kelly, who was captured soon afterwards.

Realising that the Flying Column was surrounding them, Crowley and McClure tried to break out, but after being spotted, they turned and sprinted into Kilclooney Wood. Thirty British soldiers followed and the chase was on. Darting from tree to tree in a fierce running battle, Crowley fired his rifle and McClure a revolver as they desperately raced to the Ahaphoucha. But wintertime had shed foliage, making camouflage more difficult, and British snipers twice wounded Crowley. First, a bullet hit the lock of his rifle and rebounded into Crowley's stomach, while another went straight through his back. Reaching the Ahaphoucha, both men plunged into the swift-flowing river, but weakened from loss of blood, Crowley needed McClure to hold him up. Unwittingly, McClure had also dipped his revolver into the water and soaked its old-fashioned paper cartridges. By now, Redmond had heard the gunfire, caught up, leapt into the river, and from behind grappled with McClure, who tried shooting him over his shoulder, only for the damp cartridges to misfire.

From the opposite bank, soldiers leapt into the river to bayonet McClure, but Redmond intervened just in time and had Crowley carried to the bank. There, Major Bell honoured a courageous enemy by resting Crowley's head on his greatcoat. After an army surgeon, Dr Segrave, pronounced Crowley critically wounded, Bell sent for a priest. Crowley begged for his sister Catherine to be brought from Ballymacoda, and he and McClure then briefly reminisced before the latter was handcuffed and led away. By then soldiers had intercepted a young curate, Father T. O'Connell, on his way to celebrate Mass at an outlying chapel. He witnessed Dr Segrave staunching

Crowley's stomach wound with one hand and holding Crowley's prayer book with the other as he recited the Litany of the Holy Name of Jesus:

> I saw that there was no time to lose and having made him as comfortable as circumstances would permit by means of the soldiers' knapsacks I then and there surrounded by the military and police, administered the last sacraments. The fervour and devotion for which he prepared for death – though suffering very much – were most striking.[30]

Crowley then uttered his last words: 'Father, I suppose I'll be some time in purgatory and will you tell my sister to have some masses offered up for the repose of my soul.' Segrave decided to get Crowley treated in Mitchelstown and had him placed on a cart, but shortly after setting off, Crowley died.

For days before Tuesday, 5 March, rumours had swept Cork city about an imminent rising. Young men quit their jobs, took leave of families, and on Monday evening they thronged local churches for confession. Afterwards hundreds left to rendezvous outside the city. Streets became almost entirely deserted because of harsh, windy weather and overcast skies, but also because trouble was widely anticipated. Police patrols circulated, couriers delivered messages, and mounted police, soldiers and cavalry prepared for action. Artillery was placed in the city centre. The British authorities knew something unusual was happening when a mail train from Dublin due in Cork at 2 am. on Wednesday had not even reached Charleville – 37 miles away – two hours later. Moreover, telegraph lines between Cork and Dublin, as well as Charleville and Limerick Junction, were severed, while in many places railway tracks had been torn up.

Co. Cork's most serious military action began on Wednesday morning when 1,800 Fenians assembled at Prayers Hill, on the western outskirts of Cork city. Among them was 38-year-old James Francis Xavier (J. F. X.) O'Brien. A former medical student at Queen's College Galway, he had relocated to the warmer climate of New Orleans due to ill health. There O'Brien met James Stephens and became a Fenian. When civil war began in April 1861, he enlisted in the Confederate Army as an assistant surgeon, but in late 1862, O'Brien returned to Ireland. After settling in Cork, he wrote for the *Irish People*, but after it's suppression, O'Brien briefly went underground.[31]

Aware of how few weapons the IRB possessed, O'Brien had opposed sending unarmed men out to be slaughtered, and in February 1867 he voted against a rising. However, feeling obliged to honour a majority decision, he turned out at Prayer Hill. Pessimistic from the start, O'Brien counted only one small rifle, six revolvers, two shotguns and a dozen pikes. He also doubted assurances that large IRB arms depots at Limerick Junction would equip insurgents; later, he learned that prominent Cork Fenians who had spread this disinformation never actually turned out. At Prayer Hill, O'Brien observed a complete leadership vacuum, especially as Captain Condon had been arrested:

> After waiting for leaders for the best part of an hour it was decided
> – by whom I did not know – that we should move towards Mallow.
> There was an idea among some of the men that there was a deposit of
> arms thereabouts. The men straggled along the road – a mere rabble.[32]

By a process of elimination, a leader eventually emerged. After an hour, O'Brien was made aware of two committed Fenians – Captain Mackey, the alias of Michael Mackey Lomasney, who a quarter century later would blow himself up attaching a bomb to London Bridge; and Michael O'Brien, hanged a year later as a 'Manchester Martyr'. However, when both men refused to assume command, J.F.X. O'Brien found himself last man standing. Although he soon had the rebel column marching in unison and singing rebel songs, O'Brien knew in his heart that the rising was already doomed. 'From the first I had little doubt that we were conducting one of the most forlorn of forlorn hopes.'[33] O'Brien, though, doubted that an arms depot existed at Mallow:

> I felt also that the course of that day would decide whether we should
> be an insurgent force or not. If the depot turned up, we should be in
> a position to start the revolution. While if there was no depot – as
> I felt certain would prove to be the case – we could do nothing but
> disband at once.[34]

At mid-morning, O'Brien, Mackey and fifty men diverted 6 miles outside Mallow to attack Ballyknocken police station.[35] But two constables saw them approaching and retreated inside the two-storey building, whose defenders refused to surrender. When Mackey banged on the front door with his rifle butt, a shot from inside covered him with gunpowder.

Eventually the Fenians forced entry by grabbing a small ladder propped against the barracks wall and using it as a battering ram. When the defenders fled to a second storey, O'Brien ordered the stairs set alight, after first letting the police sergeant's wife and children leave the building. At this point a villager on horseback raced towards Mallow to alert the authorities. As the blaze took hold, the policemen asked for a local priest, Father Neville, to intercede; and when he said they could surrender with honour, the policemen handed down their rifles and from a window descended down the captured ladder.

Afterwards, O' Brien rejected an offer from some policemen to join the rebels, and pleas from some Fenians to make the policemen prisoners. Believing the rising would soon end, he feared that in either case, captives could subsequently identify his men.[36] Besides Mallow, authorities had already dispatched soldiers to Ballyknocken, and soon afterwards O'Brien spotted about eighty soldiers advancing through a field. Wistfully, he thought well-armed rebels concealed behind high hedges could have slaughtered them, but now O'Brien could only order a scattering in every direction. Eventually, he found himself alone with a teenager called Murphy heading towards Limerick Junction, where Fenians had intended to rendezvous. However, after marching 35 miles without food or rest, O'Brien's feet were blistered, and despite passing Kilmallock on 7 March without incident, he soon learned of military and police checkpoints ahead. Three miles outside Kilmallock, dragoons pursued him and Murphy into a large field, discovered O'Brien's revolver, and brought them to Kilmallock police station.[37]

In Limerick, Fenians had intended marching through the county, gathering supporters, capturing arms, attacking smaller police barracks, cutting telegraph wires and ripping up railway lines. But in reality, they accomplished little. A brief assault on Ardagh police barracks in the west was a purely symbolic gesture before the rebels moved on. And when another large Fenian band attacked Adare police station, 12 miles south-west of Limerick city, it fled after defenders returned fire. Rebels did capture Kilteely barracks, 15 miles south-east of Limerick city, but only after it had already been evacuated.

Early on Ash Wednesday, 6 March, the rising's fiercest encounter happened at Kilmallock, a walled town about 20 miles from Limerick city and close to the border with Co. Cork.[38] Largely unchanged since medieval times, Kilmallock had a poorhouse, two castles, a railway station, a church, a Dominican priory and one of the strongest police barracks in southern Ireland. Captain John Dunne and Patrick Walsh, two Irish-American officers, led the rebels. Dunne was originally from nearby Charleville, while Walsh had briefly fled from Kilmallock before returning in late 1866. Dunne's plan was to capture railway stations, tear up train lines, cut telegraph wires and seize weapons from outlying police stations at Bruree and Charleville. But first, rebel columns converged on Kilmallock and joined Dunne's force in a field near the railway station, about a mile from the police barracks. Many Fenians in Kilmallock had also turned out, furious that on the previous evening police had arrested William Henry O'Sullivan, a popular hotelier who also owned a hire car establishment. Although he was not himself a Fenian, many of O'Sullivan's forty employees were in the IRB and townspeople regarded his detention as designed to intimidate the local population. After Dunne ordered Kilmallock to be searched for weapons, he, Patrick Walsh and William O'Sullivan, the hotelier's son, led 200 Fenians, most of them armed with pikes, towards the police station.

Fronted by a 3ft-high wall, the stone building was reputedly almost impossible to storm, especially as a Head Constable and thirteen policemen manned it. Apparently, they feared a night-time attack, and had remained on guard until 5 a.m. when the station lights went out. Ironically, this was the signal for an assault to begin. However, repeated and well-coordinated police return fire killed a Fenian and seriously wounded Walsh. A local doctor, Peter Clery, who had turned out in solidarity with his two Fenian brothers, treated Walsh, but soon a stray bullet from a policeman's rifle killed Clery. After trying unsuccessfully to have a hole drilled in a side wall, Dunne ordered straw and a barrel of tar to be stacked against the door and set alight, but the flames fizzled out.

Although daylight increased the risk of police recognising his men, Dunne carried the fight on into a fifth hour, even as many Fenians dumped their weapons and vanished into the darkness. However, at 9.15 a.m, a dozen police reinforcements arrived from nearby Kilfinane and caught the insurgents in withering crossfire. Crawling on hands and knees, Dunne's party first withdrew to a place of relative safety before fighting a running battle as they retreated to the town centre. Initially the Fenians intended making a last stand, but a council of war was divided on whether they should fight to the end. After Dunne advised against further resistance, he shook the hands of his men, bade them farewell, mounted a policeman's captured horse and rode off towards Charleville. Everyone else scattered. Some went on the run, but Dunne fled to America, where Fenians pilloried him for an abject performance. During Thursday afternoon, 100 armed policemen searched Kilmallock and arrested twenty men – including Patrick Walsh and William O'Sullivan junior. Later convicted of high treason, they were sentenced to between five and fifteen years' imprisonment.

Notably, the Kilmallock firefight provided the rebellion with its Tomb of the Unknown Soldier, after a third unidentified fatality was buried at the local cemetery in a grave whose headstone carried no name. Known locally as the Unknown Fenian, he was almost certainly Patrick Hassett, whose father owned a pub 2 miles outside town. After Patrick went missing on the night of Tuesday to Ash Wednesday, his family never saw him again; nor did he ever contact them. Seemingly, Patrick's father avoided visiting the police station to identify the body as he feared losing his publican's licence.

An Irish-American officer, Col. Leonard, led the rising in Drogheda. At 1.30 on 6 March, up to 1,000 insurgents assembled in a large open space known as the Potato Market, their intended headquarters. However, when twenty-seven police officers arrived and opened fire the rebels immediately scattered, leaving their weapons and ammunition behind. Police also captured twenty-five Fenians and next morning arrested forty-seven more, including eighteen men just arrived on the Liverpool steamer who planned to join the rising. Small rebel raids also occurred at Dunleer and Dundalk.

In north Queen County, rebels attempted to capture Mount Mellick police barracks but fled when defenders fired and shot one dead. Near Leixlip in Co. Kildare, rebels wounded a policeman in a brief exchange. In Co. Clare, rebels attacked a coastguard station near Kilrush and captured its armoury, while in the same county 150 insurgents mobilised outside Ennis but did not enter the town.

In Co. Tipperary, rebels blocked the main Dublin railway line near Thurles, severed the Waterford line at Bansha, and unsuccessfully attacked police stations in the Glen of Aberlow and Glenbane. But overall the Fenian rising in Tipperary was a debacle. On the night of 5 March, about 1,000 rebels turned out at Thurles, but their leader, an American officer called Joseph Gleeson, failed to show up. Demoralised, the insurgents went home. The main action in Tipperary happened at Ballyhurst, a townland on the main road between Cashel and Tipperary town. Here, the Fenian leader was 27-year-old Thomas Bourke, whose parents had migrated from Fethard fifteen years earlier. During the American Civil War, Bourke fought for the Confederacy, suffered a shattered leg at the Battle of Gettysburg, and for two years was made a prisoner of war. Returning to New York lame and in bad health, he became a successful Fenian organiser in Manhattan. On 12 January 1867, with the Fenian rank of general, Bourke sailed out of New York for England. After spending three weeks in London, he arrived at his birthplace of Fethard and began preparing Tipperary Fenians for the rising. Police knew of Bourke's presence immediately, but he spun them a tale about being a *New York Tribune* reporter in Ireland for medical treatment and to see old friends before he died. After vanishing for over a fortnight, he resurfaced at Ballyhurst on 6 March. He commanded 150 volunteers, who were already demoralised by the evident collapse of the rising. When fifty soldiers approached, a brief skirmish occurred in which one Fenian was killed, many were wounded and a large number were captured, including Bourke.

Kelly had high hopes for Co. Waterford. As one of Stephens' and Luby's first recruiting grounds, it was after Dublin, Cork, Limerick and Tipperary among the strongest Fenian areas in Ireland. The military leader in Waterford was Ricard O'Sullivan Burke, a high-level Irish-American officer who had fought for the Union throughout the entire Civil War. Besides fighting in many battles, Burke had also joined the Fenian Brotherhood and become head of a circle. After the war ended, O'Mahony sent him to Ireland, where he became close to Kelly. At the start of 1867, Burke went to London and lodged with Massey until February, when Kelly sent him to lead the Waterford rising. But arrests and arms searches had weakened Fenianism in the county, and on 5 March disappointingly few IRB volunteers gathered at the village of Kilmacow, 5 miles north of Waterford city. Burke sent all of them home.

Ulster has been called the dog that did not bark during the rising.[39] Despite IRB members there anticipating a call to arms, Kelly and the IRB leadership in Ireland had vetoed military action in the province. They feared it might provoke retaliation from the Protestant majority and incite a sectarian civil war, the same factor that later motivated an IRB Military Council to cancel mobilisation in Ulster during the Easter Rising of 1916. Besides, the Irish government had decapitated the IRB leadership there through widespread arrests during 1866, culminating in the detention of

Ulster's Fenian chief, Harbison, just days before the rising. Furthermore, despite small amounts of arms being smuggled into Belfast, Cookstown, Dungannon, Ballymoney and other towns, Fenians in Ulster were literally outgunned by a far superior British Army garrison in Belfast.

The Fenian Rising of March 1867 never became a nationwide rebellion. Geographically limited and militarily unimpressive, it did not come close to achieving its goals. Effectively it lasted two days, and within weeks the last flickering resistance was extinguished at Kilclooney Wood. Only sporadic outbreaks happened, notably in Dublin, Cork, Limerick, Tipperary, Louth, Clare and Waterford. There was almost no street fighting anywhere, not a single British Army garrison was stormed, rebels attacked just twenty-eight of 1,600 police stations in Ireland, and they captured only three – one of which had already been evacuated. Insurgents and the British Army never fought a battle and the rising was primarily suppressed by the Irish Constabulary (which soon added the prefix 'Royal' to its title) and Dublin Metropolitan Police. They did most of the fighting and inflicted the heaviest rebel casualties. Fewer than 10,000 Fenians mobilised for the rising, and although eager to fight they were mostly armed with shotguns, pikes and scythes. Edward Duffy had vetoed military action in Connaught, not a shot was fired in Ulster, and Massey's vision of thousands of Fenians converging on Limerick Junction in Munster had proved to be delusional.

Immediately after the rising, English newspapers ridiculed the (storm in a) 'Teacup rebellion'. Devoy admitted that, 'The Rising of 1867 from a military standpoint failed dismally',[40] while A.M. Sullivan scathingly declared that 'of all the insensate attempts at revolution recorded in history, this one was assuredly pre-eminent. The inmates of a lunatic asylum could scarcely have produced a more impossible scheme.'[41] Strathnairn's Military Secretary, Owen Tudor Burne, recollected that 'the Staff, were mute with surprise at our bloodless victory'.[42]

There were many reasons for this debacle. Unquestionably, the planning was defective. Paradoxically, an insurrection repeatedly promised and repeatedly delayed was eventually in unfavourable circumstances. Devoy declared that: 'The favourable elements which prevailed at the end of 1865 and the beginning of 1866 had been dissipated; significant time had not elapsed in which to remedy the weaknesses and inefficiency which characterised the situation under Stephens.'[43] Fariola acknowledged that Fenians were ill-prepared, under-resourced and grossly disorganised. 'It seemed to be the role of unmerciful disaster to follow fast and follow faster on our footsteps. There was no fight virtually speaking. There was confusion in the conveyance of orders, treason in our midst and insufficiency of arms.'[44] Consequently, only twelve people – all but one a rebel – died during one of the shortest insurrections in Irish history.

Under pressure, Kelly was forced to strike prematurely when he really needed time for meticulous preparations. Ideally, the rising should have been postponed until the autumn of 1867 at the earliest, but time was a luxury Kelly did not have. Under immense pressurise from Fenians in Ireland and revolutionary extremists in London and Liverpool, Kelly risked being ousted if he delayed – just as he himself had deposed Stephens – and Fenianism itself might have disintegrated. Cornered, Kelly, Cluseret, Fariola and Massey had only January and February 1867 to finalise arrangements for the rebellion – a completely unrealistic timescale. Moreover, based in London they had difficulty communicating military plans to Fenian leaders in Ireland. Until Massey and Fariola arrived in Ireland at the end of February, the only serious contact between these leaders and Kelly's junta was the visits of Mahony, Byrne, Harbison and Duffy to London in February, and subsequently Massey's four-day inspection tour of Ireland. As a result, Fenian leaders in Ireland and American officers distributed throughout the country were not thoroughly briefed well in advance about mobilisation arrangements, the type of warfare to be conducted and the targets to attack.

Poorly armed, many Fenians had still turned out despite atrocious weather and fought heroically, but they were badly let down by their military leaders. Just when unity at the top was essential after Stephens's overthrow, Fenianism experienced more splits as the Provisional Government and Directory fought for supremacy, while personal relations between Kelly, Cluseret, Fariola, Vifquain and Massey disintegrated. Moreover, individually, they performed dismally and sometimes abysmally. Kelly remained in London, but for reasons that did not wholly convince Fariola. Cluseret fled England before a shot was fired, citing Paris as the best place from which to observe developments. But he fooled nobody. Vifquain took Kelly's money and stayed hunkered down in Brussels. Fariola should have assumed leadership of the rising after Massey's arrest, but instead he left Ireland immediately without appointing a successor or making new military arrangements. Some lower-level commanders also performed unimpressively, like Bourke in Tipperary and Dunne at Kilmallock, while others like Gleeson at Thurles and Halpin at Tallaght never turned up at all.

Kelly's appointment of Massey as temporary commander-in-chief was a calamitous mistake. Chaos followed him everywhere, and caused even the scant preparations for rebellion to unravel as his grandiosity and recklessness confused and demoralised Fenians in the south and west. The disarray especially alienated Edward Duffy, who had already told Kelly that Connaught's involvement depended on him assigning a prestigious foreign officer to military command of the province. Kelly had responded by appointing Vifquain, but his enthusiasm had waned and he sat tight in Brussels. When Duffy's patience finally snapped in the first days of March, he sent a sister to warn Massey about the critical situation in Connaught, but all Massey did was ask Fariola to replace Vifquain in Connaught and then passively accepted his refusal. Massey's negligence gave Duffy the excuse for doing what he perhaps wanted to do all along and stand down his men. Consequently, not a shot was fired in Connaught during the rising. Massey also failed to replace Captain Condon after his arrest, leaving East Cork leaderless.

While Massey blighted the revolution openly from above, Corydon sabotaged it covertly from below. Corydon betrayed the Fenian raid on Chester and possibly prevented thousands of rifles reaching Ireland. He also told Dublin Castle the date of the rising and its military strategy, unmasked Massey as commander-in-chief, and revealed that he was travelling to Limerick Junction, thereby facilitating Massey's arrest, neutralising the Junction as a rendezvous location for the rebel army, and demoralised Fenians throughout the south and west. Corydon also expedited the capture of Captain Condon, which completely disrupted the rising in East Cork. Subsequently, at Special Commission trials he would testify against Fenian defendants like McCafferty, Flood and Bourke. Despite his relatively brief espionage career, Corydon must rank as one of the most effective government agents in Irish revolutionary history.

Fenian military resources for the rising were pitiable, proof that continuous British arms raids had had an effect. In February 1866, Kelly told Devoy that Fenians in the capital had only 800 rifles, and a year later Dublin centres said they had fewer than 3,000 weapons of all kinds. In early March 1867, Superintendent Ryan claimed the Dublin IRB possessed about 3,000 rifles and 12,000 revolvers, and even these figures were probably inflated.

An American expedition bringing officers, arms and ammunition would have greatly strengthened the rebels, and one did in fact come – but almost two months after the rising collapsed. Intent on another rebellion, Kelly's American supporters had somehow purchased and equipped a vessel with thousands of rifles, cases of ammunition and revolvers. On 15 April 1867, the ship left New York with forty American officers on board, but after reaching the west coast of Ireland five weeks later no Fenian leaders met them but extensive Crown forces were ready. Running out of provisions, the ship's master finally landed thirty-one Fenians near Dungarvan, Co. Waterford, where twenty-eight were speedily arrested. The vessel then returned to America. What might have happened had the expedition succeeded remains an intriguing question. Thousands of rifles could well have reached rebels in the south and west if Kelly had not been propelled into a premature rising. This might not have turned defeat into victory, but would surely have resulted in a more impressive and protracted insurrection. However, short-term flaws in planning and execution masked a greater truth – that long-term geopolitical factors had always made defeat inevitable.

In 1867 the United Kingdom was a great political, military and industrial power as the workshop of the world. The British Army had 172,000 soldiers who spearheaded imperial expansion across the globe, and they could reinforce the Irish garrison rapidly in the event of a rebellion. Strathnairn had already increased the garrison size from 19,500 soldiers in December 1866 to over 23,000 on 1 March 1867. Furthermore, courts martial and troop transfers had greatly reduced the likelihood of Fenian soldiers defecting to the rebels, and indeed only one did. Furthermore, an enormous material disparity existed between the two sides. Kelly said he had financed the rebellion on £1,500 and was 'almost out of my mind to know what could have been done with a little more money and what was obliged to be left undone'.[45] Far exceeding Kelly's estimate, Cluseret subsequently lamented afterwards that the rising could have succeeded 'if we had had on 7 March 100,000 in the Treasury. It failed mainly because of the total lack of money to pay the chaps who were supposed to take command.'[46] Not only was the 1867 rising a case of David against Goliath, the Irish David lacked stones for his sling.

The international situation in 1867 also strongly favoured England. Irish rebels dreamt of the enemy becoming embroiled in a major foreign conflict, but it was other European powers that went to war. Prussia and Austria defeated Denmark, before Prussia triumphed over Austria in the Seven Weeks War of 1866. Increasingly fixated on the Prussian threat, Napoleon III strengthened his army by reducing naval expenditure – considerably reducing the likelihood of him sending a French expeditionary force to Ireland.

The American schism created rival Fenian factions and an internecine struggle that complicated relations with the IRB and seriously depleted finances. By January 1867, the American movement was practically bankrupt and incapable of assisting the rising effectively. The British ambassador in Washington was mystified about how it even financed the naval expedition. And the split caused American Fenianism to lose focus, as one side wanted an attack on Canada while another remained concentrated on a rebellion in Ireland. Over time this internal wrangling exhausted the movement's military, financial and emotional resources, as well as reducing the number of officers sent to Ireland.

Finally, and completely unexpectedly, divine intervention obliterated any possibility of rebels taking to the hills and conducting protracted guerrilla warfare. The rain, sleet and gales on 5 March were a harbinger of the most terrible weather that Ireland experienced in living memory. A.M. Sullivan recalled that from next day:

> for twelve days and nights, without intermission, a tempest of snow and sleet ranged over the land, piling snow to the depth of yards on all the mountains, streets, and highways. Roads were impassable and, on the mountains, a Siberian spectacle met the view. The troops on service suffered severely; cavalry horses perished in numbers. But, after all, the troops had safe and comfortable barracks or billets to rest in at night; whereas a guerrilla warfare involving life on the unsheltered hillside was the main reliance of the insurgents. There was no attempting to cope with this fearful down-pour, accompanied as it was by a piercing hurricane.[47]

These conditions affected the rebels disproportionately by keeping many potential supporters at home, literally dampening the spirits of those men who turned out, only to shiver in the open air while police and army remained warmly ensconced in their barracks.

And yet the rising was not a complete disaster for Fenianism. At least it was militarily a more dangerous threat to British rule in Ireland than either

Emmet's Rebellion in 1803 or the 1848 rising, and Owen Tudor Burne believed that the Irish government had had a narrow escape: 'Fortunately for us, it was so badly organised that the outbreak, instead of being simultaneous in all parts of Ireland, which would have made it very formidable, fizzled, so to speak here and there like a damp squib and thus gave us plenty of warning.'[48]

Although militarily defeated, Fenians won the propaganda war, despite Dublin Castle's concerted smearing of rebels as ruffians and looters who had violated the rules of civilised warfare. Supposedly, Timothy Daly had almost murdered constable O'Donnell in Midleton, and Patrick Lennon had threatened to execute police prisoners at Glencullen. A false story also circulated that at Stepaside, Lennon had used captive policemen as human shields and ordered his men to shoot any prisoner attempting to scape. Naas claimed insurgents had committed 'a diabolical outrage' near Thurles after invading a policeman's house, trying unsuccessfully to force his brother-in-law to join the rebellion and then shooting him dead.[49] Owen Tudor Burne alleged captured Fenian papers showed a vast conspiracy among soldiers and policemen to murder colleagues, and that a bloodbath had only narrowly been averted:

> We were all marked down by name for assassination, from the Lord Lieutenant downwards, while sentries and housemaids had been bribed, in the most clever and secret manner to open the gates and doors of official and private citizens at a stated signal, for the accomplishment of these respective murders. We had really escaped what might have been a serious calamity to the peace of the country had it come off as arranged by the Irish-American Colonels.[50]

However, rebel leaders had emphatically warned Fenians against committing the massacres, drunken rampages and wanton destruction that had often disfigured Irish risings. Instead of pillaging and looting, insurgents paid for requisitioned food and drink, and they often treated the enemy chivalrously. Far from Lennon being a war criminal, one of his men, Captain Filgate, recalled that on Glencullen Mountain a police captive fell behind and he 'gently put the butt of my gun to his back and told him to keep up with the rest. Lennon saw me. In an instant he drew a revolver and threatened to kill the first person he found insulting or abusing a prisoner.'[51]

Twice, John McClure unconditionally released coastguard prisoners, who later testified that he had treated them humanely. At Ballyknocken, Captain Mackey ensured that no women and children were harmed and facilitated the escape of policemen from their burning barracks. Despite denouncing the rising, A.M. Sullivan declared that rebel behaviour at Kilmallock had redounded to their credit:

> There were two banks in the place, each containing a large sum of money in gold, silver and money; yet although any guns or pistols on the bank premises were brought away, not a penny of the money was touched. In fact, private property was most scrupulously respected, although the town was for a time completely in their hands.[52]

Robert Anderson conceded that during the previous month's Kerry rising, O'Connor's insurgents had treated a badly wounded constable Duggan very considerately. O'Connor himself apologised to the policeman for his injuries, offered a brandy flask, and left him in a neighbouring cottage after saying that a priest and doctor would be sent – a promise that was kept.[53]

Many constitutional nationalists grudgingly admired the rebels' conduct. Despite vile weather that confined many Fenians at home, thousands of mostly unarmed men had still turned out against a vastly superior enemy. And few people were surprised that frozen, badly armed insurgents at Tallaght had fled from British rifle volleys. Afterwards, British flying columns hunting rebels down often encountered sullen local populations that had actually fraternised with them. In Dublin, Col. Wellesley observed shows of sympathy for the column of captured rebels being escorted to the Castle: 'There was great excitement in the city. At most of the windows green flags were displayed and a vast concourse of people lined the route to the Castle, the gates of which were closed against the mob.'[54] Similarly, spectators cheered loudly when prisoners were led out on their way to Kilmainham Gaol. As Warren and Nagle from the *Erin's Hope* left Dungarvan for Waterford Gaol, a huge crowd bade them farewell, including many weeping women. Later, when another two of the crew arrived in Waterford, they were greeted by a large crowd. After stones were thrown at them, police charged, killing one man and wounding many others.

Fenians were heartened that their willingness to sacrifice everything for the cause had resonated widely, and nowhere more so than in East

Cork during Peter O'Neill Crowley's funeral. For two days his body lay in Mitchelstown's workhouse until his sister Catherine formally identified him. On 2 April, an inquest declared that soldiers had lawfully killed Crowley in the line of duty and Resident Magistrate Redmond turned his remains over to Catherine at the workhouse gate. Bereft, she now became like Isabella McManus six years earlier, chief mourner at her brother's funeral and the keeper of his memory. So began what an historian has called one of the most remarkable displays of sympathy and patriotic fervour in nineteenth-century Ireland – one that transformed Crowley into a revolutionary martyr.

Despite an awaiting hearse in the workhouse grounds, an immense crowd outside surged forward, took possession of the coffin, and spontaneously decided to carry it in relays every step of the 35-mile journey to Ballymacoda.[55] Almost every shop in Mitchelstown had closed out of respect for Crowley, but many men feared arrest and walked behind women streaming four deep down main street. At the front was a coffin draped with black cloth and covered in hundreds of laurel branches, Crowley's relatives, two priests and Catherine wearing a dark hood.

Silently the funeral procession snaked its way across country, passing through crowded villages and towns amidst scenes of almost unbearable grief. At dusk in Fermoy a huge gathering greeted the coffin, which children clutching little green banners led down main street, the solemnity only broken when mourner defiantly jeered at police and army barracks. As the future author and political activist Canon Patrick Sheehan, then a 15-year-old pupil, later recalled:

> It was computed that at least five thousand people took part in the procession. They shouldered the coffin of the dead patriot over mountain and valley and river. I remember how a group of us young lads shivered on the college terrace and watched the masses of men swaying over the bridge, the coffin conspicuous in their midst.[56]

On 3 April the funeral cortege reached Ballymacoda, where Crowley's body remained overnight in his own house until next day when he was buried in the local church beside his grand-uncle, Fr Peter O'Neill.

A martyr's cult grew rapidly around Crowley. A.M. Sullivan declared that his religiosity, bravery and tragic fate profoundly impressed the public mind. Reportedly, when on the run Crowley and his men had observed the customary Lenten devotions, and every night they knelt and recited the Rosary. In the telling, Crowley's final moments became an epic last stand, fighting heroically against insurmountable odds. In fact, not a single soldier suffered even a graze, although stories of police corpses secretly buried swelled the legend of Kilclooney Wood. Afterwards, locals campaigned unsuccessfully to rename Crowley's deathplace as Kilcrowley Wood, but it was soon called that anyway, a political shrine to which the IRB organised annual pilgrimages.

Initially, many Irish-Americans dismissed as British disinformation reports over the Atlantic cable that the rising had been totally defeated. Instead, messages from Col. Kelly assured O'Mahony that the situation was far from hopeless and begged him to send men and arms: 'It is war to the knife; only send us the knife.' Acting quickly, O'Mahony somehow raised enough funds for the long-promised naval expedition, though his armada consisted of only a single vessel. As already indicated, this ship, originally called the Jacknell, sailed on 12 April 1867 for Ireland carrying 5,000 rifles, 5 million rounds of ammunition, three artillery pieces and forty former army officers bound to assist an insurrection they believed was still raging in the west of Ireland. On Easter Sunday, 21 April, Captain Kavanagh fired cannon as he renamed the ship *Erin's Hope*. Skilfully evading British naval patrols, the ship reached Sligo Bay on 20 May, but for six days it cruised aimlessly while prearranged signals to the shore went unanswered by the local IRB. Eventually, Kavanagh sent ashore two crew members, who returned with Richard O'Sullivan Burke, a prominent Fenian. He explained that the revolution had collapsed, hundreds of Fenians were in gaol, and advised Kavanagh to sail south towards Skibbereen and link up with a guerrilla campaign in southern Munster. However, despite successfully avoiding British naval patrols, the ship failed to contact the Cork IRB. Kavanagh then sailed eastward to Co. Waterford. On 1 June, as provisions and water ran low, he landed twenty-seven men near Dungarvan where coastguards alerted local police, who quickly arrested the party and transferred them to Kilmainham Goal in Dublin. While *Erin's Hope* returned to America, Dublin Castle selected for trial three men whom Corydon had identified as prominent Fenians: Col. John Warren, Col. John Nagle and Captain Augustine Costello.

During April, May and June 1867, the trio and other defendants appeared at Special Commission trials in Dublin, Cork and Limerick.

Meanwhile, police captured rebels who had evaded the initial round-up. On 9 March, Edward Duffy was arrested at Boyle, Co. Roscommon, on his way to Dublin, from where he intended taking his family to America. Incarcerated in Mountjoy Gaol, Duffy bade his mother and five siblings farewell before they left Ireland. In a telegram from Liverpool on 3 July, Irish Constabulary detective McHale reported that General William Halpin, commander of rebel forces in Dublin, had just set sail for America via Queenstown. There, the informer Corydon identified him on board the liner *City of Paris*. Having fled to London, Fariola spent four desperate, poverty-stricken months surreptitiously roaming the capital with a £100 reward on his head. On 14 July, information from an informer led Metropolitan Police detectives to arrest Fariola in Oxford Street, and despite him pretending to be a German who barely spoke English, he was transferred immediately to Kilmainham Gaol.

At the Special Commissions, legal figures from the *Irish People* trials resurfaced. Butt and Lawless represented Fenian defendants, while Justices Keogh and Fitzgerald presided – though joined now by Chief Justice Monahan and Justice George. Some defendants, like McCafferty, were tried singly, but others, like Flood and Duffy, were prosecuted together. To their astonishment, Massey and Corydon gave damaging testimony for the prosecution. Having fainted at Limerick railway station, Massey was clearly no Robert Emmet and soon his resistance crumbled completely. The wife he had sent home to Ireland from New York in October 1866 visited Massey in Mountjoy Gaol, and convinced him that a new life together in a faraway country was preferable to his execution and her widowhood. Accordingly, in return for his freedom and resettlement thousands of miles away, Massey described his Fenian career and agreed to testify against former comrades. By virtually guaranteeing many convictions and discrediting Fenianism, Massey was worth every penny to Dublin Castle.

IRB fury against Corydon and Massey was immense. Fariola recalled that a few days after the rising, Kelly ordered him to establish an Avenging Committee and purchase knives with which it could dispose of both traitors.[57] On 17 April 1867, Superintendent Ryan reported rumours about assassination attempts being made on Massey and Corydon, if necessary on the witness stand in open court, and that female Fenians were prepared to stab or shoot both men.[58] Later, Ryan warned that Fenians wanted to assassinate Corydon and Massey while in protective custody at Chancery

Lane police station.[59] On 7 May, the DMP rearrested Michael Cody, the Shooting Circle's former leader who had secretly returned from England for the rising. After attempting to shoot dead a constable who recognised him, Cody was subdued by police, who found on him lists of judges, legal counsel and juries at the Special Commission. Cody himself was tried on 12 May and sentenced to twenty years' transportation in Australia, where he spent the rest of his life.

During the Special Commission trials, police guarded Massey and Corydon as they shuttled between Dublin, Cork and Limerick. Yet, despite becoming an effective double act that repeatedly and effortlessly recited damaging testimony, relations between the informers were tense, and although sharing residences, each man kept strictly to his own wing. Both men might have betrayed Fenianism, but Massey judged Corydon guilty of a higher form of treachery. Massey had only capitulated after being arrested and then pressurised by his wife, confessing that he had wanted to die after fainting at Limerick Junction. But Corydon had deliberately betrayed Fenianism and been rewarded for his perfidy. During their Special Commission appearances, Massey spoke only six words to Corydon: 'It was you got me taken.'[60]

Of 160 Fenians put on trial, 110 pleaded guilty. Some denied the charges and concocted ingenious alibis but all to no avail: John Flood claimed unsuccessfully that he was only in Chester to further his smuggling activities. Of fifty-two defendants found guilty, eight were convicted of high treason – including McCafferty – and condemned to death, though their sentences were quickly commuted to life imprisonment. Another twenty-five men received lengthy terms of penal servitude. Surprisingly, the seven defendants acquitted included Captain Patrick Condon, whose arrest had disrupted the rising in Cork.

The most important convicted Fenians, like McCafferty, went straight to high-security English prisons, and the rest were transported to Australia, where most settled permanently after being released. However, as only Western Australia was still accepting shipments and intended ending them on 26 November 1867, the Irish government raced against time to rid itself of 280 male convicts, sixty-two of them Fenians. Of the latter, seventeen were British Army soldiers sentenced at courts martial despite a long-standing British government policy of never transporting military prisoners. Some civilians were almost as senior as the IRB leaders sent to English gaols, including John Flood, Hugh Brophy, two Cork centres and Michael Moore, the IRB's most prolific pike maker.

However, one person – Octave Fariola – went voluntarily to Australia. Believing himself unappreciated by Stephens, misused by Kelly and betrayed by Massey, Fariola felt he owed Fenianism nothing. Hating prison life as his *Via Dolorosa*, Fariola protected the interests of the one person for whom he had always cared most – himself. In return for his liberty and a money grant that would take him and his wife to Australia, Fariola dictated a lengthy confession and agreed to testify if called at the Special Commission trials. On 20 December 1867, he walked out of Kilmainham Gaol a free man.

The Manchester Martyrs

Soon after the rising collapsed, Thomas Kelly went on the run, while in Ireland and London a shattered IRB pledged allegiance to his political enemy, William Roberts. Much diminished in authority, Kelly wandered from place to place in a shadowy existence, crestfallen, consumed with anger and railing against everyone he claimed had failed him. Stephens (now 'Little Baldy')[1] was supposedly luxuriating in Paris while Ireland's destiny teetered in the balance. He accused T.F. Bourke of torpedoing the rising in Tipperary and denounced McCafferty as a glory hunter who had ignored the Provisional Government's pleas to abort the Chester raid: 'But for that unfortunate affair we would have been in a position completely to surprise the government.'[2]

Soon after returning to London, Fariola accidentally encountered Kelly at London's Charing Cross railway station. Later he learned that Kelly had gone to Dublin for a meeting with the provisional government.[3] In mid-March, Kelly was definitely staying at his old lodgings in Grantham Street.[4] On 27 May, an informant told Superintendent Ryan that Kelly was living with medical students at a house on Ailesbury Road, about 2 miles south of Dublin city centre, rarely and only briefly venturing outside.[5] But T.D. Sullivan believed Kelly was living openly in the capital, 'moving about with an absence of disguise and disregard for concealment which astonished his confederates'.[6] As much of the IRB had sided with Roberts, Kelly shifted to England, where he hoped to establish a rival power base. There, he teamed up with 28-year-old Timothy Deasy, another Irish-American officer whom

Kelly had commissioned to lead the rising at Millstreet in Cork. By August 1867, both men were in Manchester for an IRB convention.

On 17 August 1867, an IRB convention in Manchester appointed Kelly Chief Executive of the Irish Republic, made Deasy responsible for the IRB in Liverpool, and designated another Irish-American officer, 28-year-old Edward Condon, as IRB leader in Manchester. Kelly and Deasy remained in Manchester for a while, but in the early hours of 11 September they left an IRB meeting in the city centre and encountered a police patrol. Challenged, Kelly and Deasy fled but were caught and, after a fierce struggle, overpowered. A loaded pistol was discovered on each man. Charged under the Vagrancy Act, Kelly said he was Martin Williams, an unemployed bookbinder, while Deasy called himself John Whyte, a hatter touring England for 'pleasure'.

Later that morning in court, Kelly and Deasy claimed they were American citizens and demanded to be discharged. Although magistrates refused, they regarded the case as routine and were about to briefly imprison them when Manchester's Chief Constable, Captain Henry Palin, intervened. Loaded revolvers did not sit well with him, while the defendants' American accents and military bearing hardly denoted innocent tradesmen down on their luck. Moreover, Dublin Castle had previously sent descriptions of Kelly and Deasy to British police forces and Palin noticed their similarity to 'Williams' and 'Whyte'. On a hunch, Palin voiced his suspicions that they were really Fenians and the magistrates remanded the pair for a week to Bell Vue Gaol in Gorton, a suburb about 4½ miles south-east of Manchester city centre. Three days later, Manchester authorities learned they had captured England's most wanted men. After Palin told Dublin Castle about the arrests it had immediately sent him Kelly's photograph. Naas, who had assumed the title Lord Mayo after his father's death on 12 August, also dispatched a senior civil servant to London, where he collected Corydon and Chief Inspector Williamson from Scotland Yard and brought them to Manchester. The informer immediately identified Kelly and Deasy.[7] On 14 September, a telegram from Manchester told Dublin Castle about Kelly and Deasy's detention. Delighted, Mayo emphasised they should be guarded round the clock, especially as he believed Manchester and Liverpool were the two British cities most vulnerable to a Fenian prison break.[8]

Edward Condon regarded Kelly's and Deasy's arrests as a serious setback, and that not responding would probably destroy the IRB in England.

Lacking the time and resources to organise a prison escape, he decided to ambush the prison van returning them to court on 18 September. After reconnoitring the Hyde Road route on which their Black Maria would travel, Condon planned to intercept the vehicle near a railway arch about half a mile from Belle Vue Gaol on its return journey, after Kelly and Deasy's court appearance confirmed they were actually inside. Afterwards, both men would be guided through an adjacent railway yard to a waiting cab and driven 6 miles east to Ashton-under–Lyne. There, Kelly and Deasy would change clothes and don disguises before travelling another 150 miles north-east to Newcastle-on-Tyne, from which they would sail first to a continental port and then return to America.

Condon's audacious plan had the elements of surprise, daring volunteers and a viable escape route. Moreover, although the Manchester IRB was penniless, Condon had secured funding from circles outside the city to buy weapons in Birmingham. Condon also instructed Belle Vue's sympathetic caterer to feed Kelly and Deasy well and strengthen them for an escape, while a friendly solicitor passed on Condon's plan. On 17 September, Condon distributed revolvers to a ten-man crew that included Michael O'Brien, a 30-year-old America Civil War veteran, William Allen, a 19-year-old joiner, and Michael Larkin, a 30-year-old tailor. Crucially, Condon had been assured that the police guard carrying keys for the door of the two-horse-drawn Black Maria always rode outside, meaning he did not regard pickaxes, crowbars and sledgehammers as necessary to break into the van.

On Wednesday, 18 September, Kelly and Deasy were back in court, but despite Mayo's appeals, their prison van travelled without armed guards or a cavalry escort. The Chief Secretary later accused Manchester authorities of overconfidence, never dreaming that Fenians would dare attack in a British city. If so, they had short memories, because only six months earlier and just 40 miles away hundreds of armed Irish republicans had converged on the city of Chester. At 5.10 p.m., a Home Office telegram urged Manchester's Lord Mayor Robert Neill to impose stricter security measures on Kelly and Deasy. So did a message at 7 p.m. from Dublin Castle.[9] But by then the prisoners were already in the wind.

That morning an IRB rescue party had gathered on Hyde Road, secreted themselves behind a wall, and waited for the prison van. Familiar with Condon's plan, Kelly and Deasy relaxed in court, even when Scotland Yard's

Chief Inspector Williamson unmasked them as prominent Fenians wanted for treason. After magistrates remanded them again, Kelly smiled, bowed to Williamson, and left the dock, straight into the custody of Sergeant Charles Brett. Aware now that two supposed vagrants were actually dangerous subversives, magistrates ordered them handcuffed and increased their security detail from three to twelve policemen. Nevertheless, they made a literally fatal mistake by allowing four non-violent offenders – three female petty criminals and a 12-year-old boy sentenced to a reformatory – to accompany Kelly and Deasy back to Belle Vue.

The dimly lit Black Maria had two rows of small cells divided by a middle passage, at the top of which sat Sergeant Brett. Some air and light entered through two roof ventilators and a door grating. Locking Kelly and Deasy inside separate cells, Brett left ajar four cages containing the three women and young boy, an understandable but critical blunder. At about half past three, a guard locked the van door from outside, passed the keys through its grating to Brett, and the vehicle departed. Two policemen sat on the driver's bench, three more rode on top, and two more stood on the rear step. Another four followed in a horse-drawn cab. Travelling unnoticed in front was another horse-drawn cab carrying Thomas Bolger, an IRB volunteer, and after passing through the railway arch at 4 p.m., Bolger alighted and signalled to Condon that the prison van was approaching.

When the Black Maria appeared, Condon recalled seeing an unexpectedly large police escort, 'apparently embracing the long and short and the fat and lean of the Manchester force'.[10] Constable Joseph Yarwood claimed Larkin grabbed a horse's head and that O'Brien fired his revolver at another horse, causing the van to crash. Dazed policemen leapt from the van and scattered in all directions, quickly followed by four officers from the following cab. Yarwood then jumped down, hit Larkin's pistol, which fired in the air, and grabbed a stone from the road and hit him hard in the mouth. As Larkin fired three shots at him, Yarwood ducked, jumped into the cab, and ordered its driver to take him to the gaol, where a scratch posse of eight warders and the chief cashier immediately set off down Hyde Road.

Discovering the van door locked, Condon's men formed a protective circle and fired shots over a hostile crowd while an IRB centre, James Lavery, unsuccessfully pounded a large stone on the roof. With time running out before police reinforcements arrived, the rescuers had to break into the van. But Brett defied shouts to throw his keys out and ignored the women's pleas. Peter Rice then fired at the lock as Brett peered through the grating, fatally wounding him in the temple and forcing an eye from its socket. A female prisoner then grabbed the keys from Brett's pocket and pushed them through the grating to Rice, who immediately opened the door. After the terrified women fled, Brett's blood-soaked body fell out upon the road, while another rescuer entered the van and released Kelly and Deasy.

Grabbing knives from a nearby house, Condon tried furiously but unsuccessfully to sever the chain links of Kelly and Deasy's handcuffs. He then ordered them taken away, while he led a rearguard action that quickly became a wild running battle with a baying mob. As Belle Vue's warders arrived, Larkin, already in bad health and now barely able to walk, was carried by Allen and O'Brien towards the railway line, but the warders and an angry mob caught up. One warder hurled a brick, which missed Allen and struck O'Brien on the forehead, knocking him to the ground. O'Brien, Larkin and Allen were then overpowered.

The whole affair had lasted only about fifteen minutes and when police reinforcements arrived most attackers had already fled. Over the following days Belle Vue warders managed to recapture escapers from the prison van, but only the three female prisoners. Condon escaped but was soon captured by a detective and taken to Albert Street police station. 'Allen, Larkin and O'Brien were brought in. We were all pretty badly battered.'[11]

Kelly's and Deasy's rescue and Sergeant Brett's death in hospital two hours later shocked London and Dublin. Shortly afterwards, the Conservative Home Secretary, Gathorne Hardy, was told at Balmoral estate in Scotland, just before an audience with Queen Victoria: 'I was rejoicing over the capture of Col. Kelly when a telegram came that an armed mob had rescued him and the other prisoner. This in Manchester! What are we coming to? The Queen took it calmly.'[12] But Mayo was furious and told Hardy that the English police had consistently disregarded his warnings.[13] Hardy immediately authorised a £300 reward for Kelly's and Deasy's recapture. Manchester detectives launched a manhunt and began rounding up the usual suspects, especially north of the river in Angel Meadow ('Irish Town'). Descriptions of alleged attackers were also telegraphed to every police station in the country, and within a day another twenty people were in custody. Condon recollected that: 'Many others picked up all over the city all through the night were brought in and thrown into our cell until it was packed with men as closely as that other British prison known as the "Black Hole of Calcutta".'[14]

During the early hours of Thursday, 19 September, at Albert Street police station witnesses walked silently down a corridor lined with Fenian suspects, pointing out men they claimed were on Hyde Road. Outside, soldiers and police stood guard against a break-out. By morning a vast crowd watched as police transferred to court an initial twenty men accused of treason felony; more spectators stood on lorries, at house windows and even on rooftops. Manchester magistrates remanded the prisoners for a week to New Bailey Prison in Salford, a couple of miles west of the city centre. By now the authorities were taking no chances and drafted 120 soldiers into the prison to repel any Fenian attack. At night, forty armed policemen patrolled the perimeter. On 22 September, tension in Manchester was high during Sergeant Brett's funeral, when a procession over a third of a mile long snaked its way along a route lined with 15,000 mourners.

By 23 September, there had been forty-eight arrests but Kelly and Deasy were still on the run, and Manchester police seemed literally clueless. However, many English Chief Constables reported sightings of Kelly and Deasy in their cities. In Liverpool, Irish detective Michael McHale reported Kelly being seen outside Dale Street police station reading his own reward poster, and that Deasy had been spotted in another part of town.[15] Condon later implied that Kelly and Deasy had reached their Ashton-under-Lynne safe house. Another Fenian account claimed they never left Manchester, but stayed underground until Deasy was smuggled to Liverpool and embarked on a liner bound for America disguised as a stoker. However, Deasy's great-grandnephew, historian Robert Bateman, has related the family tradition that both escapers separated immediately and ran in different directions. Deasy hid until darkness, when he walked through fields for two days before making his way through side streets to a friend's home in Angel Meadow ('Irish Town'). There his handcuffs were severed.[16] On 27 October 1867, in New York Harbour, Fenians welcomed Deasy ecstatically when he disembarked from the *City of Paris*. At home in Massachusetts, Deasy became a successful property dealer and hotel owner. Apparently. Kelly stayed in Manchester for some months, moving between safe houses and dodging police raids, once disguised as a priest. Finally, a cart driver for a wine merchant brought him to Liverpool, where a sympathetic crew member smuggled Kelly on board a liner and he hid in a bulkhead until after the vessel safely departed Queenstown.[17] In America, Kelly settled into relative obscurity as a New York customs officer.

On Thursday, 25 September, only twenty-three accused appeared before magistrates for committal to a Special Commission; evidence against the rest was so flimsy that prosecuting them would have destroyed the Commission's credibility. Cavalry had escorted vans to court and prisoners were manacled together, Allen to O'Brien and Condon to Larkin, a precaution that Condon regarded as humiliating: 'One could not leave the court for the most necessary purpose without dragging the other along with him.' Especially harrowing was the sight of Larkin meeting his aged mother, his wife and children. 'These were allowed to visit him during the daily recess and as we were always, except at night, chained together, I was constantly forced to witness the agony of the helpless victim and his afflicted family during their interviews.'[18]

A.M. Sullivan recalled that after the Manchester ambush, hysteria and fear gripped England:

Nothing was heard of but the Fenians; nothing was talked of but the diabolic plots and murderous designs they were said to be preparing. The Queen was to be shot at; Balmoral was to be burned down; the armouries had been attacked; the barracks were undermined; the gas works were to be exploded. the Bank blown up; the water poisoned. Panic and passion reigned supreme. Garrisons were strengthened; prison-guards were doubled; special constables were sworn in. Manchester and the surrounding towns, well-known to contain a large Irish population, were especially excited.[19]

On a report that Manchester Fenians intended kidnapping Queen Victoria and exchanging her for the prisoners, Hardy dispatched soldiers, detectives and police to Balmoral. Although nothing happened, eighteen armed policemen occupied three carriages of the royal train when the monarch returned to London.[20] Coming soon after Fenianism had supposedly been crushed, Kelly's and Deasy's escape shocked the English public. But, despite Lord Mayo's pleas, most British police forces had remained singularly indifferent to the Fenian threat. The capture of Kelly and Deasy was a coup, but it had resulted from an entirely chance encounter, not an intelligence-led operation. Mayo lamented that 'we have no police in England. During the entire time I have been in office all the warnings of the Irish government given to the English Police have been disregarded.'[21]

The person responsible for punishing the Manchester conspirators was Gathorne Hardy, a 53-year-old lawyer and protégé of Benjamin Disraeli, who, as Derby's health declined, was effectively running the government. In May 1867 he had appointed Hardy Home Secretary, after the incumbent Spencer Walpole had presided over a public order fiasco when 200,000 demonstrators occupied Hyde Park for three days and fought sporadic running battles with police as military reinforcements refused to intervene. This debacle seriously dented the government's authority and Hardy urgently needed to restore the Conservatives' reputation as a party of law and order.

Maintaining public confidence was also crucial at a time when serious crime was stoking public fear of social breakdown. Two recent murder cases in particular had transfixed the country. On 24 July 1867, John Wiggins, a 34-year-old alcoholic from London's poverty-ridden East End, slit the throat of his girlfriend after she forgot to bring him beer. Then, on 3 September in south-east London, a French leather worker, Louis Bordier, fatally stabbed his girlfriend when she tried to leave him for another man. Both slayings fed Victorian England's insatiable appetite for reading about gruesome murders, while simultaneously sensational press coverage gave respectable society a deeply unsettling glimpse into the violent world of a drink-soaked underclass whose chaotic lives seemingly revolved around petty squabbles, domestic abuse and sudden death, but whose denizens might one day wreak vengeance on their privileged rulers. The confluence of Fenian outrage, rioting and apparently endemic working-class mayhem compelled Hardy to seek speedy and exemplary punishment on the Manchester perpetrators. Hardy, though, was no diehard reactionary, but rather a pillar of Victorian rectitude, civilised, humane and deeply religious. Nevertheless, he also believed that only a strong legal framework guaranteed stability and respect for authority.

After leaving Balmoral on Sunday, 22 September 1867, Hardy reached London in an uncompromising mood: 'The public will be ready for strong measures. England will never endure that such an event should happen unpunished.'[22] Hardy had also discovered appalling incompetence: incredibly, police had known about Fenians purchasing the weapons used on Hyde Road and could possibly have prevented the ambush. 'Had arrests taken place at Birmingham when we gave notice the pistols would either have not been bought or would have been seized.'[23] Neither was Hardy much impressed by the London Metropolitan Police, whose long-time Commissioner Sir Richard Mayne was a curmudgeon who had seen off many previous Home Secretaries. Mayne had sent a Chief Inspector Adolphus Williamson to Manchester after Kelly's and Deasy's arrests, but he had failed to increase the prisoners' security.

Hardy and Disraeli agreed that in order to dispel public disquiet, a Special Commission should try the Manchester accused. Furthermore, to secure speedy convictions and executions, it should commence in Manchester on 28 October. As this was just five weeks after the ambush, Irish Nationalist MPs accused Hardy of a rush to judgement at a time when inflamed emotions made it virtually impossible to empanel an unbiased jury. Hardy dismissed their appeals for delay as stalling tactics intended to string out proceedings indefinitely, and he refused either to postpone the Commission or shift it to another city.

Promoted to one of the most difficult jobs in English politics, Hardy was unprepared for a life upended. As Home Secretary, this gentle soul encountered only brutal reality confronting 'these horrid Fenians' and deciding whether men should live or die.[24] Unrelenting pressure exhausted Hardy, who worked literally from dawn to dusk, reading reports and chairing meetings, all the time assailed by critics and damning newspaper headlines. Snatching a few days holiday in Paris on 11 and 12 October brought him no relief, as departmental papers and messages followed Hardy to the French capital. Reading the Bible as he constantly did, perhaps one verse from Job resonated: 'My groans pour out like water. What I feared has come upon me. What I dreaded has happened to me. I have no peace, no quietness. I have no rest but only turmoil.'

The Special Commission attracted national, and even international, attention. London journalists and foreign reporters flocked to Manchester and crammed into local hotels. By Monday, 28 October, the city centre resembled a fortress. One hundred and fifty soldiers garrisoned a courthouse surrounded by policemen, and every male voter had been made liable for duty as special constables. Despite typically cold and wet Manchester weather, thousands of spectators thronged the square outside court when, just before 8 a.m., five defendants arrived in a very large van escorted by cavalry and with armed police on top. Led on horseback by the Chief Constable of Salford, Captain Sylvester, the vehicle had travelled from

New Bailey Gaol along a route packed with onlookers. Condon (under his pseudonym Edward Shore), Allen, Larkin and O'Brien (using an alias, William Gould) were about to stand trial for murdering Sergeant Brett, but they must have been mystified by a fifth defendant, William Maguire, about whom they knew absolutely nothing. Maguire himself must have been even more baffled. A long-serving Royal Marine home on leave, he was an innocent victim of the hysteria that had engulfed Manchester, only connected to the ambush by his Irish accent.

Two judges presided at the Special Commission. Most senior was Sir Colin Blackburn, a 54-year-old Scot who, after an unremarkable legal career, had been surprisingly elevated to the Queen's Bench in 1859 and knighted a year later. Sir John Mellor was a 58-year-old Englishman and former Liberal MP who had joined the Queen's Bench in 1861 and was also knighted a year later. For such a high-profile case they were hardly stellar legal minds, but the government probably regarded them as safe pairs of hands who would bring the trials to a satisfactory conclusion. Attorney-General Sir John Karslake was chief prosecutor, Digby Seymour QC represented Condon, Allen and O'Brien, while Mr Sergeant O'Brien defended Larkin and Maguire. On the first day Blackburn described events on Hyde Road for a grand jury that would decide whether to indict the five defendants for murder. He declared that even if the attackers had not intended killing anyone, using weapons recklessly and causing death still constituted murder. Moreover, even without firing a gun, every participant was equally guilty by engaging in a joint enterprise. Significantly, although Fenians claimed Brett had died accidentally from a bullet fired at a door lock, Blackburn pronounced as fact that the door ventilator had been pulled aside for an attacker to intentionally shoot the policeman. After deliberating briefly, the grand jury returned at noon and issued true bills for murder against the five defendants. When the charges were read out, all of them replied, 'Not Guilty.' Apart from wanting to avoid execution, Condon, Allen, O'Brien and Larkin considered themselves innocent of a crime, morally in the right as soldiers attempting to liberate comrades. None had set out to kill anyone and they regarded Brett's death as a tragic accident. Maguire's reasoning was simpler: neither legally or morally was he guilty of any crime. Karslake was taking an all-or-nothing gamble by charging the five defendants together, since this required a single verdict for all of them, but he had cleverly imposed a heavy burden on the jury, which might think it prudent to convict one possibly innocent man rather than set four guilty Fenians free.

Next day, Tuesday, 29 October, the trial proper began. Lacking confessions, the prosecution relied entirely on eyewitness identification. This was especially true as defendants then could not testify on their own behalf or be questioned by prosecutors, preventing Karslake from discrediting them on the stand. That actually suited Seymour and O'Brien, as their Fenian clients were in fact legally guilty – something that they must have known. Consequently, for the next sixteen days, a legal war of attrition was waged in which the Attorney-General paraded witnesses who affirmed the defendants' guilt while defence counsel sought to undermine their evidence and create reasonable doubt in the jury's mind. Seymour and O'Brien had a mountain to climb. Witnesses had considerable incentives to lie. Substantial rewards were on offer, they had a chance to grandstand dramatically in court and could also help convict men widely believed to be guilty. Furthermore, identity parades conducted after the ambush had been shambolically organised and were probably rigged. Allen claimed he was made to remove his overcoat while everyone else in the line-up wore theirs, and that policemen had shown his clothes to witnesses so they could point him out. In another parade, Allen was forced to wear a handkerchief on his head.[25] John Griffiths, whose hairdressing shop was near the railway arch and who claimed he had seen an attacker wearing a white hat, pointed out Maguire at a line-up in which only the marine wore a white hat. Besides, at this time and long afterwards, juries placed considerable weight on eyewitness evidence and often convicted on that basis alone. They especially trusted policemen, respected authority figures whom judges usually protected from criticism, let alone any imputation of dishonesty. That Manchester police officers might conspire with their superiors to dovetail evidence and convict men of murdering Sergeant Brett was an idea whose time had not yet come.

On the first day, Karslake produced his star witness, Joseph Yarwood, now universally regarded as a hero. But after he fluently recalled seeing Larkin, Allen and Maguire together on the embankment, Yarwood stumbled. Claiming that Larkin and another man had attacked the prison van first, he denied ever saying the latter was Gould (O'Brien). But Seymour immediately recited his deposition at the committal proceedings when Yarwood had stated that 'Gould and Larkin rushed out from behind the archway.'[26] To Seymour's astonishment, Blackburn immediately interjected that he did not see any great discrepancy, attributing any confusion to statements being recorded rapidly and succinctly under pressure. Then, reported the *Manchester Examiner,* Yarwood insisted he had told the committal magistrates about Larkin shooting at the horses:

> Sergeant O'Brien pointed out to his lordship that this did not appear in the depositions. Mr Justice Blackburn said the witness might nevertheless have stated it. It would be a fair inference to go to the jury that the witness did not say it. Sergeant O'Brien was not entitled to do more.[27]

By sharply circumscribing what defence counsel could tell the jury, Blackburn had prevented an exploration of police perjury, dangerous territory onto which he would not let Seymour and O'Brien venture. Karslake now knew – if he did not already – that the trial was indeed in safe hands.

Furthermore, by locating Maguire at the ambush scene, Yarwood had seriously incriminated the marine. Displaying apparently total recall, successive witnesses also claimed Maguire was on Hyde Road, acting aggressively. A railway employee, John Beck, claimed Maguire had thrown stones at police. Thomas Patterson, a worker in nearby brickfields, testified that Maguire had passed stones up to Allen on the prison van roof. Another railway worker, Thomas Sperry, claimed Maguire himself had tried climbing on to the roof but slipped and fell. The cab driver who followed the prison van also said Maguire had participated in the ambush. Employing topsy-turvy logic, police constable George Shaw said, 'I did not get a clear view of Maguire's face but I believe he was the man with a white hat on who assisted in breaking into the van.'[28] Maguire might well have wondered if he had plunged headlong into a dizzying looking-glass world where illusion had replaced reality. More likely, Maguire now realised that in criminal parlance he had been fitted-up and his execution was deemed necessary for the greater good.

Tugging the jury's heartstrings at a young child's trauma, Karslake produced Joseph Partington, the 12-year-old reformatory boy. He positively recalled Allen entering the prison van and freeing Kelly. But a brickfields worker, Thomas Patterson, delivered the trial's most riveting – and embellished – testimony, which described Allen blazing away like a Wild West gunfighter:

I heard a man who wore cord trousers say, 'Shoot the b...... He's inside.' I then saw Allen run with two revolvers to the back of the van. He placed both revolvers to the ventilator and I heard a report and a woman's voice from the inside of the van. Shortly afterwards the van door was opened and Brett fell out.[29]

Allen, O'Brien and Larkin had been captured at the scene resisting arrest and a string of witnesses had testified against them, making their convictions almost a foregone conclusion. Condon was apprehended well away from Hyde Road, but he had strongly resisted arrest and a slew of witnesses placed him at the ambush scene, including a police officer in the cab following the prison van. Curiously, while Condon had acted conspicuously as a leader on Hyde Road before the attack, no evidence of this was produced at the trial.

After trial proceedings ended late on Friday afternoon, 1 November, the jury deliberated for only seventy-five minutes before delivering its verdicts. A.M. Sullivan recalled that:

The prisoners turned their eyes upward; Maguire looked towards them, half-hopefully, half-appealingly; from Allen's glance nothing but defiance could be read; Larkin fixed his gaze on the foreman, who held the fatal record in his hand, with calm resolution; while a quiet smile played round O'Brien's lips, as he turned to hear the expected words.[30]

After the foreman declared all five defendants guilty, Allen addressed the court first. He regretted Sergeant Brett's death but blamed his conviction on perjured evidence from 'prostitutes off the streets of Manchester, fellows out of work, convicted felons – aye, an Irishman sentenced to be hung when an English dog would have got off'. Defiantly, Allen refused to beg for his life. 'I want no mercy; I'll have no mercy. I'll die as many thousands have died for the sake of their beloved land and in defence of it.' Larkin looked weaker than ever but was as resolute as Allen, regretting Brett's death but insisting that he had only acted to liberate Kelly and Deasy. He did not fire a weapon and had never intended killing anyone. Larkin also excoriated witnesses, whom he claimed had perjured themselves blind. Finally revealing his true identity, O'Brien said he was an American citizen, had never been on Hyde Road, and that 'every witness who has sworn anything against me has sworn falsely.' Maguire remained composed and was not struck dumb. Passionately repudiating the verdict, Maguire denied being a Fenian, had never heard of Kelly before his own arrest, and at the time of the ambush was relaxing at home miles away. Prosecution witnesses were mistaken. He declared himself a patriot who gladly served Queen and Country, someone whose commanding officer had vouched for his loyalty.

Finally, Condon addressed the court. Most intelligent and eloquent of the Fenian defendants, he expressed incredulity at being convicted on the perjured and contradictory evidence of dishonest witnesses, swallowed wholesale by a gullible jury. Claiming he had a strong alibi, Condon said he only lacked the money to prove it; the popular press had tainted his trial by whipping up hysteria and prejudice against him. More than shading the truth, Condon declared, 'I am totally guiltless. I never threw a stone or fired a pistol; I was never at the place as they have said; it is all totally false.' A rigged trial had reached its inevitable conclusion. 'We have been found guilty and as a matter of course we accept our death as gracefully as possible. We are not afraid to die – at least I am not.' Together, Allen, Larkin and O'Brien then cried out, 'Nor I,' 'Nor I,' 'Nor I.' Broadening his oration into a defiant statement to history, Condon hoped 'that my poor country will right herself someday, and that her people, so far from being looked down on with scorn and aversion, will receive what they are entitled to, the respect not only of the civilised world but of Englishmen'. He ended by declaring that, 'You will soon send us before God and I am perfectly prepared to go. I have nothing to regret or to retract or take back. I can only say, "God Save Ireland."' Swiftly, and obviously pre-arranged, his three Fenian comrades advanced simultaneously to the front of the dock, lifted their faces, extended hands upwards and exclaimed in unison, 'God Save Ireland.' After both judges donned black caps, Mellor sentenced all five defendants to death. After shaking hands with their counsel, all the condemned men, except Maguire, shouted to weeping friends, 'God be with you, Irishmen and Irishwomen,' before being led out of court.

Hardy had dispatched the Treasury Solicitor John Greenwood to Manchester to monitor the trials and help him decide if the condemned men should die. On 6 November, Greenwood reported that although Maguire might have been at the ambush scene, 'the part he played if he was there – and the doubt that is suggested of his being there at all – entirely distinguish him from the others. The others seem to be a bad lot – very.'[31] Greenwood accepted that Brett was killed by Allen, whom he called a wrong-headed and vain individual, easily manipulated by sinister leaders. Allen, O'Brien and Larkin had been most conspicuous in the ambush, but O'Brien was 'perhaps the more odious in manner and in the exhibition which he made of himself throughout the trial and in his speech. I should judge him from all that passed, to be the worst man of all.' Intriguingly, a Fenian detainee had told Greenwood that Condon had organised the ambush and, accordingly, if four men were selected for execution, he recommended Allen, O'Brien, Condon and Larkin. However, if only three were chosen, Greenwood believed Larkin might be reprieved – 'not upon his own merits but because he seems somewhat less audacious, ill-conditioned and dangerous than the rest'. But on the other hand, while Condon might have been the real mastermind, Greenwood pointed to evidence at the trial that although he was present, his role was less violent than the others. Greenwood's scrupulous adherence to the rules of evidence led him to recommend that if Hardy reprieved anyone, it should be Condon rather than Larkin, despite the former being 'one of the most blameable of the lot'. Condon was very lucky that nobody testified he had acted as the leader on Hyde Road.

Also, on 6 November, twenty-six journalists powerfully reinforced Greenwood's lukewarm doubts about Maguire by unanimously denouncing his conviction as a travesty and petitioning Hardy for the marine's unconditional pardon.[32] Even so, Hardy could easily have stood by the jury verdict, but his deep Christian faith prevented him sending an innocent man to eternity. After consulting Justice Mellor – who clearly had his own doubts – they agreed that Maguire could safely be pardoned unconditionally once the Special Commission ended on 12 November.[33] On his release the marine was immediately reinstated in the regiment whose commanding officer had stood by him.

Pardoning Maguire actually created more problems for Hardy, as the same witnesses who wrongly convicted Maguire had also testified against Condon, Allen, O'Brien and Larkin. While they remained in Salford Gaol, campaigners claimed their convictions had been won through tainted evidence, and although Hardy stood firm and set the executions for 23 November, most people in Ireland believed they would never happen. Capital punishment for Irish rebels had generally fallen into disuse and none had been executed since Robert Emmet in 1803. Death sentences imposed in Ireland 1848 and 1867 had been commuted to imprisonment or transportation. But the ambush that freed Kelly and Deasy happened on English soil and killed an English policeman, angering the English public in a way that revolutionary violence in Ireland never did, and significantly constrained Hardy in the mercy he could bestow on the condemned men.

On Thursday, 7 November, the Cabinet met in the absence of a gout-stricken Derby and discussed Fenianism. Lord Mayo described a panicked Justice Keogh ranting about 'much blood certain to be shed unless Fenian leaders were captured'.[34] Yet, the imminent executions in Manchester were not even mentioned and no new measures against Fenians agreed. Subsequently, Disraeli aligned himself with public opinion and proposed suspending Habeas Corpus in parts of England, but Derby turned him down, fearful that anti-Fenianism would rapidly become anti-Irish violence.[35]

The two weeks after the Special Commission ended were the most hectic of Hardy's life. Nationalist MPs berated him for not reprieving the condemned men and one accused Hardy of legalising murder. Death threats inundated the Home Office. London Fenians warned 'that bloody murderer Hardy' that 'if you persist in oppressing our countrymen as you are now doing, we have solemnly sworn by the sacred throne of Almighty God to lay your worthless and lifeless body at our country's feet'.[36] An informant claimed Fenians had already chosen Hardy's assassin: 'Mr Hardy will be watched night and day till a safe opportunity presents itself.'[37] On 18 November, a Fenian mob invaded the Home Office and almost reached Hardy's office. As the execution date approached, Hardy's family and friends worried about his safety and begged him not to stroll through St James' Park, but Hardy refused to live his life in fear and drew strength from religion and the conviction that his hard-line stance had popular support: 'It would be intolerable to go about looking over one's shoulder.' The Liberal party also supported Hardy. Lord Kimberley, Mayo's predecessor, complained that:

A mawkish feeling has seized some part of the English people with regard to Fenianism which may do great harm. Either we have no right to hold Ireland in which case we ought to recognise its independence at once, or we have a right to hold it. In the latter case we are bound to enforce the law against all Irish traitors.[38]

On 15 November 1867, Justices Blackburn and Mellor sent Hardy their report on the Special Commission.[39] They fully endorsed Maguire's unconditional pardon, but consultations with fellow judges had confirmed that no other legal issues existed for the Court of Criminal Appeal to consider. 'The convictions and sentences must be considered as final.' They said Allen, Larkin and O'Brien had definitely participated in the ambush and were captured on the spot. Despite his capture some distance away, the evidence against Condon was extremely credible. Allen was especially dangerous: he had first shot at a policeman, fatally wounded Sergeant Brett, and fired on anyone trying to stop the rescue. 'We can see nothing in his favour except that he was young and probably the tool in the hands of those older than himself.' O'Brien had wounded a policeman and formed a rearguard with Allen and Larkin against pursuers, facilitating Kelly's and Deasy's escape. Interestingly, they also claimed O'Brien had been with Kelly and Deasy when they were arrested: 'We think it is established that he was a leader in the whole plot.' Although Larkin was younger than O'Brien, he had fired his weapon repeatedly 'but either from want of skill or as is more probable from inferior nerve, none of the shots which he fired took effect. It is clear that he was morally and legally as guilty as Allen.' Once again, Condon got lucky. Both judges accepted that although he had attacked the prison van and thrown stones at police, only one witness described him firing a single shot – 'a shade of distinction in his favour'.

Despite asserting that they only wanted to enlighten Hardy, Blackburn and Mellor had left him no room for mercy, except slightly in Condon's case. Accordingly, after a Cabinet meeting on 20 November, Hardy announced that Allen, O'Brien and Larkin would hang as they were ringleaders who had repeatedly fired deadly weapons. Condon had played a less prominent role and his sentence was commuted to penal servitude for life.[40] Clearly, Hardy had taken account of Greenwood, Blackburn and Mellor's minor reservations about Condon's death sentence, instinctively reluctant as ever he was to execute anyone about whom there existed even a sliver of doubt.

On the same day, 20 November, Foreign Secretary Lord Stanley passed to Hardy a letter from Charles Adams, American Minister to the United Kingdom. Adams had submitted to Secretary of State Seward a memorandum from Condon claiming to be a naturalised American wrongly convicted at the Special Commission.[41] Responding by cable, Seward instructed Adams to intercede on behalf of Condon and O'Brien. And Adams immediately urged Stanley to re-examine both cases, and next day, Stanley told him that Hardy had reprieved Condon. Adolphus Liddell, Hardy's Under-Secretary of State at the Home Office, was unmoved and strongly repudiated Condon's reprieve. 'He richly deserved to be hanged and was very lucky to escape.'[42]

Adams now decided against pressing for O'Brien's reprieve, especially as the prisoner's' guilt was not in doubt. Doing so would complicate already strained transatlantic relations at a time when Irish extremists wanted a rupture between England and America. Moreover, further reprieves would find the British government accused of caving in to foreign pressure during a political crisis that Adams described as the worst since the Gunpowder Plot of 1605. Newspapers were full of alarming reports and demanding such severe repressive measures that ministers believed the executions of O'Brien, Allen and Larkin were necessary to restore public confidence. Accordingly, Adams advised that pressing for O'Brien's reprieve would do more harm than good.[43] And Adams had the perfect cover for abandoning O'Brien. In 1866, O'Brien had often travelled between Liverpool and Dublin, bringing weapons for the rising. Tried in Liverpool for possessing rifles, he was assisted by the local American consul and acquitted after claiming American citizenship. Adams informed O'Brien that he was not going to fall for that legal manoeuvre.

On Thursday, 21 November 1867, Cabinet ministers approved Hardy's decision on Allen's, O'Brien's and Larkin's impending executions.[44] Decades later, Hardy still believed a terrible deterrent had been necessary to prevent another tragedy: 'Justice required the signal example which the Cabinet unanimously agreed should be made.'[45] The countdown to three hangings had begun.

On Wednesday morning, 20 November, Allen's uncle and three cousins had visited him for a last time while Larkin bade his wife and mother-in-law farewell. But only the prison chaplain, Father Gadd, comforted Condon and O'Brien. At this stage, though, all four men still believed Hardy would commute their sentences to life imprisonment, and indeed next evening a Home Office telegram informed Governor Holt of Condon's reprieve. However, Allen, O'Brien and Larkin remained under sentence of death. William Allen was 19 years old. Thirty-year-old Michael O'Brien had led the attack on Ballyknocken police station during the 1867 Rising, but fled afterwards to Manchester. Michael Larkin was originally from King's County (now Co. Offaly) but in 1858 he left for Manchester, where he worked as a tailor. Larkin and his wife Sarah had four children, two boys and two girls, and, in the summer of 1867, the family was joined by Larkin's recently widowed mother. In purely personal terms Larkin had more to lose than Allen and O'Brien, a burden that weighed heavily on his mind.

As preparations for the executions intensified, workmen inserted a gallows platform at the top of the prison wall. A long wooden stepladder led up from the yard to the scaffold, on each side of which stood podiums for armed soldiers. To prevent hostile demonstrations, a rescue attempt or a prison breakout, Salford's mayor swore in 500 special constables, drafted in police officers from the county force, and mobilised the town's Rifle Volunteers. Soldiers secured the gaol itself, occupied a railway station at the rear and high arches across which ran a railway line. Opposite the prison entrance stood two field guns in Stanley Street. Throughout Thursday evening, rumours circulated in Manchester that Fenians intended firebombing warehouses and other important buildings: employees, armed with revolvers, guarded them round the clock. The mayor also protected water plants and gasworks and placed the fire brigade on standby, while police patrol boats on the Irwell checked river traffic for suspicious vessels. After flocking to Manchester for the second time in a month, journalists reported a city that was apparently again under siege. New Bailey Prison itself resembled a fortified medieval castle along whose ramparts armed guards constantly patrolled.

On Friday morning, 22 November, the official hangman, William Calcraft, arrived at New Bailey Prison. Paid £10 for the first execution and £5 each for the rest, he was perhaps disappointed at Condon's reprieve. Calcraft had received death threats and the Home Office ordered troops to guard him well. From 'this side of the grave', Allen sent his uncle and aunt a defiant last letter declaring his pride that he was 'dying an honourable death; I am dying for Ireland – dying for the land that gave me birth – dying for the island of Saints and Scholars – and dying for liberty.' His only regret was dying young and being buried on English soil. On Friday evening, Allen's mother and two aunts visited him for the last time, but his tearful fiancée Mary Anne Hickey was turned away. In a steely last letter to his brother, O'Brien had denounced a trial 'unfair from beginning to end' and described himself as an innocent man convicted by a prejudiced jury. 'I must say though much I like to live I cannot regret dying in the cause of liberty, and Ireland.' As sole provider, Larkin worried desperately about his wife, children and widowed mother. Suddenly, a messenger came from the Marchioness of Queensberry. Irish born and a convert to Roman Catholicism to Irish nationalism, she had shocked London high society by fundraising for the Manchester defendants. Now, the Marchioness promised to befriend Larkin's family, a vow she kept until her death thirty-seven years later. The Marchioness also sent a £100 cheque for the other condemned men's dependents.[46]

At 6.30 p.m. on Friday, 22 November, warders locked Allen, O'Brien and Larkin in their cells for a final time. Whether each had the condemned man's last meal is unknown, but simultaneously Salford's mayor hosted a sumptuous banquet for twenty-five army officers who had kept the peace in his town. At a table decorated with corporation plate, officers tucked into a splendid repast of turkey, chicken, roast beef, pigeon pie, lobsters, grapes and other fruit. Across town, public houses near New Bailey Prison did a roaring trade as customers partied raucously through the night. Coming from afar but with nowhere to stay, many drank on, singing ribald choruses laced with gallows humour, interspersed with renditions of 'God Save the Queen' and 'Rule Britannia'. By 7 a.m. the *Manchester Courier* reported that, 'nothing but faces was to be seen in every direction looking from the scaffold'.[47] Yet surprisingly, 8,000–10,000 spectators was actually fewer than had attended New Bailey's previous execution, partly because of inclement weather and advice from Catholic priests that parishioners attend Mass but also a fear of violence. Salford's mayor had gauged the crowd's mood and was 'satisfied that at no time would it have been safe for any person to have expressed any strong Fenian sympathies'. One man who proclaimed, 'It is a great pity' was immediately howled down and forced to flee. The mayor instituted extraordinary security precautions for the executions. Across Salford, posters urged residents to stay away, mounted police patrolled the outskirts of town, and 2,000 armed special constables were on duty from 5 p.m. on Friday to 9.30 a.m. on Saturday.

A.M. Sullivan recalled that: 'Saturday, 23 November, dawned misty, murky, dull and cold over Salford. During the first hours after midnight the weather had been clear and frosty, and a heavy hoar covered the ground; but as daylight approached, a thick mist or fog crept like a pallid pall over the waking city.'[48] At quarter to five, governor Holt visited Allen, O'Brien and Larkin, and shortly afterwards Father Gadd and a Father Quick conducted Mass. At seven o'clock the three condemned men ate breakfast, and forty-five minutes later Calcraft pinioned each man's arms while both priests exhorted them to entrust their salvation to the Lord. Gadd and Quick also persuaded Allen, O'Brien and Larkin to withdraw their requests to address spectators from the gallows.

A few minutes after the prison clock struck eight o'clock, Holt, his warders and both priests escorted the three Fenians from their cells and led them to a door beyond which lay the rest of their lives. Nothing can have fully prepared Allen, O'Brien and Larkin for the shock they must have felt when the door opened – the sight of a scaffold, three hanging nooses, executioner Calcraft and a sea of faces, all of whom wanted them dead. Lines of special constables stood beside the gallows, which a strong barrier separated from the crowd. Fifty reporters occupied the nearest vantage point but a *Manchester Courier* journalist most graphically described the executions:

> The door behind the scaffold opened and a warder came forward followed by Allen. The condemned man was exceedingly pale, and looked forward on the crowd with a quick anxious gaze. His hands were convulsively clutched together, holding a small wooden crucifix, his breathing came quick and compressed and in a tremulous voice he repeated the words, 'Jesus have mercy on us.' Calcraft followed through the door and took hold of Allen's arm, leading him under the beam towards the noose.[49]

After putting a cap over Allen's head and the noose around his neck, Calcraft passed him to a warder.

Next, Calcraft turned to O'Brien. Rossa described him as courageous as a lion and the *Manchester Courier* journalist believed he was:

> by far the most self-possessed man of the three, his whole bearing was that of a man who did not fear his fate. He repeated in a firm voice, as he went along, the same responses as the other two men, and mounted the steps without the least sign of trepidation. On being put under the middle of the beam he turned around towards Allen, shook him by the hands, and kissed the cap on the unfortunate man's forehead.[50]

When Larkin saw Calcraft prepare Allen and O'Brien for death, he crumbled:

> Attended by Father Quick, Larkin had to be assisted up the steps by two warders. He had a most haggard, careworn look and as he went along, he faintly joined in the response. With him both mental and physical powers seem to have been prostrated, so that he was on the point of fainting away, especially when he saw the first glimpses of the black beams of the gallows.[51]

A warder had to support the pale and trembling Larkin as Calcraft slipped a noose around his neck.

Standing on trapdoors, all three men faced the crowd with their hands clasped, repeating the 'Litany of Jesus'. Calcraft now stepped down below the platform, followed by Fathers Gadd and Quick:

> Larkin at this moment fell completely away and fell in a dead swoon against Gould (i.e. O'Brien) with the noose tightened around his neck. The warder who was standing at his side and whose presence of mind undoubtedly served to prevent a scene instantly caught hold of him and lifted him upon his feet. Larkin still apparently unconscious fell forward, and partly supported by the gaoler and as it seemed leaning on the front screen of the scaffold he remained in that position while the others stood firm, still repeating the words, 'Lord Jesus receive us.' Then the bolt was withdrawn and the ropes tightened when the men disappeared from view behind the black screen of the scaffold.[52]

However, Calcraft realised immediately that he had botched his preparations. Although the scaffolding had been erected to conceal the dropped bodies from spectators, Calcraft could see that although Allen had died instantly, O'Brien's and Larkin's ropes were swaying backwards and forwards. Hurrying below, Calcraft grabbed Larkin's legs and pulled him until he stopped breathing. The hangman then turned to O'Brien but Father Gadd blocked his way, holding a crucifix before O'Brien for three quarters of an hour until he finally choked on his own tongue.[53]

Immediately after the bodies disappeared under the gallows, spectators had dispersed rapidly. At 9 a.m., the three corpses were cut down and buried in quicklime graves inside the prison grounds, though a year later, after New Bailey Prison was demolished, they were re-interred at Manchester's Strangeways Gaol. Finally, in 1991, the remains were exhumed again and laid to rest along with fifty-seven other executed convicts in a mass grave at Blackley Cemetery, making future identification impossible.

A jittery Calcraft could not get out of town fast enough. At 11.20 a.m. his cab swept through the prison gates and raced to London Road railway station, where he just caught a noon train for the capital.[54] At the same time, Gathorne Hardy noted:

All over at Manchester and all quiet which with the extensive precautions taken could hardly be otherwise. Poor wretches. I have thought much of them and prayed for them as for myself. Great efforts have been made on their behalf but mainly by a certain class of people many on the grounds of objection to such punishment at all. Many warnings as to my personal safety. I must take reasonable precautions and leave the rest to God.[55]

Less empathetically, Lord Kimberley tersely recorded, 'The three Fenians hanged in Manchester. I am glad the Govt. had the firmness not to resist their punishment.'[56]

Before and after 1867, the deaths of Irish patriots revived physical force nationalism. Six years earlier, Terence Bellew McManus's reburial had re-energised the Irish Republican Brotherhood, and almost half a century later, after O'Donovan Rossa died in New York, the IRB leader Tom Clarke staged a funeral that in scale and political significance surpassed any in the history of Dublin. At Glasnevin Cemetery, Patrick Pearse would deliver a graveside oration that proclaimed that 'while Ireland holds these graves, Ireland unfree shall never be at peace' and that 'the seeds sown by the young men of '65 and '67 are coming to their miraculous ripening today'. Listeners instinctively knew these words primarily alluded to Allen, O'Brien and Larkin. Their executions happened when the IRB was at its nadir after a rising was easily crushed with only twelve anonymous Fenian fatalities and without a single hero. And the Irish government had shrewdly avoided creating martyrs by commuting death sentences. Now, fortuitously, redemption had come in England through the actions and sacrifices of three obscure young men, who became republican icons through their willingness to die for the cause. This was the stuff of legend, a heroic, romantic tale around which a cult of martyrs could be woven.

In Ireland, the transformation began immediately as graphic accounts of the executions persuaded many nationalists that the British government had acted cruelly to satisfy a bloodlust fomented by the English press. A.M. Sullivan claimed Manchester crowds 'made the air resound with laughter at obscene jokes, shouts, cries, and repartees; and chorused in thousands (beneath the gallows!) snatches of "comic" ballads and pot-house songs'.[57] The *Freeman's Journal* compared spectators to Ancient Romans demanding that Christians be thrown to the lions. Irish and Irish-American newspapers emphasised the saintly dignity and bravery of three devout young men walking to their deaths after confession and communion, clutching crucifixes and reciting prayers. Furthermore, Fenians declared that Allen, O'Brien and Larkin embodied what John Devoy proclaimed was the essence of Fenianism: 'The Fenians were self-sacrificing men. They had their own share of human frailties but their worst enemies do not deny that they immolated themselves on the altar of their country.'[58] Compassion in Ireland for the executed men mingled with admiration for their courage and audacity in striking at the heart of the Empire, shaking the British government as the 1867 Rising never did.

Within hours news of the executions reached Dublin, and next day spread rapidly across rural Ireland as priests informed horrified congregations. A.M. Sullivan recalled a nationwide 'wail of grief. I never knew Ireland to be more deeply moved by mingled feelings of grief and anger.'[59] Certain that the British government had cold-heartedly used the executions to humiliate Irish nationalism, most of Ireland united spontaneously in defiance. On 8 December 1867, many towns held mock funerals in which mourners followed three empty coffins bearing the names of Allen, O'Brien and Larkin to local cemeteries. Unusually, the processions contained many young women, wearing green ribbons and keening, the distinctive form of crying heard at Irish wakes and funerals. In Dublin, tens of thousands marched the same route to Glasnevin as the Terence Bellew McManus procession six years earlier, and huge crowds also turned out in Cork, which considered Allen and O'Brien native sons. Except among Protestant loyalists, especially in Ulster, the grief encompassed every social class and variety of nationalism. John Martin led the Dublin procession and The O'Donoghue that in Killarney. Veneration of the executed men manifested itself in a multitude of songs, poems, literature, paintings, memorial cards and seventeen public monuments over the ensuing decades. Plucked from obscurity and celebrated more in death than life, Allen, O'Brien and Larkin had exhibited the same resistance to British rule as Tone, Emmet and McManus. By audaciously freeing Kelly and Deasy, defying a British court and sacrificing their lives, they had joined their famous predecessors on the pantheon of republican heroes, passing into history as the Manchester Martyrs.

Postscript

After the Liberal party won the general election of December 1868, William Ewart Gladstone became prime minister and immediately declared that his mission was to pacify Ireland. However, before tackling that country's deep-seated problems, he first needed to rid himself of eighty-one Fenian prisoners still incarcerated, forty-two in Australia and thirty-nine dispersed across England in Chatham, Portland, Millbank and Woking gaols. Gladstone preferred freeing them all in a mass amnesty but faced strong resistance from the Conservative opposition, a hostile press, and even his own Irish government. Not until late February 1869 did he win over Viceroy Lord Spencer and Chief Secretary Chichester Fortescue, and even then they only consented to the release of forty-eight low-level prisoners and a severely incapacitated Kickham. Gladstone's hopes of swiftly releasing the remaining thirty-two prominent Fenians were then set back when some pardoned men made seditious speeches in Ireland. Not until December 1870 did Gladstone override Spencer and Fortescue, but he had to make future pardons conditional on prisoners accepting banishment from the United Kingdom. The ten Portland inmates, including Luby and O'Leary, were reluctant to accept this provision – McCafferty retorted, 'Gladstone be damned' – and took their time deciding. But at Chatham's high-security prison on the Medway estuary, John Devoy, O'Donovan Rossa, John McClure, Henry Mullady and Underwood O'Connell accepted exile to America. Only W. Halpin refused.

To prevent pro-Fenian demonstrations and counter-protests, Gladstone wanted rid of the Chatham prisoners quickly and discreetly, as did Chatham's prison authorities. After a commission of inquiry had upheld

Fenian inmates' allegations of ill-treatment, the government granted them a special diet, immunity from work, a separate wing, a private exercise yard and unlimited contact with family and friends. Even then, Deputy Governor Arthur Griffiths recalled, 'It was necessary to take special precautions for the safe custody of these prisoners. Extra warders were continually on the alert and we were highly delighted to hear that they were to be speedily pardoned and released.'[1]

Within twenty-four hours, Chatham's steward's department ran up smart civilian clothing for the prisoners, and on Thursday, 5 January 1871, they were ready to leave. Griffiths remembered:

my five Fenians apparelled (by their own particular choice) in full suits of shining black, with soft felt hats, and having rather the appearance of undertaker's men starting for a 'black job' somewhere at a distance. Each carried in his hand a small black leather valise containing a few articles and necessaries for the voyage.[2]

Rossa recalled that:

we took a last fond look at our cells and descended to the courtyard. We stood and made a request that Halpin be brought down to us to bid adieu. It was granted, and it was as painful a parting as you could imagine to see us in our broadcloth bidding adieu to him in his convict grey.[3]

Trudging through heavy snow, five Fenians and four warders piled into two coaches. Griffiths occupied a gig. When the heavy prison gates swung open, the vehicles left for Chatham railway station, where everyone boarded the London train. Griffiths watched his demob-happy charges luxuriate in their new-found freedom, serenely reading newspapers and smoking cigars that he had provided. At Euston railway station, Griffith had arranged a private room in which the former prisoners tucked into their first slap-up meal in almost four and a half years – sandwiches and as much ale and wine as they desired. Five hours later the party reached Liverpool and transferred by tug across the River Mersey to the Atlantic liner SS *Cuba*. Griffiths ordered supper, and for a while once bitter enemies caroused together. Rossa recollected that:

We had a grand time of it. Jailers, convicts and ship's officers fraternized over the champagne. We tried to make ourselves as genial as possible. We toasted the Deputy's health and he toasted ours; the doctor of the ship made a speech; some of the prisoners being called upon, became humorous and gave excuses for short orations by saying they were a good while out of practice under the silent system. Altogether we had a good night of it, though we were still prisoners. It was a regular, straight-out liberty, equality and fraternity party.[4]

At 2 a.m., the Cuba Five retired to their state rooms and slept in the lap of luxury. Next morning, after the last passengers boarded, the liner finally sailed slowly down the Mersey. Below deck, Griffiths handed out a pardon and five sovereigns to each of the amnestied men and bade them farewell. 'Rossa, who called me "governor" up to the last, insisted on shaking hands; and all seemed genuinely grateful, as well as full of elation at their release.'[5] When the liner stopped briefly, a tug returned Griffiths and two warders to Liverpool, but another pair of warders stayed on board to ensure nobody absconded at Cork. Griffiths went back to Chatham, expecting never again to hear of them again.

Nearing the Cove of Cork, Rossa saw his native county tantalizingly close, but he could not set foot on land. When the *Cuba* anchored, detectives corralled him and his four comrades for six hours while the Atlantic mails were brought on board. Among the new passengers were Rossa's wife Mary Jane and their young child James, on their way to share his new life in America. Mary had alerted Rossa's Cork friends, who suddenly approached the *Cuba* in a flotilla of small boats. After they begged unsuccessfully for a chance to shake his hand, Rossa impulsively jumped over the side. Landing in a heap on one boat, he shook a few hands and exchanged words before climbing back up again and surrendering. Four or five crowded steamers also came down river from Cork and hovered around the *Cuba*, passengers cheering as a welcome committee was allowed to present new clothes and gifts of money.

On 18 January 1871, the *Cuba* docked in New York Harbour. McClure, Mullady and O'Connell immediately vanished into obscurity, but for Devoy and Rossa their political future was simplicity itself. They would start all over again.

Endnotes

Chapter One

1 Leon O Broin, Lecture on The Fenian Movement. NLI, MS27962(5).
2 Leon O Broin, *Revolutionary Underground*, Preface.
3 Charles Gavan Duffy, *Four Years of Irish History 1848–1852*, p.279.
4 John O'Leary, *Recollections of Fenians and Fenianism*, Vol 1. p.78.
5 A conclusion reached in almost identical language by both John O'Leary and William D'Arcy in their books on Fenianism.
6 For this see Kerby Miller, *Ireland and Irish America: Culture, Class and Transatlantic Migration* (Dublin, 2008) and *Out of Ireland: The Story of Irish Migration to America* (London, 1994).
7 A.M. Sullivan, *New Ireland: Political Sketches and Personal Reminiscences of Thirty Years of Irish Public Life*, p.311. Hereafter, A.M. Sullivan, *New Ireland*.
8 Ibid., p.306.
9 See Kerby Miller, *Ireland and Irish America: Culture, Class and Transatlantic Migration (Dublin, 2008)* and David Brundage, *Irish Nationalists in America: The Politics of Exile, 1798–1998* (Oxford, 2016).
10 Submission to the Cabinet by Lord Strathnairn (i.e. Sir Hugh Rose), Commander-in-Chief in Ireland, 7 June, 1867. NLI, Mayo Papers, MS 11118/14.
11 Obituary on Phelan by John O'Mahony, *Irish People* (New York), 15 January 1868.
12 Charles Gavan Duffy, *The League of North and South*, p.7.
13 Ibid.
14 For Mitchel see Brendan O Cathoir, *John Mitchel*.
15 Charles Gavan Duffy, *Four Years of Irish History, 1845–49*, p.353.
16 Ibid., p.606.
17 For Doheny see Michael Doheny, *The Felon's Track*. Also Michael O'Donnell, Lecture on Michael Doheny: Fenian Leader, 18 April 1986. Internet Posting, www.fethard.com.

18 For O'Mahony see the excellent doctoral thesis by Brian Sayers, *John O'Mahony: Revolutionary and Scholar (1815–1877)* (National University of Ireland, Maynooth, 2005). Hereafter, Sayers, John O'Mahony, *Revolutionary and Scholar*.

19 For this process see Ibid., pp.168–92.

20 Sayers, John O'Mahony, *Revolutionary and Scholar*, p.173. For the subsequent fracas with policemen see Luby's Reminiscences on O'Mahony, *Irish World* (New York), 3–24 March, 1877.

21 Sayers, Ibid., pp.175–78.

22 For this see Charles Gavan Duffy, *The League of North and South*.

23 Ibid., p.134.

24 A.M. Sullivan, *New Ireland*, p.201.

25 Charles Gavan Duffy, *The League of North and South*, p.181.

26 Ibid. p.237.

27 In a farewell address to his constituents of New Ross, Co. Wexford.

28 For Sadleir's career see A.M. Sullivan, *New Ireland*, pp.168–82.

29 Charles Gavan Duffy, *The League of North and South*, p.292.

30 A.M. Sullivan, *New Ireland,* p.239.

31 Ibid., p.259.

32 Ibid., p.258.

33 Joseph Denieffe, *A Personal Narrative of the Irish Revolutionary Brotherhood*, p.3. Hereafter Denieffe, *A Personal Narrative of the Irish Revolutionary Brotherhood*.

34 Joseph Denieffe, Memoir. NLI, MS 8002.

35 Sayers, *John O'Mahony: Revolutionary and Scholar*, pp.193–95.

36 James Stephens, *Personal Recollections of '48*, and James Stephens, *Reminiscences*. NLI. A12680. Hereafter Stephens, *Personal Recollections*.

37 Michael Doheny, *The Felon's Track*, p.229.

38 Luby's Reminiscences on O'Mahony, *Irish World* (New York), 24 March 1867.

39 Stephens, *Personal Recollections*.

40 Ibid.

41 Ibid.

42 Ibid.

43 Ibid.

44 Ibid.

45 Ibid.

46 Ibid.

47 Ibid.

48 Ibid.

49 Ibid.

50 Sayers, *John O'Mahony: Revolutionary and Scholar*, p.198.

51 Denieffe, *A Personal Narrative of the Irish Revolutionary Brotherhood*, pp.159–60.

52 Ibid., p.18.

53 Sean McConville, *Irish Political Prisoners, 1848–1922*, pp.113–14.

54 Sayers, *John O'Mahony: Revolutionary and Scholar*, pp.195–202.

55 Sean McConville, *Irish Political Prisoners, 1848–1922*, p.117.

56 O'Leary, *Recollections of Fenians and Fenianism*, Vol.1, p.81 n1.

57 Ibid., p.102.
58 Savage, *Fenian Heroes and Martyrs*, p.64.
59 Denieffe, *A Personal Narrative of the Irish Revolutionary Brotherhood*, p.29.
60 A.M. Sullivan, *The Story of Ireland*, p.571.
61 A.M. Sullivan, *New Ireland*, p.359.
62 O'Leary, *Recollections of Fenians and Fenianism*, Vol.1, p.117.
63 Ibid., p.98.
64 Letter from O'Mahony to the *Irish People* (New York), 14 December 1867. Quoted in Sayers, *John O'Mahony, Revolutionary and Scholar*, p.201.
65 Denieffe, *A Personal Narrative of the Irish Revolutionary Brotherhood*, p.36.
66 O'Donovan Rossa, *Recollections of Irish Politics*, pp.36–37.
67 Denieffe, *A Personal Narrative of the Irish Revolutionary Brotherhood*, p.27.
68 Photostat copy of a diary of James Stephens, written at Brooklyn, 1859. NLI, MS4148. Hereafter, Stephens's Diary.
69 William Dillon, *Life of John Mitchel* (London 1888), Vol. 2 pp.119–20. Quoted in Sayers, *John O'Mahony: Revolutionary and Scholar*, p.206.
70 Ibid.
71 Stephens's Diary.
72 O'Leary, *Recollections of Fenians and Fenianism*, Vol.1, p.96.
73 Luby's Reminiscences on O'Mahony, *Irish World* (New York), 24 March 1877.
74 For this see A.M. Sullivan, 'The Phoenix Conspiracy' in *New Ireland*, pp.258–69.
75 O'Donovan Rossa, *Recollections of Irish Politics*, pp.228–29.
76 Ibid., p.228.
77 John O'Leary, *Recollections of Fenians and Fenianism*, Vol.1, p.128.
78 Denieffe, *A Personal Narrative of the Irish Revolutionary Brotherhood*, p.45.
79 Luby Memoirs. NLI, MS, 331–333. Hereafter, Luby Memoirs.
80 Ibid.
81 John O'Leary, *Recollections of Fenians and Fenianism*, Vol.1, p.148.
82 Ibid., p.117.
83 Ibid., p.136.
84 For O'Mahony's visit to Ireland see Sayers, *John O'Mahony: Revolutionary and Scholar*, pp.235–39.
85 Luby's Reminiscences on O'Mahony, *Irish World* (New York), 24 March 1877.
85 Denieffe, *A Personal Narrative of the Irish Revolutionary Brotherhood*, p.60.
86 Ibid.
87 Luby, 'Luby's Reminiscences on O'Mahony', *Irish World* (New York), 24 March 1877.
88 Ibid.

Chapter Two

1 O'Donovan Rossa, *Rossa's Recollections*, p.234.
2 John O'Leary, *Recollections of Fenians and Fenianism*, Vol.1, p.132. n. For Duffy see also Savage, *Fenian Heroes and Martyrs*, pp. 374–82. Also, the obituary on Duffy, (New York), 8 February 1868.

3   For Kickham see R.V. Comerford, *Charles J. Kickham 1828–1882* (Dublin, 1979). Also Savage, *Fenian Heroes and Martyrs*, pp.358–67.

4   For Devoy, see John Devoy, *Recollections of an Irish Rebel* (New York, 1929), Terry Golway, *Irish Rebel* (New York, 1998), Terence Dooley, *The Greatest of the Fenians: John Devoy and Ireland* (Dublin, 2003).

5   Luby Memoirs.

6   John O'Mahony to Jane Mandeville, 24 October 1864. Quoted in Sayers, *John O'Mahony*, p.247. See also Toby Joyce, 'Fenianism and the American Civil War', *History Ireland*, Vol. 177, No. 2 (March–April, 2009), pp.15–16.

7   For the National Brotherhood of Saint Patrick see John Moloney, *The National Brotherhood of St Patrick and the Rise of Dublin Fenianism, 1858–1865*, M.A. Thesis, Galway University, 1976.

8   Denieffe, *A Personal Narrative of the Irish Revolutionary Brotherhood*, p.56.

Chapter Three

1   John O'Leary, *Recollections of Fenians and Fenianism*, Vol.1, p.152.

2   A.M. Sullivan, *New Ireland*, p.321.

3   For the life and political career of McManus see Thomas G McAllister, *Thomas Bellew McManus 1811–1861: A Short Biography* (Maynooth, 1972).

4   O'Leary, *Fenians and Fenianism*, Vol.1, p.152.

5   John Devoy, *Recollections of an Irish Rebel*, p.319.

6   For Doheny's revolutionary strategy see Michael Cavanagh, 'Our Dead Comrades – Col. Michael Doheny', *Celtic Monthly* 1880 (New York), pp.59–60.

7   Ibid., p.138.

8   David Brundage, *Irish Nationalists in America: The Politics of Exile, 1798–1998*, p.101.

9   Louis Bisceglia, *The Fenian Funeral of Terence Bellew McManus*, Eire-Ireland X1V:3, Fall, 1979 (pp.45–64), p.56. There are also useful accounts of McManus's re-burial in Thomas J. Brophy, 'On Church Grounds: Political Funerals and the Contest to Lead Catholic Ireland', *The Catholic Historical Review*, Vol. 9 No. 3 (July 2009), pp.491–51. Jack Morgan. '"The Dust of Maynooth": Fenian Funeral as Political Theatre', *New Hibernia Review*, 2:4, Winter 1998, pp.24–37. Also, Pauric Travers, 'Our Fenian Dead: Glasnevin Cemetery and the Genesis of the Republican Funeral', in *Dublin and Dubliners*, ed. James Kelly and E. McGearailt (Dublin, 1990), pp.52–72.

10 The McManus Obsequies, *New York Times*, 19 October 1861.

11 Sayers, *John O'Mahony, Revolutionary and Scholar 1815–1877*, p.242.

12 For the National Brotherhood of St Patrick, the IRB and McManus's funeral, see John Moloney, *The National Brotherhood of St Patrick and the Rise of Dublin Fenianism 1858–1865* (M.A. Thesis, University College, Galway, 1976).

13 Luby Memoirs.

14 Ibid.

15 Ibid.

16 For this development see Nina Ranelli, '*The Dust of Some*', *Glasnevin Cemetery and the Politics of Burial* (SIT Ireland, Fall 2001).

17 Luby Memoirs.

18 For Cullen, see, Ciaran McCarroll, Paul, Cardinal Cullen, *Portrait of a Practical Nationalist* (Dublin, 2008) and Desmond Bowen, Paul, *Cardinal Cullen and the Shaping of Modern Irish Catholicism* (Dublin, 1983).

19 Howard Lune, 'Transnational Nationalism: Strategic Action Fields and the Organisation of the Fenian Movement'. In Lune, *Research in Social Movements, Conflicts and Change* (Bingley), p.25.

20 Luby Memoirs.

21 Ibid.

22 Ibid.

23 Ibid. For Kenyon see Tim Boland, *Father John Kenyon – The Rebel Priest* (Nenagh, Co. Tipperary, 2011). Also, Seamus Pender, 'Luby, Kenyon and the McManus Funeral', *Journal of the Cork Historical and Archaeological Society*, Vol. LV1, No. 183, January–June 1951.

24 Luby Memoirs.

25 Ibid.

26 Ibid.

27 Ibid.

28 Samuel Rutherford, *The Secret History of the Fenian Conspiracy*, Vol.1, p.200.

29 Luby Memoirs.

30 Ibid.

31 Ibid.

32 Ibid.

33 O'Leary, *Recollections of Fenians and Fenianism*, Vol.1, p.153.

34 A.M. Sullivan, *New Ireland*, p.321.

35 Luby Memoirs.

36 O'Leary, *Recollections of Fenians and Fenianism*, Vol.1, p.152.

37 R.V. Comerford, *The Fenians in Context: Irish Politics and Society, 1848–82* (Dublin 1998), p.79.

38 A.M. Sullivan, *New Ireland*, pp.322–23.

39 Luby Memoirs.

40 Mervyn Busteed, *The Irish in Manchester, 1750–1921* (Manchester, 2018), p.208.

41 Stephens to O'Mahony, 25 February 1862. Denieffe, *A Personal Narrative of the Irish Revolutionary Brotherhood*, p.168.

Chapter Four

1 For this see A.M. Sullivan, *New Ireland*, pp.305–24.

2 For the Trent affair see David Brown, *Palmerston: A Biography*, pp.452–53.

3 Luby Memoirs.

4 O'Leary, *Recollections of Fenians and Fenianism*, Vol.1, p.176.

5 Ibid., p.193.

6	*A History of the Fenian Conspiracy*, Larcom Papers, NLI, MS 7517.
7	Brian Griffin, *The IRB in Connacht and Leinster, 1858–1878*, p.35. M.A. thesis. St. Patrick's College, Maynooth, 1983.
8	Devoy, *Recollections of an Irish Rebel*, p.33.
9	Luby Memoirs.
10	'Obituary on Duffy by Michael O'Rorke', *Irish People* (New York), 8 February 1868.
11	Dr Kerron O Luain (Independent Researcher), 'Ribbonism and Fenianism: Conflict and Conformity within working-class Irish Nationalism', www.academia.edu/7938933/Ribbonism_and_Fenianism_conflict_and_conformity_within_working_class_Irish_nationalism
12	For Duffy's activities see Sean O'Luing, 'A contribution to the Study of Fenianism', *Breifne*, No. 10 (1967), pp.155–74.
13	Devoy, *Recollections of an Irish Rebel*, p.31.
14	Ibid., p.33.
15	Luby Memoirs.
16	James O'Connor, in *The Irishman* (New York), Christmas edition 1874. This was in one of four articles that he published in the newspaper during December 1874 and January 1875 under the title 'Fenianism Photographed'. Hereafter O'Connor, 'Fenianism Photographed'.
17	O'Leary, *Fenians and Fenianism*, Vol.1, p.191.
18	O'Connor, 'Fenianism Photographed', 19 December 1874.
19	Luby Memoirs.
20	Ibid.
21	A.M. Sullivan, *New Ireland,* p.359.
22	O'Leary, *Recollections of Fenians and Fenianism*, Vol.1, p.97.
23	Luby Memoirs.
24	O'Connor, 'Fenianism Photographed', 2 January 1875.
25	Luby Memoirs.
26	O'Connor, 'Fenianism Photographed', 2 January, 1875.
27	Ibid., 19 December 1874.
28	Ibid., 2 January 1875.
29	A.M. Sullivan, *New Ireland*, p.359.
30	Luby Memoirs.
31	O'Leary, *Recollections of Fenians and Fenianism*, Vol.1, p.85 n1.
32	O'Connor, 'Fenianism Photographed'.
33	Luby Memoirs.
34	Ibid.
35	Ibid.
36	Ibid.
37	Ibid.
38	O'Leary, *Recollections of Fenians and Fenianism*, Vol.1, pp.232–33.
39	Ibid., pp.233–34.
40	Ibid.
41	In a letter from O'Mahony to Francis Mandeville, December 1866, NLI, MS 5018.

42 For the Irish People see Mary Leo, *The Importance of the Fenians and their Press on Public Opinion 1863–1870*, Doctoral Thesis, Trinity College, Dublin (1976).

43 Luby Memoirs.

44 T.D. Sullivan, *Recollections of Troubled Times in Irish Politics* (Dublin, 1905), pp.50–51.

45 Luby Memoirs.

46 Richard Davis, *Revolutionary Nationalist: William Smith O'Brien, 1803–1864*, p.361.

47 O'Connor, 'Fenianism Photographed', 2 January 1875.

48 A.M. Sullivan, *New Ireland*, p.332.

49 Takagami, *The Dublin Fenians, 1858–79*, pp.17–43.

50 Devoy, *Recollections of an Irish Rebel*, p.35. For the decline of NBSP see John Moloney, *The National Brotherhood of St Patrick and the Rise of Dublin Fenianism, 1858–1865*, M.A. Thesis, Galway University, 1976.

51 For Fenianism and the British Army see A.J. Semple, *The Fenian Infiltration of the British Army in Ireland 1858–1867* (1971). Also, Devoy, *Recollections of an Irish Rebel*, Chapter 19, pp.128–,32 and Takagami, *The Dublin Fenians, 1858–79*, pp.148–83.

52 Devoy, *Recollections of an Irish Rebel*, p.139.

53 Luby Memoirs.

54 Devoy, *Recollections of an Irish Rebel*, p.139.

55 In a letter to Lord Spencer, 26 December 1869, NLI, Sir Hugh Rose Papers.

56 For the Chicago Fair see Brian Griffin, '"Scallions, pikes and bog oak ornaments": The Irish Republican Brotherhood and the Chicago Fenian Fair, 1864', *Studia Hibernica*, No. 299 (1995–1997), pp.85–97.

57 R.V. Comerford, The Fenians in Context: Irish Politics and Society 1848–82 (1985), p.120.

58 O'Mahony, 'Fenianism: An Exposition', *Irish People* (New York), 1 February 1868.

Chapter Five

1 O'Mahony, 'Fenianism: An Exposition', *Irish People* (New York), 25 January 1868.

2 Ibid.

3 Ibid., 1 February 1868.

4 For Millen see his manuscript, 'An account of Fenianism from April 1865 till April 1866 written in New York 1866'. Nli 3964. Hereafter Millen, 'Account of Fenianism'.

5 Stephens to O'Mahony, 24 June 1865. Catholic University of America, Fenian Papers Digital Collection.

6 Kelly Submission, 21 June 1865. Catholic University of America Digitalised Fenian Collection.

7 Ibid.

8 Millen, 'Account of Fenianism'.

9 Ibid.

10 Millen Submission, 24 June 1865. Catholic University of America Digitalised Fenian Collection.

11 Ibid.

12 Devoy, *Recollections of an Irish Rebel*, p.55.
13 Denieffe, *A Personal Narrative of the Irish Revolutionary Brotherhood*, pp.92–93.
14 Ibid., p.92.
15 O'Connor, 'Fenianism Photographed'.
16 Millen, 'Account of Fenianism'.
17 See O'Mahony, *Irish People* (New York), 11 April 1868.
18 Millen, 'Account of Fenianism'.
19 Ibid.
20 O'Mahony, *Irish People* (New York), 8 February 1868.

Chapter Six

1 For Wodehouse see Angus Hawkins and John Powell (eds), *The Journal of John Wodehouse, First Earl of Kimberley, 1862–1902* (1998). Also, John Powell, *Liberal by Principle: The Politics of John Wodehouse, 1st Earl of Kimberley* (1996).
2 Wodehouse Journal, 31 October 1869, Kimberley Papers, Bodleian Library Oxford. Hereafter, Kimberley Papers.
3 Wodehouse to Raikes Currie, 2 December 1864, Kimberley Papers.
4 Wodehouse to Grey, 7 December 1864, Kimberley Papers.
5 Wodehouse Journal, 7 May 1865, p.159.
6 For the clash between Peel and O'Brien see Richard Davis, *Revolutionary Nationalist: William Smith O'Brien, 1803–1864*, p.357. For the dispute with Gladstone see Wodehouse Journal, 7 May 1865, p.159.
7 'A Native' (pseudonym of Percy Fitzgerald), *Recollections of Dublin Castle and Dublin Society*, p.48.
8 Col. The Hon. Frederick Wellesley, *Recollections of a Soldier-Diplomat*, p.91.
9 Ibid., pp.91–92.
10 Wodehouse to Sir George Grey, 27 November 1864, Kimberly Papers.
11 Palmerston had forwarded the letter to Grey, who then had Wodehouse investigate the matter. On 27 November, Wodehouse informed Grey that Superintendent Ryan told him that the address of the writer was bogus and that G Division did not recognise the handwriting. Kimberley Papers.
12 Wodehouse to Grey, 7 December 1864, Kimberley Papers, Bodleian Library.
13 Wodehouse to Grey, 7 December 1864, Kimberley Papers, Bodleian Library.
14 Denieffe, *A Personal Narrative of the Irish Revolutionary Brotherhood*, p.84.
15 O'Connor, 'Fenianism Photographed', 26 December 1874.
16 Ibid.
17 Luby Memoirs.
18 Copy of a letter from Wodehouse to Grey, 3 September 1865, Palmerston Papers.
19 Wodehouse to Grey, 12 September 1865, Palmerston Papers.
20 Wodehouse to the Duke of Cambridge, 13 or 14 September 1865, Kimberley Papers.
21 Wodehouse to Lord John Russell, 1 September 1865, National Archives, London, PRO30/22/28.

22 A report from the DMP Office, 23 January 1867, which represented the views of the DMP and Irish Constabulary and recounted events before and after the suppression of the *Irish People*. CSORP/1867/1316, National Archives of Ireland.

23 Savage, *Fenian Heroes and Martyrs*, p.65.

24 'A History of the Fenian Conspiracy', NLI, Larcom Papers, MS 7517.

25 Wodehouse to Grey, 16 September 1865, Palmerston Papers.

Chapter Seven

1 O'Connor, 'Fenianism Photographed', 26 December 1874.

2 Ibid.

3 Luby Memoirs.

4 Wodehouse to Grey, 16 September 1865, Kimberley Papers, Bodleian Library.

5 Wodehouse to Peel, 17 September 1865, Kimberley Papers, Bodleian Library.

6 Undated letter September 1865 from Palmerston in reply to one from Wodehouse on 15 September.

7 Rose to Wodehouse, 2 October, 1865. NLI, Larcom Papers, MS 7688.

8 Savage, Fenian Heroes and Martyrs, p.65.

9 Wodehouse to Grey, 27 September 1865, Kimberley Papers, Bodleian Library.

10 Wodehouse to Grey, 1 October 1865, Kimberley Papers, Bodleian Library.

11 Ibid.

12 Wodehouse to Lord Russell, 1 October 1865, Kimberley Papers, Bodleian Library.

13 Wodehouse to Lord Palmerston, 7 October 1865, Palmerston Papers.

14 Wodehouse to Grey, 27 October 1865, Kimberley Papers, Bodleian Library.

15 O'Connor, 'Fenianism Photographed', Christmas Edition, 1874.

16 Millen, 'Account of Fenianism'.

17 Ibid.

18 O'Leary, *Recollections of Fenians and Fenianism*, Vol. 2, p.212.

19 Superintendent Ryan's Report, DMP Office, 12 November 1865, National Archives, London, H0 45/7799.

20 Millen, 'Account of Fenianism'.

21 *The Mail,* 13 November 1865.

22 Wodehouse to Russell, 11 November 1865. National Archives, London, PRO30/22/15G.

23 *The Mail,* 13 November 1865.

24 A.M. Sullivan, *New Ireland*, p.265.

25 *Arrest and Escape of James Stephens, Head Centre of the Irish Republican Brotherhood. Trial and Sentence of Thomas Clarke Luby* by an Eyewitness (New York, 1866), p.13. The eyewitness was undoubtedly the Fenian solicitor John Lawless. Hereafter Lawless.

26 Ibid.

27 Ibid., p.24.

28 Devoy, *Gaelic American*, 14 January 1905.

29 Lawless, *Escape of Stephens*, p.39.

30 NLI, Larcom Papers, MS, 7687.

31 Ibid.
32 Devoy, *Recollections of an Irish Rebel*, p.82.
33 Denieffe, *A Personal Narrative of the Irish Revolutionary Brotherhood*, p.124.
34 Devoy, *Recollections of an Irish Rebel*, p.82.
35 McLeod at the official inquiry into Stephens's escape from Richmond Gaol. Report of the Inspectors General of Prisons to His Excellency The Lord Lieutenant with regard to the escape of James Stephens. National Archives of Ireland, CSPRP1885/24044.
36 Wodehouse to Russell, 26 November 1865, National Archives, London, PRO30/22/15G.
37 Wodehouse to Russell, 26 November 1865, National Archives, London, PRO30/22/15G.
38 Larcom, 25 November 1865, NLI, Larcom Papers, MS, 7687.
39 Ibid.
40 The judgement of the official inquiry into Stephens's escape from Richmond Gaol. Report of the Inspectors General of Prisons to His Excellency The Lord Lieutenant with regard to the escape of James Stephens. National Archives of Ireland, CSPRP1885/24044.
41 *The Nation*, 25 November 1865.
42 'All our work is undone.' Wodehouse to Larcom, 24 November 1865, NLI, Larcom Papers, MS 7687. 'rumours today …' Wodehouse Journal, 18 November 1865, p.178.
43 Wodehouse to Russell, 27 November 1865, National Archives, London, PRO30/22/15G.
44 Larcom to Lake, 26 November 1865, NLI, Larcom Papers, MS, 7687.
45 Devoy, *Gaelic American*, 21 January 1905.
46 Ibid. O'Connor, 'Fenianism Photographed'.
47 Devoy, *Recollections of an Irish Rebel*, pp.73–74.
48 O'Connor, 'Fenianism Photographed', 2 January 1875.
49 For this see O'Mahony, 'Fenianism: An Exposition', *Irish People* (New York).
50 Ibid., 4 April 1868.
51 Ibid.
52 Devoy, *Recollections of an Irish Rebel*, p.94.
53 O'Mahony, 'Fenianism: An Exposition', *Irish People*, 11 April 1868.
54 Devoy, *Recollections of an Irish Rebel*, p.90.
55 Ibid., p.96.
56 Ibid.
57 O'Mahony, 'Fenianism: An Exposition', *Irish People*, 16 May 1868.

Chapter Eight

1 Wodehouse to Gladstone, 12 February 1866, Kimberley Papers, Bodleian Library.
2 Wodehouse to Larcom, 19 November 1865, Kimberley Papers, Bodleian Library.
3 *The Mail*, 21 November 1865.

4   Ibid.

5   Wodehouse Journal, 21 January 1866, p.182.

6   M. Bonham Carter (ed.), *The Autobiography of Margot Asquith* (London, 1962), pp.100–01.

7   Wodehouse Journal, 15 November 1865, p.178.

8   Ibid.

9   Rose to the Duke of Cambridge, December 1865, NLI, Sie Hugh Rose Papers

10   Padraig Cummins Kennedy, *Political Policing in a Liberal Age: Britain's Response to the Fenian Threat, 1858–1868.*

11   Ibid.

12   Wodehouse to Rose, 18 November 1865, Kimberley Papers.

13   Lawless, *Escape of Stephens*, p.67.

14   Wodehouse to Grey, 14 November 1865, Kimberley Papers, Bodleian Library.

15   For Dublin Castle's security precautions at the 1865 Special Commission trials see Rose to Wodehouse, 11 December 1865, Kimberley Papers. Also, National Archives of Ireland., CSORP/1867/1316.

16   Lawless, *Escape of Stephens*, p.68.

17   Ibid., p.69. For Keogh see also Mary Naughten, 'Judge William Nicholas Keogh', *Journal of the Galway Archaeological and Historical Society*, Vol. 38 (1981/1982), pp.5–30.

18   Ibid.

19   Ibid., p.79.

20   Sean McConville, *Irish Political Prisoners, 1848–1922*, p.336. McConville observes that Rossa's career 'could not have been sustained but for the mercurial and sensation-seeking element in his own character'.

21   A.M. Sullivan, *New Ireland*, p.356.

22   Samuel Rutherford, *The Secret History of the Fenian Conspiracy*, Vol.1, p.145.

23   Ibid., p.146.

24   Rose to the Duke of Cambridge, December 1865, NLI, Sir Hugh Rose Papers.

25   Wodehouse, 1 December 1865. 'The sympathy with Fenianism is so widely spread amongst the class from whom warders, policemen and even soldiers are taken that treachery is to say the least not improbable wherever the prisoners are guarded, principally or exclusively by Irishmen.'

26   Letter from Rose to a Colonel Mackenzie in London, 23 November 1866. NLI, Sir Hugh Rose Papers.

27   Letter from Rose to Lord Malmesbury, 27 November 1866. NLI, Sir Hugh Rose Papers.

28   Wodehouse to Rose, 4 December, 1865. NLI, Sir Hugh Rose Papers.

29   In separate letters to Lord Russell and Grey, 10 December 1865, Kimberley Papers.

30   Wodehouse to Raikes Currie, 21 December 1865, Kimberley Papers.

31   Wodehouse Journal, 25 December 1865, p.180.

32   Wodehouse to Lord Russell, 28 December 1865, Kimberley Papers.

33   Ibid.

34   Wodehouse Journal, 8 December 1865, p.180.

35   A.M. Sullivan, *New Ireland*, p.355.

36   National Archives of Ireland, CSORP/1867/1316.

37 Superintendent Ryan, G Division Office, January 1866, National Archives, London, HO 35/7799.
38 Wodehouse to Grey, 17 January 1866, Kimberley Papers, Bodleian Library.
39 Ibid.
40 Wodehouse to Grey, 21 January 1866, Kimberley Papers, Bodleian Library.
41 Wodehouse to Gladstone, 12 February 1866. This letter in the Gladstone Papers is quoted by John Powell, *Liberal by Principle: The Politics of John Wodehouse, 1st Earl of Kimberley*, p.109.
42 Rose to Wodehouse, 13 February 1866, NLI, Sir Hugh Rose Papers.
43 Rose to Wodehouse, 14 February 1866, NLI, Sir Hugh Rose Papers.
44 For Rose's aversion to the suspension of Habeas Corpus, see his letter of 13 February 1866 to Wodehouse. For the policy of expulsion, see Rose's letter to the Duke of Cambridge, 15 February 1866. NLI, Sir Hugh Rose Papers.
45 Rose to Wodehouse, 9 February 1866, NLI, Rose Papers.
46 Wodehouse to Grey, 14 February 1866, Kimberley Papers, Bodleian Library.
47 Devoy, *Recollections of an Irish Rebel*, p.98.
48 Rose to Wodehouse, 17 February 1866, NLI, Sir Hugh Rose Papers.
49 Wodehouse to Grey, 19 February 1866, NLI, Kimberley Papers, Bodleian Library.

Chapter Nine

1 Devoy, *Gaelic American*, 14 January 1905.
2 Devoy, *Recollections of an Irish Rebel*, p.99.
3 Ibid., p.98.
4 Ibid., p.101.
5 Ibid., pp.99–100.
6 Ibid., p.103.
7 Ibid., p.105.
8 Ibid., p.421.
9 Ibid., p.111.
10 Wodehouse to Grey, 14 February 1866, Kimberley Papers.
11 Rose to Wodehouse, 17 February 1866, Sir Hugh Rose Papers.
12 A report from the DMP Office, 23 January 1867, which represented the views of the DMP and Irish Constabulary and recounted events before and after the suppression of the *Irish People*. CSORP/1867/1316, National Archives of Ireland.
13 NLI, Mayo Papers, MS 11188/21.
14 Wodehouse Journal, 25 February 1866, p.183.
15 Wodehouse Journal, 10 March 1866, p.184.
16 Wodehouse Journal, 21 April 1866, p.187.
17 Wodehouse Journal, 24 March 1866, p.185.
18 Wodehouse Journal, 1 April 1866, p.185.
19 Ibid.
20 Devoy, *Recollections of an Irish Rebel*, p.112.
21 Wodehouse Journal, 16 March 1866, p.184.

22 Wodehouse to Grey, 23 March 1866, Kimberley Papers, Bodleian Library.

23 Ibid.

24 Wodehouse Journal, 28 May 1866, p.188.

25 Superintendent Ryan, DMP Superintendent's Office, G Division, 10 February 1866; Superintendent Ryan, G Division report, 21 February 1866, National Archives, London, H0 45/7799.

26 A report from the DMP Office, 23 January 1867, which represented the views of the DMP and Irish Constabulary. CSORP/1867/1316, National Archives of Ireland.

27 For West's diplomatic efforts see Bernadette Whelan, *American Government in Ireland, 1790–1913: A History of the US Consular Service, 1789–1913* (Manchester, 2013). See also Barry Kennerk, 'A Dublin Consul Under Siege: American Reactions to the Habeas Corpus Suspension Crisis of 1866–1868', *Dublin Historical Record*, Vol. 63, No. 19 (Spring 2010), pp.18–28.

28 Wodehouse Journal, 14 June 1866, pp.189–90.

29 *Freeman's Journal*, 2 May 1866.

30 Wodehouse, 13 April 1866, Kimberly Papers, Bodleian Library.

31 NLI, Mayo Papers, MS 11188/21.

32 Superintendent Ryan, Dublin Metropolitan Police, G Division, 20 March 1866. National Archives, London, H0 45/7799.

33 Wodehouse Journal, 24 March 1866, p.185.

34 Wodehouse to Fortescue, 22 June 1866, Kimberley Papers.

35 John Devoy, *Recollections of an Irish Rebel*, p.6235.

36 In a memorandum on the Irish situation to the Cabinet on 7 June 1867. NLI, Mayo Papers, MS 11188/14.

37 Ibid.

38 Superintendent Ryan, G Division report, 21 February 1866.

39 Ibid.

40 Devoy, *Recollections of an Irish Rebel*, pp.156–57.

41 Rose to Wodehouse, 9 January 1866, NLI, Sir Hugh Rose Papers.

42 Ibid.

43 Ibid.

44 Devoy, *Recollections of an Irish Rebel*, p.38.

45 Devoy, *Gaelic American* (New York), November 1875.

46 Supt Ryan report, G Division, 1 May 1866, HO 45/7799.

47 Ibid.

48 For the attack on Warner as well as the Shooting Circle and Vigilance Committee generally, see National Archives London, Supt Ryan reports, G Division, 10 February 1866, 1 May 1866, 22 May 1866, 6 November 1867, HO45/7799.

49 Rose to a Lt Col Somerset, 14 April 1866, Sir Hugh Rose Papers.

50 Wodehouse Journal, 28 May 1866, p.188.

51 For this see Michael T. Foy, Michael Collins's *Intelligence War: The Struggle between the British and the IRA, 1919–1921*.

Chapter Ten

1   For Naas, the future Lord Mayo, see George Pottinger, *Mayo: Disraeli's Viceroy* (1990). Also, Padraig Cummins Kennedy, *Political Policing in a Liberal Age: Britain's Response to the Fenian Threat, 1858–1868*.
2   Lord Clarendon to Kimberly, 8 July 1866. Quoted in Padraig Cummins Kennedy, *Political Policing in a Liberal Age: Britain's Response to the Fenian Threat, 1858–1868*, p.222.
3   'A Native' (pseudonym of Percy Fitzgerald), *Recollections of Dublin Castle and Dublin Society*, p.46.
4   Padraig Cummins Kennedy, *Political Policing in a Liberal Age: Britain's Response to the Fenian Threat, 1858–1868* is excellent on this subject.
5   Naas, 10 December 1866, NLI, Mayo Papers, MS 11169/4.
6   Wood to Lord Naas, 15 August 1866, NLI, Mayo Papers, 11169/1.
7   Chris Payne, *The Chieftain: Victorian True Crime Through the Eyes of a Scotland Yard Detective* (2011), pp.79–80.
8   For Feilding see Padraig Cummins Kennedy, *Political Policing in a Liberal Age: Britain's Response to the Fenian Threat, 1858–1868*, especially Chapter Four, 'New Directions', pp.219–82.
9   Feilding to Naas, 24 August 1866, NLI, Mayo Papers, MS 11169/1.
10 Ibid., 9 September 1866
11 A report from the DMP Office, 23 January 1867, which represented the views of the DMP and Irish Constabulary. CSORP/1867/1316, National Archives of Ireland.
12 Ibid. The figures for detainees are from the 'A History of the Fenian Conspiracy', NLI, Larcom Papers, MS 7517.
13 Takagami, The Dublin Fenians, 1858–79, p.134.
14 Supt Ryan, Superintendent's Office, G Division, Dublin Metropolitan Police, 14 April 1867, National Archives, London, H0 45/7799.
15 'A History of the Fenian Conspiracy', NLI, Larcom Papers, MS 7517.
16 Strathnairn to Lieutenant-General Napier, 30 September 1866, Sir Hugh Rose Papers.
17 National Archives, London, H0 45/7799.
18 'A History of the Fenian Conspiracy', NLI, Larcom Papers, MS 7517.
19 Ibid.
20 Ibid.
21 Naas to Abercorn, 15 November 1866, Public Record Office of Northern Ireland, Abercorn Papers, T2541, VR 45. Quoted in Padraig Cummins Kennedy, *Political Policing in a Liberal Age: Britain's Response to the Fenian Threat, 1858–1868*, p.273.
22 Stanley to Naas, 19 November 1866, NLI, Mayo Papers, 43884/6.
23 Naas Report to Derby, 23 December 1866, NLI, Mayo Papers, MS 11189/6.
24 Strathnairn to Lord Malmesbury, 27 November 1866, Sir Hugh Rose Papers.
25 Strathnairn in a letter reassuring a loyalist Mr Osborne in Clonmel, 30 December 1866. Sir Hugh Rose Papers.
26 'A History of the Fenian Conspiracy', NLI, Larcom Papers, MS 7517.
27 7 December 1866, NLI, Mayo Papers, MS43884/4.

28 'A History of the Fenian Conspiracy', NLI, Larcom Papers, MS 7517.
29 Morris to Naas, 1 December 1866, NLI, Mayo Papers, MS 11189.
30 Ibid., Undated, December 1866.
31 Strathnairn letter to Colonel Mackenzie, 23 November 1866, NLI, Sir Hugh Rose Papers.
32 Rose to Naas, 3 December 1866, NLI, Sir Hugh Rose Papers.
33 Memorandum from Lord Mayo to Lord Strathnairn, 6 December, NLI, Mayo Papers, MS16188/77.
34 *Freeman's Journal*, 3 December 1866.
35 National Archives, London, HO45/7799.
36 Takagami, *The Dublin Fenians, 1858–79*, p.61.
37 Naas Report to Derby, 23 December 1866, NLI, Mayo Papers, MS 11189/6.
38 Strathnairn to General Peel, 26 November 1866, Sir Hugh Rose Papers.
39 Strathnairn, 25 December 1866, Sir Hugh Rose Papers.

Chapter Eleven

1 John O'Mahony, 'Fenianism: An Exposition', *Irish People* (New York). He was just Stephens's agent.
2 D. Thomas report. National Archives, London, H0 45/7799.
3 Ibid.
4 For Cluseret see Gustave Cluseret, 'My Connection with Fenianism', NLI, A15973. Reprinted from *Frazier's Magazine*, New Series, Vol. VI, No. 33. Hereafter, Cluseret, 'My Connection with Fenianism'.
5 Ibid.
6 *New York Herald,* 31 October 1866.
7 For Fariola see Octave L. Fariola, 'Amongst the Fenians'. This comprises a series of articles on his involvement with Fenianism that he published between 1 August and 24 October 1868 in *The Irishman* (New York). Hereafter, Fariola, 'Amongst the Fenians'. Also, Daniel Frankignou, 'Count Octave Fariola: A Belgian Monomaniac', Internet posting for the Confederate Historical Association of Belgium www.chab-belgium.com/pdf/english/Fariola.pdf.
8 Fariola, 'Amongst the Fenians'.
9 Ibid.
10 Ibid.
11 Ibid.
12 Cluseret, 'My Connection with Fenianism'.
13 Stephens's account of his downfall in in an undated letter 'to all who it may concern', NLI, MS 18012/115/12.
14 Ibid.
15 Ibid.
16 Ibid.
17 Ibid.
18 Ibid.

19   A.M. Sullivan, *New Ireland,* pp.358–59.
20   Ibid., p.360.
21   Ibid.
22   *A History of the Fenian Conspiracy,* Larcom Papers, NLI, MS 7517.
23   John Devoy, *Recollections of an Irish Rebel,* p.189.
24   Letter from New Orleans sent by a 'Southern Fenian' to Stephens, 20 October 1966. Catholic University of America, Fenian Papers Digital Collection.
25   Massey in numerous testimonies at trials after the rising. See, for instance, the trial of Halpin for Treason-Felony, November 1867. See also 'The statement of Patrick Condon also called Godfrey Massey when examined by the Crown Solicitor', April 1867, National Archives, HO45/7799.

Chapter Twelve

1   For the Irish in Britain see Roger Swift, Irish Migrants in the British City, 1815–1914 and The Irish in the Victorian City.
2   For the Liverpool background see John Belchem, *Irish, Catholic and Scouse: The History of the Liverpool Irish, 1800–1939.* For Fenianism more broadly in northern England, See W.J. Lowe, *The Irish in Mid-Victorian England.*
3   John Belchem, Irish, Catholic and Scouse: The History of the Liverpool Irish, 1800–1939, p.169.
4   'A History of the Fenian Conspiracy', NLI, Larcom Papers, MS 7517.
5   Fariola, 'Amongst the Fenians'.
6   Michael O'Rorke in his account of the London Directory and the Chester Affair, *The Irish People* (New York), 25 April 1868.
7   Fariola, 'Amongst the Fenians'.
8   Ibid.
9   Cluseret, 'My Connection with Fenianism'.
10   Michael O'Rorke in his account of the London Directory and the Chester Affair, *The Irish People* (New York), 25 April 1868.
11   Fariola, 'Amongst the Fenians'.
12   Ibid.
13   Obituary on Duffy by Michael O'Rorke, *Irish People* (New York), 8 February 1868.
14   Ibid.
15   Duffy to Devoy, *Recollections of an Irish Rebel,* p.187.
16   Fariola, 'Amongst the Fenians'.
17   Michael O'Rorke in his account of the London Directory and the Chester Affair, *The Irish People* (New York), 25 April 1868.
18   Fariola, 'Amongst the Fenians'.
19   Cluseret, 'My Connection with Fenianism'.
20   Corydon, in repeated testimony at many post-rising Special Commission Trials.
21   NLI, Mayo Papers, 43887/2.
22   Letters and collections in copy form by Major J.J. Greig, Head Constable of Liverpool, related to the intended Fenian attack on Chester Castle, 11 February, NLI, MS 42066.

23 For the Chester background, Roger Swift (ed.), *Victorian Chester* (Liverpool, 1996).
24 *Chester Record,* Saturday, 16 February 1867.
25 Ibid.
26 *The Irishman* (New York), 15 February 1867.
27 McHale report of an interview with Corydon, 12 February 1867, NLI, Larcom Papers, MS 7593.
28 Corydon testimony at the April 1868 Old Bailey Trial of Rickard Burke, Joseph Casey and Henry Mullady. Kelly gave similar testimony at many Special Commission trials after the rising, especially at those of McCafferty and Flood.
29 W.J. Lowe, 'Lancashire Fenianism, 1864–71', pp.173–74. In W.J. Lowe, The Irish in Mid-Victorian Victorian Lancashire: The Shaping of a Working-Class Community.
30 Diary of George Fenwick, Courtesy of Chester Public Library.
31 Argued persuasively by R.W. Durdey in his lengthy account, *The Fenians in Chester – 1867: Prelude and Aftermath* (1994). Deposited in Chester Public Library.
32 Devoy, *Recollections of an Irish Rebel*, p.189.
33 Extract from the diary of George Fenwick, Courtesy of Chester Public Library. Also, King's Hotel staff testimony at the Special Commission Trial of McCafferty.
34 *Chester Record,* Saturday, 16 February 1867.
35 For the Kerry rising see the five-part series by Sean O Luing, Kerry Archaeological and Historical Society (1971–74). Also A.M. Sullivan, *New Ireland*, pp.274–75.

Chapter Thirteen

1   Cluseret, 'My Connection with Fenianism'.
2   See also 'The statement of Patrick Condon also called Godfrey Massey when examined by the Crown Solicitor', April 1867. National Archives, HO45/7799.
3   Cluseret, 'My Connection with Fenianism'.
4   Fariola, 'Amongst the Fenians'.
5   Ibid.
6   Cluseret, 'My Connection with Fenianism'. Anderson writing as 'One Who Knows', *Contemporary Review,* February/April 1872, Part 2, p.628.
7   Fariola, 'Amongst the Fenians'.
8   Massey testimony at 1867 Special Commission Trials, in Cork. See also 'The statement of Patrick Condon also called Godfrey Massey when examined by the Crown Solicitor', April 1867. National Archives, HO45/7799.
9   Corydon testimony at the April 1868 Old Bailey Trial of Rickard Burke, Joseph Casey and Henry Mullady.
10 A History of the Fenian Conspiracy., NLI, Larcom Papers, MS 7517.
11 Supt Ryan, Superintendent's Office, G Division, Dublin Metropolitan Police, 19 February 1867, National Archives, London, H0 45/7799.
12 Supt Ryan, Superintendent's Office, G Division, Dublin Metropolitan Police, 22 February 1867, National Archives, London, H0 45/7799.
13 Supt Ryan, Superintendent's Office, G Division, Dublin Metropolitan Police, 25 February 1867, National Archives, London, H0 45/7799.

14 Brownrigg report from the Constabulary Office, Dublin Castle, 27 February 1867, NLI, Larcom Papers, MS 7593.
15 Brownrigg report from the Constabulary Office, Dublin Castle, 28 February 1867, NLI, Larcom Papers, MS 7593. Later, in a post-rising trial, Corydon also stated that military action in Ulster was ruled out as the province was considered 'a lost cause'. NLI, MS 36176.
16 Ibid.
17 Larcom, Letter of 5 March, NLI, Mayo Papers, MS 11191/5.
18 Ryan Report, 3 March 1867, Larcom Papers, NLI 7593.
19 Strathnairn, 25 February 1867 – 'I am of the opinion that I have always been.' Sir Hugh Rose Papers.
20 Fariola, 'Amongst the Fenians'.
21 J.F.X. O'Brien, *For the Liberty of Ireland*, pp.98–99.
22 Fariola Confession. National Archives, London, Robert Anderson Papers, HO 144/1537/2.
23 Fariola, 'Amongst the Fenians'.
24 Ibid.
25 Fariola, 'Amongst the Fenians'.
26 Corydon testifying in various post-rising Special Commission trials, especially that of Captain Patrick Condon.
27 Ibid.
28 Hedges Chatterton's opening speech at the trial of Captain Patrick Condon.
29 Fariola, 'Amongst the Fenians'.
30 Ibid.

Chapter Fourteen

1 Strathnairn report on the rising. National Archives, London, HO 45/7799. The best account of the Dublin rising is undoubtedly that of Shin-ichi Takagami in his doctoral thesis.
2 Strathnairn's report on military preparations for a rising was actually written by his Military Secretary, Owen Tudor Burne. 'Plan of Operations of the Garrison of Dublin in the Event of Disturbances or Insurrection on the part of the disaffected', National Archives, London, HO 45/7799.
3 Takagami, *The Dublin Fenians, 1858–79*, p.246.
4 Denieffe, *A Personal Narrative of the Irish Revolutionary Brotherhood*, p.136.
5 Larcom, NLI, Mayo Papers, MS, 11191.
6 A.M. Sullivan, *The Story of Ireland*, p.578.
7 Col. The Hon. Frederick Wellesley, *Recollections of a Soldier-Diplomat*, p.98.
8 For this early phase of the rising in Dublin see 'A History of the Fenian Conspiracy', NLI, Larcom Papers, MS 7517. Also, Takagami, *The Dublin Fenians, 1858–79*, pp.256–65.
9 Devoy, *Recollections of an Irish Rebel*, p.193.
10 Denieffe, *A Personal Narrative of the Irish Revolutionary Brotherhood*, p.141.

11 Col. The Hon. Frederick Wellesley, *Recollections of a Soldier-Diplomat,* p.98.
12 *The Irishman* (New York), 8 March 1867.
13 Col. The Hon. Frederick Wellesley, *Recollections of a Soldier-Diplomat,* p.99.
14 Sir Owen Tudor Burne, *Memories,* p.71.
15 Col. The Hon. Frederick Wellesley, *Recollections of a Soldier-Diplomat,* p.99.
16 Ibid., p.100.
17 Ibid.
18 Ibid.
19 Ibid.
20 Ibid., p.101.
21 Ibid.
22 Ibid.
23 Denieffe, *A Personal Narrative of the Irish Revolutionary Brotherhood,* p.136.
24 Col. The Hon. Frederick Wellesley, *Recollections of a Soldier-Diplomat,* p.102.
25 Ibid.
26 For the rising in Cork see also Walter McGrath, 'The Fenian Rising in Cork', *Irish Sword,* Vol. 8, 1967–68, pp.245–53. Also, Leon O Brian, 'Cork and Limerick in 1867', Lecture delivered to the Cork Old IRA, 23 November 1868, NLI, MS 27956.
27 For Crowley see Savage, *Fenian Heroes and Martyrs,* pp.261–85.
28 For the events in Middleton see especially 'Mayhem and Murder on Skellig Night – the Fenian Rising in East Cork, March 1867' (East Cork and Irish History, Ancestry and Heritage). Also see Damien Shiels, 'Middleton and the 1867 Fenian Rising', Midleton Archaeology and Heritage Project, posted on 14 December 2012: midletonheritage.com/2012/12/14/midleton-and-the-1867-fenian-rising.
29 For the events at Kilclooney Wood see Ide Ni Choindealbhain, 'Fenians of Kilclooney Wood', *Cork Historical and Archaeological Society Journal,* 49–50, 1944–45. Also, *Cork Examiner,* 2 April 1867 and Devoy, *Recollections of an Irish Rebel,* pp.213–18.
30 Father T. O'Donnell's recollections in the *Sacred Heart Review,* Vol. 1 number 12, 16 February 1889, reprinted from the *Cork Herald.*
31 For O'Brien see J.F.X. O'Brien, *For the Liberty of Ireland.*
32 Ibid., p.100.
33 Ibid., p.102.
34 Ibid.
35 For the attack on Ballyknocken police station see Ibid., pp.102–05.
36 J.F.X. O'Brien in *Gaelic American,* 10 December 1904.
37 J.F.X. O'Brien, *For the Liberty of Ireland,* pp.106–07.
38 For the attack on Kilmallock see the account by P.N. Kennedy, who participated in the attack, published in Devoy, *Recollections of an Irish Rebel,* pp.224–26.
39 For the non-rising in Ulster see Kerron O Luain, 'The Dog that Didn't Bark, in 1867', *History Ireland,* March–April 2017.
40 Devoy, *Recollections of an Irish Rebel,* p.141.
41 A.M. Sullivan, *The Story of Ireland,* p.578.
42 Sir Owen Tudor Burne, *Memories,* p.72.
43 Devoy, *Recollections of an Irish Rebel,* p.141.

44 Fariola, 'Amongst the Fenians'.
45 Kelly in a letter to Halpin in Denieffe, *Personal Narrative of the Irish Revolutionary Brotherhood*, pp.278–80.
46 Cluseret, My Connection with Fenianism'.
47 A.M. Sullivan, *The Story of Ireland*, p.578. Sullivan's memory about the snowstorm was somewhat faulty. In *A New Ireland*, p.280, he asserted that it commenced on 5 March and lasted five days. But while Strathnairn and others witnessed snow, nobody else came close to confirming the atrocious conditions that Sullivan described on that date.
48 Sir Owen Tudor Burne, *Memories*, p.71.
49 Naas Report on the rising, 10 March 1867. National Archives, London, HO 45/7799.
50 Sir Owen Tudor Burne, *Memories*, p.72.
51 Captain Filgate, *Gaelic American*, 4 February 1905.
52 A.M. Sullivan, *New Ireland*, p.278.
53 Anderson writing as 'One Who Knows', *Contemporary Review,* February/April 1872, Part 2, p.627.
54 Col. The Hon. Frederick Wellesley, *Recollections of a Soldier-Diplomat*, p.102.
55 For Crowley's funeral see *Cork Examiner*, 3 April 1867; *Freeman's Journal*, 3 April 1867.
56 Herman J. Heuser, Canon Sheehan of Doneraile: The Story of an Irish Parish Priest as told chiefly by himself in Books, Personal Memoirs and Letters (London, 1917), p.19.
57 Fariola Confession. National Archives, London, Robert Anderson Papers, HO 144/1537/2.
58 Supt. Ryan report to Assistant Commissioner Lake, 17 April 1867, Fenian Supplement 1866–69, Larcom Papers, NLI, MS 7694.
59 Supt. Ryan. G Division, 4 November 1867, National Archives, London, HO45/7799.
60 Massey during the post-rising Special Commission trials in Cork. See also 'The statement of Patrick Condon also called Godfrey Massey when examined by the Crown Solicitor', April 1867, National Archives, HO45/7799.

Chapter Fifteen

1 Denieffe, *A Personal Narrative of the Irish Revolutionary Brotherhood*, pp.278–80.
2 Ibid.
3 Fariola Confession, National Archives, London, HO 144/1537/2.
4 Denieffe, *A Personal Narrative of the Irish Revolutionary Brotherhood*, pp.278–80.
5 Supt. Ryan, G Division Report, 27 May 1867, National Archives, London, HO 45/7799.
6 A.M. and T.D. Sullivan, *Speeches from the Dock* (New York, 1904), p.239.
7 Larcom Papers, A History of the Fenian Conspiracy, MS 7517, National Library of Ireland.

8   Mayo, 16 September, National Archives, London, HO45/7799.
9   National Archives, London. Also, Mayo Papers, MS 11189, National Library of Ireland.
10 Condon's account is in F.J. Crilly, *The Fenian Movement: the Story of the Manchester Martyrs* (London 1908). There are also accounts in Joseph O'Neill, *The Manchester Martyrs* (Dublin, 2012) and Paul Rose, *The Manchester Martyrs: The Story of a Fenian Tragedy* (London 1970). For the Manchester background see Mervyn Busteed, *The Irish in Manchester, 1750–1921* (Manchester, 2018).
11 Condon in F.L. Crilly, *The Fenian Movement: the Story of the Manchester Martyrs*, p.75.
12 Earl of Cranbrook, Gathorne Hardy and Nancy E. Johnson, *The Diary of Gathorne Hardy, later Lord Cranbrook, 1866–1892*, 18 September 1867 (Oxford, 1981), p.49. Hereafter Gathorne Hardy Diary.
13 Mayo to Hardy 19 September 1867, National Archives, London, HO 45/7799 (pp.80-151).
14 Condon, in F.L. Crilly, *The Fenian Movement: the Story of the Manchester Martyrs*, p.77.
15 McHale Report, 29 September 1867, National Archives, London, HO 45/7799.
16 Robert Bateman, 'Captain Timothy Deasy, Fenian', *Irish Sword*, Vol. 8, 1967–1968, pp.130–36.
17 F.L. Crilly, *The Fenian Movement: the Story of the Manchester Martyrs*, pp.87–88.
18 Condon, Ibid., p.77.
19 A.M. and T.D. Sullivan, *Speeches from the Dock* (New York, 1904), p.256.
20 Palin to Hardy, 14 October, 1867, National Archives, London, HO 45/7799.
21 Mayo to Gathorne Hardy, 19 September 1867, NLI, Mayo Papers, MS 11189.
22 Gathorne Hardy Diary, 20 September 1867, p.50.
23 Ibid., 20 September 1867, p.49.
24 Ibid., 16 October 1867, p.57.
25 Allen in his speech from the dock at the end of the trial.
26 *Manchester Courier*, 2 November 1867.
27 Ibid.
28 Ibid.
29 Ibid.
30 A.M. and T.D. Sullivan, *Speeches from the Dock* (New York, 1904), p.258.
31 Greenwood Report, Earl Cranbrook Papers, British Library, Add 62537.
32 National Archives, London, HO 45/9349.
33 Ibid.
34 Gathorne Hardy Diary, 8 November 1867, p.53.
35 Angus Hawkins, *The Forgotten Prime Minister: The 14th Earl of Derby: Volume II, Achievement, 1851–1869* (Oxford, 2008) p.135.
36 A.E. Gathorne-Hardy, *Gathorne Hardy, first Earl of Cranbrook*, 2 Vols. (London, 1910), pp.234–35.
37 Ibid., p.235.
38 Angus Hawkins and John Powell (eds), *The Journal of John Wodehouse, First Earl of Kimberley for 1862–1902* (London, 1997), pp.212–13.
39 National Archives, London, HO 45/7799.

40 National Archives, London, HO 45/9348.
41 US State Department. Papers Relating to Foreign Affairs, 1867, Correspondence with Chalres Adams, Minister to Great Britain. Documents 1–228.
42 Liddell. Undated memo. National Archives, London, HO 45/9348.
43 United States Department of State, Diplomatic Correspondence between Minister Charles Francis Adams, London Legation and Secretary of State William Seward.
44 Gathorne Hardy Diary, 21 November 1867, pp.54–55.
45 A.E. Gathorne-Hardy, *Gathorne Hardy, first Earl of Cranbrook*, 2 Vols. (London, 1910), Vol.1, p.265.
46 A.M. and T.D. Sullivan, *Speeches from the Dock* (New York, 1904), pp.279–80.
47 *Manchester Courier*, 25 November 1867.
48 Ibid.
49 Ibid.
50 Ibid.
51 Ibid.
52 Ibid.
53 Ibid.
54 Ibid.
55 Gathorne Hardy Diary, 23 November 1867, p.55.
56 Angus Hawkins and John Powell (eds), *The Journal of John Wodehouse, First Earl of Kimberley for 1862–1902* (London, 1997), p.212.
57 A.M. and T.D. Sullivan, *Speeches from the Dock*, p.285.
58 Devoy, *Recollections of an Irish Rebel*, p.319.
59 A.M. Sullivan, *New Ireland*, p.382.

Postscript

1 Arthur Griffiths, *Fifty Years of Public Service*, p.186.
2 Ibid., p.188.
3 Jeremiah O'Donovan Rossa, *O'Donovan Rossa's Prison Life: Six Years in Six English Prisons* (1874), p.422.
4 Ibid.
5 Arthur Griffiths, *Fifty Years of Public Service*, p.191.

Sources

Primary Sources

Bodleian Library

Clarendon Papers
Kimberly Papers

British Library

Gathorne Hardy Papers
Burne Papers

Liverpool Public Record Office

Derby Papers

National Library of Ireland

Samuel Lee Anderson Papers
Larcom Papers
Michael Lennon Papers
Luby Memoirs
O'Broin Papers
Seam O'Mahony Papers
Mayo Papers
Sir Hugh Rose Papers (Microfilm Copy)
1867 Special Commission Trials
Dublin Metropolitan Police Reports
Irish Constabulary Reports

National Archives of Ireland

Chief Secretary's Registered Papers

Dublin Metropolitan Police Reports
Irish Constabulary Reports

National Archives, London

Home Office Papers
Wodehouse Correspondence
Octavia Fariola Confession

University of Southampton

Palmerston Papers
American Diplomatic Correspondence related to the Manchester Martyrs and Fenian
  prisoners in Ireland

Newspapers

Cork Examiner
Freeman's Journal
Irish Times
Irish People (New York)
The Irishman (New York)

Secondary Sources

Ambrose, Joe, *The Fenian Anthology* (Cork, 2008)
Belchem, John, *Irish, Catholic and Scouse, The History of the Liverpool Irish, 1800–1939*
  (Oxford, 2008)
Bayor, Ronald, *The New York Irish* (Baltimore, 1997)
Boland, Tim, *Father John Kenyon: The Rebel Priest* (Nenagh, 2011)
Bourke, Marcus, *John O'Leary: A Study in Irish Separatism* (Dublin, 2009)
Browne, Richard, *Famine, Fenians and Freedom, 1840–1882* (Southampton, 2011)
Brundage, David, *Irish Nationalists in America: The Politics of Exile, 1798–1998*
  (Oxford, 2016)
Bourke, Marcus, *John O'Leary: A Study in Irish Nationalism* (Dublin, 2009)
Burne, Sir Owen Tudor, *Memories* (London, 1907)
Busteed, Mervyn A., *The Irish in Manchester, 1750–1921* (Manchester, 1915)
Comerford, R.V., *Charles J. Kickham 1828–1882* (Dublin, 1979)
Comerford, R.V., *The Fenians in Context* (Dublin, 1985)
D'Arcy, William, *The Fenian Movement in the United States, 1858–1886* (Washington, 1947)
Davis, Richard, *The Young Ireland Movement* (Dublin, 1987)
Delany, Enda, *The Curse of Reason: The Great Irish Famine, 1845–52* (Dublin, 2012)
Denieffe, Joseph, *A Personal Narrative of the Irish Revolutionary Brotherhood*
  (New York, 1906)
Devoy, John, *Recollections of an Irish Rebel* (New York, 1929)
Dooley, Terence, *The Greatest of the Fenians, L. John Devoy and Ireland* (London, 2013)
Duffy, Charles Gavan, *My Life in Two Hemispheres* (London, 1898)

Sources

Duffy, Charles Gavan, *Four Years Four Years of Irish History, 1845–49* (New York, 1883)

Duffy, Charles Gavan, *The League of North and South: An Episode in Irish History, 1850–1854* (London, 1886)

Dukova, Anastasia, *A History of the Dublin Metropolitan Police and its Colonial Legacy* (Basingstoke, 1916)

Foy, Michael T., *Tom Clarke: The True Leader of the Easter Rising* (Dublin, 2014)

Gannt, Jonathan, *Irish Terrorism in the Atlantic Community, 1865–1822* (New York, 2010)

Golway, Terry, *Irish Rebel, John Devoy and America's Fight for Ireland's Freedom* (London, 1998)

Griffiths, Arthur, *Fifty Years of Public Service* (London, 1904)

Gwynn, Stephen, *Young Ireland and 1848* (Cork, 1949)

Hardy, Gathorne, *Gathorne Hardy, First Earl of Cranbrooke: A Memoir with Extracts from his Diary and Correspondence* (Whitefish, Montana, 2010)

Hawkins, Angus and Powell, John, *The Journals of John Wodehouse, First Earl of Kimberley For 1862–1902* (London, 1997)

Hawkins, Angus and Powell, John, *The Forgotten Prime Minister: The 14th Earl of Derby: Vol II: Achievement* (Oxford, 2008)

Herlihy, Jim, *The Dublin Metropolitan Police, 1836–1925* (Dublin, 2001)

Johnson, Nancy E., *The Diary of Gathorne Hardy, later Lord Cranbrooke, 1866–1892* (Oxford, 1981)

Kenna, Shane, *Jeremiah O'Donovan Rossa: Unrepentant Fenian* (Newbridge, 2015)

Kenny, Kevin, *Revolutionary Imperialist; William Smith O'Brien, 1803–1864* (Dublin, 1998)

Kenny, Kevin, *The American Irish: A History* (New York, 2000)

Keogh, Daire (ed.), *Cardinal Paul Cullen and his World* (Dublin, 2011)

Kineally, Christine, *This Great Calamity: The Irish Famine 1845–62* (Dublin, 2005)

Litton, Helen, *The Irish Famine: An Illustrated History* (Dublin, 2003)

Lyons, F.S.L., *Ireland Since the Famine* (London, 1971)

McAlister, Thomas G., *The Life and Times of Terence Bellew McManus* (Maynooth, 1972)

McConville, Sean, *Irish Political Prisoners, 1848–1922* (Abingdon, Oxon, 2003)

McGarry, Fearghal, *The Black Hand of Republicanism: The Fenians and History* (Dublin, 2009)

Miller, Kerby, *Out of Ireland: The Story of Irish Migration to America* (London, 1994)

Miller, Kerby, *Ireland and Irish America* (Dublin, 2008)

Moody, T.W., *The Fenian Movement* (Cork, 1968)

O Broin, Leon, *Fenian Fever* (London, 1971)

O Broin, Leon, *Revolutionary Underground* (Dublin, 1976)

O'Carroll, Ciaran, Paul, *Cardinal Cullen, Portrait of a Practical Nationalist* (Dublin, 2008)

O Cathoir, Eva, *Soldiers of Liberty: A Study of Fenianism 1856–1908* (2018)

O'Leary, John, *Recollections of Fenians and Fenianism, 2 Vols* (London, 1896)

Payne, Chris, *The Chieftain: Victorian Crime through the Eyes of a Scotland Yard Detective* (Stroud, 2011)

Pottinger, George, *Mayo: Disraeli's Viceroy* (Salisbury, 1990)

Powell, John, *Liberal by Principle: The Politics of John Wodehouse, First Earl of Kimberley 1843–1902* (London, 1996)

Quinlivan, Patrick and Rose, Paul, *The Fenians in England, 1845–1872* (London, 1982)

Quinn, James, *John Mitchel* (Dublin, 2008)

Rafferty, Oliver, *The Church, the State and the Fenian Threat, 1861–75* (Basingstoke, 1999)

Ramon, Marta, *A Provisional Dictator: James Stephens and the Fenian Movement* (Dublin, 2007)

Rossa, Jeremiah O'Donovan, *Rossa's Recollections: 1838–98* (New York, 1898)

Rossa, Jeremiah O'Donovan, *O'Donovan Rossa's Prison Life: Six Years in Six English Prisons* (New York, 1874)

Rutherford, John, *The Secret History of the Fenian Conspiracy*, 2 Vols (London, 1877)

Ryan Mark, *Fenian Memories* (Dublin, 1945)

Savage, John, *Fenian Heroes and Martyrs* (Boston, 1868)

Sullivan, A.M., *New Ireland* (London, 1878)

Sullivan, T.D., *Recollections of Troubled Times in Irish Politics* (Dublin, 1905)

Swift, Roger, *Victorian Chester* (Liverpool, 1996)

Wellesley, Frederick, Col. The Hon, *Recollections of a Soldier-Diplomat* (London, 1948)

Whelan, Bernadette, *American Government in Ireland, 1790–1913: A History of the US Consular Service, 1789* (Manchester, 2013)

Theses

Devitt, Jerome, *Defending Ireland from the Irish: The Irish Executive's reaction to Transatlantic Fenianism 1864–68*, Doctoral Thesis, Trinity College, Dublin (2017)

Griffin, Brian, *The IRB in Connaught and Leinster 1858–1878*, National University of Ireland, Maynooth (1983)

Johnson, Maurice, *The Fenian Amnesty Movement 1868–1879* (1980)

Kennedy, Pauric Cummins, *Political Policing in a Liberal Age: Britain's Responses to the Fenian Movement, 1858–1868*, Washington (1996)

Leo, Mary, *The Importance of the Fenians and their Press on Public Opinion 1863–1870*, Doctoral Thesis, Trinity College, Dublin (1976)

Moloney, John, *The National Brotherhood of St Patrick and the Rise of Dublin Fenianism, 1858–1865*, MA Thesis, Galway University (1976)

Quigley, Kevin, *American Financing of Fenianism, 1858–1867*, MA Thesis, National University of Ireland, Maynooth (1983)

Sayers, Brian, *John O'Mahony: Revolutionary and Scholar (1815–1877)*, Doctoral Thesis, National University of Ireland, Maynooth (2005)

Semple, A.J., *The Fenian Infiltration of the British Army in Ireland 1858–1867* (1971)

Takagami, Shin-ichi, *The Dublin Fenians, 1858–1879*, Doctoral Thesis, Trinity College, Dublin (1990)

Index